75d

PATHWAY

TO

WESTERN LITERATURE

BY

NETTIE S. GAINES

Teacher in City Schools of
Stockton, California

Cover Design by W. S. RICE

CONTENTS

iv   *Contents*

Contents

PREFACE

Western geography and history are slowly but surely gaining their rightful place in the public school system throughout the country.

For a number of years the compiler of this book has been deeply interested in the literature of the West and has directed her efforts toward having it carried along side by side with the history and geography with which it is so closely allied.

It was, therefore, a source of much gratification when James A. Barr, City Superintendent of the Stockton schools, suggested that a book be compiled composed of extracts from the works of Western writers to be used as a Supplementary Reader, for she believed that in this way children would not only gain power in reading, but that they would gradually come to possess a loyalty and love for all things Western.

With this thought constantly in mind, the work required to compile such a book has been relieved of its arduousness and the task has been one of great pleasure and profit.

It has been the aim to make the collection representative of the coast, full of local color from pioneer days to the present.

Many short extracts have been selected rather than a few long ones, hoping that a broader field may be covered. A small amount of preparation by the teacher will enable her to give a setting for any selection. This will not be required for all, as a number are complete within themselves. After the children's interest in a selection has been secured, then is the time when the author should receive recognition, and every teacher in our schools should welcome this opportunity of making the children appreciative of Western writers.

It has not been deemed advisable to classify contents, as the book is designed for use in the sixth, seventh and eighth grades in connection with the history and geography of the West. Thus the teacher will use her own judgment as to the best means of correlation.

Before submitting the manuscript of this book to the publishers, representative extracts were sent to city and county superintendents, as well as to a number of teachers, to be passed upon. The commendations received assure the success of the undertaking.

While all extracts are from the works of Western writers, yet it is hoped that the appeal of the book will not be confined to the West nor even to the confines of the school room alone.

The compiler of this book wishes to express deep appreciation to the following publishing houses for their courtesy in granting certain copyright privileges: The Macmillan Company for selections by Jack London, Gertrude Atherton and Ella Higginson; Little, Brown & Company for selections by George Wharton James and Ada Woodruff Anderson; Harper & Brothers for selections by Herman Whitaker and J. Ross Browne; Houghton Mifflin & Company for selections by Bret Harte, Florence A. Merriam and Mary Austin; Doubleday, Page & Company for selections by Stewart Edward White,

Edwin Markham and Frank Norris; Charles Scribner's Sons for selections by John C. Van Dyke and Clarence King; Paul Elder & Company for selections by Charles Keeler and Belle Sumner Angier, and Funk Wagnalls Company for poems by Richard Realf.

Special permission has been granted by the following persons and to them the compiler is deeply indebted also: Charles Keeler, Ina Coolbrith, C. F. McGlashan, Lillian Hinman Shuey, Theodore Hittell, W. E. Bartlett, Theodore Van Dyke, Idah Meacham Strobridge, A. J. Waterhouse, Henry Meade Bland, Mary B. Williams, Lowell Otus Reese, Joaquin Miller, Sharlott Hall; Out West Magazine and Pacific Monthly Magazine for illustrations.

INTRODUCTION

To present to the youth of California adequate selections from the writings of the best authors of the State is a laudable endeavor. I have long hoped to see it done. Why should our children's study of literature be confined to the works of English and Eastern authors to the exclusion of the wealth of prose and poetry produced in the West. California has made itself felt with dignity and power, as well as native force and originality, in the literature of the English-speaking world and it is appropriate that its literary contributions be placed before the future citizenship of the State.

As I have constantly affirmed, so I sincerely believe that California has a wonderful destiny as the location of the highest civilization yet to be born, and this destiny is clearly foreshadowed in its literature. Its geographic isolation, its topographic cosmos, the climatic and scenic environment it affords, the pioneer basis of its civilization, all point to this exalted destiny.

It is well, therefore, that its youth should be made familiar with what is their grave responsibility and glorious opportunity.

Mrs. Gaines has exercised great care in making the selections of this volume, and that many of them are my own especial favorites that I had the pleasure of introducing to her does not lessen my gratification in seeing them gathered together in this form.

The book as a whole will delight and interest as
well as inform and inspire the children who read
it. Other volumes undoubtedly will soon follow
and thus the mine of the rich literary treasures of
California be at least indicated to those to whom it
is a natural inheritance.

GEORGE WHARTON JAMES,

Thanksgiving Day, 1909.

Pasadena, California.

A STARTLING ADVENTURE

By J. Ross Browne

I DESCENDED several of these shafts rather to
oblige my friend the Judge than to satisfy any
curiosity I had on the subject myself. This thing
of being dropped down two hundred feet into the
bowels of the earth in wooden buckets, and hoisted
out by blind horses attached to "whims," may be
very amusing to read about, but I have enjoyed
pleasanter modes of locomotion. There was one
shaft in particular that left an indelible impression
upon my mind—so much so, indeed, that I am astonished every hair in my head is not quite gray.
It was in the San Antonia, a mine in which the
Judge held an interest in connection with a worthy
Norwegian by the name of Jansen. As I had traveled in Norway, Jansen was enthusiastic in his devotion to my enjoyment—declared he would go
down with me himself and show me everything
worth seeing—even to the lower level just opened.
While I was attempting to frame an excuse the hon-
est Norwegian had lighted a couple of candles, giv-
en directions to one of the "boys" to look out for
the old blind horse attached to the "whim," and
now stood ready at the mouth of the shaft to guide
me into the subterranean regions.

"Mr. Jansen," said I, looking with horror at the
rickety wooden bucket and the flimsy little rope
that was to hold us suspended between the surface
of the earth and eternity, "is that rope strong?"

"Well, I think it's strong enough to hold us,"

replied Jansen; "it carries a ton of ore. We don't weigh a ton, I guess."

"But the bucket looks fearfully battered. And who can vouch that the old horse won't run away and let us down by the run?"

"Oh, sir, he's used to it. That horse never runs. You see, he's fast asleep now. He sleeps all along on the down turn. It's the up turn that gets him."

"Mr. Jansen," said I, "all that may be true; but suppose the bucket should catch and drop us out?"

"Well, sometimes it catches; but nobody's been hurt bad yet; one man fell fifteen feet perpendicular. He lit on the top of his head."

"Wasn't he killed?"

"No; he was only stunned a little. There was a buzzing about among his brains for a few days after; he's at work down below now, as well as ever."

"Mr. Jansen, upon the whole I think I'd rather go down by the ladder, if it's all the same to you."

"Certainly, sir, suit yourself; only the ladder's sort o' broke in spots, and you'll find it a tolerably hard climb down; how so ever, I'll go ahead and sing out when I come to bad places."

With this the Norwegian disappeared. I looked down after him. The shaft was about four feet square; rough, black and dismal, with a small flickering light, apparently a thousand feet below, making the darkness visible. It was almost perpendicular; the ladders stood against the near side, perched on ledges or hanging together by means of chafed and ragged-looking ropes. I regretted that I had not taken Jansen's advice and committed myself to the bucket; but it was now too late. With a hurried glance at the bright world around me, a thought of home and the unhappy conditions of widows and orphans, as a general thing, I seized the rungs of the ladder and took the irrevocable dive. Down I crept, rung after rung, ladder after ladder, in the black darkness, with the solid walls of rock pressing the air close around me. Sometimes I heard the incoherent muttering of voices below, but could make nothing of them. Perhaps Jansen was warning me of breaks in the ladder; perhaps his voice was split up by the rocks and sounded like many voices; or it might be there *were gnomes* whisking about in the dark depths below. Down and still down I crept, slower and slower, for I was getting tired, and I fancied there might be poisonous gases in the air. When I had reached the depth of a thousand feet, as it seemed, but about a hundred and forty as it was in reality, the thought occurred to me that I was beginning to get alarmed. In truth I was shaking like a man with the ague. Suppose I should become nervous and lose my hold on the ladder? The very idea was enough to make me shaky. There was an indefinite extent of shaft underneath, black, narrow and scraggy, with a solid base of rock at the bottom. I did not wonder that it caused a buzzing of the brain to fall fifteen feet and light on top of the head. My brain was buzzing already, and I had not fallen yet. But the prospect to that effect was getting better and better every moment, for I was now quite out of breath, and had to stop and cling around the ladder to avoid falling. The longer I stood this way the more certain it became that I should lose my balance and topple over. With a desperate effort I proceeded, step after step, clinging to the frail wood-work as the drowning man clings to a straw, gasping for breath, the cold sweat streaming down my face, and my jaws chattering audibly. The breaks in the ladder were getting fearfully common. Sometimes I found two rungs gone, sometimes six or seven, and then I had to slide down by the sides till my feet found a resting place on another rung or some casual ledge of rock. To Jansen, or the miners who worked down in the shaft every day, all of this, of course, was mere pastime. They knew every break and resting place; and besides, familiarity with any particular kind of danger blunts the sense of it. I am confident that I could make the same trip now without experiencing any unpleasant sensation. By good fortune I at length reached the bottom of the shaft, where I found my Norwegian friend and some three or four workmen quietly awaiting my arrival. A bucket of ore, containing some five or six hundred pounds, was ready to be hoisted up. It was very nice-looking ore, and very rich ore, as Jansen assured me; but what did I care about ore till I got the breath back again into my body?

"Stand from under, sir," said Jansen, dodging into a hole in the rocks; "a chunk of ore might fall out, or the bucket might give way."

Stand from under? Where in the name of sense was a man to stand in such a hole as this, not more than six or eight feet square at the base, with a few dark chasms in the neighborhood through which it was quite possible to be precipitated into the infernal regions. However, I stood as close to the wall as was possible without backing clean into it. The bucket of ore having gone up out of sight, I was now introduced to the ledge upon which the men were at work. It was about four feet thick, clearly defined, and apparently rich in the precious metals. In some specimens which I took out myself gold was visible to the naked eye. The indications of silver were also well marked. This was at a depth of a hundred and seventy-five feet. At the bottom of this shaft there was a loose flooring of rafters and planks.

"If you like, sir," said Jansen, "we'll go down here and take a look at the lower drift. They've just struck the ledge about forty feet below."

"Are the ladders as good as those above, Mr. Jansen?" I inquired.

"Oh yes, sir; they're all good; some of the lower ones may be busted a little with the blastin'; but there's two men down there. Guess they got down somehow."

"To tell you the truth, Mr. Jansen, I'm not curious about the lower drift. You can show me some specimens of the ore, and that will be quite satisfactory."

"Yes, sir, but I'd like you to see the vein where the drift strikes it. It's really beautiful."

A beautiful sight down in this region was worth looking at, so I succumbed. Jansen lifted up the planks, told the men to cover us well up as soon as we had disappeared, in order to keep the ore from the upper shaft from tumbling on our heads, and then, diving down, politely requested me to follow. I had barely descended a few steps when the massive rafters and planks were thrown across

2

overhead and thus all exit to the outer world was
cut off. There was an oppressive sensation in being so completely isolated from the outside world—
barred out, as it were, from the surface of the earth.
Yet, how many there are who spend half their lives
in such a place for a pittance of wages which they
squander in dissipation! Surely it is worth four
dollars a day to work in these dismal holes.

Bracing my nerves with such thoughts as these,
I scrambled down the rickety ladders till the last
rung seemed to have disappeared. I probed about
with a spare leg for a landing place, but could
touch neither top, bottom nor sides. The ladder
was apparently suspended in space like Moham-
med's coffin.

"Come on, sir," cried the voice of Jansen far
down below. "They're going to blast."

Pleasant, if not picturesque, to be hanging by
two arms and one leg to a ladder, squirming about
in search of a foothold, while somebody below was
setting fire to a fuse with the design, no doubt, of
blowing up the entire premises!

"Mr. Jansen," said I, in a voice of unnatural
calmness, while the big drops of agony stood on
my brow, "there's no difficulty in saying 'Come
on, sir!' but to do it without an inch more of ladder
or anything else that I can see, requires both time
and reflection. How far do you expect me to
drop?"

"Oh, don't you let go, sir. Just hang on to that
rope at the bottom of the ladder, and let yourself
down."

I hung on as directed and let myself down. It
was plain sailing enough to one who knew the

chart. The ladder, it seemed, had been broken by a blast of rocks; and now there was to be another blast. We retired into a convenient hole about ten or a dozen paces from the deposit of Hazard's powder. The blast went off with a dead reverberation, causing a concussion in the air that affected one like a shock of galvanism; and then there was a diabolical smell of brimstone. Jansen was charmed at the result. A mass of the ledge was burst clean open. He grasped up the blackened fragments of quartz, licked them with his tongue, held them up to the candle, and constantly exclaimed: "There, sir, there! Isn't it beautiful? Did you ever see anything like it?—pure gold, almost—here it is!—don't you see it?"

I suppose I saw it; at all events I put some specimens in my pocket, and saw them afterward out in the pure sunlight, where the smoke was not so dense; and it is due to the great cause of truth to say that gold was there in glittering specks, as if shaken over it from a pepperbox.

Having concluded my examination of the mine, I took the bucket as a medium of exit, being fully satisfied with the ladders. About half way up the shaft the iron swing or handle to which the rope was attached caught in one of the ladders. The rope stretched. I felt it harden and grow thin in my hands. The bucket began to tip over. It was pitch dark all around. Jansen was far below, coming up the ladder. Something seemed to be creaking, cracking, or giving way. I felt the rough, heavy sides of the bucket press against my legs. A terrible apprehension seized me that the gear was tangled and would presently snap. In the pitchy darkness and the confusion of the moment I could not conjecture what was the matter. I darted out my hands, seized the ladder and, jerking myself high out of the bucket, clambered up with the agility of an acrobat. Relieved of my weight, the iron catch came loose, and up came the bucket banging and thundering after me with a velocity that was perfectly frightful. Never was there such a subterranean chase, I verily believe, since the beginning of the world. To stop a single moment would be certain destruction, for the bucket was large, heavy and massively bound with iron, and the space in the shaft was not sufficient to admit of its passing without crushing me flat against the ladder.

But such a chase could not last long. I felt my strength give way at every lift. The distance was too great to admit the hope of escape by climbing. My only chance was to seize the rope above the bucket and hang on to it. This I did. It was a lucky thought—one of those thoughts that sometimes flash upon the mind like inspiration in a moment of peril. A few more revolutions of the "whim" brought me so near the surface that I could see the bucket only a few yards below my feet. The noise of the rope over the block above reminded me that I had better slip down a little to save my hands, which I did in good style, and was presently landed on the upper crust of the earth, all safe and sound, though somewhat dazzled by the light and rattled by my subterranean experiences.—From "Adventures in the Apache Country."

BROWN WOLF

By Jack London

THE Klondiker's face took on a contemptuous expression as he said finally, "I reckon there's nothin' in sight to prevent me takin' the dog right here an' now."

Walt's face reddened, and the striking-muscles of his arms and shoulders seemed to stiffen and grow tense. His wife fluttered apprehensively into the breach.

"Maybe Mr. Miller is right," she said. "I am afraid that he is. Wolf does seem to know him, and certainly he answers to the name of 'Brown.' He made friends with him instantly, and you know that's something he never did with anybody before. Besides, look at the way he barked. He was just bursting with joy. Joy over what? Without doubt at finding Mr. Miller."

Walt's striking-muscles relaxed, and his shoulders seemed to droop with hopelessness.

"I guess you're right, Madge," he said. "Wolf isn't Wolf, but Brown, and he must belong to Mr. Miller."

"Perhaps Mr. Miller will sell him," she suggested. "We can buy him."

Skiff Miller shook his head, no longer belligerent, but kindly, quick to be generous in response to generousness.

"I had five dogs," he said, casting about for the easiest way to temper his refusal. "He was the leader. They was the crack team of Alaska.

Nothin' could touch 'em. In 1898 I refused five thousand dollars for the bunch. Dogs was high then, anyway; but that wasn't what made the fancy price. It was the team itself. Brown was the best in the team. That winter I refused twelve hundred for 'm. I didn't sell 'm then an' I ain't a-sellin' 'm now. Besides, I think a mighty lot of that dog. I've ben lookin' for 'm for three years. It made me fair sick when I found he'd ben stole— not the value of him, but the—well, I liked 'm. I couldn't believe my eyes when I seen 'm just now. I thought I was dreamin'. It was too good to be true. Why, I was his wet-nurse. I put 'm to bed, snug every night. His mother died, and I brought 'm up on condensed milk at two dollars a can when I couldn't afford it in my own coffee. He never knew any mother but me.

Madge began to speak:

"But the dog," she said. "You haven't considered the dog."

Skiff Miller looked puzzled.

"Have you thought about him?" she asked.

"Don't know what you're drivin' at," was the response.

"Maybe the dog has some choice in the matter," Madge went on. "Maybe he has his likes and desires. You have not considered him. You give him no choice. It has never entered your mind that possibly he might prefer California to Alaska. You consider only what you like. You do with him as you would with a sack of potatoes or a bale of hay."

This was a new way of looking at it, and Miller

was visibly impressed as he debated it in his mind. Madge took advantage of his indecision.

"If you really love him, what would be happiness to him would be your happiness also," she urged.

Skiff Miller continued to debate with himself, and Madge stole a glance of exultation to her husband, who looked back warm approval.

"What do you think?" the Klondiker suddenly demanded.

It was her turn to be puzzled. "What do you mean?" she asked.

"D'ye think he'd sooner stay in California?"

She nodded her head with positiveness. "I am sure of it."

Skiff Miller again debated with himself, though this time aloud, at the same time running his gaze in a judicial way over the mooted animal.

"He was a good worker. He's done a heap of work for me. He never loafed on me, an' he was a joe-dandy at hammerin' a raw team into shape. He's got a head on him. He can do everything but talk. He knows what you say to him. Look at 'm now. He knows we're talkin' about him."

The dog was lying at Skiff Miller's feet, head close down on paws, ears erect and listening, and eyes that were quick and eager to follow the sound of speech as it fell from the lips of first one and then the other.

"An' there's a lot of work in 'm yet. He's good for years to come. An' I do like him."

Once or twice after that Skiff Miller opened his mouth and closed it again without speaking. Finally he said:

"I'll tell you what I'll do. Your remarks,

ma'am, has some weight in them. The dog's worked hard, and maybe he's earned a soft berth an' has got a right to choose. Anyway, we'll leave it up to him. Whatever he says goes. You people stay right here settin' down; I'll say 'good-bye' and walk off casual-like. If he wants to stay, he can stay. If he wants to come with me, let 'm come. I won't call 'm to come an' don't you call 'm to come back.''

He looked with sudden suspicion at Madge, and added, ''Only you must play fair. No persuadin' after my back is turned.''

''We'll play fair,'' Madge began, but Skiff Miller broke in on her assurances.

''I know the ways of women,'' he announced. ''Their hearts is soft. When their hearts is touched they're likely to stack the cards, look at the bottom of the deck, an' lie—beggin' your pardon, ma'am—I'm only discoursin' about women in general.''

''I don't know how to thank you,'' Madge quavered.

''I don't see as you've got any call to thank me,'' he replied; ''Brown ain't decided yet. Now, you won't mind if I go away slow. It's no more'n fair, seein' I'll be out of sight inside a hundred yards.''

Madge agreed and added, ''And I promise you faithfully that we won't do anything to influence him.''

''Well, then, I might as well be gettin' along,'' Skiff Miller said, in the ordinary tones of one departing.

At this change in his voice, Wolf lifted his head

quickly, and still more quickly got to his feet when the man and woman shook hands. He sprang up on his hind legs, resting his fore paws on her hip and at the same time licking Skiff Miller's hand. When the latter shook hands with Walt, Wolf repeated his act, resting his weight on Walt and licking both men's hands.

"It ain't no picnic, I can tell you that," were the Klondiker's last words, as he turned and went slowly up the trail.

For the distance of twenty feet Wolf watched him go, himself all eagerness and expectancy, as though waiting for the man to turn and retrace his steps. Then, with a quick, low whine, Wolf sprang after him, overtook him, caught his hand between his teeth with reluctant tenderness and strove gently to make him pause.

Failing in this, Wolf raced back to where Walt Irvine sat, catching his coatsleeve in his teeth and trying vainly to drag him after the retreating man.

Wolf's perturbation began to wax. He desired ubiquity. He wanted to be in two places at the same time, with the old master and the new, and steadily the distance was increasing. He sprang about excitedly, making short, nervous leaps and twists, now toward one, now toward the other, in painful indecision, not knowing his own mind, desiring both and unable to choose, uttering quick, sharp whines and beginning to pant.

He sat down abruptly on his haunches, thrusting his nose upward, his mouth opening and closing with jerky movements, each time opening wider. The jerking movements were in unison with the recurrent spasms that attacked the throat, each spasm severer and more intense than the preceding one. And in accord with jerks and spasms the larynx began to vibrate, at first silently, accompanied by the rush of air expelled from the lungs, then sounding a low, deep note, the lowest in the register of the human ear. All this was the nervous and muscular preliminary to howling.

But just as the howl was on the verge of bursting from the full throat, the wide open mouth was closed, the paroxysms ceased, and he looked long and steadily at the retreating man. Suddenly Wolf turned his head, and over his shoulder just as steadily regarded Walt. The appeal was unanswered. Not a word nor a sign did the dog receive, no suggestion and no clew as to what his conduct should be.

A glance ahead to where the old master was nearing the curve of the trail excited him again. He sprang to his feet with a whine, and then, struck by a new idea, turned his attention to Madge. Hitherto he had ignored her, but now, both masters failing him, she alone was left. He went over to her and snuggled his head in her lap, nudging her arm with his nose—an old trick of his when begging for favors. He backed away from her and began writhing and twisting playfully, curvetting and prancing, half rearing and striking his fore paws to the earth, struggling with all his body, from the wheedling eyes and flattening ears to the wagging tail, to express the thought that was in him and that was denied him utterance.

This too he soon abandoned. He was depressed by the coldness of these humans who had never been cold before. No response could he draw from

them, no help could he get. They did not consider
him. They were as dead.

He turned and silently gazed after the old master. Skiff Miller was rounding the curve. In a
moment he would be gone from view. Yet he
never turned his head, plodding straight onward,
slowly and methodically, as though possessed of no
interest in what was occurring behind his back.

And in this fashion he went out of view. Wolf
waited for him to reappear. He waited a long
minute, quietly, silently without movement, as
though turned to stone—withal stone quick with
eagerness and desire. He barked once, and waited.
Then he turned and trotted back to Walt Irvine.
He sniffed his hand and dropped down heavily at
his feet, watching the trail where it curved emptily
from view.

The tiny stream slipping down the mossy-lipped
stone seemed suddenly to increase the volume of its
gurgling noise. Save for the meadow-larks, there
was no other sound. The great yellow butterflies
drifted silently through the sunshine and lost themselves in the drowsy shadows. Madge gazed tri-
umphantly at her husband.

A few minutes later Wolf got upon his feet.
Decision and deliberation marked his movements.
He did not glance at the man and woman. His
eyes were fixed up the trail. He had made up his
mind. They knew it. And they knew, so far as
they were concerned, that the ordeal had just begun.

He broke into a trot and Madge's lips pursed,
forming an avenue for the caressing sound that it
was the will of her to send forth. But the caressing

sound was not made. She was impelled to look at her husband, and she saw the sternness with which he watched her. The pursed lips relaxed, and she sighed inaudibly.

Wolf's trot broke into a run. Wider and wider were the leaps he made. Not once did he turn his head, his wolf's brush standing out straight behind him. He cut sharply across the curve of the trail and was gone.—From "Love of Life."

COLUMBUS

By Joaquin Miller

BEHIND him lay the gray Azores,
    Behind the gates of Hercules;
Before him not the ghost of shores;
    Before him only shoreless seas.
The good mate said: "Now must we pray,
    For lo! the very stars are gone.
Brave Adm'r'l, speak; what shall I say?"
    "Why, say: 'Sail on! sail on! and on!'"

"My men grow mutinous day by day;
    My men grow ghastly wan and weak."
The stout mate thought of home; a spray
    Of salt wave washed his swarthy cheek.
"What shall I say, brave Adm'r'l, say,
    If we sight naught but seas at dawn?"
"Why, you shall say at break of day:
    'Sail on! sail on! sail on! and on!'"

They sailed and sailed, as winds might blow,
  Until at last the blanched mate said:
"Why, now not even God would know
  Should I and all my men fall dead.
These very winds forget their way,
  For God from these dread seas is gone.
Now speak, brave Adm'r'l; speak and say"—
  He said: "Sail on! sail on! and on!"

They sailed. They sailed. Then spake the mate:
  "This mad sea shows his teeth to-night.
He curls his lip, he lies in wait,
  With lifted teeth, as if to bite!
Brave Adm'r'l, say but one good word;
  What shall we do when hope is gone?"
The words leapt like a leaping sword:
  "Sail on! sail on! sail on! and on!"

Then, pale and worn, he paced his deck,
  And peered through darkness. Ah, that night
Of all dark nights! And then a speck—
  A light! A light! At last a light! A light!
It grew, a starlit flag unfurled!
  It grew to be Time's burst of dawn.
He gained a world; he gave that world
  Its grandest lesson: "On! sail on!"
                    —From "Book of Poems."

THE PASSING OF THE SPANISH HOME

By Helen Hunt Jackson

THE Señora Moreno's house was one of the best specimens to be found in California of the representative house of the half barbaric, half elegant, wholly generous and free-handed life led there by Mexican men and women of degree in the early part of this century, under the rule of the Spanish and Mexican viceroys, when the laws of the Indies were still the law of the land, and its old name, "New Spain," was an ever-present link and stimulus to the warmest memories and deepest patriotisms of its people.

It was a picturesque life, with more of sentiment and gayety in it, more, also, that was truly dramatic, more romance, than will ever be seen again on those sunny shores. The aroma of it all lingers there still; industries and inventions have not yet slain it; it will last out its century—in fact it can never be quite lost, so long as there is left standing one such house as the Señora Moreno's.

When the house was built Señora Moreno owned all the land within a radius of forty miles—forty miles westward, down the valley to the sea; forty miles eastward into the San Fernando Mountains; and a good forty miles, more or less, along the coast. The boundaries were not very strictly defined; there was no occasion in those happy days to reckon land by inches. It might be asked, perhaps, just how General Moreno owned all this land, and the question might not be easy to answer. It was not and could not be answered to the satisfaction of

the United States Land Commission, which, after
the surrender of California, undertook to sift and
adjust Mexican land titles, and that was the way it
had come about that the Señora Moreno now called
herself a poor woman. Tract after tract, her lands
had been taken away from her; it looked for a time
as if nothing would be left. Every one of the
claims based on deeds of gift from Governor Pio
Pico, her husband's most intimate friend, was dis-
allowed. They all went by the board in one batch,
and took away from the Señora in a day the greater part of her best pasture lands. They were lands
which had belonged to the Buenaventura Mission,
and lay along the coast at the mouth of the valley
down which the little stream which ran past her
house went to the sea; and it had been a great
pride and delight to the Señora, when she was
young, to ride that forty miles by her husband's
side, all the way on their own lands, straight from
their house to their own strip of shore. No wonder
she believed the Americans thieves, and spoke of
them always as hounds. The people of the United
States have never in the least realized that the taking possession of California was not only a conquering of Mexico, but a conquering of California
as well; that the real bitterness of the surrender
was not so much to the empire which gave up the
country, as to the country itself which was given
up. Provinces passed back and forth in that way,
helpless in the hands of great powers, have all the
ignominy and humiliation of defeat, with none of
the dignities or compensation of the transaction.

Mexico saved much by her treaty, in spite of having
to acknowledge herself beaten; but California lost

all. Words cannot tell the sting of such a transfer. It is a marvel that a Mexican remained in the
country; probably none did, except those who were
absolutely forced to it.

Luckily for the Señora Moreno her title to the
lands midway in the valley was better than to
those lying to the east and to the west, which had
once belonged to the missions of San Fernando
and Buenaventura; and after all the claims, coun-
terclaims, petitions, appeals and adjudications were
ended, she still was left in undisputed possession
of what would have been thought by any new-
comer into the country to be a handsome estate,
but which seemed to the despoiled and indignant
Señora a pitiful fragment of one. Moreover, she
declared that she would never feel secure of a foot
of even this. Any day, she said, the United States
Government might send out a new land commission to examine the decrees of the first, and revoke
such as they saw fit. Once a thief, always a thief.
Nobody need feel himself safe under American
rule. There was no knowing what might happen
any day; and year by year the lines of sadness, resentment, anxiety and antagonism deepened on the
Señora's fast aging face.

It gave her unspeakable satisfaction when the
commissioners, laying out a road down the valley,
ran it at the back of her house instead of past the
front. "It is well," she said. "Let their travel be
where it belongs, behind our kitchens; and no one
have sight of our front doors, except friends who
have come to visit us." Her enjoyment of this
never flagged. Whenever she saw, passing the
place, wagons or carriages belonging to the hated

Americans, it gave her a distinct thrill of pleasure to think that the house turned its back on them. She would like always to be able to do the same herself; but whatever she, by policy or in business, might be forced to do, the old house, at any rate, would always keep the attitude of contempt—its face turned away.

One other pleasure she provided herself with, soon after this road was opened—a pleasure in which religious devotion and race antagonism were so closely blended that it would have puzzled the subtlest of priests to decide whether her act was a sin or a virtue. She caused to be set up, upon every one of the soft rounded hills which made the beautiful rolling sides of that part of the valley, a large wooden cross; not a hill in sight of her house left without the sacred emblem of her faith. "That the heretics may know, as they go by, that they are on the estate of a good Catholic," she said, "and that the faithful may be reminded to pray. There have been miracles of conversion wrought on the most hardened by a sudden sight of the Blessed Cross."

There they stood, summer and winter, rain and shine, the silent, solemn, outstretched arms, and became landmarks to many a guideless traveler who had been told that his way would be by the first turn to the left or the right, after passing the last one of the Señora Moreno's crosses, which he couldn't miss seeing. And who shall say that it did not often happen that the crosses bore a sudden message to some idle heart journeying by, and thus justified the pious half of the Señora's impulse? Certain it was, that many a good Catholic

3

halted and crossed himself when he first beheld
them, in the lonely places, standing out in sudden
relief against the blue sky; and if he said a swift,
short prayer at the sight, was he not so much the
better?—From "Ramona."

INDIAN BASKETRY

By Ella Higginson

INDIAN basketry is poetry, music, art and life
itself woven exquisitely together out of dreams,
and sent out into a thoughtless world in appealing
messages which will one day be farewells, when
the poor lonely dark women who wove them are
no more.

At its best, the basketry of the islands of Atka
and Attu in the Aleutian chain is the most beautiful in the world. Most of the basketry now sold as
Attu is woven by the women of Atka, we were told
at Unalaska, which is the nearest market for these
baskets. Only one old woman remains on Attu
who understands this delicate and priceless work;
and she is so poorly paid that she was recently reported to be in a starving condition, although the
velvety creations of her old hands and brain bring
fabulous prices to some one. The saying that an
Attu basket increases a dollar for every mile as it
travels toward civilization is not such an exaggera-
tion as it seems. I saw a trader from the little
steamer Dora—the only one regularly plying those
far waters—buy a small basket, no larger than a

pint bowl, for five dollars in Unalaska; and a month later, on another steamer, between Valdez and Seattle, an enthusiastic young man from New York brought the same basket out of his stateroom and proudly displayed it.

"I got this one at a great bargain," he bragged, with shining eyes. "I bought it in Valdez for twenty-five dollars, just what it cost at Unalaska. The man needed the money worse than the basket. I don't know how it is, but I'm always stumbling on bargains like that!" he concluded, beginning to strut.

Then I was heartless enough to laugh, and to keep on laughing. I had greatly desired that basket myself.

He had the satisfaction of knowing, however, that his little twined bowl, with the coloring of a Behring Sea sunset woven into it, would be worth fifty dollars by the time he reached Seattle, and at least a hundred in New York; and it was so soft and flexible that he could fold it up meantime and carry it in his pocket, if he chose—to say nothing of the fact that Elizabeth Propokoffono, the young and famed dark-eyed weaver of Atka, may have woven it herself. Like the renowned "Sally-Bags," made by Sally, a Wasco squaw, the baskets woven by Elizabeth have a special and sentimental value. If she would weave her initials into them, she might ask, and receive, any price she fancied. Sally, of the Wascos, on the other hand, is very old; no one weaves her special bag, and they are becoming rare and valuable. They are of plain, twined weaving, and are very coarse. A small one in the writer's possession is adorned with twelve fishes, six eagles, three dogs, and two and a half men. Sally is apparently a woman suffragist of the old school, and did not consider that men counted for much in the scheme of Indian baskets; yet, being a philosopher, as well as a suffragist, concluded that half a man was better than none at all.

At Yakutat "Mrs. Pete" is the best known basket weaver. Young, handsome, dark-eyed and clean, with a chubby baby in her arms, she willingly and with great gravity posed against the pilothouse of the old Santa Ana for her picture. Asked for an address to which I might send one of the pictures, she proudly replied, "just Mrs. Pete, Yakutat." Her courtesy was in marked contrast to the exceeding rudeness with which the Sitkan women treat even the most considerate and differential photographers; glaring at them, turning their backs, covering their heads, hissing and even spitting at them.

Basketry is either hand-woven or sewed. Hand-woven work is divided into checker work, twilled work, wicker work, wrapped work and twined work. Sewed work is called coiled basketry.

Twined work is found on the Pacific Coast from Attu to Chile, and is the most delicate and difficult of all woven work. It has a set of warp rods, and the weft elements are worked in by two-strand or three-strand methods. Passing from warp to warp, these weft elements are twisted in half-turns on each other, so as to form a two-strand or three-strand twine or braid, and usually with a deftness that keeps the glossy side of the weft outward.

"The Thlinkit, weaving," says Lieutenant Emmons, "sits with knees updrawn to the chin, feet close to the body, bent-shouldered, with arms around the knees, the work held in front. Sometimes the knees fall slightly apart, the work held between them, the weft frequently held in the mouth, the feet easily crossed. The basket is held bottom down. In all kinds of weave, the strands are constantly dampened by dipping the fingers in water. The finest work of Attu and Atka is woven entirely under water. A rude awl, a bear's claw or tooth, are the only implements used. The Attu weaver has her basket inverted and suspended by a string, working from the bottom down toward the top.

Almost every part of plants is used—roots, stems, bark, leaves, fruit and seeds. The following are the plants chiefly used by the Thlinkits: The black shining stems of the maiden-hair fern, which are easily distinguished and which add a rich touch; the split stems of the bromegrass as an overlaying material for the white pattern of spruce-root baskets; for the same purpose, the split stem of blue-joint; the stem of wood reedgrass; the stem of tufted hairgrass; the stem of beach rye; the root of horsetail, which works in a rich purple; wolf moss, boiled for canary-yellow dye; mannagrass; root of the Sitka spruce tree; juice of the blueberry for a purple dye.

The Attu weaver uses the stems and leaves of grass, having no trees and few plants. When she wants the grass white, it is cut in November and hung, points down, out-doors to dry; if yellow be desired, as it usually is, it is cut in July and the two youngest full-grown blades are cut out and split into three pieces, the middle one being rejected and the others hung up to dry out-doors; if green is wanted, the grass is prepared as for yellow, except that the first two weeks of curing is carried on in the heavy shade of thick grasses, then it is taken into the house and dried. Curing requires about a month, during which time the sun is never permitted to touch the grass.

Ornamentation by means of color is wrought by the use of materials which are naturally of a different color; by the use of dyed materials; by overlaying the weft and warp with strips of attractive material before weaving; by embroidering on the texture during the process of manufacture, this being termed "false" embroidery; by covering the texture with plaiting, called imbrication; by the addition of feathers, beads, shells and objects of like nature.

Some otherwise fine specimens of Atkan basketry are rendered valueless, in my judgment, by the present custom of introducing flecks of gaily-dyed wool, the matchless beauty of these baskets lying in their delicate, even weaving, and in their exquisite natural coloring—the faintest old rose, lavender, green, yellow and purple being woven together in one ravishing mist of elusive splendor. So enchanting to the real lover of basketry are the creations of those far lonely women's hands and brains, that they seem fairly to breathe out their loveliness upon the air, as a rose.

This basketry was first introduced to the world in 1874 by William H. Dall, to whom Alaska and those who love Alaska owe so much. Warp and weft are both of beach grass or wild rye. One who has

never seen a fine specimen of these baskets has
missed one of the joys of this world.

The Aleuts perpetuate no story or myth in their
ornamentation. With them it is art for art's sake;
and this is, doubtless, one reason why their work
draws the beholder spellbound. The symbolism of
the Thlinkit is charming. It is found not alone in
their basketry, but in their carvings in stone, horn,
and wood, and in Chilkaht blankets. The favorite
designs are shadow of a tree, water drops, salmon
berry cut in half, the Arctic tern's tail, flaking of
the flesh of a fish, shark's tooth, leaves of the fireweed, an eye, raven's tail, and the crossing. It
must be confessed that only a wild imagination
could find the faintest resemblance of the symbols
woven into the baskets to the objects they represent. The symbol called "shadow of a tree" really
resembles sunlight in moving water.

With the Haidah hats and Chilkaht blankets it
is very different. The head, feet, wings and tail
of the raven, for instance, are easily traced. In
more recent basketry the Swastika is a familiar
design. Many Thlinkit baskets have "rattly" covers. Seeds found in the crops of quail are woven
into these covers. They are "good spirits" which
can never escape, and will insure good fortune to
the owner. Woe be to him, however, should he
permit his curiosity to tempt him to investigate;
they will then escape, and work him evil instead of
good all the days of his life.

In Central Alaska, the basketry is usually of the
coiled variety, coarsely and very indifferently ex-
ecuted. Both spruce and willow are used. From
Dawson to St. Michael, in the summer of 1907,

stopping at every trading post and Indian village, I did not see a single piece of basketry that I would carry home. Coarse, unclean and of slovenly workmanship, one could but turn away in pity and disgust for the wasted effort.

The Innuit in the Behring Sea vicinity make both coiled and twined basketry from dried grasses; but it is even worse than the Yukon basketry, being carelessly done—the Innuit infinitely preferring the carving and decorating of walrus ivory to basket weaving. It is delicious to find an Innuit, who never saw a glacier, decorating a paperknife with something that looks like a pond lily and labelling it Taku Glacier, which is three thousand miles to the southeastward. I saw no attempt on the Yukon, nor on Behring Sea, at what Mr. Mason calls imbrication—the beautiful ornamentation which the Indians of Columbia, Frazer and Thompson Rivers and of many Salish tribes of Northwestern Washington use to distinguish their coiled work. It resembles knife-plaiting before it is pressed flat. This imbrication is frequently of an exquisite dull, reddish brown over an old, soft yellow. Baskets adorned with it often have handles and flat covers; but papoose baskets and covered long baskets, almost as large as trunks, are common.

The serpent has no place in Alaskan basketry for the very good reason that there is not a snake in all Alaska, and the Indians and Innuit probably never saw one. A woman may wade through the swampiest place or the tallest grass without one shivery glance at her pathway for that little sinuous ripple which sends terror to most women's hearts in warmer climes. Indeed, it is claimed that no poisonous thing exists in Alaska.

There was once a tide in my affairs which, not being taken at the flood, led on to everlasting regret.

One August evening several years ago I landed on an island in Puget Sound where some Indians were camped for the fishing season. It was Sunday; the men were playing the fascinating gambling game of slahal, the children were shouting at play, the women were gathered in front of their tents, gossiping.

In one of the tents I found a coiled, imbricated Thompson River basket in old red-browns and yellows. It was three and a half feet long, two and a half feet high, and two and a half wide, with a thick, close-fitting cover. It was offered to me for ten dollars, and—that I should live to chronicle it! —not knowing the worth of such a basket, I closed my eyes to its appealing and unforgetable beauty, and passed it by.

But it had, it has, and it always will have its silent revenge. It is as bright in my memory to-day as it was in my vision that August Sunday ten years ago, and more enchanting. My longing to see it again, to possess it, increases as the years go by. Never have I seen its equal, never shall I. Yet I am ever looking for that basket, in every Indian tent or hovel I may stumble upon—in villages, in camps, in out-of-the-way places. Sure am I that I should know it from all other baskets, at but a glance.

I knew nothing of the value of baskets, and I fancied the woman was taking advantage of my

ignorance. While I hesitated, the steamer whistled.
It was all over in a moment; my chance was gone.
I did not even dream how greatly I desired that
basket until I stood in the bow of the steamer and
saw the little white camp fade from view across
the sunset sea.—From "Alaska."

AN ENGINEERING TRIUMPH

By DAN DE QUILLE

ANOTHER work that has been of great benefit
to the towns along the Comstock, and to all
the mining and milling companies in and about the
towns, and along the canons below, was the bringing of an ample supply of pure water from the
Sierra Nevada Mountains.

In the early days, when the first mining was done
at Virginia City and Gold Hill, natural springs
furnished a supply of water for the use of the few
persons then living in the two camps. For a time
after the discovery of silver, these springs, and a
few wells that were dug by the settlers, sufficed for
all uses, but as the towns grew in population an
increased supply of water was demanded. A water
company was formed and the water flowing from
several tunnels, that had been run into the mountains west of Virginia City for prospecting purposes, was collected in large wooden tanks, and distributed about the two towns by means of pipes.
At length the tunnels from which this supply was
obtained began to run dry, and a water famine was
threatened. It then became necessary to set men to

work at extending the tunnels further into the hills
to cut across new strata of rock. This increased
the supply for a time, but at length the whole top
of the hill into which the tunnels extended appeared to be completely drained.

Early in the spring, when the snow was melting,
they afforded a considerable supply; but in the
summer, when water was most needed, the tunnels
furnished but feeble streams and these were much
impregnated with minerals, one of the least feared
of which was arsenic. The ladies rather liked
arsenic, as it improved their complexion; made
them fair and rosy-cheeked—almost young again,
some of them. The miners did not object to arsenic, as, while it did not injure their complexion,
it strengthened their lungs—made them strong-
winded, and able to scale mountains. (Every man
of them hungered to hunt the wild chamois.) But
there were other minerals held in solution in the
water—that were not so well thought of.

The nearer hills having thus been drained, tunnels were run into such of those further away as
were of sufficient altitude to permit of streams
from them being brought to the two towns. These
tunnels were run for no other purpose than to
find water. A hill was examined with a view to
its water-producing capacity. It was found that
those which rose up in a single sharp or rounded
peak were not rich in water. The best water-pro-
ducers were hills on the tops of which there were
large areas of flat ground. That portion of a
range of mountains which contained on the summit
a large, shallow basin surrounded by clusters of
hills or peaks was found to yield largely and for a

long time, when tapped by a tunnel run under the basin or sink at the depth of three or four hundred feet.

Dams were constructed across the outlets of these basins to hold back the water from the melting snow, in order that it might filter down through the earth to the tunnels. At the mouths of the tunnels heavy bulkheads of timber and plank were constructed, to keep back and dam up the water where it could be kept cool and pure. Where deep shafts stood near the line of these tunnels, ditches were dug to them along the sides of the hills, and the water formed by the melting of the snow in the spring was let into them. All manner of devices, in short, were resorted to for the purpose of keeping in and upon the hills all of the moisture from snow or rains that fell upon them. Yet, one after another these hills failed. When once the tops had been thoroughly drained it appeared to require all of the water that fell on them in any shape during winter to reach down into and moisten them to the level of the tunnels. Finally, there were, in all, many miles of these horizontal wells. All the hills from which water could be brought, for miles away to the northward and southward of Virginia City and Gold Hill, were tapped, thousands on thousands of dollars being expended in this work. When a reservoir of water was first tapped in a new hill there would be poured out a great flood for a few days; this would then fall to a moderate stream and so remain for a month or two, when it would begin to dwindle away. The water from the many tunnels was collected by means of small wooden flumes or troughs, winding about the curves of the hills for miles, and in summer, when most wanted, the sickly streams from the more distant tunnels were lost by leakage and evaporation before having finished half their course to the towns.

Virginia City and Gold Hill were frequently placed upon a short allowance of water, and it was seen that a great water famine must soon prevail in both towns, in case the tunnels that had been run into the mountains were depended upon for a supply. The Virginia and Gold Hill Water Company then determined to bring a supply of pure water from the streams and lakes of the Sierra Nevada Mountains—from the regions of eternal snow.

The distance from Virginia City to the first available streams in the Sierras was about twenty-five miles; but between the Virginia range of mountains and the Sierras lay the deep depression known as Washoe Valley—in one part of which is situated Washoe Lake. The problem to be solved in bringing water from the Sierras to Virginia City was how to convey it across this deep valley.

Mr. H. Schussler, the engineer under whose supervision the Spring Valley Water Works, of San Francisco, were constructed, was sent for, and crossing the Sierras he made an examination of the route over which it was proposed to bring the water. He acknowledged that the undertaking was one of great difficulty. To convey the water across the deep depression formed by Washoe Valley would demand the performing of a feat in hydraulic engineering never before attempted in any part of the world. This was to carry the water through an iron pipe under a perpendicular pressure of 1,720 feet. This feat, however, Mr. Schussler said could be performed, and he was ready to undertake it at once.

Surveys were made, in the spring of 1872, and orders given for the manufacture of the pipe. To make the pipe was the work of nearly a year. The manufacturers were furnished with a diagram of the line on which it was to be laid and each section was made to fit a certain spot. When the route lay round a point of rocks the pipe was made of the required curve, and other curved sections were required when the line crossed deep and narrow ravines.

The first section of pipe was laid June 11th, 1873, and the last on the 25th of July the same year. The whole length of the pipe is seven miles and one hundred and thirty-four feet. Its interior diameter is twelve inches, and is capable of delivering 2,200,000 gallons of water per twenty-four hours. It lies across Washoe Valley in the form of an inverted syphon. The end at which the water is received rests upon a spur from the main Sierras at an elevation of 1,885 feet above Washoe Valley. The outlet is on the crest of the Virginia range of mountains, on the eastern slope of which are situated the towns of Virginia and Gold Hill. The perpendicular elevation of the inlet above the outlet is four hundred and sixty-five feet. Thus is brought to bear a great pressure which forces the water rapidly through the pipe.

The water is brought to the inlet through a large wooden flume, and at the outlet is delivered into a similar flume, twelve miles in length, which conveys it to Virginia City. The pipe is of wrought iron, and is fastened by three rows of five-eighths-inch rivets. At the lowest point in the ground crossed, the perpendicular pressure is one thousand seven hundred and twenty feet, equal to eight hundred pounds to the square inch. Here the iron is five-sixteenths of an inch in thickness, but as the ground rises to the east and west, and the pressure is reduced, the thickness of the iron decreases through one-fourth, three-sixteenths. down to one-sixteenth.

In its course the pipe crosses thirteen deep gulches, making necessary that number of undulations, as it is throughout its length laid at the depth of 2½ feet below the surface of the earth. Besides these, there are a great number of lateral curves round hills and points of rocks. There was just one place and none other for each section of pipe as received from the manufactory. At each point where there is a depression in the pipe there is a blow-off cock, for the removal of any sediment that may collect, and on the top of each ridge is an air-cock, for blowing off the air when the water was first let in, and at other times when the pipe is being filled. The pipe contains no less than 1,150,000 pounds of rolled iron, is held together by 1,000,000 rivets, and there were used in securing the joints 52,000 pounds of lead, which was melted and poured in from a portable furnace that moved along the line as the work of laying the pipe progressed. Before being put down, each section of the pipe was boiled in a bath of asphaltum and coal-tar at a temperature of 380 degrees. At the first filling of the pipe a stream of water, about the thickness of a common lead-pencil, escaped through

the lead packing of a joint, at a point where the
pressure was greatest. This struck against the
face of a rock and, rebounding, played upon the
upper side of the pipe. The water brought with it
from the rock a small quantity of sand or grit, perhaps, but at all events it soon bored a hole through
the pipe, and from this hole, which shortly became
two or three inches in diameter, a jet of water as-
scended to the height of two hundred feet or more,
spreading out in the shape of a fan toward the top.

When this break occurred, a signal smoke was
made in the valley, and the lookout at the inlet on
the mountain spur shut off the water. Over each
joint in the pipe was placed a cast-iron sleeve or
band, weighing 300 pounds, and within this sleeve
was poured the molten lead which served as packing. In all there were used 1,475, or 442,500
pounds, of these sleeves, and but three out of the
whole number proved faulty and failed to sustain
the strain brought upon them, and of 12,640 sheets
of iron used in the pipe but one bad one was found.
As it would have been a great task to test each
section of the pipe by hydraulic pressure at the
manufactory, the engineer proposed to bring the
whole under the required strain at once, after they
were put down. He began the pressure with a
perpendicular height of 1,250 feet in the column
of water, increased it to 1,550, to 1,700, and finally
to 1,850, being 130 feet more than the pipe would
be required to sustain when in actual use.

During these experiments, men were stationed at
the inlet of the pipe, at its outlet on the summit of
the Virginia range, and at various points through
the valley, as lookout men. They made their sig-

nals by means of smoke during the day, and a fire by night—a trick learned from the Piute Indians.

As the water came surging down through the great inverted syphon from the elevated mountain spur, and began to fill and press upon the parts lying in the deeper portions of the valley, one after another the blow-off cocks on the crests of the ridges crossed, opened, and allowed the escape of the compressed air. Compared with what was heard when these cocks blew off, the blowing of a whale was a mere whisper. The water finally flowed through the pipe and reached Gold Hill and Virginia City on the night of August 1, 1873. Early that evening a signal fire was lighted in the mountains at the inlet of the pipe, showing that the water had again been turned on.

As the pipe filled, the progress of the water in it could be traced by the blowing off of the air on the tops of the ridges, through the valley and at last, to the great joy of the engineer and all concerned in the success of the enterprise, the signal fire at the outlet, on the summit of the Virginia range, was for the first time lighted, showing that the water was flowing through the whole length of the pipe.

When the water reached Virginia City there was great rejoicing. Cannons were fired, bands of music paraded the streets, and rockets were sent up all over the city. Many persons went out and filled bottles with this first water from the Sierras, and a bottle of it is still preserved in the cabinet of the Pacific Coast Pioneers.—From ''The Big Bonanza.''

NOBILITY

By Richard Realf

CAN'T man be noble unless he be great,
  With a patrimonial hall;
And heaps of gold and vast estate,
  And vassals at his call?

Can't man be noble unless there be
  A title to his name,
Unless he live in luxury
  Or loll in the seats of fame?

Can't man be noble unless his voice
  Be heard in the senate band;
Or his eye flash bright and his words breathe light
  Through all his native land?

Ah yes! at the forge and the weaver's loom,
  As well as in hall of state,
At the desk and in the cottage room,
  There are noble ones and great.

They are springing up on every side,
  In hamlet and in town;
Where the stream pours and ocean roars,
  They are wreathing a laurel crown.

They are weaving the mighty robe of truth,
  And bold are the throws they make,
As they are teaching age and guilt
  Oppressive bonds to break.

Yes, these are the noble and the great
  Who will shine at a distant day,
Where titled ones of hall and state
  Shall have been but far away.
                    —From "Poems."

A UNIQUE HOUSE

By W. C. Bartlett

THE loftiest house, and the most perfect, in the
matter of architecture, I have ever seen, was that
which a wood-chopper occupied with his family one
winter in the forests of Santa Cruz County. It
was the cavity of a redwood tree two hundred and
forty feet in height. Fire had eaten away the
trunk at the base, until a circular room had been
formed, sixteen feet in diameter. At twenty feet
or more from the ground was a knot-hole, which
afforded egress for the smoke. With hammocks
hung from pegs, and a few cooking utensils hung
from other pegs, that house lacked no essential
thing. This woodsman was in possession of a house
which had been a thousand years in process of
building. Perhaps on the very day it was finished
he came along and entered it. How did all jack-
knife and hand-saw architecture sink into insignificance in contrast with this house in the solitudes
of the great forest! Moreover, the tenant fared
like a prince; within thirty yards of his coniferous
house a mountain stream went rushing past to the
sea. In the swirls and eddies under the shelving
rocks if one could not land half a dozen trout

within an hour he deserved to go hungry as a penalty for his awkwardness. Now and then a deer came out into the openings, and, at no great distance quail, rabbits and pigeons could be found. What did this man want more than nature had furnished him? He had a house with a "cupola" two hundred and forty feet high, and game at the cost of taking it.—From "A Breeze From the Woods."

IN BLOSSOM TIME

By Ina Coolbrith

IT'S O my heart, my heart,
    To be out in the sun and sing—
To sing and shout in the fields about,
    In the balm and blossoming!

Sing loud, O bird in the tree;
    O bird, sing loud in the sky,
And honey-bees, blacken the clover beds—
    There is none of you glad as I.

The leaves laugh low in the wind,
    Laugh low, with the wind at play;
And the odorous call of the flowers all
    Entices my soul away!

For O but the world is fair, is fair—
    And O but the world is sweet!
I will out in the gold of the blossoming mould,
    And sit at the Master's feet.

And the love my heart would speak,
  I will fold in the lily's rim,
That the lips of the blossom, more pure and meek,
  May offer it up to Him.

Then sing in the hedgerow green, O thrush,
  O skylark, sing in the blue;
Sing loud, sing clear, that the king may hear,
  And my soul shall sing with you!
          —From "Songs of the Golden Gate."

AUTUMN IN SOUTHERN CALIFORNIA

By Theodore Van Dyke

THERE is nothing about autumn here that is at all saddening or sentimental. It is only the long-lingering afternoon of a long-lingering summer day. There are dreamy hazes and filmy atmospheres enough, but they are not at all peculiar to autumn. The spider occasionally weaves his thin shroud and the gossamer rides the air; dead leaves rustle to the rabbit's tread; the crow caws from the tree-top; the jay jangles and the quail pipes; but they have been doing it all summer, and, in truth, much of it in the spring. It is a bad country for "the singer," although one occasionally ventures "a poem" in which no one without looking at the title could tell which season it described.

September brings no change along the rolling hills, except a little ashen tint upon the ramiria and the chorizanthe, a paler brown upon the dodder that clambers over the chemisal or buckwheat, a grayer shade upon the white sage and the dead

phacelias, a grayer brown upon the plains and
table-lands. Smiling from unclouded skies, the sun
passes the central line, the nights grow a trifle
cooler, the ocean breeze a trifle fresher; but instead of rain there is merely a dryer air. The lin-
net and the mocking-bird are heard no more; the
cooing of the dove sounds more seldom from the
grove; the brooding call of the quail has ceased
along the hills and dales, and the young coveys
gather into large bands. The mimulus that has
lingered long among the shady chinks of the granite piles begins to close its crimson bugles; the ivy
that twines the oak above it shows a strong tinge
of scarlet; the sand-verbena and other summer
flowers begin to fade; the wild gourd ripens on the
low grounds, and the meadows along the edge turn
a trifle sere. But in nearly all else it is summer.

October comes, but the summer sun still rules
the land. The low hills that are free from chaparral grow paler where the dead mustard, wild oats,
clover, alfileria and foxtail have so long lain bleach-
ing. The chaparral bushes look, perhaps, a trifle
weary; the green of the sumac is a little less bright
than in July; the elder and the wild buckwheat
look unmistakably worse for wear, and even the
ever-vigorous cactus seems to think it has done full
duty. But all these changes are very slight and
would scarcely be noticed by the casual observer.
For the whole host of bushes and trees that cover
the hills, the living grass that covers the moist
lands, and the dead grass that carpets the plains,
all wear the same general appearance as in July;
while some plants, such as goldenrod in the meadows, are just coming into bloom, and on the dry

lands the baccharis is rearing its snowy plumes. Many days will now be cooler than most days of the summer, hoar-frost will be found along the mountain valleys, some skies will be a little overcast, perhaps rain enough may fall to start the weather prophets; but the whole will be soft and bright like the sunset hour of a lovely summer day.

November: Yet no leaden skies; no sodden leaves on soaking ground; no snowflakes riding on howling blasts; no sloughs of mud in the roads to-day, frozen hummocks to-morrow; no robin chirping out a dismal farewell high above one's head; no fish-ducks whistling down the icy margin of the pond where of late the mallard quacked; no sparrows sitting around with ruffled feathers. Only a little colder nights and shorter days; only a little frost along the bottoms of the valleys; only a little stiller, drier air, often clearer than in summer, except where brush-fires make it thick or hazy. The evaporation being checked by the longer and cooler nights, the water rises in the springs and runs in places where two months ago was nothing but dry sand. The wild duck appears along the sloughs, the honk of the goose is heard again in its winter haunts, the bluebird and robin come down from the high mountains, and the turtledove almost disappears. The sycamore and cottonwood begin to look sere, the grapevine leaves are yellowing, and the willows are fast fading. But in nearly all else it is still summer.

December comes at last, but few would suspect it. The nights are still colder, and the hoar-frost creeps higher up along the slopes of the valleys, and thin ice may form at daylight on some of the

lowest grounds. Yet the days are nearly like those
of summer, though the seabreeze is almost gone
and the wind comes often from the north and east.
The berries of the manzanita are now black and
shining; the heteromeles is aglow with scarlet clusters; the goldenrod that lately blazed along the
meadows is grown gray and fuzzy; the acorns pat-
ter on the roof beneath the spreading live-oak; the
plains look a little grayer, the table-lands a little
browner. But the grand old oaks, the sumacs, the
lilac, fuchsia, manzanita, madrona—all the chaparral bushes, in fact—are very nearly as green as
ever. We might as well call the whole of it summer, for it is only summer a little worn out.

"How fearfully monotonous all that must be!"
remarks one who has never passed through it. "I
like something positive, some distinctive features
about the seasons. It is so pleasant to sit by the
fire and hear the snowstorm howl without; sleigh-
riding is so delightful, skating is such a luxury!
And then the winter air is so bracing and sends
the pulse bounding, and makes the cheek glow with
health!"

To which it might be replied: There are some
things that are not always objectionable even when
monotonous; such things as health and wealth, for
instance. It is possible that such things appear
monotonous to those who do not possess them; and
also possible that after a thorough trial of them
they might change their opinion of them. One
who has never spent an autumn outside of an um-
brella or an overcoat, and all whose winters have
been largely spent sitting by the fires and listening to the raging of the storm without, is hardly a

competent judge compared with one who has given
both sides of the case a fair trial, as have most of
the residents of California. At all events, there is
always one resource for any one whom such monotony troubles—to return to the East and try
once more those good old days by the fire. Few
ever stay East long enough to test them again thoroughly; from those that do, "monotony" is the
least complaint ever heard after their return to
California.—From "Southern California."

LEAF AND BLADE

By Ina Coolbrith

I AM a lowly grass blade,
    A fair green leaf is she,
Her little fluttering shadow
    Falls daily over me.

She sits so high in sunshine,
    I am so low in shade,
I do not think she ever
    Has looked where I am laid.

She sings to merry music,
    She frolics in the light;
The great moon plays the lover
    With her through half the night.

The swift, sweet winds they flatter
    And woo her all the day—
I tremble lest the boldest
    Should carry her away.

Only a little grass blade
    That dare not look so high,
Yet, oh! not any love her
    One-half so well as I.

My little love—so happy!
    My love—so proud and fair!
Would she might dwell forever
    In the sweet summer air.

But, ah! the days will darken,
    The pleasant skies will pall,
And pale, and parched, and broken,
    My little love down fall.

And yet the thought most bitter
    Is not that she must die,
But that even death should bring her
    To lie as low as I.
—From "Songs From the Golden Gate."

THE ASCENT OF MT. TYNDALL

By Clarence King

THERE was no foothold above us. Looking
down over the course we had come, it seemed,
and I really believe it was, an impossible descent;
for one can climb upward with safety where he
cannot downward. To turn back was to give up in
defeat; and we sat at least half an hour, suggesting
all possible routes to the summit, accepting none,
and feeling disheartened.

About thirty feet directly over our heads was another shelf which, if we could reach it, seemed to offer at least a temporary way upward. On its edge were two or three spikes of granite; whether firmly connected with the cliff, or merely to blocks of debris, we could not tell from below. I said to Cotter, I thought of but one possible plan: It was to lasso one of these blocks, and to climb, sailor fashion, hand over hand, up the rope.

In the lasso I had perfect confidence, for I had seen more than one Spanish bull throw his whole weight against it without parting a strand. The shelf was so narrow that throwing the coil of rope was a very difficult undertaking.

I tried three times, and Cotter spent five minutes vainly whirling the loop up at the granite spikes.

At last I made a lucky throw, and it tightened upon one of the smaller protuberances. I drew the noose close, and very gradually threw my hundred and fifty pounds upon the rope; then Cotter joined me and, for a moment, we both hung our united weight upon it.

Whether the rock moved slightly or whether the lasso stretched a little we were unable to decide; but the trial must be made, and I began to climb slowly. The smooth precipice-face against which my body swung offered no foothold, and the whole climb had, therefore, to be done by the arms, an effort requiring all one's determination. When about halfway up I was obliged to rest, and curling my feet in the rope, managed to relieve my arms for a moment. In this position I could not resist the fascinating temptation of a survey downward.

Straight down, nearly a thousand feet below, at the foot of the rocks, began the snow, whose steep, roof-like slope, exaggerated into an almost vertical angle, curved down in a long white field, broken far away by rocks and polished, round lakes of ice.

Cotter looked up cheerfully and asked how I was making it, to which I answered that I had plenty of wind left. At that moment, when hanging between heaven and earth, it was a deep satisfaction to look down at the wild gulf of desolation beneath, and up to unknown dangers ahead, and to feel my nerves cool and unshaken.

A few pulls hand over hand brought me to the edge of the shelf, when, throwing an arm around the granite spike, I swung my body upon the shelf and lay down to rest, shouting to Cotter that I was all right, and that the prospects upward were capital. After a few moments' breathing I looked over the brink and directed my comrade to tie the barometer to the lower end of the lasso, which he did, and that precious instrument was hoisted to my station, and the lasso sent down twice for knapsacks, after which Cotter came up the rope in his very muscular way without once stopping to rest. We took our loads in our hands, swinging the barometer over my shoulder, and climbed up a shelf which led in a zigzag direction upward and to the south, bringing us out at last upon the thin blade of a ridge which connected a short distance above with the summit. It was formed of huge blocks, shattered and ready, at a touch, to fall.

So narrow and sharp was the upper slope that we dared not walk, but got astride, and worked slowly along with our hands, pushing the knapsacks in advance, now and then holding our breath when loose masses rocked under our weight.

Once upon the summit, a grand view burst upon us. Hastening to step upon the crest of the divide, which was never more than ten feet wide, frequently sharpened to a thin blade, we looked down the other side, and were astonished to find we had ascended the gentler slope, and that the rocks fell from our feet in almost vertical precipices for a thousand feet or more. A glance along the summit toward the highest group showed us that any advance in that direction was impossible, for the thin ridge was gashed along in notches three or four hundred feet deep, forming a procession of pillars, obelisks, and blocks piled upon each other, and looking terribly insecure.

We then deposited our knapsacks in a safe place, and, finding that it was already noon, determined to rest a little while and take a lunch at over thirteen thousand feet above the sea.

The view was so grand, the mountain colors so brilliant, immense snowfields and blue alpine lakes so charming, that we almost forgot we were ever to move, and it was only after a swift hour of this delight that we began to consider our future course.

"We're in for it now, King," remarked my comrade, as he looked aloft, and then down; but our blood was up and danger added only an exhilarating thrill to the nerves.

The shelf was barely more than two feet wide and the granite so smooth that we could find no place to fasten the lasso for the next descent; so I determined to try the climb with only as little aid as possible. Tying it around my breast again,

I gave the other end into Cotter's hands, and he, bracing his back against the cliff, found for himself as firm a foothold as he could, and promised to give me all the help in his power. I made up my mind to bear no weight unless it was absolutely necessary; and for the first ten feet I found cracks and protuberances enough to support me, making every square inch of surface do friction duty, and hugging myself against the rocks as tightly as I could. When within about eight feet of the next shelf, I twisted myself round upon the face, hanging by two rough blocks of protruding feldspar, and looked vainly for some further handhold; but the rock, beside being perfectly smooth, overhung slightly, and my legs dangled in the air. I saw that the next cleft was over three feet broad, and I thought possibly I might, by a quick slide, reach it in safety without endangering Cotter. I shouted to him to be very careful and let go in case I fell, loosened my hold upon the rope, and slid quickly down. My shoulder struck against the rock and threw me out of balance; for an instant I reeled over upon the verge, in danger of falling, but, in the excitement, I thrust out my hand and seized a small alpine gooseberry bush, the first piece of vegetation we had seen. Its roots were so firmly fixed in the crevice that it held my weight and saved me.

I could no longer see Cotter, but I talked to him, and heard the two knapsacks come bumping along till they slid over the eaves above me, and swung down to my station, when I seized the lasso's end and braced myself as well as possible, intending, if he slipped, to haul in slack and help him as best

I could. As he came slowly down from crack to crack, I heard his hobnailed shoes grating on the granite; presently they appeared dangling from the eaves above my head. I had gathered in the rope until it was taut, and then hurriedly told him to drop. He hesitated a moment and let go. Before he struck the rock I had him by the shoulder and whirled him down upon his side, thus preventing his rolling overboard, which friendly action he took quite coolly.

The third descent was not a difficult one, nor the fourth; but when we had climbed down about two hundred and fifty feet the rocks were so glacially polished and water-worn that it seemed impossible to get any farther. To our right was a crack penetrating the rock perhaps a foot deep, widening at the surface to three or four inches, which proved to be the only possible ladder. As the chances seemed rather desperate, we concluded to tie ourselves together, in order to share a common fate, and with a slack of thirty feet between us and our knapsacks upon our backs, we climbed into the crevice and began descending with our faces to the cliff. This had to be done with unusual caution, for the foothold was about as good as none, and our fingers slipped annoyingly on the smooth stone; besides, the knapsacks and instruments kept a steady backward pull, tending to over-balance us. But we took pains to descend one at a time and rest whenever the niches gave our feet a safe support. In this way we got down about eighty feet of smooth, nearly vertical wall, reaching the top of a rude granite stairway, which led to the snow; and here we sat down to rest and found to our astonishment that we had been three hours from the summit.

After breathing a half minute we continued down, jumping from rock to rock, and, having by practice become very expert in balancing ourselves, sprang on, never resting long enough to lose the aplomb, and in this way made a quick descent over rugged debris to the crest of a snow-field, which, for seven or eight hundred feet more, swept down in a smooth, even slope, of very high angle, to the borders of a frozen lake.

Without untying the lasso which bound us together, we sprang upon the snow with a shout and glissaded down splendidly, turning now and then a summersault and shooting out like cannonballs almost to the middle of the frozen lake, I upon my back, and Cotter feet first, in a swmming position. The ice cracked in all directions. It was only a thin, transparent film, through which we could see deep into the lake. Untying ourselves we hurried ashore in different directions, lest our combined weight should be too great a strain upon any point.

With curiosity and wonder we scanned every shelf and niche of the last descent. It seemed quite impossible we could have come down there, and now it actually was beyond human power to get back again. But what cared we? "Sufficient unto the day." We were bound for that still distant, though gradually nearing, summit; and we had come from a cold, shadowed cliff into deliciously warm sunshine and were jolly, shouting, singing songs and calling out the companionship of a hundred echoes.—From "Mountaineering in the Sierra Nevadas."

A TRIP TO THE FARALLONES

By Charles Keeler

AT daylight, on a Sunday morning in July, I found myself with one companion standing upon Fisherman's Wharf in San Francisco and waiting for the signal to start upon a trip to the Farallones. The early hour had been chosen on account of the tide, which was then on the ebb, a circumstance of no little importance in undertaking to beat out to sea through the Golden Gate against the fresh head wind which was then blowing. The sun was just flushing the misty sky over the Berkeley hills across the bay, and the staunch craft of the Greek fishermen were bobbing about at their moorings beside us. One or two were already starting off and spreading their graceful lateen sails to the morning breeze. A group of bronzed fishermen, in their blue shirts, rubber boots and bright sashes, were at work making ready some of the boats for the day's labor, washing seines, hauling them in to dry and cleaning off the decks.

The captain and two hands, composing the crew of our little boat, were late in arriving, but presently appeared on the wharf with supplies for the trip. Like most of the fishermen, our men were Greeks, understanding but little English and speaking less. Our boat was the largest of the fishermen's one-masted craft with lateen sails, and was

5

decked over, leaving an apartment below in which one might sit or crawl about in the darkness. All being ready, the anchor was drawn in and stowed below, and the long oars were brought into use to carry us well out into the stream. By this time the breeze had freshened so that the water was flecked with big white combers. Several fishing boats had started out before us and a number followed closely after, making a picturesque little flotilla scudding along under closely reefed sails. The raising of our mainsail in so stiff a breeze was attended with no little difficulty, but at last, after much pulling, jumping about, shouting and dodging of flapping canvas and swinging boom, it was up and we were started on our voyage.

My companion and I were safely stowed out of harm's way below deck, with the hatch tightly closed over our heads and the odors of unsavory viands and bilge water about us in the darkness. The boat was bobbing about like a cork and the one controlling passion of our lives was to get out of our prison into the sunlight. This we presently insisted on doing, and, upon opening the hatch and standing up in the well, life took on quite a different aspect. The cold, salt air soon restored us to a more comfortable frame of mind, although, every few minutes, a vigorous wave would come *cathud* against the bow and hurl a bucketful of water in our faces. The fortunate possession of a rubber coat saved me from being completely drenched, and, with the exception of the seepage from an occasional shower of spray running down my neck, and a pair of wet shoes, I kept tolerably dry. The case was otherwise with my companion, however;

he had no rubber coat and was accordingly soon compelled to go below, drenched and disconsolate.

We passed the ships anchored in the stream. Alcatraz, with its array of fortifications, was on the right of us and Black Point on the left. As we stood out past Lime Point, in the teeth of a stiff breeze, I occupied myself watching the California murres disporting in the water. The murre is one of the low forms of sea bird which nest along the exposed rocky cliffs of both the Atlantic and Pacific Oceans. The breeze was still blowing and our little craft tumbling about as it approached the bar of the Golden Gate. When a little way out at sea, we noticed, slightly isolated from the mainland, a large rock completely whitened with the guano of this bird, a fact indicating the presence of a large rookery.

The wind, which had been uncomfortably brisk inside the bay, left us almost entirely after we were well off the shore, and we were soon rolling aimlessly on the broad ocean swells, with only now and then a puff of air to make the sails flap. Thus we spent the rest of the day, the great glassy undulating surface of the sea rocking us about upon the very threshold of our journey, with the bleak coast-line visible far behind us—bold, bare and black in hue, save for some yellow patches of dead grass—and the Farallones lost in the mist at sea. The sun went down behind them and out of the west came the cold, pervasive fog, folding us in its mantle of utter darkness. Ships were near us, becalmed in like manner. At intervals their foghorns blew and our captain responded upon a dismal tin horn. One ship drew so near that we could hear the cries of the men as they tugged at the ropes, the voice of the mate calling orders and the noise of the flapping sails.

We went supperless to bed, our stomachs not admitting of experiments with the coarse fare of the fishermen, and lay in our close, damp quarters in uneasy sleep. At daybreak next morning the dark, lead-colored water and foggy air looked cheerless enough, but we were consoled by the information that we were sailing under a good breeze directly toward our destination. Soon the North Farallones loomed up through the fog—little bare rocks visible only as we rose on the crest of a wave, with the surf dashing against their sides. Presently Midway Rock was passed and at last we were in sight of South Farallone. Almost before we knew it the mainsail had been lowered. As we rounded a projecting rock the jib was taken in and we slipped past Sugar Loaf Rock into Fisherman's Bay, where the anchor was dropped and the fog-horn blown to summon the eggers on shore to send us a skiff in which to land. Drawing near the island we found ourselves in a new and strange wonderland. There was but a bare, jagged ridge of rock cut out in places into great cones and pyramids. Yonder was one shaped like a titanic bee-hive and about it swarmed a vast throng of sea birds in lieu of bees. Off toward the farther end was a rock with a little archway cut through it near the top. The rocks were of a light pinkish or cream color, from the guano upon them, interspersed with patches of pale green where some mosses or lichens had taken root. Lower down, where the waves dashed upon them, they were clean and almost black in color, while in beautiful contrast to their somber hue the breakers were shattered into white foam and pale green opaline tints. But that which interested us most was the vast assemblage of birds. Every cranny upon the face of the rough, granitic cliffs was alive with murres, uttering their characteristic note, some at rest, some fluttering and scrambling or bobbing their heads, the whole scene being one of indescribably weird animation, and unlike anything else imaginable unless it be the witches in Faust on Walpurgis night. Here and there the black figure of a cormorant upon her nest was noticed, or one would fly past with a fish in her bill, headed toward her young. Occasionally a puffin, or sea parrot, as he is aptly called—a queer fellow with his immense red bill—would pass our way. The most familiar birds were the western gulls, which flocked about the boat in considerable numbers, displaying their beautiful slate-blue mantles and yellow, scarlet-spotted bills. They were attracted by the refuse of the men's breakfast which had been thrown overboard in the cove, but in spite of their fine plumage and graceful actions they proved to be disagreeable, noisy, quarrelsome birds.

After our half hour of impatient waiting the eggers appeared on the cliff above us, and, lowering a skiff which hung suspended from a sling, rowed out to take us ashore. Once safely landed we climbed up the long, ladder stairway to the level bluff whence the roadway leads around to the lighthouse settlement. Having fasted for thirty-six hours it was annoying to be overcome by seasickness and to be compelled to take a cup of tea in lieu of breakfast. However, time was precious, and, as we had come on a scientific excursion, we were determined to make the best of it. The eggers started early on their morning's round, so we trudged along after them as briskly as we could.

It may be well to digress a few moments to explain the vocation of egging as carried on at the Farallones a few years ago. The egg of the California murre was found to have possibilities, as a marketable commodity, of being converted into omelettes and sundry other mysterious dishes in the San Francisco restaurants. The shell is so tough that the eggs may be tossed about almost as freely as so many cobblestones, thus making the cargo an especially easy one to handle. A party of Greek fishermen made a practice of camping upon the Farallones during the egging season and gathering enough eggs to keep one of their largest craft constantly employed transporting them to town. Upon establishing themselves upon the island they would first go about the accessible area occupied by the birds and destroy every egg which could be found. A day or two later they would repeat their visit, gathering a large supply of fresh eggs. These visits were continued every second or third day of the season, until the resources of the birds were about exhausted. The eggers wore rope shoes to make their footing secure upon the dangerous, rocky ledges, and the fronts of their shirts were converted into great pockets in which to carry the plunder. Ropes, to which the men could cling as they advanced, were secured to the rocks in the more perilous places. The government has now wisely put a stop to this traffic, which was rapidly

depleting this locality of its sea birds.—From
"Bird Notes Afield."

THE OAKS OF TULARE

By Lillian Hinman Shuey

GO up the broad valley, the far land, the fair
    land,
  Where the plain stretches on like a slumbering
    sea;
Where rivers flow down from high mountains
    snow-crowned,
  And the wind seeks the desert to roam and be
    free.
Go there when sweet April her soft showers carry
  To the wonderful grove land, the oaks of Tulare.

Go there in bright June when the slow-creeping
    shadows,
  In the rank meadow grasses lie dewy and cool;
The boughs all attune with the sky-larks and lin-
    nets,
  While the soft winds of summer the leafy courts
    rule.
One still autumn day in thy green aisles to tarry
  Is forever to love thee, dear oaks of Tulare.

I see the blue sky and the high fretted arches,
  And the moss-tangled branches all knotted and
    gray;

Fond memory pictures the calm, sacred places
　Where I waited and loitered that happy June
　　day.
While Hope, eager-winged as some comforting
　fairy,
　Is alluring me back to the oaks of Tulare.

Great oaks leading up to the steep sunny hillsides,
　Stretching down to the banks of the slow, wind-
　　ing stream,
I see, through thy vistas, the homestead, the cot-
　tage,
　And the pink-tinted orchards in radiance gleam.
Some day may I rest there, long, glad years to
　tarry,
　In my wonderful grove land, the oaks of Tulare.
　　　　　　　—From "California Sunshine."

FROM YUMA TO SALTON SEA

By George Wharton James

PURCHASING two boats at Yuma, one a flat-
bottomed ordinary gig, stoutly built, with six
oars, and the other a mere tub, or light scow, with
flat bottom and stub nose, such as miners and prospectors have made to float down the Colorado River,
our party of six whites left "the city of torrid
heat." There were Brown (partner of Burton
Holmes, the well-known lecturer); Gripton, of New
York; Van Anderson, of New York; Judson, dean
of Fine Arts Department of University of South-

[From "The Wonders of the Colorado Desert," by George
　Wharton James.　Copyright, 1906, by Edith E. Farns-
　worth.]

electric light plants, all revealing the great activity and determined pressure of the work. All the men that could possibly be used were working day and night on the construction of the Rockwood headgate.

Here our Indians joined us for the main part of the trip. Talk about Indians being fools! They were both keen, observing, wide-awake, daring, serene in the face of danger, self-contained and hard-working. There's many a white man who would look down on these "savages" who could not begin to compare with them in intelligence and practical usefulness.

Leaving the lower intake in three boats with six whites and these two Indians we started down the Alamo—as the canal should properly be termed. For the first ten miles it was plain, easy, smooth floating on the bosom of a great river, for, as I have shown, all the water of the Colorado was pouring through the "temporary cut" into it. The great volume had widened and deepened the channel until now it was no longer a "canal," but a mighty river, nearly 1,000 feet across.

At the end of this ten miles our troub'es began. As we had been warned, we found the river had left its bed and overflowed the country in every direction, in all of which was a mesquite forest. The mesquite, for all practical purposes where man is concerned, should be called the *mescratch,* for its thorns are large, sharp and penetrating. As the diminished current bore us on we ran end on, stern on, sidewise, anyhow, into these mesquite thorns. I was in the front boat, in the bow, seeking the way. As the stream divided and subdivided it required speedy observation to tell which was the larger current and follow it, and Jim and I were kept very busy. There was no time given for decision, for we were borne on into one of the waiting trees, ready to pierce us from "stem to stern" with its poisonous thorns. I learned to "take" them head on as a goat takes its foes. Pulling my broad-brimmed sombrero over my ears, lifting up my coat collar and lowering my head I "butted in." But the fun came when we stuck there. Fun? Oh, it was great, to find yourself lodged in the heart of the branches of a mesquite, the thorns making fresh punctures in your tires at very movement, and the uneasy current beneath swaying and swinging you to and fro! Many a time we had to resort to machete, hatchet or axe and literally chop our way through. Then, as the many divisions and diversions of the current reduced the flow of water, we ran on to sandbars in these mesquites and for hours at a time we had to wade in the water, up to our middles, often sinking in the quicksands up to our knees and higher, lifting, pushing, pulling, straining to get our boats along, while the mesquite thorns got in their work.

And the *joy* of it was increased as night came on. We were still in the thick of it. No place to camp. Not a sign of dry bank anywhere. There was nothing for us but to stop in the first break big enough for three boats to be tied side by side, for misery loves and needs company, and eating our cold supper, scratched from top to toe, wet through, muddy, bedraggled, and wretched in appearance, our "joy" was added to by a heavy downpour of rain. Physically we were so miserable that it made us laugh.

Where were we to sleep?

Nowhere but in the boats. Now it cannot be conceded that the slats at the bottom of a boat are at all conducive to sleep, especially when the slats are wet and very muddy. With evident shrinking these scions of noble houses stretched out their blankets. Brownie and Lea took the scow, the two Indians the bow of the big boat, Grippie the wide stern-seat, to which he built an extension for his feet, and Van on the slats below, while I had the other small boat to myself.

My! how it did pour, and I guess those boats leaked extra on purpose. Wet through, I awoke to find Van wringing out his blankets, and at another time to hear Grippie laughing as if he would burst. "What's up?" I asked, to which he gave the intelligible response, "I'm laughing because I'm so miserable."

No hot coffee! no hot steak! no steaming fried onions! no hot anything, except a hot temper! But we had vowed we would "grin and bear" whatever came along, so with "brave hearts and dauntless spirits" we swallowed a cold biscuit and started on.

It was four times worse that morning than it had been the preceding day. Hour after hour we toiled along, up to the waist in water, chopping, cutting, pushing, pulling, and getting scratched, mainly the latter. Several times we had to cut down mesquite trees that completely blocked our way, and I never knew before how hard it was to cut down a tree below the water line. For, of course, if the stump was left high enough to prevent our boats going over them, we might as well have left the trees standing.

Hour after hour it kept up, until at last peace reigned within, for we were back again in the main current and channel. The contour of the country here is such that, while a small part of the water had escaped and flowed off by way of the Rio Padrones, the larger amount converges and re-enters the banks of the Alamo at a point called Seven Wells. As soon as we could we camped, spread out our bedding to dry, while Brownie made sweet music with steak, onions, potatoes and corn on the frying-pan and stew-kettles.

That night in camp on the Alamo we uneasily tossed on our blankets, for all of us had a number of thorns deep seated in various and many parts of our systems. While the thorns in our bodies made our sleep that night somewhat disturbed, it was a great improvement upon the night we spent in the boats.

The following day we had reasonably good rowing, though the wind arose and blew dead against us for several miles. But with a fair current in our favor we were able to make headway.

That afternoon we reached Sharps, the point in Mexico where the waters of the river are taken and diverted into the canals of the Imperial region. Leaving one of our boats here, we were soon gliding easily along down the strong current. There was a trifle of nervousness at first, lest we get too far apart, and one or the other of us get into trouble, so the order was, "Keep close together, and listen for each other's signals." Our first rapid gave us quite a little thrill. It was nothing very great or dangerous, but to hear the roar and rush, and swish and dash of the water, and to see the rising and falling, the spray and spume, and the marked descent of the whole river for fifty feet or more, led us to wonder if we'd get through all right. Indian Jim at the oars and I with the steering oar, we sent our boat right into the heart of it, and in a moment we were rising and falling, tossing and bouncing, from one wave to another. We shipped a little water, but not enough to scare us, so it was with bolder hearts we ran the next and the next.

Soon the lookout called, "Two water-tanks ahead," and when we all arose to see, there loomed before us on the right, the tanks of the power house at Holtville. We tied up here, for three of our party, Brownie, Gripton and Lea, had to leave us, and Indian Joe went with them. They took team for Imperial, while Van Anderson, Indian Jim and I were left to run the rapids alone.

The question arose in my mind: Shall we go in two boats or one? The square-nosed scow had served us so well I hated to part with it, so without consulting the others I decided to handle it myself. We started, and almost immediately ran into a "nasty" place. The railway bridge crosses the Alamo a short distance from where we were camped. It rests upon piles which stand obliquely to the course of the river. The result was that my boat was swept down and struck the piles, swerved into a snag with a lot of branches which had caught in nearly the same spot, and came near upsetting. There I was, held fast by the force of the current, and imprisoned in the arms of the snag. It took quite a time of pulling, pushing and cutting before I got loose. Then on we went again.

That was the beginning of the real fun of the trip. That afternoon and the next day we must have run over fifty rapids, some short, some long, some rough and dangerous, but most of them just exhilarating and exciting. How one's blood tingled with the dash and roar, the speed and the tossing, and how one's hands, wrists and arms had to work to keep the boat safe while in the middle of the rapids! We had no great rocks to contend with, but something equally dangerous. The rapids were filled with heavy masses of "nigger-head" clay, and once or twice I got ugly bumps on these "heads" that shook the boat from end to end and nearly toppled me head over heels.

In several places the river widened out for half a mile, or even a mile, and the flats were covered with ducks, geese and pelicans. I think I saw more of these aquatic birds in these two or three days than I had seen in the whole of my previous life. In some cases we were allowed to come as near to them as fifty feet, and with a gun an expert could have had his choice out of the thousands.

And now we experienced the reality of one of the dangers against which we had been warned and that I had all along foreseen. The boats were about fifty feet apart. We were in the radius of a great curve. The mad river was here boring under the bank, which was fully forty feet high. No one who has not seen the cutting, or, literally, the auger-like boring power, of this river in such places can believe the extent of its work. It cut in deeply and removed the entire foundation of the bank for ten, fifteen, even twenty feet. Then, without a pre-monitory warning, the whole bank for fifteen or twenty feet back, dropped with a terrific splash into the river. And it fell off as if cut with some gigantic machine, almost as straight as the cutter slices a bar of soap. Both boats were almost swamped by the great waves that ensued, but fortunately neither of us was immediately under the bank, or this account would have had a more somber ending.

That night we camped at the deserted shack of a settler who had "taken up" a homestead. We saw many pathetic evidences of a woman's presence in the rude and simple efforts to care for a woman's comfort. Just before the shack, the rapids dashed on to the sea. Early in the morning we started and for an hour had hard rowing. The banks were all gone, there was nothing but flats over which the river distributed itself, making it very hard to find the main current. The wind began to blow and ere long a perfect gale made waves which added to our difficulties. Soon I was completely stranded. I had been aground several times before, but this was permanent. The wind was blowing furiously and my companions could not hear my shouts, but fortunately one of them saw my predicament and they ran ashore and waited. There was but one thing to do. That was for me to go to them. Jumping into the water, and sinking up almost to the middle in quicksands, I struggled against the wind to reach them. Each time I pulled myself out of the treacherous sand the wind blew me back, and for a while I despaired of making headway. But keeping desperately at it I succeeded at last in

6

reaching their boat, where I fell over breathless,
speechless and exhausted. When I was able to
move we all jumped out into the water and lifted
and pushed the boat back to where the other was
stranded. There we took out everything of value,
and said our final farewell to it.

But our difficulties were not over. Though the
three of us handled the oars, the six of them made
so little headway that two hours' rowing advanced
us not more than half a mile. By this time the
waves were running high and furious, and Jim,
the Indian, got scared. He cried out: "I no like
this river. Pretty soon we tip over and this boat
he sink. We no get there."

"Are you scared, Jim?" I asked.

"No!" he responded quickly, "no scared, but I
no like 'em this river."

Each time we got into the trough we shipped so
much water that finally I decided to abandon the
attempt to cross the sea. Giving the order, we
turned stern to the wind and soon rowed over the
flats, the water having been blown over them to a
depth of several inches with the wind, and ran
ashore opposite a large volcanic butte that stood
out in the heart of the desert.

We anchored the boat as well as we could and
then proceeded to carry everything from the boat
to the butte, where, pretty well above the then
level of the sea, we piled them up, covered them
with our bed-canvas and tied them down to the
anchoring rocks.

Then we started, each heavily laden with cameras, canteens and food, for the nearest point on
the railway. The efflorescing salts made a yielding

crust on the alkali soil in which we sank over the
ankles at every step. One of my ankles was soon
cut through and I suffered intensely. To add to
our difficulties we soon came to the brink of a
wide slough, far too deep for us to ford, and it
was impossible to swim across heavy laden as we
were. There was no other course than to go around
it, and this added several weary miles to our tramp.
At length, after full eighteen miles of a walk,
wearied out but glad at the accomplishment of our
trip, we reached Imperial Junction, from which
point Indian Jim and I went to Yuma, while Van
Anderson remained there all night, taking the
morning train for Mecca.—From "The Wonders of
the Colorado Desert."

LINCOLN, THE MAN OF THE PEOPLE

By Edwin Markham

WHEN the Norn-Mother saw the Whirlwind
Hour,
Greatening and darkening as it hurried on,
She bent the strenuous Heavens and came down
To make a man to meet the mortal need.
She took the tried clay of the common road—
Clay warm, yet with the genial heat of Earth,
Dashed through it all a strain of prophecy;
Then mixed a laughter with the serious stuff.

The color of the ground was in him, the red earth;
The tang and odor of the primal things—
The rectitude and patience of the rocks;
The gladness of the wind that shakes the corn;

The courage of the bird that dares the sea;
The justice of the rain that loves all leaves;
The pity of the snow that hides all scars;
The loving kindness of the wayside well;
The tolerance and equity of light
That gives as freely to the shrinking weed
As to the great oak flaring to the wind—
To the grave's low hill as to the Matterhorn
That shoulders out the sky.

And so he came
From prairie cabin up to Capitol,
One fair Ideal led our chieftain on.
Forevermore he burned to do his deed
With the fine stroke and gesture of a king.
He built the rail-pile as he built the State,
Pouring his splendid strength through every blow,
The conscience of him testing every stroke,
To make his deed the measure of a man.

So came the Captain with the mighty heart;
And when the step of Earthquake shook the house,
Wrenching the rafters from their ancient hold,
He held the ridge pole up, and spiked again
The rafters of the Home. He held his place—
Held the long purpose like a growing tree—
Held on through blame and faltered not at praise.
And when he fell in whirlwind, he went down
As when a kingly cedar, green with boughs,
Goes down with a great shout upon the hills,
And leaves a lonesome place against the sky.

—From "Lincoln and Other Poems."

THE DESERT'S CALL

By Mary Austin

IF one is inclined to wonder at first how so many dwellers came to be in the loneliest land that ever came out of God's hands, what they do there and why they stay, one does not wonder so much after having lived there. None other than this long-brown land lays such a hold on the affections. The rainbow hills, the tender bluish mists, the luminous radiance of the spring, have the lotus charm. They trick the sense of time, so that once inhabitating there you always mean to go away without quite realizing that you have not done it. Men who have lived there, miners and cattlemen, will tell you this, not so fluently, but emphatically, cursing the land and going back to it. For one thing there is the divinest, cleanest air to be breathed anywhere in God's world. Some day the world will understand that, and the little oases on the windy tops of the hills will harbor for healing its ailing, house-weary broods. There is promise there of great wealth in ores and earths, which is no wealth by reason of being so far removed from water and workable conditions, but men are bewitched by it and tempted to try the impossible.

You should hear Salty Williams tell how he used to drive eighteen and twenty-mule teams from the borax marsh to Mojave, ninety miles, with the trail wagon full of water barrels. Hot days the mules would go so mad for drink that the clank of the water bucket set them into an uproar of hideous, maimed noises and a tangle of harness chains, while Salty would sit on the high seat with the sun glare heavy in his face, dealing out curses of pacification in a level, uninterested voice until the clamor fell off from sheer exhaustion. There was a line of shallow graves along that road; they used to count on dropping a man or two of every new gang of coolies brought out in the hot season. But when he lost his swamper, smitten without warning at the noon hour, Salty quit his job; he said it was "Too hot." The swamper he buried by the way with stones upon him to keep the coyotes from digging him up, and seven years later I read the penciled lines on the pine headboard, still bright and un-weathered.

But before that, driving up on the Mojave stage, I met Salty again crossing Indian Wells, his face from the high seat, tanned and ruddy as a harvest moon, looming through the golden dust above his eighteen mules. The land had called him.

The palpable sense of mystery in the desert air breeds fables, chiefly of lost treasure. Somewhere within its stark borders, if one believes report, is a hill strewn with nuggets; one seamed with virgin silver; an old clayey water-bed where Indians scooped up earth to make cooking pots and shaped them reeking with pure gold. Old miners drifting about the desert edges, weathered into the semblance of the tawny hills, will tell you tales like those convincingly. After a little sojourn in that land you will believe them on their own account.—From "The Land of Little Rain."

THE GREAT BASIN

By Col. John C. Fremont

IN arriving at Utah Lake, we had completed an immense circuit of twelve degrees diameter north and south, and ten degrees east and west; and found ourselves, in May, 1844, on the same sheet of water which we had left in September, 1843. The Utah is the southern limb of the Great Salt Lake; and thus we had seen that remarkable sheet of water both at its northern and southern extremity, and were able to fix its position at these two points. The circuit which we had made, and which had cost us eight months of time, and 3,500 miles of traveling, had given us a view of Oregon and of North California from the Rocky Mountains to the Pacific Ocean, and of the two principal streams which form bays or harbors on the coast of that sea. Having completed this circuit, and being now about to turn our backs upon the Pacific slope of our continent, and to recross the Rocky Mountains, it is natural to look back upon our footsteps and take some brief view of the leading features and general structure of the country we had traversed. These are peculiar and striking, and differ essentially from the Atlantic side of the country. The mountains all are higher, more numerous and more distinctly defined in their ranges and directions; and, what is so contrary to the natural order of formations, one of these ranges, which is near the coast (the Sierra Nevada and the Coast Range), presents higher elevations and peaks than any which are to be found in the Rocky moun-

tains themselves. In our eight months' circuit, we
were never out of sight of snow; and the Sierra
Nevada, where we crossed it, was near 2,000 feet
higher than the South Pass in the Rocky Mountains. In height, these mountains greatly exceed
those of the Atlantic side, constantly presenting
peaks which enter the region of perpetual snow;
and some of them volcanic, and in a frequent state
of activity. They are seen at great distances and
guide the traveler in his course.

The course and elevation of these ranges give
direction to the rivers and character to the coast.
No great river does, or can, take its rise below the
Cascade and Sierra Nevada range; the distance to
the sea is too short to admit of it. The rivers of
the San Francisco Bay, which are the largest after
the Columbia, are local to that bay, and lateral to
the coast, having their sources about on a line with
the Dalles of the Columbia, and running each in
a valley of its own, between the Coast range and
the Cascade and Sierra Nevada range. The Columbia is the only river which traverses the whole
breadth of the country, breaking through all the
ranges, and entering the sea. Drawing its waters
from a section of ten degrees of latitude in the
Rocky Mountains, which are collected into one
stream by three main forks (Lewis's, Clark's and
the North fork) near the center of the Oregon
Valley, this great river thence proceeds by a single
channel to the sea, while its three forks lead each
to a pass in the mountains, which opens the way
into the interior of the continent. This fact in relation to the rivers of this region, gives an immense
value to the Columbia. Its mouth is the only inlet

and outlet to and from the sea; its three forks lead
to the passes in the mountains; it is, therefore, the
only line of communication between the Pacific
and the interior of North America; and all operations of war or commerce, of national or social
intercourse, must be conducted upon it. This gives
it a value beyond estimation, and would involve
irreparable injury if lost. In this unity and concentration of its waters, the Pacific side of our continent differs entirely from the Atlantic side, where
the waters of the Alleghany Mountains are dispersed into many rivers, having their different en-
trances into the sea, and opening many lines of
communication with the interior.

The Pacific Coast is equally different from that
of the Atlantic. The coast of the Atlantic is low
and open, indented with numerous bays, sounds
and river estuaries, accessible everywhere and
opening by many channels into the heart of the
country. The Pacific Coast, on the contrary, is
high and compact, with few bays, and but one that
opens into the heart of the country. The immediate coast is what the seamen call *iron-bound*. A
little within, it is skirted by two successive ranges
of mountains, standing as ramparts between the
sea and the interior of the country; and to get
through which there is but one gate, and that narrow and easily defended. This structure of the
coast, backed by these two ranges of mountains,
with its concentration and unity of waters, gives
to the country an immense military strength, and
will probably render Oregon the most impregnable
country in the world.

Differing so much from the Atlantic side of our

continent, in coast, mountains and rivers, the Pacific side differs from it in another most rare and singular feature—that of the Great Interior Basin, of which I have so often spoken, and the whole form and character of which I was so anxious to ascertain. Its existence is vouched for by such of the American traders and hunters as have some knowledge of that region; the structure of the Sierra Nevada range of mountains requires it to be there; and my own observations confirm it. Mr. Joseph Walker, who is so well acquainted in those parts, informed me that, from the Great Salt Lake west, there was a succession of lakes and rivers which have no outlet to the sea, nor any connection with the Columbia, or with the Colorado or the Gulf of California. He described some of these lakes as being large, with numerous streams, and even considerable rivers falling into them. In fact, all concur in the general report of these interior rivers and lakes; and, for want of understanding the force and power of evaporation, which so soon establishes an equilibrium between the loss and supply of waters, the fable of whirlpools and subterraneous outlets has gained belief, as the only imaginable way of carrying off the waters which have no visible discharge. The structure of the country would require this formation of interior lakes; for the waters which would collect between the Rocky Mountains and the Sierra Nevada, not being able to cross this formidable barrier, nor to get to the Columbia or the Colorado, must naturally collect into reservoirs, each of which would have its little system of streams and rivers to supply it. This would be the natural effect; and what I saw went to confirm it. The Great Salt Lake is a formation of this kind, and quite a large one; and having many streams and one considerable river, 400 or 500 miles long, falling into it. This lake and river I saw and examined myself; and also saw the Wah-Satch and Bear River Mountains, which enclose the waters of the lake on the east, and constitute, in that quarter, the rim of the Great Basin. Afterwards, along the eastern base of the Sierra Nevada, where we traveled for forty-two days, I saw the line of lakes and rivers which lie at the foot of that Sierra and which Sierra is the western rim of the basin. In going down Lewis's fork and the main Columbia, I crossed only inferior streams coming in from the left, such as could draw their water from a short distance only; and I often saw the mountains at their heads white with snow—which, all accounts said, divided the waters of the *desert* from those of the Columbia, and which could be no other than the range of mountains which form the rim of the basin in its northern side. And in returning from California along the Spanish trail, as far as the head of the Santa Clara fork of the Rio Virgen, I crossed only small streams making their way south to the Colorado, or lost in sand (as the Mo-hah-ve); while to the left, the lofty mountains, their summits white with snow, were often visible, and which must have turned water to the north as well as to the south, and thus constituted, on this part, the southern rim of the basin. At the head of the Santa Clara fork, and in the Vegas de Santa Clara, we crossed the ridge which parted the two systems of waters. We entered the basin at that point, and have traveled in it ever since, having its southeastern rim (the Wah-satch Mountain) on the right, and crossing the streams which flow down into it. The existence of the basin is, therefore, an established fact in my mind; its extent and contents are yet to be better ascertained. It cannot be less than 400 or 500 miles each way, and must lie principally in the Alta California, the demarcation latitude of 42 degrees probably cutting a segment from the north part of the rim. Of its interior but little is known. It is called a *desert*, and, from what I saw of it, sterility may be its prominent characteristic; but where there is so much water, there must be some *oasis*.

The great river and the great lake, reported, may not be equal to the report; but where there is so much snow, there must be streams; and where there is no outlet, there must be lakes to hold the accumulated waters, or sands to swallow them up. In this eastern part of the basin, containing Sevier, Utah, and the Great Salt Lakes, and the rivers and creeks falling into them, we know there is good soil and good grass, adapted to civilized settlements. In the western part, on Salmon Trout River, and some other streams, the same remark may be made.

The contents of this great basin are yet to be examined. That it is peopled, we know; but miserably and sparsely. From all that I heard and saw, I should say that humanity here appeared in its lowest form, and in its most elementary state. Dispersed in single families; without firearms; eating seeds and insects; digging roots (and hence their name)—such is the condition of the greater part. Others are a degree higher, and live in communities upon some lake or river that supplies fish and from which they repulse the miserable *digger*. The rabbit is the largest animal known in this desert; its flesh affords a little meat; and their bag-like covering is made of its skins. The wild sage is their only wood, and here it is of extraordinary size— sometimes a foot in diameter and six or eight feet high. It serves for fuel, for building material, for shelter to the rabbits, and for some sort of covering for the feet and legs in cold weather. Such are the accounts of the inhabitants and productions of the Great Basin; and which, though imperfect, must have some foundation, and excite our desire to know the whole.

The whole idea of such a desert, and such a people, is a novelty in our country, and excites Asiatic, not American, ideas. Interior basins, with their own systems of lakes and rivers, and often sterile, are common enough in Asia; people still in the elementary state of families, living in deserts, with no other occupation than the mere animal search for food, may still be seen in that ancient quarter of the globe; but in America such things are new and strange, unknown and unsuspected, and discredited when related. But I flatter myself that what is discovered, though not enough to satisfy curiosity, is sufficient to excite it, and that subsequent explorations will complete what has been commenced.

This account of the Great Basin, it will be remembered, belongs to the Alta California, and has no application to Oregon, whose capabilities may justify a separate remark. Referring to my journal for particular descriptions, and for sectional boundaries between good and bad districts, I can only say, in general and comparative terms, that in that branch of agriculture which implies the cultivation of grains and staple crops it would be inferior to the Atlantic States, though many parts are superior for wheat, while in the rearing of flocks and herds it would claim a high place. Its grazing capabilities are great; and even in the indigenous grass now there, an element of individual and national wealth may be found. In fact, the valuable grasses begin within one hundred and fifty miles of the Missouri frontier and extend to the Pacific Ocean. East of the Rocky Mountains it is the short, curly grass, on which the buffalo delights to feed (whence its name of buffalo), and which is still good when apparently dry and dead. West of those mountains it is a larger growth, in clusters, and hence called bunch-grass, and which has a second or fall growth. Plains and mountains both exhibit them, and I have seen good pasturage at an elevation of ten thousand feet. In this spontaneous product the trading or traveling caravans can find subsistence for their animals, and in military operations any number of cavalry may be moved, and any number of cattle may be driven; and thus men and horses may be supported on long expeditions, and even in winter, in the sheltered situations.

Commercially, the value of the Oregon country must be great, washed as it is by the North Pacific Ocean—fronting Asia—producing many of the elements of commerce—mild and healthy in its climate—and becoming, as it naturally will, a thoroughfare for the East India and China trade.—From "A Narrative of Adventures and Explorations."

THE MAN OF THE TRAIL

By Henry Meade Bland

A SPIRIT that pulses forever
  Like the fiery heart of a boy;
A forehead that lifts to the sunlight,
  And is wreathed forever in joy;
A muscle that holds like the iron
  That binds in the prisoner steam:
Yea, these are the trail-man's glory!
  Yea, these are the trail-man's dream!

An eye that catches the beauty
  That gleams from the mountain and sky;
And an ear that awakes to the song
  Of the storm, as it surges on high;
A sense that garners the splendor
  Of sun, moon, or starry gleam:
Lo, these are the trail-man's glory!
  Lo, these are the trail-man's dream!

The wild, high climb o'er the mountains;
  The lodge by the river's brim;
The glance at the fierce cloud-horses
  As they plunge o'er the range's rim;
The Juniper's balm for the nostrils;
  The dash in the cool trout-stream:
Yea, these are the trail-man's glory!
  Yea, these are the trail-man's dream!

The ride down fair river canyon,
  Where the wild oats grow breast high;
And the shout of the quail on the hillside;
  The turtle-dove flashing by;

An eye 'round the fragrant fire,
　Where the eyes of a comrade beam:
Yea, these are the trail-man's glory!
　Yea, these are the trail-man's dream!

　　　　　　—From "Out West Magazine."

ON AN ALASKAN TRAIL

By Ella Higginson

THE trip over "the trail" from Valdez to the
Tanana country is one of the most fascinating in Alaska.

At seven o'clock of a July morning five horses stood at our hotel door. Two gentlemen of Valdez had volunteered to act as escort to the three ladies in our party for a trip over the trail.

I examined with suspicion the red-bay horse that had been assigned to me.

"Is he gentle?" I asked of one of the gentlemen.

"Oh, I don't know. You can't take any one's word about a horse in Alaska. They call regular buckers 'gentle' up here. The only way to find out is to try them."

This was encouraging.

"Do you mean to tell me," said one of the other ladies, "that you don't know whether these horses have ever been ridden by women?"

"No, I do not know."

She sat down on the steps.

"Then there's no trail for me. I don't know how to ride nor to manage a horse."

After many moments of persuasion, we got her

upon a mild-eyed horse, saddled with a cross saddle. The other lady and myself had chosen side saddles, despite the assurance of almost every man in Valdez that we could not get over the trail sitting a horse sidewise, without accident.

"Your skirt'll catch in the brush and pull you off," said one, cheerfully.

"Your feet'll hit against rocks in the canyon," said another.

"You can't balance as even on a horse's back sideways, and if you don't balance even along the precipice in the canyon your horse'll go over," said a third.

"Your horse is sure to roll over once or twice in the glacier streams, and you can save yourself if you're riding astride," said a fourth.

"You're certain to get into quicksand somewhere on the trip, and if your weight is all on one side of your horse you'll pull him down and he'll fall on top of you," said a fifth.

In the face of all these cheerful horrors, our escort said:

"Ride any way you please. If a woman can keep her head, she will pull through everything in Alaska. Besides, we are not going along for nothing!"

So we chose side-saddles, that having been our manner of riding since childhood.

We had waited three weeks for the glacial flood at the eastern side of the town to subside, and could wait no longer. It was roaring within ten steps of the back door of our hotel; and in two minutes after mounting, before our feet were fairly settled in the stirrups, we had ridden down the sloping bank into the boiling, white waters.

One of the gentlemen rode ahead as guide. I watched his big horse go down in the flood—down, down; the water rose to its knees, to its rider's feet, to *his* knees—

He turned his head and called cheerfully, "Come on!" and we went on—one at a time, as still as the dead, save for the splashing and snorting of our horses. I felt the water, icy cold, rising high, higher; it almost washed my foot from the red-slippered stirrup; then I felt it mounting higher, my skirts floated out on the flood, and then fell, limp, about me. My glance kept flying from my horse's head to our guide and back again. He was tall, and his horse was tall.

"When it reaches *his* waist," was my agonized thought, "it will be over *my* head!"

The other gentleman rode to my side.

"Keep a firm hold of your bridle," said he gravely, "and watch your horse. If he falls—"

"Falls! *In here!*"

"They do sometimes; one must be prepared. If he falls—of course you can swim?"

"I never swam a stroke in my life; I never even tried!"

"Is it possible?" said he, in astonishment. "Why we would not have advised you to come at this time if we had known that. We took it for granted that you wouldn't think of going unless you could swim."

"Oh," said I, sarcastically, "do all the women in Valdez swim?"

"No," he answered, gravely, "but then, they

don't go over the trail. Well, we can only hope that he will not fall. When he breaks into a swim—"

"Swim! Will he do that?"

"Oh, yes, he is liable to swim any moment now."

"What will I do then?" I asked, quite humbly; I could hear tears in my own voice. He must have heard them, too, his voice was so kind as he answered.

"Sit as quietly and as evenly as possible, and lean slightly forward in the saddle; then trust to heaven and give him his head."

"Does he give you any warning?"

"Not the faintest—ah-h!"

Well might he say "ah-h!" for my horse was swimming. Well might we all say "ah-h!" for one wild glance ahead revealed to my glimmering vision that all our horses were swimming.

I never knew before that horses swam so *low down* in the water. I wished when I could see nothing but my horse's ears that I had not been so stubborn about the saddle.

The water itself was different from any water I had ever seen. It did not flow like a river; it boiled, seethed, whirled, rushed; it pushed up into an angry bulk that came down over us like a deluge. I had let go of my reins and, leaning forward in the saddle, was clinging to my horse's mane. The rapidly flowing water gave me the impression that we were being swept down the stream.

The roaring grew louder in my ears; I was so dizzy that I could no longer distinguish any object; there was just a blur of brown and white water, rising, falling, about me; the sole thought

that remained was that I was being swept out to
sea with my struggling horse.

Suddenly there was a shock which, to my tor-
tured nerves, seemed like a ship striking on a rock.
It was some time before I realized that it had been
caused by my horse striking bottom. He was walking—staggering, rather—and plunging; his whole
neck appeared, then his shoulders; I released his
mane mechanically, as I had acted in all things
since mounting, and gathered up the reins.

"That was a nasty one, wasn't it?" said my
escort, joining me. "I stayed behind to be of service if you required it. We're getting out now, but
there are at least ten or fifteen as bad on the trail
—if not worse."

As if anything *could* be worse!

I chanced to lift my eyes then, and I got a clear
view of the ladies ahead of me. Their appearance
was of such a nature that I at once looked myself
over—and saw myself as others saw me! It was
the first and only time that I have ever wished
myself at home when I have been traveling in
Alaska.

"Cheer up!" called our guide, over his broad
shoulder. "The worst is yet to come."

He spoke more truthfully than even he knew.
There was one stream after another—and each
seemed really worse than the one that went before.
From Valdez Glacier the ice, melted by the hot
July sun, was pouring out in a dozen streams that
spread over the immense flats between the town and
the mouth of the Lowe River. There were miles
and miles of it. Scarcely would we struggle out of
one place that had been washed out deep—and

how deep we never knew until we were into it—
when we would be compelled to plunge into another.

At last, wet and chilled, after several narrow
escapes from whirlpools and quicksand, we reached
a level road leading through a cool wood for several miles. From this, of a sudden, we began to
climb. So steep was the ascent and so narrow the
path—no wider than the horse's feet—that my
horse seemed to have a series of movable humps on
him, like a camel; and riding sidewise, I could only
lie forward and cling desperately to his mane, to
avoid a shameful descent over his tail.

Actually, there were steps cut in the hard soil
for the horses to climb upon! They pulled themselves up with powerful plunges. On both sides of
this narrow path the grass, or "feed," as it is called,
grew so tall that we could not see one another's
heads above it as we rode; yet it had been growing only six weeks.

Mingling with young alders, fireweed, devil's
club and elderberry—the latter sprayed out in scarlet—it formed a network across our path, through
which we could only force our way with closed
eyes, blind as Love.

Bad as the ascent was, the descent was worse.
The horse's humps all turned the other way, and
we turned with them. It was only by constant
watchfulness that we kept ourselves from sliding
over their heads.

After another ascent, we emerged into the open
upon the brow of a cliff. Below us stretched the
valley of the Lowe River. Thousands of feet below wound and looped the blue reaches of the

river, set here and there with islands of glistening sand or rosy fireweed, while over all trailed the silver mists of morning. One elderberry island was so set with scarlet sprays of berries that from our heights no foliage could be seen.

After this came a scented, primeval forest, through which we rode in silence. Its charm was too elusive for speech. Our horse's feet sank into the moss without sound. There was no underbrush; only dim aisles and arcades fashioned from the gray trunks of trees. The pale green foliage floating above us completely shut out the sun. Soft, gray, mottled moss dripped from the limbs and branches of the spruce trees in delicate, lacy festoons.

Soon after emerging from this dream-like wood we reached Camp Comfort, where we paused for lunch.

This is one of the most comfortable road houses in Alaska. It is situated in a low, green valley; the river winds in front, and snow mountains float around it. The air is very sweet.

It is only ten miles from Valdez, but those ten miles are equal to fifty in taxing the endurance.

We found an excellent vegetable garden at Camp Comfort. Pansies and other flowers were as large and fragrant as I have ever seen, the coloring of the pansies being unusually rich. They told us that only two other women had passed over the trail during the summer.

While our lunch was being prepared, we stood about the immense stove in the immense living room and tried to dry our clothing.

The room was at least thirty feet square. It had

a high ceiling and rough board floor. In one corner was a piano, in another a phonograph. The ceiling was hung with all kinds of trail apparel used by men, including long boots and heavy stockings, guns and other weapons, and other articles that added a picturesque and even startling touch to the big room.

In one end was a bench, buckets of water, tin cups hanging on nails, washbowls, and a little wavy mirror swaying on the wall. The gentlemen of our party played the phonograph while we removed the dust and mud which we had gathered on our journey; afterward, *we* played the phonograph.

Then we all stood happily about the stove to "dry out," and listened to our host's stories of the miners who came out from the Tanana country laden with gold. As many as seventy men, each bearing a fortune, have slept at Camp Comfort on a single night. We slept there ourselves on our return journey, but our riches were in other things than gold, and there was no need to guard them. Any man or woman may go to Alaska and enrich himself or herself forever, as we did, if he or she have the desire. Not only is there no need to guard our riches, but, on the contrary, we are glad to give freely to whomsoever would have.

Each man, we were told, had his own way of caring for his gold! One leaned a gunny-sack full of it outside the house, where it stood all night unguarded, supposed to be a sack of old clothing, from the carelessness with which it was left there. The owner slept calmly in the attic, surrounded by men whose gold made their hard pillows.

They told us, too, of the men who came back, dull-eyed and empty handed, discouraged and foot-sore. They slept long and heavily; there was nothing for them to guard.

Every road house has its "talking machine," with many of the most expensive records. No one can appreciate one of these machines until he goes to Alaska. Its influence is not to be estimated in those far, lonely places, where other music is not.

In a big store "to Westward" we witnessed a scene that would touch any heart. The room was filled with people. There were passengers and officers from the ship, miners, Russian half-breeds, and full-blooded Aleuts. After several records had filled the room with melody, Calvé, herself, sang "The Old Folks at Home." As that voice of golden velvet rose and fell, the unconscious workings of the faces about me spelled out their life tragedies. At last, one big fellow in a flannel shirt started for the door. As he reached it, another man caught his sleeve and whispered huskily:

"Where you goin', Bill?"

"Oh, anywheres," he made answer roughly, to cover his emotion; "anywheres, so's I can't hear that—piece"—and it was not one of the least of Calvé's compliments.

Music in Alaska brings the thought of home; and it is the thought of home that plays upon the heart-strings of the North. The hunger is always there—hidden, repressed, but waiting—and at the first touch of music it leaps forth and casts its shadow upon the face. Who knows but that it is this very heart-hunger that puts the universal human look into Alaskan eyes?

After a good lunch at Camp Comfort we resumed our journey. There was another bit of enchanting forest; then, of a sudden, we were in the famed Keystone Canyon.

Here the scenery is enthralling. Solid walls of shaded gray stone rise straight from the river to a height of from twelve to fifteen hundred feet. Along one cliff winds the trail, in many places no wider than the horse's feet. One feels that he must only breathe with the land side of him, lest the mere weight of his breath on the other side should topple him over the sheer, dizzy precipice.

It was amusing to see every woman lean toward the rock cliff. Not for the gold of Klondike would I have willingly given one look down into the gulf, sinking away, almost under my horse's feet. Somewhere in those purple depths I knew that the river was roaring, white and swollen, between its narrow stone walls

We finally reached a place where the descent was almost perpendicular and the trail painfully narrow. The horses sank to their haunches and slid down, taking gravel and stones down with them. I had been imploring to be permitted to walk; but now, being far in advance of all but one, I did not ask permission. I simply slipped off my horse and left him for the others to bring with them. The gentleman with me was forced to do the same.

We paused for a time to rest and to enjoy the most beautiful waterfall I saw in Alaska—Bridal Veil. It is on the opposite side of the canyon, and has a slow, musical fall, of six hundred feet.

When we went on, the other members of our

party had not yet come up with us, nor had our horses appeared. In the narrowest of all narrow places I was walking ahead, when, turning a sharp corner, we met a government pack-train, face to face.

The bell horse stood still and looked at me with big eyes, evidently as scared at the sight of a woman as an old prospector who has not seen one for years.

I looked at him with eyes as big as his own. There was only one thing to do. Behind us was a narrow, V-shaped cave in the stone wall, not more than four feet high and three deep. Into this we backed, Grecian-bend wise, and waited.

We waited a very long time. The horse stood still, blowing his breath loudly from steaming nostrils, and contemplating us. I never knew before that a horse could express his opinion of a person so plainly. Around the curve we could hear whips cracking and men swearing; but the horse stood there and kept his suspicious eyes on me.

"I'll stay here till dark," his eyes said, "but you don't get me past a thing like *that!*"

I didn't mind his looking, but his snorting seemed like an insult.

At last a man pushed past the horse. When he saw us backed gracefully up into the V-shaped cave, he stood as still as the horse. Finding that neither he nor my escort could think of anything to say to relieve the mental and physical strain, I called out graciously:

"How do you do, sir? Would you like to get by?"

"I'd like it—well, lady," he replied, with what I felt to be his very politest manner.

"Perhaps," I suggested sweetly, "if I came out and let the horse get a good look at me—"

"Don't you do it lady. That 'u'd scare him plumb to death!"

I have always been convinced that he did not mean it exactly as it sounded, but I caught the flicker of a smile on my escort's face. It was gone in an instant.

Suddenly the other horses came crowding upon the bell-horse. There was nothing for him to do but to go past me or to go over the precipice. He chose me as the least of the two evils.

"Nice pony, nice boy," I wheedled as he went sliding and snorting past.

Then we waited for the next horse to come by; but he did not come. Turning my head, I found him fixed in the same place and the same attitude as the first had been; his eyes were as big and they were set as steadily on me.

Well—there were fifty horses in that government pack train. Every one of the fifty balked at sight of a woman. There were horses of every color— gray, white, black, bay, chestnut, sorrel, and pinto. The sorrel were the stubbornest of all. To this day I detest the sight of a sorrel horse.

We stood there in that position for a time that seemed like hours; we coaxed each horse as he balked; and at the last were reduced to such misery that we gave thanks to God that there were only fifty of them and that they couldn't kick sidewise as they passed.

I forgot about the men. There were seven men,

and as each man turned the bend in the trail he
stood as still as the stillest horse, and for quite as
long a time; and naturally I hesitated to say, "Nice
boy, nice fellow," to help him by.

There were more glacier streams to cross. These
were floored with huge boulders instead of sand
and quicksand. The horses stumbled and plunged
powerfully. One misstep here would have meant
death; the rapids immediately below the crossing
would have beaten us to pieces upon the rocks.

Then came more perpendicular climbing; but at
last, at five o'clock, with our bodies aching with
fatigue and our senses finally dulled, through sheer
surfeit, to the beauty of the journey, we reached
"Wortman's" road house.

This is twenty miles from Valdez; and when we
were lifted from our horses we could not stand
alone, to say nothing of attempting to walk.

But "Wortman's" is the paradise of road
houses. In it, and floating over it, is an atmosphere
of warmth, comfort and good cheer that is a rest
for body and heart. The beds are comfortable and
the meals excellent.

But it was the welcome that cheered—the spirit
of genuine kind-heartedness.

The road house stands in a large clearing, with
barns and other buildings surrounding it. I never
saw so many dogs as greeted us, except in Valdez
or on the Yukon. They crowded about us, barking
and shrieking a welcome. They were all big mala-
mutes.

After a good dinner we went to bed at eight
o'clock. The sun was shining brightly, but we
darkened our rooms as much as possible, and in-

stantly fell into the sleep of utter exhaustion.—
From "Alaska."

THE WAY OF THE DESERT

By Idah Meacham Strobridge

UNDER the palms and pepper trees that grow
by Pacific waters I sit, and say, "This is
home;" and I keep saying it over and over again,
as a child repeats a lesson that is hard to learn.
But repeating the words of a lesson a hundred
times and more is not learning it. Therefore, I do
not know my lesson yet. I have driven my tent
pegs here among California roses, and under a California sky. I have stretched the ropes tight and
have anchored them down—to stay. Yet this is
not home. If you would ask me "Why?" remember that the tent-canvas was weathered in a Desert
wind, and the ropes bleached by a Desert sun.
Then the tent stood there for long, in that land,
very long. And tent pegs pull hard when driven
long in one place. So—though there are lilies
and roses about me and the wind brings the salt
smell of the sea, yet would I have the Desert alkali
in my nostrils, and smell the smoke from a grease-
wood camp-fire.

Into a gray Desert (a land of gray sage and gray
sand; of lizards, and little horned toads that are
gray; where the coyote drifts by you like a fragment from gray fog-banks blown by the wind),
half a century ago, they came—the prospectors—
seeking the Desert's treasure-trove, where the Des-

ert had none hidden away. Some are yet seeking —following the mirage still.

Once—long ago—my horse and I went away into the mirage—land of these old miners; and there I heard them voice the stories of their hopes—the dreams that they believe will, some day, surely come true. By camp-fire smoke, or in the dim light of sod cabins, I have sat in that silence the Desert teaches you, and have listened as they talked, and believed as I listened. Yes, even believed; as you, too, will believe if you hear from their own lips the fables that seem so true during the hour you are under the story-teller's charm, with no sound breaking in save the crooning of the Desert wind, or the cry of a lone coyote.

It may be that the twilight hour that lies at the end of some day that is now far in the future will find you there at the grease-wood camp-fire of one of these old men. Then you will know these things as I have known them.

Go up into the mountains and you will find the old prospectors who came into the country in the days of their youth, and stay on now through the unrewarding, quiet years. To the last chapter of your own life the memories of them and their stories will be with you, to link you yet closer to the old days when you found the trail that led you to the heart of the Desert.

Then live in the big, still plains that tend to a big and a serene life, learning the best the Desert may teach you. These things you learn:

That we are what we think and feel, not what others think and feel us to be; that mankind is a brotherhood, each needing the other, and not one can be spared from the unit; brothers are we, born of a common parentage; and there is small difference between man and man, except in so far as they are good or bad.

Therefore I repeat to you that you, too, may some day learn the Desert's lure—the Desert's charm. Some time your destiny may lead you there; and lying awake in your blankets at night under the purple-black sky that is crowded with palpitating stars, with the warm Desert wind blowing softly over you, caressing your face and smoothing your hair as no human hands ever could, and bringing with it the hushed night-sounds that only the land of the grease-wood and the sage knows! then—all alone there with only God and the Desert—you will come to understand the old prospector and his ways; the Red Man who was there before him; and all who, by reason of years of dwelling there, have made it their own. But not now; not till you and the Desert are lovers.

So I say to you: "Go! go to the gray land and search till you find its heart!" If you go, and live there long enough, you will learn to love it. And if you love it and go away, you will never for one instant forget it in after years. It will be with you in memory ever afterward—a something so cherished that it has no counterpart elsewhere in all the world. And always—though you go to the end of the earth—you will hear the still voice calling and calling!—From "In Miner's Mirage Land."

HEIMWEH

By Lowell Otus Reese

NOW the mountain breeze is blowing 'round a
    little cabin hiding
  Down among the cedar windfalls of the far Sier-
    ra hills;
And the music of the torrent on the wind of morn-
    ing riding,
  Through the balsam-laden air in sweet harmonic
    measure thrills;
Oh, the mellow, mellow murmur! I can hear the
    Naiads singing
  'Mid the bending boughs of alder where the hid-
    den waters flow;
And the echo of their music in an ecstacy is ringing
  Night and morning 'round the windows of a cab-
    in that I know.

Sweet, sweet, waiting to greet,
Over and over the tongues repeat,
Deep in the woodland gloam,
"Cool, cool is the hidden pool—
When are you coming home?"

Tell me what it is that deep within the bosom low is
    crying,
  When across the distant mountain comes the
    whisper of the pine;
When you wake at night and listen to the mystic
    voices sighing
  From the far-off slopes all heavy with the scent
    of columbine;

Tell me from what ancient era comes the restless
    spirit stirring
  In my breast when summer beckons and the
    haunted breezes blow,
Till I hear the stealthy footsteps and the wild wings
    nervous whirring
  In the leafy forest temples 'round a cabin that I
    know.

Oh, the magic of the mountains when the voice of
    Nature calling,
  With a flood of homesick longing all the yearn-
    ing spirit fills!
When you spend the long night's dreaming of the
    early glory falling
  In a flood of gold and purple on the greenness
    of the hills:
Who shall turn my heart against her? Who shall
    keep my feet from straying
  To the far-off rocky valley where the hidden
    waters flow—
Where all summer long I listen the enchanted
    breezes playing
  In the pine and cedar waving 'round a cabin that
    I know!

        Hark, hark! Out in the dark,
        Whippoorwill's cry and the fox's bark,
          Under a starry dome;
        Near, clear, comes to my ear—
          "When are you coming home?"

SAN FRANCISCO'S OLD CHINATOWN

By Frank Norris

THEY looked swiftly around them, and the bustling, breezy water-front faded from their recollections. They were in a world of narrow streets, of galleries and overhanging balconies. Craziest structures, riddled and honey-combed with stairways and passages, shut out the sky, though here and there rose a building of extraordinary richness and most elaborate ornamentation. Color was everywhere. A thousand little notes of green and yellow, of vermilion and sky blue, assaulted the eye. Here it was a doorway, here a vivid glint of cloth or hanging, here a huge scarlet sign lettered with gold, and here a kaleidoscopic effect in the garments of a passer-by. Directly opposite and two stories above their heads, a sort of huge "loggia," one blaze of gilding and crude vermilion, opened in the gray cement of a crumbling facade, like a sudden burst of flame. Gigantic pot-bellied lanterns of red and gold swung from its ceiling, while along the railing stood a row of pots—brass, ruddy bronze and blue porcelain—from which were growing red, saffron, purple, pink and golden tulips without number. The air was vibrant with unfamiliar noises. From one of the balconies near at hand, though unseen, a gong, a pipe and some kind of stringed instrument wailed and thundered in unison. There was a vast shuffling of padded soles and a continuous interchange of singsong monosyllables, high-pitched and staccato, while from every hand rose the strange aromas of the

East—sandalwood, punk, incense, oil, and the smell of mysterious cooking.

"Chinatown!" exclaimed Travis. "I hadn't the faintest idea we had come up so far. Coudy Rivers, do you know what time it is?" She pointed a white kid finger through the doorway of a drug store, where, amid lacquer boxes and bronze urns of herbs and dried seeds, a round Seth Thomas marked half-past four.

"And your lunch?" cried Coudy. "Great heavens! I never thought."

"It's too late to get any at home. Never mind; I'll go somewhere and have a cup of tea."

"Why not get a package of Chinese tea, now that you're down here, and take it home with you?"

"Or drink it here."

"Where?"

"In one of the restaurants. There wouldn't be a soul there at this hour. I know they serve tea any time. Coudy, let's try it. Wouldn't it be fun?"

Coudy smote his thigh. "Fun!" he vociferated. It is—it would be *heavenly!* Wait a moment. I'll tell you what we will do. Tea won't be enough. We'll go down to Kearney street, or to the market, and get some crackers to go with it."

They hurried back to the California market, a few blocks distant, and bought some crackers and a wedge of new cheese.

"First catch your restaurant," said Travis, as they turned into Dupont street with its thronging coolies and swarming gayly clad children. But they had not far to seek.

"Here you are!" suddenly exclaimed Coudy, halting in front of a wholesale tea-house bearing a sign in Chinese and English. "Come on, Travis!"

They ascended two flights of a broad, brass-bound staircase leading up from the ground floor and gained the restaurant on the top story of the building. As Travis had foretold, it was deserted.

The restaurant ran the whole depth of the building, and was finished off at either extremity with a gilded balcony, one overlooking Dupont street and the other the old Plaza. Enormous screens of gilded ebony, intricately carved and set with colored glass panes, divided the room into three, and one of these divisions, in the rear part, from which they could step out upon the balcony that commanded the view of the Plaza, they elected as their own.

It was charming. At their backs they had the huge, fantastic screen, brave and fine with its coat of gold. In front, through the glass-paned valves of a pair of folding doors, they could see the roofs of the houses beyond the Plaza, and beyond these the blue of the bay with its anchored ships, and even beyond this the faint purple of the Oakland shore. On either side of these doors, in deep alcoves, were divans with mattings and headrests for opium smokers. The walls were painted blue and hung with vertical Cantonese legends in red and silver, while all around the sides of the room small ebony tables alternated with ebony stools, each inlaid with a slab of mottled marble. A chandelier, all a-glitter with tinsel, swung from the center of the ceiling over a huge round table of mahogany.

PREFACE

The supermarket today is regarded as an established institution, yet only thirty years ago it was but an embryonic idea. Already, this marketing innovation has left an indelible imprint on most aspects of food manufacturing, processing, wholesaling, and retailing. The lack of a text devoted to a comprehensive appraisal and analytical study of the industry has prompted the writing of this book.

Directed toward a broad audience, *Supermarketing* is intended as an aid to food and related-industry entrepreneurs, executives, key employees and those aspiring to positions of responsibility, and marketing students at the university level. It is hoped that all will find something helpful here. Top executives, for example, who must be well informed about all the many facets of supermarket operation, will find of particular interest the chapters on financial considerations, the impact of the supermarket on the food industry, and managerial policy and practice. Superette managers who want to attain supermarket status for their enterprises will find of value the store-operation sections and the appendix. Food brokers, manufacturers' salesmen, processors, and wholesalers will be interested in the entire text, especially the sections on buying operations and the supermarket's impact on the industry. Executives of retailing operations affected by the supermarket may find information relevant to the increasing competition they face from the supermarkets. Finally, students of marketing at universities, particularly in the areas of retailing, can learn principles and practices which will be of value in their future business careers. The book may also be of use as a supplement in many different courses in marketing.

The author owes a debt of gratitude to the library of the Super Market Institute for the use of its excellent research facilities. Research there was facilitated by the cheerful cooperation of the librarian, Catherine McAndrews. Other invaluable aid in the gathering of pertinent data was rendered by the Institute's Research Department, directed by Curt Kornblau. The book has benefited greatly from the counsel of Dr. Richard M. Clewett, Professor of Marketing at Northwestern University. The analytical criticism of Dr. W. Tate Whitman, Professor of Economics at Emory University, has been equally helpful. Dr. Patrick Kemp, also of Emory University, edited the sections on financing, operations, and managerial policy and perspective. Facilities for research and the mechanical work of compiling the text were provided by Emory University's School of Business through the assistance of Dean Guy W. Trump and the late Dean Gordon Siefkin. Thanks go also to all the other university colleagues and business associates who were so helpful.

Above all, credit is due my wife, Theodora, for her help with the editing and other intricate details and for her encouragement and inspiration. Nor do I forget my son, Jimmy, who always wanted to help.

FRANK J. CHARVAT

Atlanta, Georgia

CONTENTS

TABLES

1 | INTRODUCTION

SIGNIFICANCE OF THE SUPERMARKET INDUSTRY

The supermarket, which is a relatively new institution, already transacts more dollar volume per year than all department, variety, and drugstores combined. Furthermore, as comparative statistics in Table 1-1 indicate, the supermarket industry has surpassed volume-wise all other types of nondurable-goods stores and now ranks as "volume king" of traditional retailing.[1] Only the automobile dealers —durable-goods outlets with large dollar-unit sales—exceeded the supermarket industry in 1958 on a dollar-volume basis. But consumers basically do not envisage an automobile dealer as a retailer.

The 20,413 supermarkets, supermarts, or supers in the United States in 1958 transacted an estimated volume of $28.7 billion. This phenomenal $28.7 billion volume, averaging more than $1,404,000 per supermarket, represented 64 per cent of all grocery store sales and 57 per cent of the total food store sales in the country.

Yet, 30 years ago, the supermarket industry was comprised of only a few hundred stores scattered throughout the Far West and the Southwest. Statistics in Table 1-2 evidence the phenomenal growth of this industry, which literally has leaped into national prominence. However, statistics in Table 1-2 do not show the complete extent of food sales in large markets inasmuch as the volume prerequisite for admission to the "charmed circle" was changed twice in the past nine years. Prior to 1951, a qualifying super needed to transact a yearly volume of $250,000. In 1951, the standard was raised to

---

[1] The term *traditional retailing* includes bakery, clothing, confectionery, delicatessen, department, drug, furniture and appliances, grocery, hardware, shoe, variety, and vegetable and fruit stores, and service stations.

1

TABLE 1-1 *

Total Sales by Selected Types of Retail Outlets for the Year 1958.

Type of outlet	Sales (in billions)
Automobile dealers	$31.63
Supermarkets †	28.66
Gasoline service stations	15.73
Department stores	12.50
Furniture and appliance stores	10.32
Drug stores	6.59
Variety stores	3.59

* U.S. Bureau of the Census, *Survey of Current Business,* Government Printing Office, Washington, D.C., March, 1959, p. s–9.

† "Industry Survey," *Super Market Merchandising,* XXIV, no. 3, April, 1959, p. 42.

$375,000; and in 1954, the volume requirement was lifted to $500,000 per year. Under the $375,000 requirement, the number of supermarkets in 1956 was 22,567, with sales of $23.2 billion.[2]

COMPOSITION OF THE INDUSTRY IN 1958

It is difficult to visualize an American who hasn't shopped in a supermarket. Supers seem to abound everywhere. Yet, what is the current status as to components of this industry that literally revolutionized not only food distribution but the entire retailing system?

Data in Table 1-3 indicate 20.7 per cent or 4,236 of the supermarkets are individual units as far as ownership and operation are concerned. Many started as small stores. Whatever profits were made have gone into building up the store into a sizable venture, inasmuch as more facilities are needed constantly. An individual super can require ownership capital of several hundred thousand dollars invested at one location. Obviously, close supervision is needed to manage a business of this scope, which averages over $1,000,000 volume per year. However, an additional 6.6 per cent, or 1,343 of the supers, have branched out into two- and three-unit

[2] "Super Market Boom Rides out Another Year," *Super Market Merchandising,* XXII, no. 4, April, 1957, p. 104.

TABLE 1-2

Number of Supermarkets in the U.S., Estimated Sales Volume, and Per Cent of Grocery Store Sales and of Food Store Sales Transacted by Supermarkets for the Years 1935 to 1958.

Year	Number of supermarkets *	Estimated supermarket sales * (in millions)	Supermarket sales as a per cent of grocery store sales †	Supermarket sales as a per cent of food store sales †
1935	300	$ 150	—	1.7
1936	1,200	500	—	5.6
1937	3,066	800	—	8.2
1938	3,700	1,000	—	10.5
1939	4,982	1,500	19.4	14.7
1940	6,175	2,000	24.0	18.3
1941	8,175	2,500	26.0	19.8
1942	9,011	3,000	24.7	19.0
1943	9,100	3,500	26.4	20.0
1944	9,460	3,600	26.4	18.9
1945	9,575	4,500	31.4	22.7
1946	10,057	5,500	29.8	22.7
1947	10,846	7,000	31.3	24.6
1948	11,970	7,780	32.3	25.1
1949	13,089	8,507	35.2	27.4
1950	14,217	10,250	40.3	31.3
1951 ‡	15,383	12,356	40.7	32.9
1952	16,501	14,096	43.7	35.4
1953	17,550	16,092	47.9	39.4
1954 ‡	13,598	15,980	45.8	38.5
1955	15,153	18,644	50.5	42.7
1956	17,024	21,797	55.7	47.4
1957	18,843	25,235	59.5	52.8
1958	20,413	28,664	64.3	56.9

* Yearly surveys published in April editions, *Super Market Merchandising*.

† Calculated by dividing supermarket sales by total grocery store sales and total food store sales, obtained from U.S. Department of Commerce, *Survey of Current Business*, Government Printing Office, Washington, D.C., March editions.

‡ Statistics for the years prior to 1951 were for stores with a minimum volume of $250,000. Data for the years 1951 through 1953 were for stores with a minimum volume of $375,000. Since 1954, data include stores with a minimum volume of $500,000.

TABLE 1-3 *

Ownership of Supermarkets Classified by
Size of Organization for the Year 1958.

Size of organization	Number of stores	% of stores	$ Sales (in millions)	% of sales
1 store	4,236	20.7	5,224	18.2
2–3 stores	1,343	6.6	1,813	6.3
4–10 stores	1,244	6.1	1,835	6.4
11 or more stores . .	13,590	66.6	19,792	69.1
	20,413	100.0	28,664	100.0

* "True Look at the Super Market Industry," *Super Market Merchandising*, XXIV, no. 4, April, 1959, p. 102.

operations in an effort to increase earnings, to diversify risk, and to afford a source for reinvestment of earnings. An additional 1,244 stores, or 6.1 per cent of the supers, have grown into larger operations of from four to ten units in a given community or region. Consumers frequently refer to these as *chains*. However, by definition, a chain must contain eleven or more units. Most of the concerns in this four- to ten-unit group are the result of expansion from one store. And, over the years, through opening new stores and acquiring existing ones by exchange of stock or outright purchase, the corporate chain has become the dominant force in the industry, with 66.6 per cent of the stores and 69.1 per cent of the volume. Chains tend to operate the larger stores.

While 33 per cent, or 6,813, of the supers are listed as nonchains or independents, the bulk of these (more than 70 per cent) are members of wholesale- or retail-sponsored voluntary chains.[3] These voluntaries, exemplified by the Independent Grocers Alliance of America and the Red and White Corporation, operate primarily as buying organizations for their members, although they also offer

[3] *Facts in Grocery Distribution* (New York: Progressive Grocer, 1958), p. F-15.

merchandising, advertising, and promotional services. Thus the buying power in supermarts tends to be concentrated.

Statistics in Table 1-4 reveal that 9,223, or about 45 per cent, of the supers transacted a yearly volume of from $500,000 to $1,000,-000. The markets transacting between $1,000,000 and $2,000,000 yearly represented only 39.9 per cent of the supers but were the major class volumewise. If $110 per square foot of space in a super

TABLE 1-4 *

Number and Sales of Supermarkets Classified
by Dollar Volume for the Year 1958.

$ Volume	Number of markets	% of markets	$ Sales (in millions)	% of sales
500,000– 999,000	9,223	45.2	$ 6,641	23.2
1,000,000–1,999,000	8,139	39.9	12,045	42.0
2,000,000–4,999,000	2,869	14.1	8,492	29.6
5,000,000–and over	182	0.8	1,485	5.2

* "True Look at the Super Market Industry," *Super Market Merchandising,* XXIV, no. 4, April, 1959, p. 102.

is used as an approximate standard, the latter market would range from 11,000 sq ft to 22,000 sq ft of space, exclusive of any outside facilities.[4] The colossuses with sales of over $5,000,000 are insignificant numerically but transact 5 per cent of supermarket sales.

Where are the supers located geographically? Although supermarkets are found in every state, plus the District of Columbia, they have tended to concentrate (obtain a larger share of the food business) in the newer growing areas. Supermarts transacted more than 70 per cent of the grocery store sales in Arizona, California, Colorado, Florida, Louisiana, and Nevada.[5] Texas has also been a mecca for supermarkets. In Florida alone, supers transacted 87 per cent of the grocery sales. Supermarkets also are especially dominant in New

[4] "Super Market Boom Rides out Another Year," *Super Market Merchandising, op. cit.*
[5] *Ibid.*

Jersey and Michigan, two original "hot beds" of supers in the early
1930's.

The 1958 supermarket had 23.6 full-time and 6.7 part-time employees per store.[6] These data include central office and warehouse
personnel as well as store employees. Roughly projecting these statistics to a total industry basis would indicate 400,000 to 500,000
full-time and 125,000 part-time workers.

APPROACH OF THE BOOK TO STUDY OF THE SUPERMARKET INDUSTRY

The size, significance, and composition of the industry have been
presented to show the importance of the supermarket in the area of
distribution. This is a field in which firms are big business. In trac-
ing the development of the supermarket to its present status, it is
necessary to examine certain issues: What is a supermarket? Why
did the industry start? Why did the industry develop so rapidly?
What practices and policies did supermart management adopt to
generate expansion? Furthermore, since such rapid growth was certain to have its impact upon the existing marketing order, what
changes in the food store sales pattern resulted? What shifts occurred in the sales and major product lines of other types of stores
that were encroached upon by the invading supermarket? An examination of these issues forms the core of this text.

Definition of a Supermarket

First consider the term *supermarket,* which did not appear in
Webster's Unabridged New International Dictionary until 1956.[7]
Basically the definition evolves around the two terms *super* and
market.

Super means "above," "over beyond," "that which surpasses."

---

[6] "True Look at the Super Market Industry," *Super Market Merchandising,*
XXIV, no. 4, April, 1959, p. 102.

[7] Certain organizations and authorities who pioneered in this field employed
the term *super market* as two words instead of one, as Webster lists it. As a
result of usage over the years, this spelling also has found wide support in the
industry.

Market refers to a "place" where merchandise is displayed or available for sale. Marketing can be considered the act of selling or purchasing in, or as in, a market. Therefore, in a broad sense, supermarketing can be considered the act of marketing on a large scale or in a manner that surpasses ordinary marketing.

However, the term *supermarket* first became associated with the large food stores that developed in the Far West in the 1920's, and through usage the term became synonymous with this type of food retailing. It is in this sense that the term "supermarketing" is used in this text; namely, it describes the marketing activity in the large type of retail food store known as a supermarket.

Next, the specific definition of a supermarket must be considered. This is imperative in order to gather statistical material and to analyze the industry. Literally scores of definitions have been formulated over the years. These have been subject to changes because of wide diversity and extremely rapid growth. Diversity has existed in (1) number of stores by owners, (2) sales volume per unit, (3) product lines handled, and (4) regional features. In this book the accepted definition is:

A supermarket is a departmentalized retail food store having four basic food departments—self-service groceries, meat, produce, and dairy—plus any number of other departments, with the establishment doing a minimum yearly volume of $500,000.[8]

Innovation

The question of definition was answered at the start. Next, what brought about the advent of the supermarket? In the 1920's the food

---

[8] Authorities in the field have differed as to what the minimum volume of a supermarket should be. Prior to 1951, the two major sources of statistical information in the industry—the magazine, *Super Market Merchandising,* and the trade association, Super Market Institute—were in accord on the $250,000 minimum volume. In order to make adjustment for the change in the rising level of food prices and for the trend toward larger stores, both raised their minimum volume in 1951. The $375,000 volume was selected by *Super Market Merchandising* because it corresponded to the O.P.S. classification for Type 4 stores. The Super Market Institute in 1951 raised its minimum volume to $500,000. In 1954 *Super Market Merchandising* did likewise, and both sources once again were in agreement as to volume.

store industry was composed of many single- or limited-line outlets
such as dairy stores, grocery stores without meat, meat markets, con-
fectioners, and delicatessens. The movement toward multi-line operation, however, in the form of the combination market had started.
The two major outlets were the grocery store without meat and the
combination market. Whether independently owned or members of
chains, these were generally small, were located close to the consumer, and offered a variety of services such as credit and delivery.

A marketing innovation, the supermarket, appeared in California
in the late 1920's and several years later in the East. The underlying
forces behind each of these movements were different. Even the
stores were not the same, but each offered a key to the growing importance of the supermarket movement and to changes in the pattern
of retail sales. This subject of development is discussed compre-
hensively in Chapter 2.

Internal and External Factors

The growth of the supermarket industry occurred in an era in
which a maze of particular external influences were present that had
a bearing on its development. Consumer buying habits changed. A
desire for one-stop shopping came into vogue. The automobile came
into wider use for everyday living; refrigeration became a "must"
for most homes. From the depths of a depression, personal disposable income rose to an unprecedented height by 1958. These and
other factors are presented in Chapter 3 to ascertain what influence
they had on the development of the supermarket industry.

How did the food store industry as a group fare in this economic,
technological, and psychological setting? Did the supermarket gain
more in volume than other types of food stores? It was found that it
did. Therefore internal features are examined to discern what practices the supermarket operators adopted that attracted customers
to them. These techniques are grouped under operational and financial factors and are given close scrutiny in Chapters 4 through 7.
Such features as buying practices, selling techniques, pricing, ex-

pense control, profit relationships, and investment requirements are highlighted. These chapters, which basically contain the principles of supermarketing, are of special interest to management, owners, and students.

Impact on Pattern of Food Store Sales

Specifically, what changes occurred in the pattern of food store sales by 1958 compared with those of 1929 when supermarkets were for practical purposes nonexistent? An answer to this requires a detailed statistical study of (1) the number of different kinds of food stores, (2) sales by type of food stores, and (3) sales of major product lines transacted by types of food stores. These three constitute the pattern of food store sales as defined in this book. The impact of the supermarket is examined in Chapters 8 through 11. The final chapter, 12, is devoted to industry trends and conclusions of this study, written from a management point of view so as to aid present and future policy and decisions. This final chapter is entitled, "Managerial Policy and Perspective."

SCOPE OF THE STUDY

The growth of the supermarket industry influenced other phases of food and nonfood distribution besides the food sales pattern. The supermarket's successful exploitation of self-service influenced other forms of retailers to review their selling techniques and possibly to adopt this principle. The addition of nonfood lines by supermarkets tended to shift the sales pattern by kind of retail outlet for items such as health and beauty aids, housewares, and certain soft goods.

Manufacturers and wholesalers of food products reviewed their marketing programs in an attempt to obtain greater distribution of their lines in supermarkets. Frequently manufacturers sold directly to supers. Food wholesalers were able to reduce their costs of operation through cost-plus plans;[9] many worked closely with

[9] R. D. Tousley, "Reducing Distribution Costs in the Grocery Field," *Journal of Marketing*, XII, no. 4, April, 1948, p. 455.

supers on narrow margins or even sponsored their own supermarts.

All these salient aspects offer challenging facets for study. While these and other factors are considered in this text, attention is mainly centered on the innovation, growth, operational features, and impact of the supermarket on the pattern of food store sales which occurred simultaneously with the supermarket development.

2 | DEVELOPMENT OF THE SUPERMARKET

INTRODUCTION

In the preceding chapter, the significance of the supermarket industry, its definition, the plan of approach, and the scope of this text were considered. It is the objective of this chapter to study the development of large markets in the United States from the time of the earliest Boston public market to the modern supermarkets of today. Included are the forces that had a bearing on the start of supermarkets in the Los Angeles area and the East. For convenience in presentation, the data are examined in chronological time periods. These are as follows:

1. Large markets prior to 1930
2. The era of the "cheapy" supermarket, 1930 to 1935
3. The period of experimental growth and development, 1935 to 1946
4. The postwar period of "modern" supermarket expansion, 1946 to date

LARGE MARKETS PRIOR TO 1930

In this section the history of early large markets prior to 1930 is reviewed to ascertain if any met the accepted definition of a supermarket as outlined in this book. This includes an examination of: (1) early public and private concession-type markets, (2) Piggly Wiggly stores, (3) "market stores" of the Los Angeles area, and (4) large markets in the Southwest.

Early Public and Private Concession-Type Markets

The concept of a large market is not a recent innovation in the United States.[1] Large markets operating under public ownership date back to 1658 in Boston.[2] Some of the very early ventures were the Faneuil Hall Market of Boston, the Lexington Market of Baltimore, and the Catherine Market of New York City. The Catherine Market by 1860 had 60 enclosed stalls in addition to the areas used by the open-air vendors. By 1918 the U.S. Bureau of the Census listed 174 of these large retail markets in cities of over 30,000 population.[3]

Not all the early markets were publicly owned. Privately financed and operated markets included the Reading Terminal Market of Philadelphia, the Euclid and 46th Street Market of Cleveland, and the Pike Place Market of Seattle.

These early markets were housed in a variety of buildings, varying from sheds or booths (frequently built on public property to enable farmers to sell their products) to the more elaborate structures found in New Orleans and San Francisco. They all had common characteristics: (1) a large area, (2) many stalls, booths, or departments leased to various proprietors who operated individually, and (3) a large over-all volume for the market, although each section had a relatively small sales volume.

Were these supermarkets? A brief description of the mode of operation of one—the Crystal Palace Market of San Francisco—is presented to see how it measured against our current definition of a supermarket.

Crystal Palace Market

This establishment, founded in 1922 and controlled by the owners of the Emporium, was housed in a 68,000-sq ft building located in

[1] Paul H. Nystrom, *Economics of Retailing* (New York: The Ronald Press Co., 1936), Vol. 1, p. 335.
[2] Arthur E. Goodwin, *Markets Public and Private* (Seattle: Montgomery Printing Co., 1939), p. 22.
[3] *Ibid.*, p. 27.

the downtown district.[4] Public transportation was good; 80 per cent of all street cars in the city passed its door. In addition, a 4,350-car parking lot was immediately adjacent. The multimillion dollar sales volume of 1929 was divided among the following product classes: [5]

	% sales
Meat	18
Fruit and vegetable	16
Grocery	15
Delicatessen	13
Drugs, tobacco, etc.	12
Restaurant	10
Dairy	7
Fish and poultry	5
Bakery	3
Miscellaneous	1
	100

There were 110 departments, with concessions leased on a minimum guarantee basis and every lease containing a percentage-of-gross-sales clause. Management had control over the kind and quality of merchandise sold. Extensive advertising was done, with the market drawing 150,000 people weekly. The appeal was not one of price; rather, extensive promotions were planned, including car raffles and public drawings.

This operation, founded in the 1920's, certainly had many of the characteristics attributed to a supermarket in Chapter 1. While it was not a supermarket as defined, since it lacked self-service, it certainly was a forerunner of the modern super. The lack of self-service also characterized the other typical, large early markets of the United States.

Piggly Wiggly Stores

During 1916 in Memphis, Tennessee, Clarence Saunders started his first revolutionary self-service store in a location formerly oper-

[4] The Emporium is a San Francisco department store.

[5] Emil Dollenger, "Quality, Not Price, Built San Francisco's Grand Crystal Market," *Super Market Merchandising*, II, no. 1, January, 1937, p. 3.

ated by a regional chain.[6] He emphasized basic principles of standardization and simplification found in industrial management books
of today.

In the first six months of operation, this store did $114,000 gross
sales at an expense of $3,400—a 3 per cent of sales expense rate—
and experienced a stock turnover of 39 times a year.[7] This success
was partly attributed to the innovation of self-service. The idea
grew into a chain of owned and leased stores, with the latter li-
censed to use the name, equipment, and method of operation.

After a series of financial maneuvers, Saunders lost control in
1923. However, the chain continued to expand, and by 1928 reached
a peak of 2,700 stores in 41 states; this was prior to sale of its stores
to Safeway Stores and the Kroger Company.[8]

Unfortunately, only fragmentary information is available on the
complete operating results of this chain. It was reported in 1920
that the operating subsidiary, Piggly Wiggly Store Company, had
404 units with a yearly volume of almost $60,000,000.[9] The average
yearly store volume was $150,000, although the peak store did a
$10,000 weekly sales volume while operating as a self-service com-
bination grocery and meat market.[10] The resulting net profits of this
chain from 1919 to 1925 as a percentage of sales were mediocre
(less than 1 per cent); however, detailed expense breakdowns were
not published.[11]

A separately controlled chain, Piggly Wiggly Western States
Company, reported for the fiscal year 1923 a gross margin of 11.8
per cent and an operating expense of 8.3 per cent.[12] These extremely favorable results compare with today's supermarket, but
they steadily declined thereafter until the chain was sold in 1927.

[6] Walter Hayward and Percival White, *Chain Stores* (New York: McGraw-
Hill Book Co., Inc., 1922), p. 180.
[7] *Ibid.*
[8] *Ibid.*, p. 186.
[9] R. P. Crawford, "Piggly Wiggly, How It Has Grown," *Forbes*, October,
1921, p. 15.
[10] *Ibid.*
[11] *Moody's Industrial Manual*, 1920–1926.
[12] *Ibid.*

Based on the available information, a few of the Piggly Wiggly Stores were supermarkets according to our current definition. The limited data indicated the system, in part, operated at a smaller expense rate than the existing independent grocer or the chain economy store whose clerks serviced the trade. But in the era of the 1920's, the chains were concentrating on clerk-service economy stores and did not develop the potentialities of self-service.

"Market Stores" of the Los Angeles Area

Two kinds of "market stores" that flourished in the Los Angeles area prior to 1930 were also supermarkets according to the definition set forth in this book. These were:

1. The large, self-service food store, which was operated under centralized control and which, by current standards, would be judged as an excellent example of a supermarket

2. The open-front, drive-in market, which comprised a group of independent units in a single building

Ralph's Grocery Company. The first type of these market stores was exemplified by Ralph's Grocery Company, although there were others such as Carty Brothers and Alpha Beta Food Markets. Ralph's, still a large supermarket operator today, started in downtown Los Angeles in 1872 with one store.[13] By 1911 the company had built a flourishing operation featuring clerk-service and delivery. As the city grew, attractive branches were opened in modern, elaborate buildings. The units recognized the advantages of self-service and started conversion in 1926. By 1928 delivery was abandoned: 74 trucks were auctioned in one day. By 1929 the chain had 16 large, well-developed supermarkets.[14]

Drive-in markets. The second type of market store was the open-front, drive-in market that appeared in the Los Angeles area about 1925.[15] This type of operation comprised a group of food stores in

[13] Lucius Flint, "The Los Angeles Super," *Chain Store Age*, Grocery Executive Edition, June, 1950, p. j34.
[14] *Ibid.*
[15] Walter Van de Kamp, "An Innovation in Retail Selling," *Magazine of Business*, July, 1929, p. 28.

a one-story building located in neighborhood and outlying sections. Parking was immediately adjacent. Each of the units of the large market store was individually owned and operated; yet, shoppers looked on the market as a single entity. Certain of these units met our current definition of a supermarket. One of the most elaborate of these drive-ins was Chapman Park Drive-in Market of Los Angeles. The land and building alone represented an investment of over $400,000.[16]

Factors influencing the supermarket innovation in the Los Angeles area.   It is not known definitely whether all these units met the self-service requirement. But writers in this era were of the opinion that the following reasons were responsible for this development: [17]

1. Los Angeles had no elevated, subway, or other good means of transportation to the central business district. Thus, individuals were forced to use private motor cars as the chief source of transportation. In 1928 the population of California was 4,556,000.[18] Passenger car registrations were 1,799,890; approximately 35 per cent of the inhabitants had cars.[19] This percentage of the population owning cars was substantially higher than the national average.

2. Parking in the central area was limited, and restrictions were severe. Therefore, secondary or outlying sections developed. These invariably had some facilities for parking.

3. The wide use of the automobile for shopping prevailed. People throughout the year were able to circulate more freely. The climate was favorable for outdoor living and activity.

4. The open-front, drive-in markets did not have to be erected

---

[16] "495 Autos Can Park in This New Drive-In Market," *Progressive Grocer*, XIII, no. 10, October, 1929, p. 30.

[17] These are synopses of the opinions of three authors: Walter Van de Kamp, "An Innovation in Retail Selling," *Magazine of Business,* July, 1929, p. 28; S. L. Brevit, "Drive-In Department Stores Gaining Popularity in the West," *Sales Management*, XXX, no. 3, January 17, 1931, p. 118; and H. M. Foster, "Threat of the Supermarket," *Sales Management*, XXXII, no. 9, April 20, 1933, p. 436.

[18] U.S. Bureau of Census, *Statistical Abstract of the United States, 1929*, Government Printing Office, Washington, D.C., 1930, p. 7.

[19] *Ibid.*, p. 387.

as substantially as in colder communities. The required building investment was less, and therefore business men were more likely to
experiment with a new type of market.

5. Land was plentiful and reasonably priced. This growing territory spread over a large area and was not subject to central transportation limitations.

6. The people had a pioneer spirit, believed in change, and were
more adaptable to innovations than the inhabitants of the East or
Middle West.

It was surprising to note that none of the literature in this era
prior to 1930 mentioned low price appeal in connection with these
"market stores." These factors indicate that this supermarket development was viewed as a regional affair suitable for California
or possibly the Southwest.[20]

Large Markets in the Southwest

One of the earliest and the largest supermarket operations in the
Southwest was Henke & Pillot of Houston, Texas. This firm had its
origin in 1872.[21] By 1900 its downtown store had 50,000 sq ft of
space and operated 13 departments, including its own bakery and
coffee-roasting plant. The store grew to a yearly volume of $5,-
000,000. As Houston spread out and the automobile came of age,
two modern and well-equipped outlying stores featuring large parking lots were added in 1926 and 1928. Some self-service operation
was adopted in the following year, and the concern became a full-
fledged supermarket.[22]

Other supermarket operators in the Southwest at this time were
J. Weingarten, Incorporated, and the ABC Stores, Incorporated.
Mr. Joe Weingarten, chairman of the board of J. Weingarten, In-
corporated, has stated that his first large market operation which

[20] C. B. Larrabee, "Grocery Manufacturers Condemn Supermarket Price
Cutters," *Printers Ink*, CLXII, no. 9, March 2, 1933, p. 41.
[21] Charles N. Bunnell, "Henke & Pillot Supermarket Grew from Houston Public Demand," *Super Market Merchandising*, II, no. 2, February, 1937, p. 3.
[22] "Big Volume in 1922," *Chain Store Age*, Grocery Executive Edition, June,
1950, p. j22.

could be considered a supermarket was started in 1918.[23] This store had both self-service grocery and dairy departments.

ERA OF THE "CHEAPY" SUPERMARKET, 1930 TO 1935

A new type of supermarket developed in 1930. It was a depression product and was very different in appearance from the attractive California and Texas markets. Yet this "cheapy," as it was referred to, still conformed to our definiton, and its development in New York and New Jersey awakened the country to this retailing innovation.

King Kullen and Big Bear Markets

Michael Cullen, an ex-chain-store executive, opened the first successful "cheapy" in August, 1930, in Jamaica, Long Island, New York.[24] By the end of 1932, the King Kullen Markets had increased to eight outlets. Big Bear, a similar "cheapy" supermarket, followed King Kullen. In December, 1932, Roy O. Dawson and Robert M. Otis, together with the American House Grocers, a local wholesaler, opened the Big Bear in Elizabeth, New Jersey. The location was an abandoned factory of the Durant Motor Car Company.[25]

The word "cheapy" was synonymous with price structure and appearance. The interior had no partitions, crude floors, bare ceilings, unpainted fixtures, glaring lights, gaudy signs, and merchandise piled everywhere. The units thrived in low-rent locations on the fringe of thickly populated sections. Later, other "cheapy" units were opened in abandoned warehouses, empty department stores, garages, and factories.

The price structures were even more fantastic when compared with the existing forms of food merchandising. Their promotional names (King Kullen, The Price Wrecker; and Big Bear, the Price Crusher) were in conformity with their price schedules. Compare

[23] M. M. Zimmerman, *The Super Market* (New York: McGraw-Hill Book Co., Inc., 1955), p. 26.
[24] "The Cheapy Thrives," *Business Week,* no. 179, February 8, 1933, p. 11.
[25] M. M. Zimmerman, *Super Market Spectacular Exponent of Mass Distribution* (New York: Super Market Publishing Co., 1937), p. 25.

the following King Kullen Market prices with those of other stores: [26]

	Elsewhere	King Kullen
All 10-cent drug items	$ 0.10	$ 0.09
Campbell's tomato soup	0.07	0.04
U.S. Rubber tires for Fords	5.50	3.78
General Electric vacuum cleaners . .	35.00	11.94

The greater portion of space in King Kullen Markets was allocated to the grocery, meat, bakery, and dairy departments. The remainder of the space was leased to utensil, produce, paint, hardware, and auto accessory concessionaires. A King Kullen Market required an investment of $30,000, which included $23,000 for merchandise, $2,500 for grocery equipment, and $4,500 for meat department equipment.[27]

Two of King Kullen's operating principles were (1) the other departments must all sell merchandise at reduced prices, and (2) the income from the concessions should pay the rent of the entire establishment.[28]

During this time Big Bear operated only the grocery department, which occupied 30 per cent of the 50,000-sq ft floor space.[29] It leased concessions for meat, produce, dairy, bakery, candy, tobacco, drugs, luncheonette, and paints. The concessionaires were charged 5.13 per cent on their gross sales in lieu of rent and other overhead expenses. The Big Bear made a substantial profit on the leased departments.

The markets that mushroomed following King Kullen and Big Bear were generally of the same "cheapy" type. Many of these early supers—The Whale, Giant Tiger, Big Chief, Little Bear—were strange stores, frequently referred to as monstrosities because of their method of operation, location, appearance, and type of structure occupied.[30] The King Kullen markets in modified form are still in operation.

26 "The Cheapy Thrives," *op. cit.*
27 Zimmerman, *The Super Market, op. cit.*, p. 32.
28 Zimmerman, *Super Market Spectacular Exponent of Mass Distribution, op. cit.*, p. 10.
29 *Ibid.*
30 Carl W. Dipman, "Merchandise Trend in Food Trade," *Journal of Marketing*, III, no. 3, January, 1939, p. 269.

Factors Influencing the Development
of the "Cheapy" Supermarket in the East

The innovation of the "cheapy" supermarket in the East was attributed to the fact that low income and unemployment made low price of paramount importance in the early 1930's.[31] The supermarket was a lower-cost type of operation than the existing food stores. It passed on to the consumer some of its savings, in the form of lower prices.

Income and employment statistics. The year 1932 was a depression year. Statistics in Table 2-1 indicate that the number of em-

TABLE 2-1 *

National Income and Employment in the
United States for the Years 1929 to 1936.

Year	National income (in billions)	Number of gainfully employed
1929	$83.3	35,563,000
1930	68.9	33,122,000
1931	54.3	29,715,000
1932	40.0	26,222,000
1933	42.5	26,133,000
1934	50.3	28,402,000
1935	55.9	29,725,000
1936	65.1	31,858,000

* U.S. Bureau of the Census, *Statistical Abstract of the United States,* Government Printing Office, Washington, D.C., 1940, p. 315.

ployed persons dropped 9,341,000 between 1929 and 1932, or by 27 per cent. Unemployment stood at an all-time twentieth century high of 12,300,000 persons.[32] Wages were sharply cut; many of the working population were on a part-time basis. The national income dropped from $83.3 billion in 1929 to a low of $40.0 billion in 1932.

[31] Larrabee, *op. cit.*

[32] Bureau of Labor Statistics, *Monthly Labor Review,* Vol. 35, no. 1, Government Printing Office, Washington, D.C., 1933, p. 140.

The country as a whole was "dissaving"—living on past capital accumulation. This was the economic setting for the "cheapy" supermarket.

Early price policies of supermarkets. Low price was the basic appeal of the "cheapy" supermarket as it invaded the food store field.[33] Everything about the market had an air of cheapness. Nationally advertised brands were placed on sale at ridiculously low prices. Loss leaders were common. Many of the customers drove as far as 50 miles to the Big Bear.[34]

King Kullen's pricing format [35] was to sell

> 300 items at cost
> 200 items at 5% above cost
> 300 items at 15% above cost
> 300 items at 20% above cost

The appeal of low price was nothing new.[36] Chains had used it successfully for years and generally undersold the independents.[37] But the supers "stole the thunder" from the chains and were able invariably to quote lower prices than the economy stores or independents.[38]

Charles F. Phillips cited that on June 20, 1935, he checked the prices on 34 well-known branded items in the Big Bear and in a chain store. The chain store prices for these items averaged 12.8 per cent in excess of those of Big Bear.[39] A study of advertised staple merchandise prices made by M. M. Zimmerman in 16 cities throughout the country in 1935 found that the supers undersold the chains on comparable products from 4.8 to 22.9 per cent.[40]

[33] Zimmerman, *The Supermarket Spectacular Exponent of Mass Distribution, op. cit.*, p. 10.

[34] *Ibid.*, p. 11.

[35] Zimmerman, *The Super Market, op. cit.*, p. 33.

[36] Charles F. Phillips, "The Supermarket," *Harvard Business Review*, XVI, no. 2, Winter, 1938, p. 192.

[37] Federal Trade Commission, *Chain Stores, Final Report on the Chain Store Investigation,* submitted to 74th Congress, 1st session, Senate, Document 4, Government Printing Office, Washington, D.C., Dec. 14, 1934, p. 67.

[38] Phillips, *op. cit.*, p. 196.

[39] *Ibid.*, p. 198.

[40] Zimmerman, *The Supermarket Spectacular Exponent of Mass Distribution, op. cit.*, p. 53.

With regard to their loss-leader policies, Phillips stated:

There is no doubt but that many supermarkets have been large users
of loss leaders in the sense that many items have been sold at prices only
slightly above their actual cost to the operator. This practice, of course,
gives the supermarket the appearance of being a low price institution. At
the same time it is evident that much of the cry against this type of operation for the use of loss leaders is not valid because many supermarkets are
in a position to quote prices below those of their competitors primarily
because of their low cost of operations, but also in some degree because
of their buying practices.[41]

*Comparative margins, expenses, and profits of independents,
chains, and early supers.*   Prior to the development of the supermarket industry in the 1930's, the retail grocery distribution industry
had its battle lines drawn between chains and independents. The
operating costs of independents in the Louisville area in the late
1920's are indicated in Table 2-2.

TABLE 2-2 *

Profit and Loss Statement for the Average Grocery Store in the
Louisville Survey as a Percentage of Sales for the Year 1929.

Sales		100.00
Cost of sales		74.19
Gross margin		25.81
Expenses		
Miscellaneous	2.53	
Owners' salary	4.01	
Other salaries	6.31	
Rent	.98	
Utilities	1.23	
Delivery	2.77	
Advertising	.31	
Insurance	.15	18.29
Net profit		7.52

* U.S. Department of Commerce, *Distribution Cost Studies Number 1,
Louisville Grocery Survey, Part IIIA*, Government Printing Office, Washington,
D.C., 1932, pp. 15–23.

[41] Phillips, *op. cit.*

Other studies of independent store operations showed gross margins to be closer to 20 per cent and profits varying from 1.6 to 2.6 per cent of sales, depending upon the type of operation.[42]

The Great Atlantic and Pacific Tea Company for the year 1929 operated 15,150 smaller-type economy stores, with the average weekly sales of $1,317 per store. A breakdown of these operations for 1929, 1933, and 1935 is shown in Table 2-3. The gross margin

Table 2-3 *

Condensed Profit and Loss Statement of the Retail Store
Operation of the Great A & P Tea Company as a
Percentage of Sales for the Years 1929 to 1935.

	1929	*1933*	*1935*
Sales	100.00	100.00	100.00
Cost of sales	81.64	78.10	80.50
Gross margin	18.36	21.90	19.50
Total operating expenses . .	15.52	19.08	17.56
Net profit	2.84	2.82	1.94

* *United States* v. *The Great A & P Tea Company*, U.S. Circuit Court of Appeals, 7th district, Docket 9221, Records & Briefs, Vol. II, p. 162.

for chain stores as a group for 1929 was 18.99 per cent, and for independents, 23.01 per cent of sales.[43] These statistics, published later, support Professor Schmalz's contention that, generally, the chains were in a position to undersell the independent grocer at that time.

When the "cheapy" supermarket entered the field in the depression years, it operated at even a lower gross margin than the chain. The operating statement of the Big Bear super in Elizabeth, New Jersey, for 1933 is shown in Table 2-4.

Big Bear earned a substantial profit from concessions and was in a position to operate its grocery department on a 12 per cent gross.

[42] A series of studies made in the 1920's were quoted by Carl N. Schmalz, "Independent Stores vs. Chains in the Grocery Field," *Harvard Business Review*, IX, no. 4, July, 1931, p. 431.
[43] Federal Trade Commission, *Chain Stores, op. cit.*

TABLE 2-4 *

**Operating Statement of the Big Bear, Elizabeth, New Jersey,
for the Year 1933.**

	Dollar		% of sales
Grocery department sales	$2,188,403		100.00
Cost of sales	1,925,795		87.99
Gross profit	$ 262,608		12.01
Expenses			
Rent $15,516		.71	
Payroll 79,545		3.64	
Light and heat 7,881		.35	
Advertising 28,974		1.32	
Handling 20,157		.93	
Administration 11,248		.51	
Clerical 6,915		.32	
Insurance 3,523		.16	
Miscellaneous 7,462		.34	
Taxes 1,094		.05	
Depreciation 219	182,534	.01	8.34
Net profit from			
grocery operators	$ 80,074		3.67
Rental from concessions	86,434		
Net profit	$166,508		

* M. M. Zimmerman, *The Supermarket Spectacular Exponent of Mass Distribution* (New York: Super Market Publishing Company, 1937), p. 14.

Furthermore, the accounting system did not adequately show the operating profit because all rental and light for the store was charged to Big Bear grocery department even though it occupied only 30 per cent of the space.

Similarly, King Kullen stores made a gross profit of 9 per cent on grocery and fruit and vegetables and a net profit of 2½ per cent! Their net profit on meat sales was 3 per cent. These remarkable operating results and profits were the result of the innovation of the "cheapy" supermarket.

During the early 1930's other mushrooming supermarkets maintained an operating advantage over the chain economy stores and the small independents. Gross margins varied from 10 to 14 per cent of sales.[44] John Hartford, president of the A & P, reported that supermarket competitors in Detroit during this period operated on a 12.5 per cent gross and earned a 2.5 per cent net.[45] He said that the established A & P aim was to operate at a 12 per cent gross and 2 per cent net.[46]

The statistics on supermarket operation in this era indicate that it was extremely difficult for the conventional A & P economy store and the average independent combination market to compete with supers.

PERIOD OF EXPERIMENTAL GROWTH AND DEVELOPMENT, 1935 TO 1946

The markets that mushroomed following King Kullen and Big Bear were generally of the same "cheapy" variety. This type of store, however, rapidly lost its appeal when more attractive supermarkets were opened, starting in 1935.[47] By this time the principle of the supermarket operation had been proved sound. National income and employment had risen; new capital began to be attracted to the industry. "Traded up" supermarkets began to multiply in superior locations. Larger investments in equipment and buildings followed and resulted in improved external and internal appearances of the stores, which began to take on the semblance of supermarkets as we know them today.

Statistics on supermarkets kept yearly, beginning in 1936, are recorded in Table 1-2 and indicate the number of supers and their volume increase every year thereafter. Such chains as A & P, Kroger, First National Stores, and American Stores opened experimental supermarket units at this time.[48] But it was not until 1937, that the

---

[44] Phillips, *op. cit.,* p. 192.

[45] *United States* v. *The Great A & P Tea Company,* U.S. Circuit Court of Appeals, 7th district, Docket 9221, Records & Briefs, Vol. II, p. 194.

[46] *Ibid.,* p. 194.

[47] Carl W. Dipman, "Merchandise Trend in Food Trade," *Journal of Marketing,* III, no. 3, January, 1939, p. 269.

[48] M. M. Zimmerman, "The Supermarket and the Changing Retail Structure," *Journal of Marketing,* VI, no. 2, April, 1941, p. 403.

TABLE 2-5 *

**Operating Statement of an Average Independent Combination
Market as a Percentage of Sales for the Year 1935.**

Sales		100.0
Cost of sales		81.7
Gross margin		18.3
Expenses		
Utilities	.8	
Advertising	.6	
Rent	1.4	
Wages	5.4	
Owner's	4.7	
Taxes	.4	
Other	3.4	16.7
Net profit		1.6

* *Standard Ratios for Retailing* (New York: Dun & Bradstreet, Inc., 1936),
p. 8.

industry leader, the A & P, decided to make the supermarket the
next step in its development.[49] Some of the first chain supers were
opened under different names; for example, the Kroger Company
operated stores in Cincinnati under the name "Pay'n Takit." The
increase in the number of supermarkets in the late 1930's was due
largely to the switch of chains to supers (see Table 1-2). From 1936
to 1938 the number of supermarkets skyrocketed from 1,200 to 4,982.
Statistics on the number of supers for the industry leader (A & P)
are given in Table 2-6; they indicate the rapid shift to supermarket
operation. In many urban areas the most strategic locations for
supermarkets already were well developed with such outlets.[50]

The first supermarket convention in 1937 gave the industry a degree of unity. At that time the industry's trade association, Super
Market Institute, was founded. The Institute, which has lent organization to the industry and has furnished the widely scattered

[49] *United States* v. *The Great A & P Tea Company, op. cit.,* p. 192.
[50] William Applebaum, "Adjustment of Retailing to 1941 Conditions," *Journal
of Marketing,* V, no. 4, April, 1941, p. 438.

TABLE 2-6 *

**Number of A & P Supermarkets and Small Economy Stores
for the Years 1936 to 1943.**

Year	Number of supers	Number of small economy stores
1936	20	14,426
1937	282	12,776
1938	771	9,900
1939	1,119	7,902
1940	1,396	5,677
1941	1,552	4,490
1942	1,633	4,188
1943	1,646	4,105

* *United States* v. *The Great A & P Tea Company,* U.S. Circuit Court of Appeals, 7th district, Docket 9221, Records and Briefs, Vol. I, p. 323.

members a common bond, has grown from 32 pioneer members to the point where it currently embraces over 744 companies operating 11,388 outlets.[51] In addition to sponsoring the annual meetings at which current major industry problems are discussed, the Super Market Institute fosters educational activities, establishes ethical business practices, promotes research activities, and serves as a clearing house for information. More recently adopted activities include the intra-industry figure exchange and the executive training program. Credit also must be given to M. M. Zimmerman for the development and guidance of this industry, especially in the formative years. In 1936 he founded the publication, *Super Market Merchandising,* which has been a major source of information for the supermarket operators.

The years 1941 and early 1942 showed one of the largest increases in the number of supers. The number of units increased by 2,000. Many chains and independents displayed feverish activity, apparently in an attempt to beat the impending building restriction that

[51] *The Super Market Industry Speaks—1959* (Chicago: Super Market Institute), p. 15.

resulted from World War II.[52] During the ensuing war years, the
industry showed little or no expansion. This was accounted for by
building material shortages, lack of adequate help, food rationing,
price controls, rationing which limited the use of the automobile,
desire of people to know their grocers more intimately so as to obtain advantages in food purchasing, reduced significance of price
as a result of swollen consumer incomes, and food shortages.[53]
Nevertheless the supers survived this era, partly through the increased employment of women, the addition of nonfood lines, the
maintenance of as large an inventory of national brands as possible,
and self-service expansion.[54]

Prior to World War II supermarkets as a whole concentrated
mainly on the sale of foods. During the war the supers began to feature more nonfood lines. The success of this policy led to the addition of more nonfood departments after the war.[55]

POSTWAR PERIOD OF MODERN SUPERMARKET EXPANSION

The industry again experienced renewed impetus in 1946. The
population increase and outward push from the center of cities, plus
the building of new homes in the suburbs, offered new location opportunities. Satisfactory profit margins continued to make this a
mecca for expansion. Furthermore the industry was able to obtain
capital. Many of the firms which less than 15 years earlier were small
operations or nonexistent entered the capital markets by publicly
selling securities in order to obtain funds for expansion. Many of
the independent food retailers realized they could not compete with
this new method of merchandising and converted their stores into
supermarkets. In this they were aided by voluntary chains and alert

[52] Carl W. Dipman, "Changes in Food Distribution," *Journal of Marketing*,
VI, no. 4, April, 1942, p. 48.
[53] M. M. Zimmerman, "Super Market Sales & Profit Trends 1941–43," *Journal
of Marketing*, X, no. 2, October, 1944, p. 162.
[54] M. M. Zimmerman, "Tomorrow's Super Market," *Journal of Marketing*, X,
no. 4, April, 1946, p. 384.
[55] M. M. Zimmerman, *Super Market—Its Growth and Future* (New York:
Super Marketing Merchandising Publishing Co., 1948), p. 4.

wholesalers who helped them to streamline their methods of operation. New stores were built with greater floor space and parking facilities. Many stores were remodeled. More elaborate interiors and exteriors became the vogue, with services such as music and air conditioning added. The statistics in Table 1-2 indicate an increase of 213 per cent in the number of supers from 1945 to 1958 and a rise in sales volume of 637 per cent for the same period. By 1958 the number of supermarkets had reached 20,413 units.

Other features that aided this tremendous postwar expansion included the further shift of local, regional, and national chains from small to large store operation. In addition, the increased promotion and ballyhoo techniques of supermarket operators to increase store traffic made the suburban shopping center and the supermarket a sociological mecca for the American family. Finally, the constant pressure to reinvest earnings into profitable merchandising operations aided the expansion movement.

One of the most recent trends in the postwar era is the increased emphasis on horizontal integration through acquisition on the part of the larger concerns. Examples of this are the recent foragings of the National Tea Company and the ACF–Wrigley Stores, Incorporated. The keynote seems to be "acquire or expire." More and more the emphasis is not on "big business" but on "bigger business."

SUMMARY

The first supers were a relatively few Piggly Wiggly stores. These were followed by the California supers and drive-in markets, which appeared to be a product of primarily local forces. Then came a new supermarket, the "cheapy," which flourished in the depression years of the 1930's and which made low price its basic appeal. This was followed by the policy of "trading-up" the stores. The national food chains joined the movement after 1936 and gave it impetus. The World War II period saw changes in policies but relatively no change in number of markets. The postwar period was one of vast expansion in number of units, size of stores, services, and dollar volume. The industry has become one of bigger and bigger business.

3
EXTERNAL FACTORS THAT INFLUENCED THE GROWTH OF THE SUPERMARKET INDUSTRY

INTRODUCTION

The development of the supermarket, including the factors that influenced its innovation, was discussed in the preceding chapter. It was shown that the early supers, with the exception of California and the Southwest, were largely of the "cheapy" variety. But from 1935 on, the supermarket industry continued to gain new members at a remarkable rate and began to improve the appearance, equipment and location of its stores.[1]

This chapter and the subsequent four analyze the factors that aided this remarkable growth. For expedience these are broken down into external and internal considerations. The former are examined in this chapter and include:

1. Changes in personal disposable income and personal consumption expenditures
2. Shifts in upper income shares
3. Changes in expenditures in food stores
4. Changes in the pattern of food consumption

[1] Charles F. Phillips, "The Supermarket," *Harvard Business Review*, XVI, no. 2, Winter, 1938, p. 192.

5. Technological developments and their adoption
6. Population growth and shift to the suburbs
7. Retail trend toward decentralization
8. Shifts in consumer buying habits (including one-stop shopping and scrambled merchandise) [2]
9. Additional external factors

Still other external influences were present in the economy such as industrial decentralization, concentration of power among food manufacturers and higher literacy; but the above listed factors appeared to be the most pertinent to the problem.

CHANGES IN PERSONAL DISPOSABLE INCOME AND PERSONAL CONSUMPTION EXPENDITURES

As previously indicated, the national income of the United States suffered a substantial drop from $83 billion in 1929 to $40 billion in 1932.[3] Employment decreased from 35,563,000 in 1929 to 26,222,000 in 1932.[4] It was at this time that the "cheapy" supermarket started its expansion—offering "food for less." But the "cheapy" depression product was short-lived and soon was replaced by the more elaborately equipped and housed super.

From 1935 to date, the total and the per capita disposable personal income and personal consumption expenditures increased substantially. These statistics are shown in Table 3-1 together with the cost of living index which also rose in this interval, although by a lesser amount than the per capita income and expenditures. The trend thus has been for each person to have more income to spend and to need relatively less of this larger income for basic living purposes. The large personal consumption expenditures indicate that

---

[2] The term *scrambled merchandise* was used by Malcolm P. McNair to indicate the merchandising of a commodity in retail stores in which the product was basically foreign. This discussion is found in an article by Malcolm P. McNair, "Trends in Large-Scale Retailing," *Harvard Business Review*, X, no. 1, Fall, 1932, p. 31.

[3] These statistics are contained in Table 2-1.

[4] *Ibid.*

TABLE 3-1

Total Disposable Personal Income, Total and Per Capita
Personal Consumption Expenditure, and the Cost of
Living Index in the United States for
the Years 1935 to 1958.

Year	Disposable personal income * (billions)	Personal consumption expenditures † (billions)	Per capita personal consumption expenditure ‡	Cost of living index §
1935	$ 58.0	$ 56.2	$ 443	58.7
1936	66.1	62.5	486	59.3
1937	71.1	67.1	520	61.4
1938	65.5	64.5	496	60.3
1939	70.2	67.5	508	59.4
1940	75.7	72.1	545	59.9
1941	92.0	82.3	616	62.9
1942	116.7	91.2	673	69.7
1943	132.4	102.2	745	74.0
1944	147.0	116.6	841	75.2
1945	151.1	123.1	879	76.9
1946	158.9	146.9	960	83.4
1947	169.5	165.6	1,150	95.5
1948	188.4	177.9	1,200	102.8
1949	186.4	180.6	1,210	101.8
1950	204.3	194.0	1,280	102.8
1951	225.0	208.3	1,358	111.0
1952	237.4	218.3	1,401	113.5
1953	250.2	230.5	1,456	114.4
1954	254.4	236.5	1,467	114.8
1955	274.4	254.0	1,546	114.5
1956	290.4	269.4	1,602	116.2
1957	305.1	284.4	1,661	120.2
1958	311.6	290.6	1,669	123.5

* Statistics for 1935 to 1950, U.S. Bureau of the Census, *1951 Supplement, Survey of Current Business,* Government Printing Office, Washington, D.C., 1952, p. 8. Statistics for 1951 to 1956, U.S. Bureau of the Census, *Statistical Abstract of the U.S.,* Government Printing Office, Washington, D.C., 1959, p. 305.

† *Ibid.*

‡ This is the Bureau of Labor Statistics Cost of Living Index in which statistics for the years 1947–49 equal 100. U.S. Bureau of the Census, *Statistical Abstract of the U.S.,* 1959, *op. cit.,* p. 338.

§ Calculated by dividing Personal Consumption Expenditure by total population data contained in the *Statistical Abstract of the U.S., op. cit.,* p. 5.

people did spend liberally in this era; and as shown later in this chapter, food stores did capture a greater portion of the consumer dollar through the sale of "luxury" food items and newly added nonfood lines.

SHIFTS IN UPPER INCOME SHARES

A parallel to the above is the study by Simon Kuznets on the upper income shares of the national income.[5] During the interwar decades (1919–1938) before income taxes, the top 5 per cent of the population had 30 per cent of the income; during 1947–1948, they had only 18 per cent of the income.

Up to 1938 the income percentage of the top 5 per cent varied only by 4.7 percentage points in either direction from the 1919–1938 average of 30 per cent; [6] but from 1938 on, the upper-share income declined steadily. This decline was unparalleled in the financial records for its magnitude and persistence.

The most recent statistics on the distribution of personal income indicate that the basic trend in upper-share income has continued. Between 1946 and 1955, the top 20 per cent of the income units dropped from 46.1 per cent to 44.6 per cent of total personal income.[7] The biggest gains were registered by the middle income groups.

There were various causes for this shift. The most important were (1) the reduction of unemployment, (2) the growth of unions, (3) the tax structures, and (4) the marked increase in total income that flowed to the lower income groups, particularly the farmers and wage earners.[8] This increase in income that precipitated to the lower income groups was more likely to be spent on food as well as other purchases.

[5] Simon Kuznets, *Shares of Upper Income Groups in Income and Savings* (New York: National Bureau of Economic Research, Inc., 1953).

[6] *Ibid.*, p. XXXV.

[7] U.S. Department of Commerce, *Survey of Current Business,* Government Printing Office, Washington, D.C., July, 1958, p. 13.

[8] Kuznets, *op. cit.*

CHANGES IN THE PATTERN OF FOOD CONSUMPTION

Shifts in the dietary habits of the American people significantly altered the pattern of food store sales from 1929 to 1954. The trend in consumption was away from less expensive bulk foods such as potatoes and grain products and toward the more costly leafy green vegetables, fresh fruits, and meat and dairy products as noted in Table 3-2. On a per capita basis the consumption of potatoes in 1954 was only 106 lb as compared with 169 lb in 1929. The consumption of dairy products in the same period rose from 379 lb to 417 lb per person; and meat, poultry, and seafood increased on a per capita basis from 134 to 169 lb. These changes in food consumption habits benefited in general the food store industry and in particular the supermarket. The latter increased its volume in the above lines and realized larger margins.[9]

TABLE 3-2 *

Yearly Consumption of Food Products per Capita, Retail-Weight Equivalent (in pounds), by Major Food Groups for the Years 1929, 1948, and 1954.

Product	1929	1948	1954
Dairy products	379	412	417
Eggs	40	47	52
Meat, fish, and poultry	134	151	169
Potatoes and sweet potatoes	169	116	106
Leafy green and yellow vegetables	102	111	112
Citrus fruit and tomatoes	79	116	108
Flour and cereal products	234	169	156
Ice cream	11	18	17

* Bureau of Agricultural Economics, U.S. Department of Agriculture, *Consumption of Food in the U.S.*, Agriculture Handbook No. 62, Government Printing Office, Washington, D.C., October, 1955, p. 43.

[9] Herman L. Myers and Forrest Scott, *The Rise of the Super Market*, U.S. Department of Agriculture, Bureau of Agricultural Economics, MTS–103, Government Printing Office, Washington, D.C., December, 1951, p. 10.

CHANGES IN EXPENDITURES IN FOOD STORES

Statistics in Table 3-3 indicate that food store sales, both on a total and a per capita basis, rose substantially from 1935 to 1958. This gain has been attributed not only to a rise in prices but also to an increase in total and per capita quantities of products sold in food stores.[10]

Furthermore, the food store group not only gained absolutely in dollar sales but captured a greater portion of the consumer's dollar. The statistics in Table 3-4 show that 15 cents out of every dollar of personal consumption expenditure went to the food store in 1935. The trend from 1935 to 1958 has been upward, and in 1958, 17.31 cents out of every consumer dollar spent went to the food store group.

TECHNOLOGICAL DEVELOPMENTS AND THEIR ADOPTION

Technological developments such as the automobile and the refrigerator, and their wide use in daily living, enabled a change to take place in the food store sales pattern. These developments influenced changes in buying habits, which in turn benefited certain types of food stores (particularly the supermart) to the detriment of other kinds of food store outlets. Of the many developments that occurred, three are selected for study as logically being the most important:

1. The automobile
2. Refrigeration
3. New food manufacturing and processing techniques

[10] The Retail Food Price Index of the Bureau of Labor Statistics (recorded in Table 3-3) increased from 49.7 in 1935 to 120.3 in 1958. However, this rise was relatively less than the total food store sales and the per capita food store sales.

TABLE 3-3

Total Food Store Sales, Per Capita Food Store Sales,
and Retail Food Price Index for the Years 1935 to 1958.

Year	Food store sales (in billions) *	Per capita food store sales †	Retail food price index ‡
1935	$ 8.4	$ 66	49.7
1936	9.0	72	50.1
1937	9.7	75	52.1
1938	9.5	73	48.4
1939	10.2	78	47.1
1940	10.9	83	47.8
1941	12.6	95	52.2
1942	15.8	117	61.3
1943	17.5	128	68.3
1944	19.0	138	67.4
1945	19.8	141	68.9
1946	24.2	171	79.0
1947	28.4	197	95.9
1948	31.0	210	104.1
1949	31.0	208	100.0
1950	32.8	215	101.2
1951	37.6	244	112.6
1952	39.8	254	114.6
1953	40.8	255	112.8
1954	41.6	257	112.6
1955	42.0	264	110.9
1956	44.2	274	111.7
1957	47.8	280	115.4
1958	50.3	289	120.3

* These statistics do not contain sales of the country general store. U.S. Bureau of the Census, *Statistical Abstract of the U.S.*, Government Printing Office, Washington, D.C., 1959, p. 833.

† Calculated by dividing food store sales by the total population statistics contained in the *Statistical Abstract of the U.S.*, 1959, p. 5.

‡ *Ibid.*, p. 328.

TABLE 3-4 *

Percentage of Personal Income Expenditure
Spent in Food Stores.

Year	%
1935	15.00
1940	15.18
1945	16.15
1950	16.75
1955	17.17
1956	17.29
1957	16.83
1958	17.31

* Calculated by dividing total food store sales (data contained in Table 3-3) by total personal consumption expenditures (statistics found in Table 3-1).

Automobile

Statistics on car registrations are shown in Table 3-5. From 1915 to 1920, motor vehicle registration increased 308 per cent. From 1920 to 1930 an additional 190 per cent gain was experienced. By 1930 cars in operation totaled 26.5 million. These substantial increases on a national basis occurred when the supermarket, except in the Los Angeles area, was a rarity. In California there was early acceptance and wide use of the automobile for shopping.

The "cheapy" supermarket of the early 1930's had "low prices" as the basic appeal, and the significance of the automobile was to furnish transportation to the supers and to haul away the food bargains, since the units in general were located in fringe areas poorly serviced by public transportation.

From 1930 to 1950 car registrations increased from 26,532,000 to 48,567,000. By 1958 registrations rose to 68,299,000 cars. These statistics are contained in Table 3-5. This substantial gain occurred concomitantly in the era of vast supermarket growth. Not only did car registration increase, but cars were distributed widely among the population. They were used more in daily living, driven more by women, and used actually for shopping. It was in this manner that the automobile and its use can be said to have played an integral part in the supermarket development.

Refrigeration

A second technological development that influenced the pattern of food store sales was the principle of refrigeration. In Table 3-6

TABLE 3-5 *

Motor Vehicle Registrations (in thousands) in the
United States for the Years 1915 to 1958.

1915	2,491
1920	9,239
1925	19,941
1930	26,532
1935	32,035
1940	30,638
1945	44,140
1950	48,567
1955	62,020
1956	64,437
1957	67,131
1958	68,299

* U.S. Bureau of Census, *Statistical Abstract of the U.S.*, Government Printing Office, Washington, D.C., 1959, p. 559.

are statistics on manufacturers' unit sales of refrigerators. The adoption for home use started in the late 1920's and continued through the 1930's, although unit sales varied in some years because of economic conditions.

The major influence of the refrigerator on buying habits was to reduce the frequency of shopping trips. The refrigerators enabled the storage of foods, particularly meat, for longer periods of time than the old conventional ice box.[11] Following World War II, a variation of the refrigeration principle—the deep freeze or home freezer—enabled storage of foods for even longer periods. The sales of home freezers, which totaled 8,983,800 units through 1956, along

[11] A. A. Brown, "Competition in Refrigeration Demands the Retelling of the Food Protection Story," *Edison Electric Institute*, April, 1937, p. 123.

TABLE 3-6

Manufacturers' Sales by Number of Units of Refrigerators and Home Freezers for the Years 1926 to 1956.

Year	Refrigerators	Home Freezers
1926 *	205,000	
1927	375,000	
1928	535,000	
1929	778,000	
1930	791,000	
1931	906,000	
1932	798,000	
1933	1,016,000	
1934 †	1,283,000	
1935	1,568,000	
1936	1,996,000	
1937	2,310,000	
1938	1,254,000	
1939	1,900,000	
1940	2,700,000	
1941	3,500,000	(None recorded
1942 ¶	520,000	before 1946)
1945	263,860	
1946	2,100,000	210,300
1947 ‡	3,400,000	607,000
1948	4,766,000	690,000
1949	4,450,000	485,000
1950	6,020,000	884,000
1951	3,731,000	1,032,500
1952	3,196,000	1,118,200
1953 §	3,287,000	1,049,800
1954	3,135,000	943,000
1955	3,820,000	1,045,000
1956	3,382,000	919,000

* Sales from 1926 to 1934 are found in *Electrical Merchandising*, Vol. 55, no. 1, January, 1936, p. 3.

† Sales from 1934 to 1945 are found in *Electrical Merchandising*, Vol. 76, no. 1, January, 1946, p. 37.

‡ Sales from 1947 to 1952 are found in *Electrical Merchandising*, Vol. 85, no. 1, January, 1953, p. 75.

§ Sales from 1953 to 1956 are found in *Electrical Merchandising*, Vol. 90, no. 1, January, 1957, p. 102.

¶ None were manufactured during the years 1943 and 1944.

with the growing popularity of refrigerators with frozen food compartments also influenced the pattern of frozen food sales.

In addition to reducing the frequency of shopping trips, refrigeration brought about still another and more revolutionary change in the food pattern. It made possible the development of a myriad of new frozen food products which gained popularity. The supermarkets took greater advantage of this new food trend than the small food store by providing the space and the large capital for the refrigerated units required to store and display these new foods.[12]

New Food Manufacturing and Processing Techniques

Manufacturers developed products that made it more convenient to prepare and serve foods. For example:

1. Baby foods, which got their start in 1925, built up to a $251,-000,000 retail volume in 1958.[13]

2. The preservation of foods by quick freezing was pioneered by Clarence Birdseye in 1925.[14] The first line was introduced in the food stores by General Foods in 1930. Frozen foods, which not only included the conventional fruit juices and vegetables but also complete dinners, attained an estimated retail volume of $2.331 billion in 1958.[15] Dehydrated food processing currently looks promising.

3. New, instant-type desserts, ready cake mixes, and beverages (to name but a few) were developed. These new products generally were more expensive than the older types of products which they replaced.[16] The distribution of gourmet specialties by General Foods is a recent innovation.

4. Packaging changes have resulted that not only facilitate self-service selling but also require additional display space. One example is the growing use of multiple packaging that requires room

---

[12] Edwin T. Gibson, "Frozen Foods in the Super Market," *Super Market Merchandising*, XV, no. 6, June, 1950, p. 72.

[13] *What the Public Spends for Grocery Store Products* (New York: Food Topics Publishing Co., 1959), p. 3.

[14] *Frozen Food Industry* (Philadelphia: Curtis Publishing Co., 1952), p. 4.

[15] *What the Public Spends for Grocery Store Products, op. cit.*

[16] "Stocks Have Trebled," *Progressive Grocer*, XXXI, no. 10, October, 1952, p. 41.

for display in order to differentiate the product from the 5,710 other items in supermarkets.[17] Another example is the innovation of larger packages for soap and cleansers, which require additional space for proper merchandising.

The many new items and innovations required the food store to carry larger inventories, to provide more display space, and to have sizable investments in refrigerated cases. These new products, easily sold by self-service techniques, in the main benefited the supermarket as compared to the small grocer who lacked the needed facilities.[18]

POPULATION GROWTH AND SHIFT TO THE SUBURBS

The population of the United States increased during the years 1930 to 1950 from 123,070,000 to 151,240,000.[19] By January, 1958, the number of inhabitants soared to 171,970,000.[20] This rise of 23.4 per cent was associated with a rising food store volume. However, locational shifts in the population appeared to affect more significantly the shifting of the pattern of food store sales than did the increase in the number of inhabitants.

Data on 140 central cities in the United States, which in 1940 had 50,000 or more population, are given in Table 3-7. From 1930 to 1940 the percentage increase of population in the central cities was 6.1 per cent, while the areas adjacent rose 16.9 per cent, as calculated from statistics contained in Table 3-7.

In the period of 1940 to 1950 the number of central cities increased to 168, as noted from the figures in Table 3-8. The central city population grew 13.9 per cent, but the areas adjacent rose 35.5 per cent. National population from 1940 to 1950 increased from 131,936,000 to 151,240,000, or only 14 per cent. The estimated

---

[17] Frank J. Charvat, "Growth Trend in Multiple Packaging," *Advertising Agency,* Vol. 51, no. 17, August 15, 1958, p. 16.

[18] "Stocks Have Trebled," *Progressive Grocer, op. cit.*

[19] U.S. Bureau of the Census, *Number of Inhabitants, U.S. Summary 1950 Census of Population,* Government Printing Office, Washington, D.C., 1952, pp. 1–51.

[20] U.S. Bureau of the Census, *Current Population Reports,* Government Printing Office, Washington, D.C., 1958, p. 1.

TABLE 3-7 °

Shift in Population in 140 Central Cities of the
United States with 50,000 Population and Over,
for the Years 1930 and 1940.

	1930 Population	1940 Population	% increase 1940 over 1930
Central cities	40,343,442	42,796,170	6.1
Outside central city area †	17,259,423	20,109,603	16.9

° U.S. Bureau of the Census, *Sixteenth Census of the U.S., 1940 Population,*
Vol. 1, Government Printing Office, Washington, D.C., 1942, p. 61.
† The area "outside the central city" is, by census definition, immediately
adjacent to the city.

changes in population to 1958 indicate a continuation of this trend,
with the inhabitants literally racing to the suburbs to live.

An additional factor of this national shift to suburban living was
the composition of the population.[21] The median family income in
1950 for the suburban area was $5,100 against $3,600 for the city
proper. About 75 per cent of the suburban families owned their
homes, as compared with 41 per cent for the city. Approximately 27
per cent of the residents in the suburbs were under 14 years of age,
whereas in the city itself, this age group claimed only 21.4 per cent.

These changes in urban and suburban population were attributed
in part to World War II, to the desire for home ownership, to the
requisite for larger space around homes, to more families, and to
the increase in personal disposable income. The automobile was a
tool in this development, since it helped to provide transportation.
These outlying areas, not so densely populated per square mile as
the cities, required shopping facilities. New secondary shopping
centers mushroomed; some assumed major significance. The extent
to which supermarkets and other forms of retailing took advantage
of these new suburban markets is examined in the next section.

[21] "The Lush New Suburban Market," *Fortune,* XLVIII, no. 5, November,
1953, p. 131.

TABLE 3-8 *

Shift in Population in 168 Central Cities of the
United States with 50,000 Population
and Over, for the Years 1940 and 1950.

	1940 Population	*1950 Population*	*% increase 1950 over 1940*
Central city	43,391,718	49,412,792	13.9
Outside central city area	25,887,957	35,087,888	35.5

* U.S. Bureau of the Census, *Number of Inhabitants, U.S. Summary, 1950 Census of Population,* Government Printing Office, Washington, D.C., pp. 1–69.

RETAIL TREND TOWARD DECENTRALIZATION

The development of outlying shopping sections was an adjunct to the suburban movement of the population. The supermarket was part of this movement. While it can be contended that the locating of supermarkets is a management prerogative and should be included in the next chapter under operating practices, the whole retail movement to the suburbs was pronounced. This forced retail management generally to open outlets in the suburbs.[22] The need for retail outlets was made greater when manufacturing plants were given special tax advantage to encourage new factories in outlying areas.[23]

In Table 3-9 are statistics on retail sales volume by size of city. Generally, the period from 1939 to 1954 showed a trend toward a greater percentage of sales in smaller communities. However, the movement by large retailers to the suburbs has further gained momentum.[24] Companies participating in shopping centers read like a "Who's Who of Merchandising." Many of these outlying shop-

[22] "The Changing American Market," *Fortune,* XLVIII, no. 2, August, 1953, p. 232.

[23] V. B. Smith, "Industry Disperses Plants," *Engineer-News,* March 27, 1952, p. 241.

[24] "The Changing American Market," *op. cit.*

TABLE 3-9 *

Retail Trade by City Size for the Years 1954, 1948, and 1939.

Size	Sales (in billions)			Percentage distribution		
	1954	1948	1939	1954	1948	1939
500,000 and over	$ 35.8	$ 30.3	$10.2	21.1	23.2	24.3
250,000 to 499,999	13.4	9.9	3.9	7.8	7.6	9.4
100,000 to 249,999	15.9	12.5	3.8	9.4	9.6	8.9
50,000 to 99,999	14.5	11.0	3.5	8.5	8.4	8.3
10,000 to 49,999	34.6	26.3	8.0	20.4	20.1	19.1
5,000 to 9,999	12.8	9.7	3.0	7.5	7.4	7.2
2,500 to 4,999	9.9	7.0	2.3	5.8	5.4	5.6
Under 2,500	33.1	24.0	7.3	19.5	18.3	17.2
Total	$170.0	$130.7	$42.0	100.0	100.0	100.0

* Data for 1939 and 1948 from U.S. Bureau of Census, *Census of Business, 1948, Retail Trade, Part 11*, Vol. II, Government Printing Office, Washington, D.C., 1952, p. 14. Data for 1954 from U.S. Bureau of Census, *Census of Business, 1954*, Bulletin R-2-2, Government Printing Office, Washington, D.C., 1957, pp. 2–309.

ping centers located in unincorporated areas in order to obtain low-cost land and to avoid annoying local ordinances. This phenomenal shift is reflected in the data contained in Table 3-9. Total retail sales made in areas of under 2,500 rose from 17.2 per cent of all retail sales in 1939 to 19.5 per cent of all retail volume by 1954.

Three types of centers have developed.[25] The smallest—5 to 10 acres with a maximum of ten stores and referred to as the neighborhood type—has one dominant store in the group acting as the magnet to attract shoppers. This core store frequently has been a large supermarket. The investment ranges from several hundred thousand dollars to several million dollars. The second type—the intermediate community center of 10 to 25 acres with a junior department store as the focal point—needs a minimum of 5,000 families for its support. This type of center is reflected by Lincoln Village in the Chicago suburbs, which required an investment of about $3,000,000. The third type is a regional center with a minimum of 35 acres and serv-

[25] "Shopping Centers," *Barrons*, XXXVI, no. 32, August 6, 1956, p. 3.

ing 100,000 persons. Examples of the latter are the $100,000,000 extravaganza of Lakewood Center in Los Angeles, which has a 12,000-car parking lot, or the new $25,000,000 Roosevelt Field center in New York, which contains 110 stores and expects to transact an $80,-000,000 yearly volume.

In 1957, 35 regional centers, 200 intermediate community centers, and 600 of the neighborhood type of center were opened.[26] Shopping centers continue to flourish, but they appear to be losing some of their momentum. A 1958–59 directory of the large suburban shopping centers lists 1,914 centers with 14,750 tenant stores.[27]

The decentralization movement was a factor in supermarket development.[28] The "cheapy" supers were first located in low-rent districts adjacent to densely populated areas of New Jersey and New York. It was considered that a population of 75,000 to 100,000 was required to support a million-dollar yearly volume market and that the saturation point of the number of these units would be reached quickly.[29]

With the shift to better equipped and housed supers, stores were opened in a variety of other sections and communities throughout the country. Many of the new locations were selected to house larger stores and to provide necessary parking. The changing pattern is shown by the statistics in Table 3-10. In 1940, 28.4 per cent of the supers were in cities with a population of 500,000 and over, and 50 per cent in cities with an excess of 100,000 inhabitants. Although the number of supermarkets increased numerically in these large cities during the next 14 years, there was an over-all trend toward small-town locations; and the large cities lost relatively in the number of supers by almost 13 per cent. All classes of communities under 100,000 population gained relatively in this 14-year period. More than 38 per cent of all supermarkets in 1954 were in towns of less

[26] *Business Week*, no. 1499, May 24, 1958, p. 50.

[27] *Directory of Shopping Centers in the United States and Canada 1958–59* (Chicago: National Research Bureau, Inc., 1959).

[28] "Store Locations," *Chain Store Age*, Grocery Executive Edition, January, 1950, p. 143.

[29] Carl Dipman, "Merchandising Trends in the Food Trade with Special Reference to Supermarkets," *Journal of Marketing*, III, no. 3, January, 1939, p. 272.

TABLE 3-10 *

Number of Supermarkets in the United States by Size of the Community
for the Years 1940, 1950, and 1954, and the Percentage That
Each Community Is to the Total.

	1940		1950		1954	
Population	Number	%	Number	%	Number	%
500,000 and over	2,119	28.4	2,854	20.1	3,073	17.8
100,000 to 499,999	1,599	21.4	2,929	20.7	3,441	19.9
25,000 to 99,999	1,647	22.0	3,276	23.5	3,938	22.8
10,000 to 24,999	967	12.9	2,218	15.8	3,025	17.5
5,000 to 9,999	545	7.3	1,289	9.1	1,592	9.2
2,500 to 4,999	352	4.7	784	5.3	1,038	6.0
Under 2,500	244	3.3	814	5.5	1,191	6.8
Total	7,473	100.0	14,164	100.0	17,298	100.0

* *Super Markets in the United States* (Philadelphia: Curtis Publishing Co.,
1954), p. 7.

than 25,000 inhabitants. These statistics indicate that supermarkets
followed the trend of the population to the outlying areas. The
supermarkets were here at an advantage in that they could erect
facilities suitable to the shopping needs. Moreover, in these outlying
locations, there tended to be less competition from small food stores
than in the older sections where rental facilities for small food stores
were greater.

SHIFT IN CONSUMER BUYING HABITS, INCLUDING ONE-STOP SHOPPING AND SCRAMBLED MERCHANDISING

Certain consumer buying habits underwent a considerable change
after the 1920's. These shifts were associated with the supermarket
development inasmuch as the supers adopted practices in line with
the change in shopping wants.[30] Supermarkets were thus in a more

[30] The changes in shopping habits occurred concomitantly with the development of the supermarket. No attempt is made to determine which preceded the
other. The entire movement was part of a trend toward "simplified selling."

favorable position than other types of food stores to benefit from these changes.

Thirty-seven different studies were reviewed to determine changes in shopping habits that differed from those of the pre-supermarket era.[31] An example is the *McCall's Magazine* "Consumer Diary Study," the results of which are found in Table 3-11. The findings of the various research projects are summarized as follows:

1. There has been a decided increase in one-stop shopping preference. Women shoppers first go to stores they believe will give them the best opportunity of making all their purchases. This desire has led to the diversified lines of merchandise handled by supers.

2. Visits to the food store have become less frequent. The average seems to be about three times per week. There is a decided increase in the number of people who shop once a week.

3. There has been a substantial increase in the use of the automobile for shopping.

4. The average expenditure per customer in the stores has increased substantially, more than the rise in price level.

5. Shopping seems concentrated on certain days of the week, with Friday and Saturday the key days.

6. People tend to travel farther to shop than they did prior to the supermarket development.

7. While shopping is still done predominantly by women alone, the increase in number of men shoppers has been substantial. The general findings indicate men alone, or accompanied by women, purchase about 40 per cent of the food.

8. Impulse buying has become a significant factor in food shopping. Display techniques and ability of the buyer to wander through the store have resulted in the purchase of a significant number of items that the customer had not intended to buy upon entering the store.

[31] A comprehensive file of consumer-shopping studies is contained at the library of the Super Market Institute. These studies were made by advertising agencies, private research firms, universities, and the research departments of corporations, newspapers, and periodicals.

9. Preference for self-service is indicated by answers to surveys and also by the heavy patronage of self-service food stores.

10. There is a desire for more convenient and attractive shopping.

TABLE 3-11 °

Findings from McCall's Magazine Consumer Diary
Study of Food Purchases Made by 1,090
Families for One Week in the Year 1956.

A. FOOD PURCHASES MADE BY THE PANEL:

Products purchased	Number of families that purchased these products	Total number of purchases of each product made	Dollar value of purchases
Meat, poultry, fish	1,051	4,515	$ 6,066
Produce	1,030	4,211	1,951
Dairy	1,067	7,278	4,530
Frozen foods	653	1,603	974
Baked goods	1,069	4,984	1,723
Grocery items	1,090	23,491	11,378

B. FOOD PURCHASING HABITS:

1. Approximately 86.6 per cent of the food shoppers always use an automobile, and an additional 1.8 per cent use an automobile for food shopping only part of the time.

2. Approximately 90.7 per cent of the families do some shopping at supermarkets, and 75.8 per cent shop exclusively at supermarkets.

3. Major reasons for shopping at supermarkets expressed as a percentage of total responses:

Large selection	49.0%
Economy	37.8%
Self-service selection	28.7%
One-stop shopping	22.2%
Easy-to-find items	20.5%
Freshness	13.9%

4. Two major dislikes are (a) impersonal relationship due to large size of store, and (b) difficulty of finding items because of the size of the store.

° Home Testing Institute, Inc., *McCall's Food and Grocery Products Diary Study* (New York: McCall Corp., 1956).

11. Advertising helps women in their search for merchandise. They examine the newspapers prior to making shopping expeditions.

These changes in buying habits in general have favored the supermarket industry as compared to other types of food stores.[32] Perhaps the most significant of these changes in shopping in relation to the growth of supermarkets has been the preference for one-stop shopping.[33] This in turn has been one of the reasons that has intensified competition among different types of retailers in selling the same product—scrambled merchandising.[34] Supermarkets have always been one of the proponents of scrambled merchandising. Aided by large customer traffic, supers have added many lines of merchandise that were foreign to food stores in the 1920's and have turned them into substantial sources of profit.[35]

ADDITIONAL EXTERNAL FACTORS THAT INFLUENCED THE SUPERMARKET DEVELOPMENT

An examination of the literature in this field has disclosed a variety of additional external factors that had varying degrees of influence on the supermarket growth. Some of the most important of these are summarized below.

1. There was a trend following the early 1930's for a greater percentage of married women to work outside the home. Generally they were able to spend this income, or at least part of it, as they wished. The display techniques of supermarkets and the addition of nonfood lines have attempted to capture this income.[36]

2. Manufacturers of food products increased the brand and package advertising of their merchandise in an effort to presell the customers.[37]

---

[32] The operating practices of supermarkets that enabled them to benefit more from these buying habit changes than other types of food stores are presented in Chapters 4 through 7.

[33] *Here's How We Shop for Our Big Grocery Order* (New York: Batten, Barton, Durstine & Osborne, 1959).

[34] Richard Alt, "Competition among Types of Retailers in Selling the Same Commodity," *Journal of Marketing*, XIV, no. 3, January, 1948, p. 444.

[35] Milton Alexander, "Where We Stand in Non-Foods Merchandise," *Progressive Grocer*, XXXI, no. 10, October, 1952, p. 197.

[36] "Supermarket Revolution in Retailing," *Business Week*, no. 1189, June 28, 1952, p. 38.

[37] John R. Gilman, "Why Package Products Face Super Competition in Supermarkets," *Advertising Agency*, Vol. 45, no. 6, June, 1952, p. 64.

3. There was a growing trend for manufacturers to identify their products in the mind of the consumer as to constant quality and value. This ready recognition and acceptance of brand names aided the self-service movement, one of the keystones of the supermarket.[38]

4. Following World War II there was a trend toward larger family units than in the 1930's. With more members of the family to take care of, women found it difficult to shop frequently. When they did go to the store, they bought in greater quantity and tended to patronize supermarkets because of price appeal and convenience offered.[39]

5. The scarcity of cheap household help today, compared to the availability in the 1930's, influenced women to seek easier-to-prepare foods. This in turn necessitated that the merchant carry a greater variety of these foods. The larger facilities and resources of the supers enabled them generally to benefit more than the small food store.[40]

6. The growing baby crop, which began during World War II and which has continued unabated since then, has placed an ever-larger percentage of the population under 21 years of age. These growing bodies have made it necessary for families, in order to sustain this age group, to place an increasing portion of their expenditures into food and related items sold in supers.

MARKET OF THE 1960's

Continuation of a favorable market for the "sizzling sixties" is portrayed by the recent forecast of the magazine *Life*.[41] The 55 million families of 1960 are expected to increase to 66 million by 1970. One out of every four 18-year-old girls would be married by the

---

[38] E. B. Weiss, "Food Supers Will Find Going Tougher," *Printers Ink*, Vol. 239, no. 13, June 27, 1952, p. 71.

[39] Charlotte Montgomery, "The Woman and the Modern Market," *Progressive Grocer*, XXXI, no. 10, October, 1952, p. 170.

[40] *Ibid.*

[41] The magazine *Life* employed many market research experts to plan a research project forecasting the market of the 1960's. The findings were published in a booklet entitled *The Market of the Sixties* (New York: Time, Inc., 1960).

end of 1960, the survey predicted. Prior to World War II, 53 per cent of the women between 20 and 24 were married; in 1960, 65 per cent of the women in this age group would be married, and the continued outlook is for a leveling off at that percentage. Furthermore, women of today are bearing larger families, with the 1970 population estimated at 210 million persons. A new baby boom is anticipated to start around 1965 when the girl babies born in the early postwar years reach marriageable age. The 1970 birth rate is expected to be over 5 million compared with slightly more than 4 million currently in 1960.

Families with teen-agers, which comprise the major market of the 1960's, will continue to spend out of proportion to their number, especially for food and soft drinks. The number of inhabitants over 65 will increase by 19 million; and for the first time, this class will have sizable incomes to spend. Wives between the ages of 35 and 64 are expected to have continued increase in income as a result of their employment outside their homes. From 1940 to 1960, the number of working women between the ages of 35 and 64 more than doubled.

During the 1950's, the population of suburban areas of metropolitan markets grew seven times as fast as the rest of the United States. Suburbs are expected to continue to expand. Overlapping areas from one metropolitan center to another will create vast new interrelated markets. Continued decentralized industry and service organizations will strengthen the tendency toward convenience shopping, with greater dependence on cars. The consumer will be of a higher intellectual level.

In 1947, family units in the $4,000 to $7,500 income bracket represented about 23 per cent of all units but had 43 per cent of all disposable income. This group destroyed the traditional gap between a mass market for necessities and the small class market for luxuries. By 1960, 22 million family units comprised this middle income group, a gain of 30 per cent over 1947. The families earning more than $7,500 yearly have doubled since 1947 to over 12 million. The number of family units under $4,000 annual income has declined both relatively and absolutely since World War II and comprises today only two-fifths of the families, whereas in 1947 they represented about 70 per cent of the family units. By 1970, 45 per cent of all families will have annual incomes over $7,500; approximately 39 per cent will be middle income units from $4,000 to $7,500 income, and only 16 per cent will have incomes under $4,000. This substantial group of high income families will have broad, discretionary purchasing power, from caviar and champagne to world travel.

The market of special interest to the supermarket industry, that for food, drink, and tobacco, is currently estimated at $91 billion. This is expected to rise to $117 billion in 1970, a gain of 29 per cent. Household and recreation goods, which totaled $35 billion in 1960, are expected to rise to $53 billion by 1970, a gain of 51 per cent. Another item of possible interest to the supermarket industry is clothing. This totaled $35 billion in 1960 and will increase 18 per cent by 1970 to $43 billion. The supermarket industry, faced with these optimistic forecasts, can plan accordingly.

SUMMARY

The economic setting in which the supermarket developed was pictured statistically in this chapter. These data, including shifts in upper income shares, the rise in personal disposable income, and increased expenditures in food stores, were presented to support the qualitative discussions. The technological and psychological environment in which the supermarket grew was depicted. The acceptance of the automobile as a shopping aid and the shift in consumer buying habits were but two aspects covered. No numerical claim was made as to the extent of the association between the supermarket development and each of these external factors, individually or as a group. The contention presented has been that the growth of the supermarket industry since the "cheapy" development occurred concomitantly with various external factors which furnished a favorable atmosphere. Simply, the economic, technological, and psychological setting for the development of the supermarket was extremely favorable. And the period of the "sizzling sixties" promises more of the same.

4 | SELLING OPERATIONS

INTRODUCTION

The preceding chapter covered the favorable economic, technological, and psychological setting in which the supermarket industry grew. Statistics in Table 4-1 indicate that the total retail sales rose from $48.3 billion in 1929 to $170 billion in 1954. Almost 15 per cent of this $121.7 billion increase was accounted for by the supermarket. By 1954 supermarket sales of $18.2 billion represented almost 11 per cent of all retail store sales of $170 billion. The supermarket volume grew far more than that of the other food store members. Yet, all were in the same economic setting during this period. Therefore the supermarkets must have adopted or developed operating practices that induced consumers to come to them in preference to competitors.

The purpose of this and the subsequent three chapters is to examine what the supermarket industry did to promote such progress. What practices within the control of the operators themselves were pursued? Whereas diversity among the members is great, certain general or common characteristics of operation set the supermarket apart from other types of retailers.

These characteristics are discerned through study of operating and financial statistics of individual concerns as well as industry surveys. The operating data are examined in this and the subsequent two chapters in the framework of the main sections of an operating statement; i.e., sales, cost of sale and gross margin, cost or expense, and profit divisions. Selling practices are reviewed first; cost of sales and margins will be examined in Chapter 5; expense and profit analysis will be contained in Chapter 6. The financial prin-

53

TABLE 4-1 °

Sales of Certain Classes of Retail Stores
and Total Retail Sales
in the United States for the Years
1929, 1939, 1948, and 1954 (in billions of dollars).

Type of outlet	1929	1939	1948	1954
All retail store sales	$48.3	$42.0	$130.5	$170.0
Nonsuper grocery stores	7.3	6.2	16.9	16.2
Supermarkets †	—	1.5	7.8	18.2
Specialty food stores	3.4 §	2.4 ‡	6.2 ‡	5.4
All retail sales except food store group ¶	37.6	31.9	99.6	130.2

° Data for 1929, 1939, and 1948 are found in U.S. Bureau of the Census, *Retail Trade—General Statistics, Part 1,* Vol. 1, Government Printing Office, Washington, D.C., 1952, p. 1.04. Data for 1954 are found in U.S. Bureau of the Census, *1954 Census of Business,* Bulletin R-2-2, Government Printing Office, Washington, D.C., 1957, p. 2–2.

† These statistics are found in Table 1-2.

‡ U.S. Bureau of the Census, *Statistical Supplement, 1951 Survey of Current Business,* Government Printing Office, Washington, D.C., 1952, p. 25.

§ U.S. Bureau of the Census, *Food Retailing—Retail Distribution,* M–93, Government Printing Office, Washington, D.C., 1934, p. 9.

¶ Calculated by subtracting total food store sales from total retail sales for the respective years.

ciples of supermarketing will be studied in Chapter 7 in the framework of the major asset and liability classifications of a balance sheet.

At the outset, to exemplify approximate supermarket operations, the published results of two different operations are presented in Tables 4-2 and 4-3. The findings of the Harvard Business School Study of Food Chains, expressed as a percentage of sales, are contained in Table 4-2. The operating results of Wilt's, an independent supermarket located in Elkhart, Indiana, are presented in Table 4-3. These statements are submitted to exemplify approximate supermarket operations for both chains and independents. They are not presented to show chain versus independent operation; nor are the data to be considered as typical for the entire industry. The operating statements indicate merely approximate margin, expense, and profit relationships for a supermarket. Operating policies adopted by management can result in variations from these statistics.

TABLE 4-2 *

Operating Statistics of Selected Food Chains Expressed as a Percentage of Sales for the Years 1955 to 1958.

	1958	*1957*	*1956*	*1955*
Sales	100.00	100.00	100.00	100.00
Cost of sales	79.50	79.63	80.61	81.89
Gross profit	20.50	20.37	19.39	18.11
Expenses				
Payroll	10.07	10.01	9.74	9.68
Real estate	1.77	1.64	1.54	1.45
Equipment costs	1.38	1.42	1.39	1.36
Utilities	0.67	0.62	0.61	0.60
Supplies	1.14	1.18	1.11	1.08
Services purchased	0.25	0.26	0.26	0.27
Advertising (includes stamps) .	1.88	1.87	1.44	0.82
Traveling	0.10	0.09	0.08	0.08
Insurance (except real estate) .	0.14	0.13	0.15	0.16
Taxes (except real estate or income)	0.53	0.54	0.49	0.48
Miscellaneous	0.61	0.61	0.63	0.56
Interest paid	0.24	0.25	0.27	0.24
Total expense	18.78	18.62	17.71	16.78
Net operating profit	1.72	1.75	1.68	1.33
Other income (primarily cash discounts earned and interest) . .	1.17	1.21	1.22	1.17
Less income tax	1.48	1.50	1.48	1.28
Net profit	1.41	1.46	1.42	1.22

* Wilbur B. England, *Operating Results of Food Chains in 1958* (Cambridge: Harvard Business School, Bulletin No. 156, 1959), p. 2.

VOLUME—A SUPERMARKET NECESSITY

The stress on volume in a supermarket is inherent in the basic nature of operation of this type of retail institution. The early super,

OVER

TABLE 4-3 *

Operating Statistics of Wilt's Supermarket, Elkhart,
Indiana, Expressed as a Percentage of Sales
for the Year 1956.

Sales	100.0
Cost of sales	80.7
Gross profit	19.3
Expenses	
Premiums	1.1
Advertising	0.6
{Regular payroll	9.2
16%{Executive payroll	0.5
Supplies	1.0
Utilities	0.3
Insurance	0.4
Rent	0.3
Taxes	0.9
Depreciation	0.7
Interest	0.2
Other expense	1.5
Total expense	16.7
Net operating profit	2.6
Cash discounts	0.3
Net profit before income tax	2.9

* "Change or Die, Says Wilt's," *Super Market Merchandising*, XXIII, no. 8,
August, 1958, p. 47.

appealing on a price basis, needed volume to compensate for a
narrow gross margin and net profit. The market of today, operating
on a larger but still relatively small gross margin compared with
other types of retailers, also needs volume operation to compensate
for tight gross margins. In addition, the modern market has added
materially to its expense of doing business and its investment. Competitive conditions prevent most markets from operating continuously at a level which will yield the greatest dollar net return. Un-
used capacity appears to exist in most markets. Therefore stress
must be placed on added possibilities for volume to bring the market

more in line with its capacity and optimum profit potential. These relationships are examined in detail in Chapter 7.

SALES PRACTICES OF SUPERMARKETS

The basic technique of supermarket operation has been to transact a large dollar volume.[1] This has been accomplished by devices such as:

1. Price appeal
2. Display techniques
3. Self-service
4. Attractive and convenient shopping facilities
5. Advertising and promotion
6. Large inventories but well regulated with regard to turnover
7. Addition of diversified lines of merchandise including nonfood items

Each of these devices for building volume is examined in detail in the remainder of this chapter.

Price Appeal

With regard to price, from the inception of the "cheapy" supermarket to the modern supers of today, the general practice has been to sell for less.[2] Through its low-cost methods, the supermarket, more than any other food store, has passed on to the customer over the past 25 years greater values plus additional services.[3] The "cheapy" super rode to fame by its "price wrecking" policies and large volume. Supers still stress low prices as a means of attracting customers and building volume. Witness the full-page newspaper ads of special values offered by supers. Price studies dating back to the "cheapy" supers indicate the constant endeavor of modern supers to sell for less, and this is further substantiated by the small gross

[1] M. M. Zimmerman, "Ten Years of Supermarket Growth," *Super Market Merchandising*, XI, no. 12, December, 1946, p. 45.

[2] Victor Lebow, "What Department Store Managers Should Know About Supermarkets," *Journal of Retailing*, XXIX, no. 1, Spring, 1953, p. 17.

[3] William Applebaum, "Is Supermarket Efficiency Slipping?" *Chain Store Age*, Grocery Store Executive Edition, February, 1952, p. 169.

margin of the supermarkets in comparison with that of other forms
of retailing.[4] Even though supers generally have modernized their
stores and made them attractive, studies have revealed customers
still have the "opinion" that supermarkets quote low prices.[5] Akin to
price appeal is the concept of quality. In the main, whether it be
nationally advertised, branded merchandise, or chain store brands,
supermarkets have been associated with the concept of giving satisfactory quality in relation to price.[6] One of the keystones of supermarket operation, self-service, is in part predicated on the customer's
recognition of price bargains on known lines.

Pricing Policies

The pricing policies of individual supermarkets can vary widely
as a result of local factors. In the main, however, supers basically
follow a policy of normal markup pricing, tempered by competitive
conditions and price leadership. As a simple example consider that
a can of tomato soup costs a super 10 cents and the normal markup
is 9. 2 per cent, based on selling price; then

$$\text{Selling price} = \frac{\text{cost} \times 100\%}{100\% - \text{markup \% at retail}} = \frac{10\cancel{c} \times 100\%}{(100\% - 9.2\%)}$$
$$= 11 \text{ cents}$$

or, the soup would sell at 11 cents per can.

Most comparable concerns in that immediate trading area, unless a particular store is differentiated by offering different services,
will price the soup competitively. However, if a store faces little
competition, markup on the tomato soup could range as high as 23
per cent, with the soup selling at 11.5 cents per can, or 2 cans for
23 cents. Chain stores in a given city, except for advertised specials

---

[4] Gross margins are discussed in detail in Chapter 5.

[5] In a study conducted by the magazine *Super Market Merchandising* in 1948,
the number two reason advanced for trading in supermarkets was "Low Price."
The findings of the *1958 Survey of Super Market Shoppers, Their Buying Habits
and Attitudes,* published by Burgoyne Grocery and Drug Index, Inc., and the
results of a study by Newel Comish, "What Influences Customer Choice of Food
Store?" *Journal of Retailing,* Summer, 1958, indicate price is still a significant
factor in the patronage of supers.

[6] Lebow, *op. cit.*

which are announced throughout the area, have marked similar merchandise at different prices at different locations.

A smaller independent supermarket, not associated with a whole-sale or retail-sponsored voluntary chain, may even be forced to operate on a smaller markup in a highly competitive area or differentiate the store because of its lack of buying power. To attract customers to the market some stores have differentiated by offering unusually high quality meat or by remaining open longer hours.

A manufacturer of soup, desiring more display space and a resulting greater share of the market, may offer comparable buyers a deal involving cooperative advertising or price concessions. The tomato soup possibly can be advertised and sold at 10 cents a can. Deals such as this on a wide variety of merchandise occur daily and constantly upset the market equilibrium. Witness the week-end, advertised specials offered in the Thursday night ads in which supers still use the price appeal as an attraction to customers.

The particular store or stores accepting the special soup deal in a certain trading area will have a temporary price advantage. Stores not participating in the arrangement may either cut the price of tomato soup to 10 cents or push some other price special in their weekly promotions, continuing to sell tomato soup at 11 cents per can to the shoppers attracted by other bargains or patron-buying motives. At the end of the special promotion (several days to a week) the price of tomato soup will revert back to the original equilibrium price of 11 cents per can. No one company can continue to enjoy indefinitely the advantages of a special promotion or purchase because the normal markups established for the various classes of commodities in the industry are a function of cost of selling and profit on the one hand and giving the consumer what he or she desires on the other. Supers are forced by their customers to handle some products that yield low profits per linear foot of display space. The establishment of normal markups or margins is discussed in Chapter 5.

Produce marketing is complicated further by varying degrees of product deterioration, fluctuations in supply, and great number of products handled. Managers apply suggested markups on the individual products to make an over-all initial markup for the department of 30 to 35 per cent and a maintained markup of about 25 per cent after allowances for markdowns. Spoilage losses average from 1 to 3 per cent of sales.

Meat pricing is complicated by the wide fluctuations that occur in wholesale prices for meat. Furthermore, production costs are incurred in the super to prepare the meat in proper cuts and packages for the consumer. While an over-all yearly markup percentage generally is set as a standard, a super must operate daily in the approximate spread between selling prices set by competition plus what consumers will pay and the cost of the meat set by factors over which the super has no control. The supermarket must know the fixed and variable costs of handling all kinds of meat, as well as which types of meat cuts pay off. Skill in pricing joint products (for example, short ribs and roasts from the same rib) is essential to maintain the general gross margin and still attract customers on a price basis.

Display Techniques

A second means of developing large volume is to display mass stocks of inventory.[7] At an early date in its history the super found that mass displays of merchandise psychologically tended to make people buy. Mock-ups, mirrors, and lighting have been used to give the illusion of bigness. Modern display fixtures, refrigerators, and freezers have been developed. Manufacturers constantly have studied package design to make the product more appealing. Studies have been made on the value of display space to increase sales.[8] Multiple packaging has been developed to create "billboard illusions" in stores, as well as make display space more usable directly on floors of supermarkets. The placing of related merchandise, such as wash cloths adjacent to toilet soap, has boosted sales. Other re-

[7] William S. Ireland, "Mass Sells More," *Chain Store Age*, Grocery Executive Edition, August, 1950, p. 68.
[8] "Merchandise Location," *Chain Store Age*, Grocery Executive Edition, December, 1958, p. 52.

lated items include cellophane wrapped footballs with vitamin pills and table cloths with baby food.[9] Studies on impulse buying have indicated that approximately 25 per cent of the purchase in supers are unplanned. Other surveys have shown that 77 per cent of women who shop with children purchase items at the suggestion of children who see the item on display. Shoppers, surrounded by an assortment of related merchandise such as health and beauty aids in a supermarket, respond to the display of the merchandise and do not take into account the type of store in which they are shopping.[10] The supermarket has been an unusually lucrative source of unplanned purchases. Increased volume is thus obtained.

Self-Service

Akin to mass displays is the policy of self-service. Supermarket operators generally are of the opinion that letting people roam with push carts has paid off in increased sales.[11] Shoppers can feel, pinch, smell, and handle the merchandise; they can compare brands and read labels. To feel is reassuring. No clerk anxiously stands by to finish the sale or hurry the customer. Shoppers can budget as they go along. The *McCall's* study of 1,090 families disclosed 28.7 per cent of the respondents preferred to shop in supermarkets because they could make their own selection.[12]

While the supers originally had only self-service in groceries, they have adapted this technique to meat, dairy, produce, and bakery departments, with outstanding results. The facts are that when a supermarket operator puts in a self-service meat department, his sales usually increase because customers [13]

1. Hate to wait.
2. Want to search among a broad variety of kinds of meat.

[9] "New Angles on Related-Item Display," *Super Market Merchandising,* XXII, no. 4, May, 1957, p. 99.

[10] John R. Gilman, "Why Package Products Face Super Competition in Supermarkets," *Advertising Agency,* 45, no. 6, June, 1952, p. 64.

[11] *Ibid.*

[12] Home Testing Institute, Inc., *McCall's Food and Grocery Products Purchase Diary Study* (New York: McCall Corp., 1956).

[13] Don Parsons, "The Supermarket Formula," *Food Business,* Vol. 6, no. 5, May, 1958, p. 17.

3. Like to make their own choice.
4. Like to see what they are getting.
5. Like to take their own time to select purchases.

The self-service technique originated in supers was adopted by other forms of retailing on a growing scale since about 1950. Walgreen, Woolworth, and Kresge are examples in the drug and variety store field. Self-service, called "quick service," had swept the variety industry to the point in 1958 where 42 per cent of total variety stores had adopted quick service.[14] Department stores have re-examined the problem of determining the amount of assistance to be given to a customer and have developed new store layouts and display techniques with the aim of not only increasing sales but of also reducing selling costs.[15] This simplified selling, as it is referred to in department store terminology, is exemplified by the Fedway Stores division of Federated Department Stores, Incorporated.

Attractive and Convenient Shopping Facilities

Another device to increase volume has been to make the store attractive, convenient, and pleasant for shopping.[16] The "cheapy" super maintained an air of cheapness which contributed to the feeling of obtaining bargains. Since the advent of the supers, the general policy has been to make the stores more appealing through more attractive interiors, better lighting, music, air conditioning, rest rooms, and parking lots. This trend of "trading up" the stores has been questioned as an unnecessary expenditure, since it has tended to increase expenses and raise gross margins.[17] These expenditures possibly could result in the super losing its basic competitive advantage of price appeal. On the other hand, it has been contended that these expenses for comfortable shopping are a rela-

[14] "Self-service in Variety, 1958," *Variety Store Merchandiser*, Vol. 54, no. 4, May, 1958, p. 67.
[15] C. W. Barker, I. D. Anderson, and J. D. Butterworth, *Principles of Retailing* (New York: McGraw-Hill Book Co., Inc., 1956), p. 136.
[16] "Appearance Counts at Penn Fruit," *Super Market Merchandising*, XIII, no. 9, October, 1949, p. 74.
[17] "Schwegmann Brothers, Inc.," *Business Week*, no. 1136, June 9, 1951, p. 120.

tively small percentage of sales; the resultant increase in volume has improved the earnings effectively.[18]

An example of a recently opened modern super with decor is Eavey's Super Market in Fort Wayne, Indiana. It has 50,250 sq ft of selling space, a "kiddie korral," post office, flower shop, liquor department, utility payment booth, and a carillon for time and weather.[19] Despite the cost of these attractions, advertised prices are in line with chain competition and the concern appears to be successful.

The term "convenience of the supermarket to the customer" is concerned with the ease by which the consumer gets to the supermarket. This varies by particular kind of store location—central business district, neighborhood location, planned outlying shopping center, or highway market. Management has come to realize that nearness in itself is not a basic prerequisite per se, inasmuch as from 80 to 90 per cent of the customers use a car for grocery shopping.[20] General factors to be considered in selecting a supermarket site to make the location convenient include:

1. Street walking traffic
2. Street driving traffic
3. Congestion of streets to get to the market
4. Intersection of other streets
5. Availability of parking
6. Ease of access or egress of the parking lot
7. Public transportation
8. Zoning in the neighborhood

Furthermore, management must examine other location factors in the selection of a market site, including:

1. Land size
2. Suitability of store rental property
3. Number of competing stores

[18] Applebaum, *op. cit.*
[19] "Eavey's Young Giant," *Super Market Merchandising*, XXII, no. 1, January, 1957, p. 85.
[20] Home Testing Institute, Inc., *McCall's Food and Grocery Products Purchase Diary Study, op. cit.*

4. Standards of competition
5. Population trends
6. Income trends
7. Diversity of income sources
8. Type of customers
9. Population density
10. Taxes
11. Neighborhood changes
12. Size of trading area

The *McCall's* Food Study disclosed that the average family spends $25.27 per week or $1,314.04 per year on grocery store products. If $110 of yearly sales per square foot of space is used as a standard, a market of 10,000 sq ft of total covered space would need 837 families in order to transact a yearly volume of $1,100,000. This average figure can vary in specific instances, but it is presented to illustrate the importance of having sufficient potential in the area from which patronage is drawn.

Rules of thumb are difficult to establish in locating a supermarket. In a built-up neighborhood of one- and two-family units, a supermarket should control at least 20 per cent of all food business in its primary trading area of a 1-mile radius of the store, at least 10 per cent within the 1- and 2-mile radius, and an additional 1 to 2 per cent within the 2- to 5-mile radius of the store. Mr. Ray Harb, general sales manager for Red and White, Incorporated, reported that a metropolitan location can pull customers who buy all requirements from a distance that takes a maximum of 20 minutes to drive.[21] In rural areas the allowance for driving should be 30 to 40 minutes. Other results of a study made by *Food Topics* on the maximum trading area of a supermarket are shown in Table 4-4. In a city with inhabitants of 500,000 or more, a super can draw from a radius of 7.1 miles from the store. In a small town of less than 10,000 persons, the trading-area radius ranges up to 22.4 miles. Again it is cautioned that locational problems of each store are unique and subject to individual variation.

[21] "Store Locations," *Food Topics*, January 23, 1956, p. 1.

Trends in supermarket location indicate that management has followed the movement of the population to outlying residential or suburban areas in an endeavor to make the facility convenient for shopping. In fact, even highway locations have been pioneered in recent years to satisfy this demand.

TABLE 4-4 *

Maximum Trading Area Radius for a $500,000
Yearly Volume (and over) Supermarket by
Size of Community.

City size	Trading area radius (miles)
500,000 and over	7.1
100,000–499,000	8.8
25,000–99,000	10.4
10,000–24,000	12.1
Under 10,000	22.4

* "Store Locations," *Food Topics*, January 23, 1956, p. 1.

Advertising and Promotion

Promotion and advertising have been attempted to increase sales. Attractions for inducing people to shop at supers have ranged from automobile and money raffles to guest appearances by movie stars.[22] While stores differ as to the extent of promotion, an endeavor has been made to make the super a family place to shop, a source of evening entertainment, a place to go. Snack bars, magazine sections for children, soda fountains, kiddyland rides, and special attractions galore have abounded in certain supers. Yet, the food-chain operating statements for 1958, shown in Table 4-2, indicated advertising and promotion expense (including trading stamps) to be 1.88 per

[22] Pragmatic operators will find of extreme value a series of articles entitled *1,000-and-one Super Promotion Ideas*, which started in the March, 1951, issue of *Super Market Merchandising* and continued intermittently until September, 1952. These ideas, together with practical illustrations, cover the topics of grand openings, storewide promotions, institutional campaigns, anniversaries, and specific product promotions. Also of value is an article "51 Public Relations Ideas," *Super Market Merchandising*, XXIV, no. 5, May, 1959, p. 113.

cent of sales. Surveys conducted by the magazine *Super Market Merchandising* indicated that advertising expenditures (excluding stamps) in 1955 and 1956 were 0.84 and 0.93 per cent of sales, respectively.[23]

Promotion can take two directions. One is the special, short-run type; the other is the long-run, regular promotion, usually of a premium nature. The former is exemplified by the following:

1. Grand openings: free gifts or night club shows
2. Storewide promotions: airplane ride with the purchase of $25 or more, mystery shopper sale, or finder's keepers sale
3. Institutional: polio campaign or set-up of art galleries
4. Anniversary: serve breakfast or give birthday cakes to all babies born the week of the sale
5. Holiday: free trimmings if you purchase a turkey at Thanksgiving
6. Product lines: half-cent sale or shopping bag specials full of canned goods

The regular or constant type of promotion typically involves a premium. There are four types.

1. Giveaways: Have a lottery every week or give a certain dish of a china set with a stated dollar purchase. Stagger the kind of dish given away so that it will take several months to get a whole set.
2. Discount-on-purchase plan: Offer certain merchandise at a discount if customers purchase a certain dollar amount. The merchandise sold at a discount can range from special premiums to regular merchandise carried.
3. Cash register receipt: Save receipts, and after they total a certain prescribed amount, offer the customer a premium such as a dollar salad bowl.
4. Stamp or coupon plan: Give coupons or certificates to be applied to the purchase of merchandise carried by the store. Or use the conventional type of stamp plan whereby stamps are given generally at the rate of one stamp for each 10-cent purchase. The stamps

[23] "How's Business," *Super Market Merchandising*, XXII, no. 8, August, 1957, p. 113.

are saved in a booklet and redeemed for a great variety of merchandise premiums.

Of all the regular type of promotion plans, trading stamps have become the most vital promotional tool for supermarket operators. A study made by *Progressive Grocer* indicates that the typical super which issues stamps spends 2.03 to 2.06 per cent of the sales dollar for this device.[24] The general use of trading stamps has grown unevenly and cyclically since the 1890's, with a department store generally as the core. While some supers introduced trading stamps earlier, their general acceptance dates from about 1950. For a supermarket to use this promotional tool successfully, certain prerequisites must be met. There are six discernible features.[25]

1. The user should be part of a group of different stores reasonably close to each other geographically. All should handle the same stamp, with the super or a department store as the center of influence.

2. Stamps are promotional; customers must be encouraged to save them and associate the stamps with that particular store.

3. Stamps must obtain and hold additional volume; while the volume increase varies, at least a 10 per cent increase in sales is needed to break even on the stamp cost.

4. The super must be able to handle added volume without materially increasing the overhead.

5. Stamps are not a panacea for supers whose quality and type of service are inferior to that offered by competitors.

6. Stamps do not permit much, if any, independence in pricing.

The use of trading stamps reached its zenith in 1956 when 39 per cent of the supermarkets reported using this premium.[26] In 1957 the upward trend finally halted when only 38 per cent reported using stamps; in 1958 only 35 per cent reported stamp plans in opera-

[24] *Facts in Grocery Distribution* (New York: Progressive Grocer, 1958), p. F–19.

[25] Albert Haring and Wallace O. Yoder, *Trading Stamp Practice and Pricing Policy* (Bloomington: Indiana University, 1958), p. 284.

[26] *Facts in Grocery Distribution* (New York: Progressive Grocer, 1959), p. F–13.

tion. However, there is no indication that stamps will fade into the position of relative insignificance as their past history purports, inasmuch as the major factors that led to stamp ascendency will continue to influence the market.[27] Indications are that certain industry giants may adopt stamps as a promotional tool, with market tests being conducted on a limited experimental basis.

Large Inventory

Merchandising is defined as the adaptation of a product to fit the requirements of the buyer, coupled with the effective presentation of such goods.[28] Supermarkets merchandise through their buyers and buying committees who screen the veritable horde of items and deals presented. Merchandising is completed by the various display and sales techniques that result in the movement of goods to the ultimate consumers.

Supermarkets have carried larger and more diversified inventories in an effort to increase sales. Examine the increase of the number of items carried: [29]

Year	Items
1928	867
1946	3,000
1950	3,750
1955	4,723
1957	5,144
1958	5,600

This increase resulted in part from the shopper's desire to select from many lines. In addition, manufacturers produced and promoted new items in accord with the strong desire of the housewife to want convenience in food preparation.[30] Ingenuity and skill of food processors created new and better products, such as frozen juices and

[27] Eugene Beem, "Who Profits from Trading Stamps," *Harvard Business Review*, Vol. 35, no. 6, November–December, 1957, p. 121.

[28] T. N. Beckman, H. H. Maynard, and W. R. Davidson, *Principles of Marketing* (New York: The Ronald Press Co., 1952), p. 5.

[29] *Facts in Grocery Distribution, op. cit.*, p. F–3.

[30] "The Fabulous Market for Food," *Fortune*, XLVIII, no. 4, October, 1953, p. 135.

cake mixes. Most supers are cramped for space; it is a constant fight to get merchandise on display. Manufacturers' salesmen do not sell merchandise to supermarket buyers; instead they sell dollar profits to the supers for granting them location and display space in the store. In the case of many new items or brands, advertising done to presell the customer is not sufficient inducement to buy. Various promotions, premiums, coupons, and deals are required to get the item carried.

Basically, an item is judged for stocking in supermarkets on turnover, gross margin, and expense of handling and selling.[31] Inherent in these major features are space for display, storage, competing lines handled, advertising allowances, promotional support, items given a store, and merchandise-returns policy. These criteria, which influence profits, vary for different kinds of merchandise. The supermarket has attempted to attain a large volume (and its resultant advantages) through a high rate of turnover.[32] Rates for selected supermarket chains for 1956 are shown in Table 4-5.[33] These range from a low of 7.8 for A. J. Bayless Markets, Inc., to a high of 14.94 for Daitch Crystal Dairies, Incorporated. A turnover of about 12 times per year, or once a month, appears to be average. The Harvard Study of Selected Food Chains indicated a stock turnover of 12.3 for 1958.[34]

The wide variation in turnover rates is in part attributed to the lines of merchandise stressed by the respective companies. The trend toward larger stores in the postwar period has offered additional shelf space for display and has made the super a bonanza for visiting salesmen. The increase in number and kind of food items carried, coupled with nonfood lines, has tended to lower turnover rates in the postwar period for many concerns. As an example, be-

[31] Malcolm P. McNair, "Thinking Ahead in Retailing," *Super Market Merchandising*, XV, no. 8, August, 1950, p. 106.

[32] Milton Alexander, "Where We Stand on Non-food Merchandising," *Progressive Grocer*, XXXI, no. 10, October, 1952, p. 200.

[33] The supermarket chains listed in Table 4-5 were those whose detailed operating statistics were published in *Moody's Industrial Manual*.

[34] Wilbur B. England, *Operating Results of Food Chains in 1958* (Cambridge: Harvard Business School, Bulletin 156, 1959), p. 33.

tween 1950 and 1956 the turnover for Colonial Stores, Incorporated, dropped from 15.0 to 10.3; for Lucky Stores, Incorporated, from 10.8 to 7.9; and for Market Basket, Incorporated, from 11.7 to 10.2. This is a merchandising trend that management must watch. How-

TABLE 4-5 *

Annual Inventory Turnover of Selected Supermarket Chains for the Year 1956.

Company	Turnover
American Stores Co.	11.7
A. J. Bayless Markets, Inc.	7.8
Century Food Markets Co.	11.3
Colonial Stores, Inc.	10.3
Daitch Crystal Dairies, Inc.	14.9
Fisher Bros., Co.	11.2
Food Fair Stores, Inc.	14.8
Food Mart, Inc.	9.5
Grand Union, Inc.	11.2
Jewel Tea Co., Inc.	10.8
Kroger Co.	11.5
Lucky Stores, Inc.	7.9
Market Basket	10.2
Purity Stores	13.0
Safeway Stores, Inc.	10.9
Shaffer Stores Co.	10.2
Shopping Bag Food Stores	10.2
Sunrise Supermarkets Corp.	13.7
Thriftmart, Inc.	7.9
Weingarten, J., Inc.	9.8

* These statistics are calculated from data contained in *Moody's Industrial Manual.* Cost of sales is divided by average inventory at cost.

ever, profits have not appeared to suffer inasmuch as gross margins generally have improved for concerns that lower turnover to carry more lines. As a generalization from the 1956 data, stores with the lower inventory turnover rates tend to have the higher gross margins.[35]

Supermarkets have enjoyed a high inventory turnover as compared with that of other retailers, as shown by the statistics in Table

[35] Gross margins are discussed in Chapter 5.

4-6. The average turnover of about 12 times per year is approximately triple that for department, drug, and variety stores, which average about four times per year. Simply, the velocity of goods in and out of a super is three times that for a department, drug, or variety store; or, a supermarket buys, stocks, sells, makes a profit, and repeats the cycle about three times while a drug, department, or variety store is doing it once with the same dollar inventory. This is a vital consideration in the handling of nonfood lines.

Addition of Nonfood Products

Akin to the problem of controlling a large inventory is that of adding nonfood products to the line. The supermarket has incorporated in its operation the rapidly moving meat, dairy, and produce

TABLE 4-6

Annual Inventory Turnover of Various Lines of Retailing for the Year 1954.

Department stores	3.7 *
Drug stores	3.9 †
Hardware stores with sales over $200,000	2.3 ‡
Jewelry stores with sales over $500,000	1.1 §
Variety stores	4.2 ¶

* Controllers Congress, *1954 Merchandise and Operating Results* (New York: National Retail Dry Goods Association, 1955), p. 1.
† *Lilly Digest* (Indianapolis: Eli Lilly and Company, 1955), p. 21.
‡ "1954 Retail Hardware Survey," *Hardware Retailer*, June, 1955, p. 14.
§ *1954 Operating Statistics* (New York: American National Retail Jewelers Association, 1955), p. 4.
¶ "Harvard Report on Variety Chains," *Chain Store Age*, Variety Store Managers Edition, XXXI, no. 8, August, 1955, p. 62.

items; but it also has concentrated on fast-turnover nonfoods which have experienced higher markup and profits. For the year 1958, food stores sold $1.82 billion in nonfood items exclusive of tobacco products. Of this group, health and beauty aids, with sales of $1.10 billion, were the largest group.[36] This substantial $1.10 billion total

[36] *Facts in Grocery Distribution, op. cit.*

represented 60 per cent of the entire national volume of health and
beauty aids. Other classes of nonfoods included greeting cards, magazines and books, toys, records, stationery, clothing, dry goods, and
film. In addition, tobacco products of $1.8 billion were sold in
grocery stores during the year 1957.[37] A study made by *Chain Store
Age* disclosed that the 1959 supermarket transacted 4.3 per cent of
total sales in tobacco products, 2.3 per cent in health and beauty
aids, 1.1 per cent in housewares, and 0.5 per cent in magazines and
books.[38]

The super is basically a food store; many of these nonfood lines
create a problem of buying, stocking, rotating, and selling that differs from the food departments. While the bulk of nonfoods are
handled through the supermarket buying division, the tasks of merchandising nonfoods have been simplified partly by the use of rack
jobbers for at least part of the needs, as shown by the data in Table
4-7. The rack or short-order jobber performs the function of stock-

TABLE 4-7 *

Source of Nonfood Products in Supermarkets
Expressed as a Percentage of Stores
Using the Source.

Source	Drugs	Housewares	Toys	Soft Goods
Manufacturer	67.2	58.3	65.5	79.2
Rack jobber	24.1	66.8	28.4	46.6
Food wholesaler	7.6	3.6	2.0	4.8
Other wholesaler	12.1	36.4	11.4	4.7
Concessionaire	0.0	0.1	0.6	0.4

* "Non-Foods Jump to Major Rank," *Super Market Merchandising*, XIX, no.
1, January, 1954, p. 36.

ing and rotating merchandise and keeping the shelves clean. The
general practice has been for the store to receive 25 per cent as its

[37] *Supermarket News*, April 14, 1958, p. 52.
[38] "What Do Food Chains Sell?" *Chain Store Age, Grocer's Manual Issue,*
July, 1959, p. 109.

share of all merchandise sold.[39] Stock left in the store by the rack jobber normally remains the property of the jobber until sold. Merchandise is sold in the regular manner, and the consumer does not know that consigned products are being purchased.

In a study covering the influence of nonfood merchandise on food products, the following data were disclosed: [40]

1. Supers reduced the amount of space for food products by less than 10 per cent in order to stock nonfoods.

2. New stores were built larger so as to handle both lines.

3. The food lines that suffered most were the slow turning, less profitable ones.

4. The nonfood lines carried had to turn over rapidly, to take up little room, and to be adapted to self-service sale and not require technical selling.

Furthermore, studies revealed that visits to food stores were about four times more than those to every drug store and eight times more than to every hardware store.[41] Mathematically there was greater chance for displayed merchandise to be purchased in a super. The trend toward the sale of nonfoods in supers has been pronounced in the postwar period.

One of the more recent nonfood trends has been the marriage of the discount house and the supermarket in the form of giant merchandising colossi.[42] Safeway Stores, Incorporated, has opened a discount center within one of its food markets in Bakersfield, California, in which appliances, sporting goods, and related items are featured. Schwegmann Brothers has opened a store in New Orleans with 189,000 sq ft of space on the first floor and 55,000 sq ft of selling space on the mezzanine to merchandise an infinite variety of stock. Two Guys from Harrison and the National Grocery Company

[39] Interview with Chris Tarrant, Secretary, Grocerland Co-operative, Inc., Chicago, Illinois, on June 20, 1957.

[40] "Supers Bid Welcome to Soft Goods," *Super Market Merchandising*, XVIII, no. 7, July, 1953, p. 27.

[41] Gilman, *op. cit.*

[42] "The Super Super Market," *Super Market Merchandising*, XXII, no. 7, August, 1957, p. 56.

have opened a 110,000-sq ft operation estimated to do $20,000,000 in food, durable goods, auto accessories, and promotional items. Merchandise is received directly from the manufacturer in drop shipments. Retailing innovations of this type may cause an upheaval in the world of retailing.

SUMMARY

Supermarkets have adopted practices that have led toward increased sales per store. These practices have included low price policies, mass displays, large stocks (but carefully selected as to turnover), self-service, promotions, addition of certain nonfood departments, and improved appearance and services. Excellent merchandising practices to obtain increased sales per square foot of floor space and linear display space have been pursued. Management has taken advantage of the desire of the consumer for one-stop shopping by selection of merchandise and expanding store building programs. Simply, the policy is to attract the consumer and attractively display a variety of fast-turning merchandise that can be purchased as a result of planned purchases as well as impulse buying.

These selling policies are a must if a store is to realize its full potential during its lifetime, the length of which is governed by unpredictable factors. Detrimental population shifts may take place in a store's trading area, competition may move in, or the facilities of the store may become outmoded. A given store has certain facilities with which to make a profit, and in the main, these resources do not always appear to be used at maximum capacity. Thus management must strive to make the most out of the facilities over a predetermined period of time. In a store's trading area, management must strive to obtain its maximum share of the available market commensurate with the store facilities. The marginal customer attracted or the extra dollar of sales to the established customer has a significant impact on profits of a store. Not only does the added sales dollar reflect in the normal profit percentage, but it also contributes to an increased profit percentage. This interesting phenomenon will be presented in Chapter 7 after margin, expense, and profit relationships have been examined.

5 | BUYING OPERATIONS AND MARGINS

INTRODUCTION

The preceding chapter pointed out the necessity for a large volume per super and examined the selling techniques designed by supermarkets to generate this needed large volume. It is the purpose of this chapter to continue the study of supermarketing principles, still in the framework of an operating statement. Attention in this section is focused on (1) cost of goods sold and (2) principles involved in the establishment of gross margins. The former includes a review of buying practices and techniques developed by this industry.

COST OF GOODS SOLD

There is a maxim in retailing that anything well bought can be sold at a profit. Department stores recognized this principle early, as did food chains. Buying is an area of specialization in itself, and the demise of the small food store can be attributed to a large extent to improper or inept purchasing.

Balance of Buying Power Favors Supers

Supermarkets in 1958 had sales of $28.7 billion.[1] Inasmuch as cost of goods sold in a supermarket averages about 79.50 per cent of the sales dollar, merchandise purchases approximated $22.8 billion in 1958, assuming no major change in inventory position by the members.[2] Supers, in the aggregate, wield a powerful buying force.

[1] See Table 1-2.
[2] See Table 4-2.

Furthermore, the strong trends toward larger stores and more
stores under a common ownership through horizontal integration
have given the individual members of this industry more potent bargaining power. Even an individually owned store with typical yearly
sales of $1,000,000 is a highly respected customer, since purchases
for that operation approximate $800,000. As a result, transactions to-
day between the buyer (the super) and the seller (the manufacturer) are more of a cooperative venture in which the manufacturer
needs the assistance and cooperation of the supermarket.

Routine Buying Policies

Many of the purchases of a supermarket are of a routine nature
from established sources of supply. It would be difficult to envisage
a super without Ritz crackers or Campbell's tomato soup. Responsibility for buying, the actual placing of the order, varies according
to the size and organizational structure of the company. Specialized
buyers are used by the large chains for routine buying, with store
managers requisitioning from the warehouses. In some smaller organizations the entire buying responsibility for routine purchases
is handled by one individual. Some firms become members of wholesale or retail voluntary chains in order to procure staple items at
low cost. Department managers, specializing in certain areas such
as produce and meat, have assisted in routine procurement for the
one-or-few unit operations. Ordering and shelf stocking of certain
items frequently are handled by manufacturers' salesmen under the
authorization of the owner, manager, or person responsible for buying.

Yet, even in the purchase of regular items, care must be taken
to make certain that the best possible prices and deals are obtained. The purchase of routine merchandise must be an integral
part of the selling program. The buyer must be aware of special promotions, displays, local and national advertising, economical handling of merchandise, warehousing, promptness of delivery, and
turnover. Some of the larger firms, such as Jewel Tea Company,
have acquired electronic computers to handle the logistics problem

of most economical handling and warehousing of merchandise. In turn, manufacturers must not be complacent about their established brands in a super. Commodity analysis constantly takes place, either subjectively by a busy owner or manager or objectively by accountants and statisticians who compute dollar profit per linear foot of display space. No item on the shelves of a super is in a haven. It must sell or be eliminated.

New Products—Life Blood of a Super

Merchandise that is well established in a supermart under a system of cooperation between the manufacturer and the supermarket is "bread and butter" volume. These items reflect customers' needs and wants and move off the shelves. However, a dynamic supermarket that is striving for added volume and a greater profit percentage must evaluate successfully new products on a continuous basis. New items that sell are the volume builders that a super needs to add increased profits to the store. A supermarket retains its basic competitive position in a trading area by [3]

1. Offering an expanding variety of merchandise.
2. Developing a good reputation for offering new items.
3. Functioning as the purchasing agent for the community.
4. Differentiating its store from competition.
5. Associating with the news value inherent in new products.

The problem of adding new merchandise to the line becomes more acute because of the difficulty in defining exactly what a new product is. A new item can be [4]

1. A product that hasn't existed previously or a product so changed as to make most existing items obsolete.

2. A product that has been changed in varying degree in construction, design, color, size, or package.

3. A product on the market not previously handled by the particular super.

[3] E. B. Weiss, *Winning Chain Store Distribution for New Products* (New York: Doyle, Dane, Bernbach, Inc., 1956).
[4] *Ibid.*

4. An old item made by a new manufacturer.

Supermarket attitude toward new items will vary, depending upon how new products fall into these divisions as well as upon the prestige and record of the supplier.

Buying Committee

As a result of buying complexities of stocking the myriad of new items and the importance of integrating purchasing, sales, advertising, and promotion into a unified merchandising program, supermarkets have developed buying or merchandise committees. Approximately 88 per cent of the supermarkets have these committees, which replaced food retailing by a federation of individual apron-stringed grocers with a select group of skilled merchandisers having the power to match giant manufacturers.[5] The stated purpose of these committees is to [6]

1. Remove buying decisions from an emotional atmosphere.

2. Prevent a buyer's personal likes and dislikes from entering into a decision.

3. Help store and field personnel to understand buying operations at headquarters better through rotating participation of some members.

4. Capitalize on collective knowledge.

5. Provide for the orderly continuity of buying operations.

Buying committees range from 3 to as many as 17 members. They are made up of a buyer and other top advertising, promotion, merchandising, and sales executives. Frequently store managers are included to make their operation more democratic. Each member on the committee has one vote, and it takes a simple majority to add a new item to the line. Faced with the problem of buying many lines of merchandise, some firms have organized two buying committees.

Activities of these committees are as varied as their composition. Some assemble once every week, and depending upon the number

---

[5] From an address by William C. Nugent to the Grocery Manufacturers of America, Inc., on November 12, 1957, at New York City.
[6] *Ibid.*

of products to be considered, the meetings run from 1 to 6 hours. A buying committee's decision is binding in that a buyer cannot overrule or ignore it. The group decision, however, is not irrevocable. For example, if a product is rejected, another presentation generally can be given in a period of from 60 to 90 days after the rejection. Some committees will review an item as many as three times. After a merchandise group selects a product, store managers must introduce the item. But if it doesn't sell, a manager need not reorder. In turn, store managers in some supermarket chains can request buying committees to adopt a product. It must be remembered that the buying committee decisions involve the entire store system and not just one store.

The results of merchandise committee decisions have been examined in several studies. One large food chain reports that its buying office has presented for consideration as many as 150 to 200 new items per week.[7] If all were accepted, 10,000 new items per year would be added to this chain, which normally carries 4,000 items. A study of the activities of 12 buying committees of some of the largest supermarket chains showed that out of 496 products examined, 220 were voted favorably, 61 were deferred, and 215 were rejected.[8] In another study, the buying practices of eight chains were examined for the period of March, 1954, to June, 1955.[9] Thousands of items were presented to the buyers. They in turn screened new items and submitted only 1,433 products to the respective merchandise committees. These committees disposed of the new items as follows: [10]

Rejected	987
Held for reconsideration	16
Accepted for testing	10
Recommended for special promotion only	13

---

[7] Weiss, *Winning Chain Store Distribution for New Products, op. cit.*
[8] Nugent, *op. cit.*
[9] William Applebaum and Richard Moulton, *An Exploration into Reasons Why Supermarkets Add and Discontinue Items* (New York: McCall Corp., 1956).
[10] *Ibid.*

Accepted part of the line	29
Accepted	378
Items reviewed	1,433

In all, 69 per cent of the items presented to the committees of these eight chains were rejected and only 26 per cent were accepted unconditionally.

As a corollary to this same study of the eight chains, the major reasons for discontinuing 3,725 items from the line during this same 16-month period were: [11]

	Per cent
Slow movement	42
Did not fulfill expectations	22
Replaced by superior product	15
Due to manufacturers' action	11
Other	10

Merchandise that doesn't sell is eliminated.

In cases where a decision to add an item is questioned, some companies resort to consumer panels of up to 16 housewives whose opinions are respected. Other companies have a designated test-store group where product tests are regularly conducted in order to assist the merchandise group.

This trend of employing the buying committee has shifted the duties of a buyer from one of making decisions to one of communications. Buyers make decisions on the original screening. After this, they generally present the product to the merchandise committee for a group decision. In the committee the buyer carries but one vote. In turn, this has made selling on the part of the manufacturer more impersonal, since the salesmen seldom appear personally before the committee. The salesman merely sells the buyer and fills out comprehensive data sheets so that the buyer in turn can do a creditable job of presenting the proposal. Table 5-1 contains a suggested form of the Super Market Institute to be filled out by the salesman for use in the buying function. This type of impersonal selling in turn requires manufacturers to

[11] *Ibid.*

1. Open up channels of communication with all executives having a voice in new-item determination.

2. Develop new methods of presenting data to the buying committee.

3. Understand problems confronting chains and their difficulties in adopting new products.

Supermarkets in turn must review and improve the functioning of the committee as to operating techniques and organization in order to make it more effective.

TABLE 5-1 *

Grocery Promotion and New Item Fact Sheet.

1. ITEM _____   PROMOTION NUMBER _____
2. Date presented _____   Buyer _____
3. Starting date _____   Accepted (date) _____
4. Closing date _____   Rejected (date) _____
5. Type of promotion _____

	FOR BUYER'S USE	
This Item		*Reg. Mdse.*
$____	cost/case	$____
$____	cost/unit	$____
$____	suggested retail	$____
$: %	profit/unit	$: %
$: %	profit/case	$: %

6. Pack and size _____
7. Invoice price per case _____
8. Freight, if any _____
9. Terms (cash discount) _____
10. Promotional allowance _____
11. Total cost per case _____
12. Performance requirements for promotional allowance _____
13. Promotional allowance paid by: Check___ Off invoice___ Free mdse.___.
14. Display allowance: Yes_____ No_____.
15. Advertising allowance: Yes___ No___. If "yes," is it in addition to promotion and display allowance?___ Tear sheet to be furnished?   Yes___ No___
16. Are allowances over and above regular contract?   Yes___ No___
17. Floor stock protection on regular merchandise?   Yes___ No___
18. Will regular merchandise be picked up while deal is in effect? Yes___ No___
19. Display material available? Yes___ No___ Delivered to: Store___ Warehouse___.
20. Will deal be advertised by manufacturer? Yes___ No___. If "yes," to what extent? _____
    National media _____
    Local media _____

* Super Market Institute.

21. Will case be marked "Deal?" Yes___ No___ How many sides?_____
22. Is sale guaranteed? Yes___ No___ If "yes," what basis?_____
23. Is price guaranteed against decline? Yes___ No___ If "yes," what limits, if any? _____
24. Manufacturer's name _____
25. Manufacturer's address _____
26. Local representative _____
27. Local representative's address _____
    Additional information: _____
    _____
    _____

NEW ITEMS
(Complete in addition to first sheet)

1. Who handles this product in this market?
   Name_____ SRP †_____
   Name_____ SRP _____
   Name_____ SRP _____
2. What advertising and promotion is being done in this market by manufacturer? _____
3. What advantage is there in stocking this item? _____
4. If approved, when will item be available for delivery? _____
5. Shipping point _____
6. Transit time _____
7. Best routing _____
8. What quantities must be purchased to obtain lowest cost? _____
9. LCL price_____ Pool car price_____ Car price_____
   Minimum_____ Minimum_____ Minimum_____
10. Are drop shipments available? Yes_____ No_____.
    Additional Information _____
    _____
    _____

† Suggested retail price.

Factors Involved in Selecting Individual Products

While buying committees vary as to composition and method of operation, they generally are in accord as to the factors involved in the selection of merchandise. Following are criteria used to judge a product: [12]

[12] Address by William C. Nugent presented at the United States Wholesale Grocers' Convention, April 21, 1957, St. Louis, Missouri.

1. Will product return a fair dollar profit in terms of potential volume and shelf space?
2. Does the consumer want the product?
3. What is its sales potential?
4. Is there a need for the product?
5. How will the product be advertised and promoted?
6. Are there advertising, promotional, or display allowances available?
7. Is there a retailer incentive (deal goods)?
8. Is a product of good quality?
9. Is packaging proper?
10. Is the manufacturer reliable?
11. Does competition have the item?
12. Was the product market-tested?
13. Is the product timely—in season?
14. Is the introduction timely?
15. Will it bring new customers to the store?
16. How many items are in a carton?
17. Does stock of item conflict with company policy?
18. What is the merchandise returns policy of the manufacturer?
19. What is the quantity that must be bought?
20. What discounts are offered?

A manufacturer will do well to weigh these factors in merchandising his line to fit in with these requirements. There is an ever-increasing problem of obtaining distribution of new products in the supermarkets.

Make or Buy

Akin to the problem of product selection is the alternative of a supermarket: whether to manufacture or to purchase. Different stores have different policies in this regard, and it is difficult to generalize.

The industry leader, the Great Atlantic and Pacific Tea Company, has long been an advocate of manufacturing as well as marketing. Other large chains have entered manufacturing operations on a

more limited scale, primarily in bakery and coffee lines. The factors
that determine whether a product should be manufactured or purchased include:

1. Investment in manufacturing facilities
2. Alternative use of funds
3. Frequency of depressed conditions in the line so that advantageous purchases can be made
4. Total dollar volume of the specific item
5. Total dollar volume of any one item within a line
6. Strength of brand preference for competing products
7. Strength of the emotional buying motive for the item as a result of strong brand preference (e.g., baby food)
8. Need for a yardstick to insure proper costs for the product

Policy on Packer versus Private Brands

Closely related to the problem of "make or buy" is that of brand
selection. Supermarkets got their start in the self-service sale of
nationally known brands. In today's market, however, there are both
packer and private brands crowding the shelves. Packers' brands
include nationally known products—Del Monte and Dole—as well
as little known or unadvertised brands of small and medium-sized
packers. Private labels exist at both retail and wholesale levels and
include chain brands. The private labelers acquire their merchandise
from manufacturers of various sizes. Some of the private brands also
are packed by the chain factories and sold as chain brands. Thus
chain brands can be both private brands and packers' brands.

For example, in the canned goods field, nationally advertised
products generally command a higher price than private labels or
unknown packers' brands. Competition between them is primarily
on a price basis. Major packers who know possible total demand
and supply conditions, inventory carry-over, costs, and profit possibilities attempt to establish prices on their branded products, quality
considered. In turn, they are underpriced by unknown brands that
arrive on the market at various times and in varying quantities. A
retailer may never again carry a particular private brand. In bumper

crop years, the price spread between the two tends to increase as smaller packers literally dump their pack on the market and force the major packers to take a new price position.

Add to this the growing importance of chain-branded goods that are brought into the store under the broad family brand of the retailer and which embrace a variety of food products, from bread to cheese. Little advertising or promotional expense is incurred other than that related to the store special sales. As a result of astute buying, display policies, and tie-in of the product with the general reputation of the store, the chain labels have been taking an increasingly larger share of the market.

Factors involved in the decision to use chain brands are for the most part similar to those involved in the decision whether to manufacture or to purchase. One additional feature is that funds need not be expended for plant and equipment because chains have been able to obtain items under their brand from small manufacturers as well as large national sellers of branded products.

Use of Buying Associations

Food chains and large, independent supermarkets have integrated their operations by performing more and more of the wholesale marketing functions and even some of the manufacturing activities. For example, approximately 80 per cent of the supermarkets obtain their grocery products through their own central warehouses, from 9 to 10 per cent obtain their merchandise through retailer-owned cooperatives, 3 per cent through voluntary chain wholesalers, and 7 per cent through no central warehouse or affiliation.[13] As a result of their own wholesale operations, the integrated retailers generally have been able to place merchandise in their stores at a cost less than that of small independent merchants who buy from service wholesalers. This has placed the large operators at a competitive advantage in this high-volume, narrow-profit industry in which a 10 cent price advantage on a case of tomato catsup is significant. To adjust for this competitive disadvantage in buying,

[13] *Super Market Industry Speaks* (Chicago: Super Market Institute, 1956).

many of the independent merchants have cooperated with each other for the purpose of purchasing primarily staple merchandise. In 1957 there were 88,000 food stores that were members of voluntary and cooperative buying organizations.[14] Although most of these units were not supermarkets according to the definition established in this text, inasmuch as their volume was under $500,000 annually, a fair amount of their sales of $20.46 billion was transacted by supermarket members. Independent Grocers Alliance of America, commonly referred to as IGA, is the largest of the voluntary chains. The 5,300 member stores in 1957 transacted approximately $2.9 billion sales.[15] While only 234 of their United States outlets and 20 Canadian stores were classified as supermarkets, these units are reported to have done at least 5 per cent of the retail volume of this voluntary organization. Therefore this procurement channel must be considered in a text on supermarkets even though the voluntaries were developed to aid the smaller merchant.

There are basically two types of buying associations in the food industry. One is the wholesale-sponsored voluntary chain, such as the Red and White Corporation or IGA. Red and White is owned by its wholesale members throughout the country. Its headquarters in Chicago conducts many varied activities. It makes arrangements with manufacturers to pack merchandise for its wholesalers, handles all quantity and net buying arrangements which are available to the wholesalers on a national basis, and arranges for quantity discounts on a national basis where available. Red and White also arranges for private labeling, furnishes advertising service, and works with the member stores at the retail level to improve their operation. The independent retail stores in turn agree to purchase a certain portion of their requirements through the respective local wholesale member. There is no requirement that an individual retailer purchase all requirements through this wholesaler. In the similarly operated IGA

[14] *Facts in Grocery Distribution* (New York: Progressive Grocer, 1958), p. F–5.
[15] Interview with Mr. Don R. Grimes, assistant to the president, IGA, July, 1957.

voluntary chain, the retailer members pay 2 per cent above cost of the merchandise to their IGA local wholesaler, who gets "cash on the barrel head." Cash discounts vary from 1 to 2 per cent, and the local retailer also pays drayage.

The other principal method of purchasing through an affiliation is that of the retail-sponsored voluntary chain in which a group of retailers form a cooperative to purchase some or all of their joint requirements. The association is financed by its retail members, whereas financing is done by the wholesaler in the method described previously. Some cooperatives require members to have on deposit funds equal to each week's purchases. In return, merchandise is delivered to the respective members at cost plus a slight percentage for operation of the association plus drayage. In some cases the cooperative even owns and operates its own warehouse facilities. Cooperative profits paid to the members are based on the ratio of the percentage of each member's purchases through the cooperative to the total sales of the cooperative. This type of operation is used primarily to procure staple merchandise.

Consigned Merchandise

The final method of acquiring merchandise is that of consignment selling. The vast majority of the merchandise sold by supers is purchased outright. It turns over rapidly, and thus inventory investment is kept at a minimum. Yet, some manufacturers and wholesalers leave merchandise with supermarts who become the agents for the purpose of selling the goods. Title remains with the manufacturer, and the super receives its compensation in the form of a percentage of the selling price at which the goods actually are sold. A supermarket will use this arrangement in cases in which it does not desire to tie up capital in merchandise that may prove to be unsalable. This situation arises primarily with unknown new grocery products of questionable merit or nonfood items with which the super has limited experience. It is in conjunction with the latter case, nonfood merchandise placed in supers by rack jobbers, that consignment selling is significant. Nonfood sales in a 1958 super averaged 5 per cent of total sales.[16]

Basically, a rack jobber sets up display equipment in a supermarket, arranges the merchandise, services the account by exchanging defective goods and rebuilding stocks, and suggests how the store manager can tie in with national advertising. The super receives, as its compensation for rental of space and for the selling of the product, from 25 to 35 per cent of the sales price of each item. The margin depends upon the type of goods handled by the particular rack merchandiser. Some jobbers carry a complete line; others specialize in certain merchandise categories. It is possible for a large super to be serviced by as many as ten specialized rack jobbers in such areas as hardware, housewares, health and beauty aids, tobacco, soft goods, toys, stationery, auto supplies, pet food, and electrical items.

Wide diversity exists among members of the supermarket industry in the use of rack jobbers. Even divisions within the same company may vary as to policy. For example, the stores of the Great Atlantic and Pacific Tea Company in Baltimore employ an old drug wholesale house to handle their health and beauty aids on a rack-jobbing basis.[17] The same company in Jacksonville, Florida, buys all stationery items and health and beauty aids direct from manufacturers.[18] As supers become more familiar with the merchandising of nonfood items, they take over certain lines of this activity. The items taken over from rack merchandisers generally are small in size and moderately priced; they contain a minimum of style obsolescence, sell in volume, are consumed quickly, display easily, and offer a fair profit margin. The extent of consignment selling by rack jobbers is shown by the data in Table 4-7. Consignment sellers are the second most important source of nonfood merchandise in supers.

---

[16] *The Super Market Industry Speaks* (Chicago: Super Market Institute, 1959).

[17] "How Rack Jobbers Open Doors for Sale of Non-foods in Supers," *Sales Management,* Vol. 82, no. 7, April 3, 1959, p. 44.

[18] *Ibid.*

GROSS MARGINS

In the preceding section, buying practices and techniques developed by this industry were reviewed. The importance of scientific purchasing was stressed as a vital requisite to the fundamental method of operation of this volume merchandiser. The vast array of merchandise carried must be sold at relatively low prices in order to represent good value to the customer. This in turn requires skillful buying.

Like all retailers, a supermarket purchases merchandise at one price and in turn sells it at a higher price. In turn, out of its sales dollar it must obtain the cost of the merchandise and leave a balance (gross margin) to cover expenses and net profit. In order for a balance to exist in the form of gross margin, the supermart must, of necessity, furnish services for which its customers are willing to pay. While a super does nothing to the fundamental form or shape of the goods, it does give them added value in the form of time, place, and ownership utility. For example, it enables butter produced in the summer in Wisconsin to be purchased and consumed by a family in New York in the winter. This measure of value added by the supermarket to the products it sells is its gross margin.

Margins differ within product lines and among individual supermarkets and various types of retailers. Markups also vary over time. It is the purpose to examine these facets in the remainder of this chapter.

Trends in Margins

The early supermarkets were able to operate on gross margins varying from 10 to 14 per cent of sales.[19] This was a considerable reduction from the generally accepted 19 to 20 per cent for the chain economy store and the independent grocers in the early 1930's.[20]

---

[19] Charles F. Phillips, "The Supermarket," *Harvard Business Review*, XVI, no. 2, Winter, 1938, p. 192.

[20] *United States* v. *The Great A. and P. Tea Company*, U.S. Circuit Court of Appeals, 7th district, Docket 9221, Records and Briefs, Vol. II, p. 162.

The Great Atlantic and Pacific Tea Company strove for a 12 per cent gross profit once it had adopted supermarket operation.[21]

(Industry studies on gross margin first were made in the period following World War II. The magazine, *Super Market Merchandising*, conducted an industry-wide survey in the years 1947 to 1956 and reported that the average gross margins were: [22]

Year	% sales
1947	18.2
1948	17.7
1949	17.6
1950	17.7
1951	17.4
1952	17.9
1953	18.4
1954	18.8
1955	19.0
1956	19.6

The food chain supermarkets indicated gross margins that ranged from 18.11 to 20.50 per cent of sales, as shown by the data in Table 4-2.)

Statistics in Table 5-2 comprise the gross margins for selected supermarket chains. The 1956 range was 16.27 for Shaffer Stores Company and 22.98 for A. J. Bayless Markets, Incorporated. The general trend of gross margins for the selected chains has been upward in line with that for the industry. For example, between 1950 and 1956 the gross margin for Colonial Stores, Incorporated, rose from 17.7 to 18.7 as a percentage of sales; for Food Fair Stores, Incorporated, from 17.1 to 18.7; and for Market Basket, Incorporated, from 18.8 to 19.6. The much publicized Schwegmann Brothers, Incorporated, New Orleans, constantly strove for a gross margin of only 10 per cent, but in recent years legal difficulties in connection with fair trade laws have forced it upward.[23]

---

[21] *Ibid.*

[22] These statistics from 1947 through 1951 are from the yearly surveys published in the May editions, 1948 through 1952, respectively, of *Super Market Merchandising*. Statistics for 1952 through 1956 are from the yearly surveys published in August 1953 through 1957 editions of *Super Market Merchandising*.

[23] "Schwegmann Bros., Inc.," *Business Week*, no. 1136, June 9, 1951, p. 120.

Forces Behind Increases in Margins

Four movements have been present since the 1930's, particularly since World War II, which have tended to force gross margins upward.

TABLE 5-2 *

Gross Margin, Expense, and Net Profit (Before Taxes) as a Percentage of Sales for Selected Supermarket Chains for the Year 1956.

Company	Gross margin	Expense	Net profit
American Stores Co.	17.72	15.15	2.57
A. J. Bayless Markets, Inc.	22.98	17.75	5.23
Century Food Markets Co.	20.54	18.59	1.95
Colonial Stores, Inc.	18.68	15.94	2.74
Daitch Crystal Dairies, Inc.	19.91	18.36	1.55
Fisher Bros., Co.	17.01	14.23	2.78
Food Fair Stores, Inc.	18.68	15.24	3.44
Food Mart, Inc.	19.33	15.88	3.45
Grand Union Co.	19.68	16.99	2.69
Jewel Tea Co., Inc.	19.32	15.48	3.84
Kroger Co.	17.83	15.52	2.31
Lucky Stores, Inc.	20.92	17.36	3.56
Market Basket	19.63	16.34	3.29
Purity Stores, Ltd.	18.46	16.09	2.37
Safeway Stores, Inc.	17.75	15.07	2.68
Shaffer Stores Co.	16.27	15.01	1.26
Shopping Bag Food Stores	22.22	19.34	2.88
Sunrise Supermarkets Corp.	18.60	16.20	2.40
Thriftimart, Inc.	16.54	13.77	2.77
Weingarten, J., Inc.	19.84	17.13	2.71

* Calculated from statistics contained in *Supermarket News Food Industries Financial Manual* (New York: Fairchild Publications, Inc., 1957).

1. The first is a tendency during and since the postwar era to expand into nonfood lines which earn a higher markup than grocery products. For example, health and beauty aids are handled at about 28 to 31 per cent gross margin as shown by the statistics in Table

5-3. Toys and certain of the soft goods are handled at about 30 per cent markup. Arrangements with rack jobbers return to the super about 25 to 35 per cent of the selling price. Moreover, many of the nonfood lines are fair traded.[24]

2. Second is a tendency for families to purchase better and more convenient kinds of food products. Per capita consumption of meat and fresh produce has increased. While margins vary depending upon store policies, meat returns a gross margin of about 17 to 22 per cent and produce from about 25 to 31 per cent, as shown by the data in Table 5-3. Frozen foods, including prepared dinners, currently account for about 5 per cent of supermarket sales and re-

TABLE 5-3

Gross Margins in Supermarkets by Major Product Lines.

Product	Food Town study [*]	Super Valu study [†]
Meat	16.9%	21.3%
Produce	25.4	30.8
Frozen foods	22.2	20.3
Bakery	18.0	17.8
Paper products	23.9	23.4
Health and beauty aids	27.7	31.3
Food specialties	24.9	23.9
Beer and wine	26.3	
Toys	. . .	29.5

[*] "The Foodtown Study," *Progressive Grocer*, XXXIV, no. 1, January, 1955, p. 43.

[†] *Facts in Grocery Distribution* (New York: Progressive Grocer, 1958), p. F–18.

turn from 20 to 22 per cent gross margin. Stores incur added expense for stocking and displaying the assortment of frozen foods. Per capita use of paper products has mounted, and these products gross from 23 to 24 per cent margin.

3. Third is the fact that supermarkets in recent years have adopted

[24] Milton Alexander, "Where We Stand on Non-food Merchandising," *Progressive Grocer*, XXXI, no. 10, October, 1952, p. 200.

merchandising policies in line with consumer desires and habits that necessitate more diversified inventories. Merchandise turnover, which is a vital factor in determining retail price, has decreased. General price policy in supers has been for the fastest movers, usually products essential to the health and well being of the family, to carry the lowest margins. As sales movement declines, percentage of margin usually increases. This realistic pricing philosophy builds volume, strengthens consumer confidence in the store, and at the same time produces a satisfactory competitive over-all store margin.[25]

4. Fourth is a tendency to increase customer services and comfort—"trade up" the supers. This trend has resulted in larger expenses and, in turn, higher margins.[26]

Comparison of Margins with Other Retailers

Although these four pressures have tended to force gross margins upward, supermarkets still operate at a lower over-all markup than the chain economy stores and the small independent grocers of the 1920's. In comparison with other types of retailers, few maintain such low markups as the supermarket, as shown by the statistics in Table 5-4. Department and variety stores have both maintained margins of over 35 per cent or about double that for the supermarket. The nature of the products sold, competitive conditions, and policies of manufacturers, wholesalers, and retailers are a few of the factors that have a bearing on the margins. But the fact that the super could operate on such a narrow margin influenced other retailers. Those who handled the same nonfood products easily sold in supers attempted to improve their competitive position.

The average 1957 margin for a small, combination grocery and meat market was 18.25 per cent of sales.[27] This was lower than the

---

[25] "The Food Town Study," *Progressive Grocer*, XXXIV, no. 1, January, 1955, p. 43.

[26] Actually margins could have been left the same and profits reduced. This has not been the case, as will be seen in the next section on expenses.

[27] *Facts in Grocery Distribution* (New York: Progressive Grocer, 1958), p. F–17.

margin for its counterpart in the 1920's. Supermarket margins, as shown by the data in Table 4-2, ranged from 18.11 to 20.50 for chain units. Because of differences in products handled by various supers, no attempt can be made to compare their margins with those for

TABLE 5-4

Gross Margin for Various Kinds of
Retail Establishments for the Year 1954.

Type of store	Gross margin as % of sales
Department store	36.5 [a]
Drug store	33.2 [b]
Furniture store (large)	39.0 [c]
Hardware store	29.5 [d]
Meat market	21.4 [e]
Supermarket	18.8 [f]
Variety store	37.7 [g]

[a] Controllers Congress, *1954 Merchandise and Operating Results* (New York: National Retail Dry Goods Association, 1955), p. 1.

[b] Lilly Digest (Indianapolis: Eli Lilly & Co., 1955), p. 21.

[c] *1954 Furniture Operating Experiences* (Chicago: National Retail Furniture Association, 1955), p. 5.

[d] "1954 Retail Hardware Survey," *Hardware Retailer,* June, 1955, p. 77.

[e] *Meat Markets—Operating Results in 1954* (New York: Dun & Bradstreet, Inc., 1954), p. 2.

[f] *Facts in Grocery Distribution* (New York: Progressive Grocer, 1957), p. F–15.

[g] "Harvard Report on Variety Chains," *Chain Store Age,* Variety Store Managers Issue, XXXI, no. 8, August, 1955, p. 65.

the small combination market. The comparison should be by product classes. For staple food items, supers continue to be the price leaders.

This trend of rising gross margins has resulted from policies of supers endeavoring to furnish goods and services desired by the consumer. However, the supermarket managements must not fail to realize that they have an Achilles heel in rising gross margins necessitated by increased expenses. Since 1957 the full-line but limited-brand "vest pocket" super has gained popularity in the Southeast,

Southwest, and in some areas of the Pacific Coast.[28] These stores, with from 2,000 to 4,000 sq ft of space, sell every type but not every size or brand of product at low prices. This and other innovations in retailing must be watched by supermarket management.

Margins by Product Lines

While the over-all gross margin of a supermarket averages about 18 to 20 per cent of the sales dollar, individual departments and products within these departments have gross profit percentages and dollar gross margins that vary widely from the store average. Furthermore, sales by product lines and the resulting dollar margins are not equally important. For example, the 1957 Harvard Study of Food Chains disclosed the following product-line sales of the medium-sized food chains:

Item	*% total sales*
Groceries	66.2
Produce	9.9
Meat	23.9

In turn, these same food chains had product-line, gross-margin percentages as follows:

Groceries	17.4
Produce	26.9
Meat	20.8

The percentages of total-dollar gross margin earned by product classes for these same stores were:

Groceries	61.3
Produce	13.5
Meat	25.0

Therefore all three product classes did not contribute equally to the store margin of 18.9 per cent. For example, if these percentages were applied to a store doing $1,000,000 volume, the dollar gross margin for the entire store would be $189,379. However, produce sales

---

[28] *Facts in Grocery Distribution, op. cit.,* p. F–4.

would total only $99,000 but would return $24,479 gross margin. Thus, while produce sales were only 9.9 per cent of the total volume, they returned 13.5 per cent of the store's dollar gross profit.

A further breakdown of margins of grocery items suggested by *Progressive Grocer* in its widely distributed margin card include the following:

Margin %	Item
9 or less	Butter, coffee, sugar
10–15	Eggs, cereals, soup, soap
16–19	Dog food, flour mixes, syrup
20–22	Catsup, frozen food, canned fruits
23–25	Jelly, olives, paper towels
26–28	Pie filling, waxes, brooms, pectin
29 and over	Drug sundries, napkins, facial tissue

These margin percentages illustrate the wide variation in gross profit among different products. Gross profit percentage is a function of the competitive situation in the respective market areas, volume and resulting turnover of each item, handling and display costs, and the nature of the product. A super generally must price its products competitively, and thus it is limited in its control over specific product margins. In addition, if a product such as coffee has a high turnover and sells in volume, the margin percentage may be small, but the total-dollar gross margin may be large. A premium margin normally is placed on products that are bulky and difficult to display, such as brooms and paper goods.

Improvement in Supermarket Margins

Gross margin is the difference between the selling price and the cost of the goods sold. Management is under constant pressure to improve store margins in order to increase the profit possibilities. It can do this by holding selling prices constant and reducing cost of sales, raising selling prices generally and holding cost of sales constant, raising selling prices generally and lowering cost of sales, or concentrating effort on selling products which normally have the largest gross margin percentages.

Any activity on the part of management that can reduce the cost of the merchandise which the super sells can increase the gross margin. That is why scientific purchasing has played such a vital role in the development of this industry. Astute purchasing is the heart of a super's merchandising strategy. Management also must strive to keep cost of sales down through close control of inventory in order to prevent losses or shrinkages from accruing. Losses that appear in inventory increase the cost of goods sold during that period and thus reduce the dollar margin. Losses occur as a result of:

1. Failure to get the merchandise that was purchased. This involves proper inspection.

2. Excessive discounts offered to employees on merchandise bought for their own consumption.

3. Pilferage on the part of customers, personnel, or suppliers. This can vary from 0.35 per cent to 0.50 per cent of the sales dollar and thus increase the cost of sales by a like amount.[29]

4. Spoilage or shrinkage of merchandise, particularly in produce and meat departments.

The competitive situation in the respective trading area of a super has a bearing on prices charged. An individual store normally may find it difficult to raise prices above competition unless the store is differentiated in some manner. But the merchandising skill of the store executives can augment margins. Special promotions or sales can be used more effectively to draw customers who buy related merchandise not on sale and which carries larger margin percentages. A store executive may be able to merchandise specific products to advantage through knowledge of local factors and flexible operations. A product in short supply in the market may be raised in price and return a higher margin. Merchandising skills must be developed and employed to plan operations more completely, take advantage of special events, promote seasonal merchandise sales and display merchandise more effectively.

[29] These figures were obtained from a letter from Mr. G. L. Mattei, District Manager, William J. Burns International Detective Agency, to the Super Market Institute on January 22, 1958.

Managerial ability is important to make certain that selling prices are not understated. This can occur if checkers undercharge for merchandise or do not record the sale of every item. Improperly marked merchandise can lower margins. It is vital to get the money due the super. The proper combination of merchandising and managerial skills on the part of the store executives, coupled with skillful buying, can improve the gross margin in a super.

SUMMARY

Merchandise "well bought" can be sold at a profit. This is a cardinal rule in the supermarket industry which purchases over $20 billion in merchandise each year. The term "well bought" means the purchase of merchandise that meets the needs and wants of the customer and which can be sold at a price that reflects good value.

Trends within the industry toward larger stores and more stores under a common ownership, coupled with the development of group purchasing (the buying committee), have given the industry advantageous bargaining power with suppliers. Furthermore, the wide use of the buying committee has resulted in a more unified merchandising program—greater coordination of buying, selling, advertising and promotion. The role of the buyer has changed. Although he performs executive tasks, he must also be a communication expert, taking the manufacturer's message to the committee. This impersonal buying has forced food manufacturers to revamp their selling programs.

In turn, the margins in the supermarket industry have tended upward. This has been brought about by four fundamental forces present in the industry. There has been a tendency during and since the postwar era to expand into nonfood lines that earn a higher markup than grocery products. Second is the tendency for families to purchase better and more convenient kinds of food products that carry a wider margin. Third, supermarkets have adopted merchandising policies in line with consumer desires and habits that necessitate more diversified inventories to be handled. This has lowered turnover and resulted in higher margins. Finally, there has been a tendency to increase customer services and comfort. This trend has resulted in greater expenses and, in turn, higher margins. Yet, the supermarket continues to afford the consumer values in its respective area substantially better than those offered by other forms of retailing.

6 | EXPENSES AND PROFITS

INTRODUCTION

The preceding chapter examined (1) the buying practices of supermarkets and (2) the principles involved in the establishment of gross margins. The purpose of this section is to continue the study of the principles of supermarketing within the framework of an operating statement. Attention in this chapter is focused on operating expense and net profit relationships.

OPERATING EXPENSES

The third step in the plan to identify characteristics of supermarket operation that set it apart from other forms of retailing is to study expense relationships.

At the outset, reference is made to the data in Tables 4-2 and 4-3, which list detailed expenses as a percentage of sales for supermarket food chains and for an independent supermart. Other expense ratios can be found in Table 6-1 which presents operating data from the annual surveys conducted by the Super Market Institute among its members for the years 1954 through 1958. Akin to other retailers, the major expense items of supermarkets are for store payroll, administrative salaries, occupancy or real estate, advertising, and store supplies.

Trends in Supermarket Total Operating Expense

Yearly surveys conducted by the staff of *Super Market Merchandising* for 1947 through 1956 indicate that operating expenses as a percentage of sales were: [1]

[1] The statistics for the years 1947 to 1950 are from the yearly surveys published in the May editions, 1948 through 1951, respectively, of *Super Market*

Year	% sales
1947	14.8
1948	14.9
1949	13.9
1950	14.3
1951	15.4
1952	15.7
1953	16.1
1954	15.8
1955	16.1
1956	16.9

These data are comparable with the total expense statistics of the Super Market Institute figure exchange data shown in Table 6-1. This organization reported in its 1958 study that total operating ex-

TABLE 6-1 *

Operating Statistics of Selected Super Market Institute
Members as a Percentage of Sales
for the Years 1954 to 1958.

	1958 †	1957	1956	1955	1954
Sales	100.00	100.00	100.00	100.00	100.00
Cost of sales	81.88	81.89	.82.06	82.24	82.63
Gross profit	18.12	18.11	17.94	17.76	17.37
Expense					
Store labor	10°%	6.87	7.10	7.08	7.16
Advertising	—	0.87	1.00	0.89	0.90
Store supply	—	0.88	0.88	0.80	0.80
Store rent and real estate . . .	—	1.12	1.07	1.07	1.01
Heat, light, power . .	—	0.50	0.50	0.48	0.47
All other expenses . .	—	5.80	5.41	5.05	4.38
Total expenses . .	16.19	16.04	15.96	15.37	14.72
Net profit ‡ . .	2.20	2.26	2.13	2.56	2.46

* *Facts in Grocery Distribution* (New York: Progressive Grocer, 1959), p. F–21.

† *The Super Market Industry Speaks* (Chicago: Super Market Institute, 1959), p. 17.

‡ These statements do not include other income and expense items. Therefore net profit cannot be added to total expense to obtain gross margin.

Merchandising. Data for 1951 through 1956 are found in the August editions, 1952 through 1957, respectively, of the same magazine.

penses ranged from 14.54 to 17.49 per cent of sales for the middle range of respondents and 16.19 per cent for the typical supermarket.[2]

The expense rates as a percentage of sales for certain supermarket chains for 1956 are shown in Table 5-2. These rates ranged from a low of 13.77 for Thriftimart, Incorporated, to a high of 19.34 for Shopping Bag Food Stores. The diversity of characteristics of stores within the industry, including the method of operation and lines stressed, had a direct bearing on these ratios.

The expense rate for supers in the postwar period was considerably larger than that for supermarkets in the late 1930's. And the expense trend each year has continued upward. The rise is attributed to improved customer shopping conveniences and services and to a higher percentage of sales expended for salaries and wages. It was not unusual for the expense rate of supers in the 1930's to average 10 to 11 per cent of sales.[3] In 1941 the entire supermarket operation of the A & P worked on a 10.51 expense ratio.[4] However, the expense rate for supers in recent years has still been lower than that for the grocery stores and combination markets, including the A & P economy stores of the early 1930's.

Comparison of Total Expense with Other Retailers

The general trend of total expense in a supermarket has shown consistent increase over the years. Yet, the supermart is still a low cost marketer when compared to other types of retailers. The total expense rate of the supermarket industry compared with that of the variety and department stores is substantially lower; in fact, it is about 50 per cent less, as illustrated by statistics in Table 6-2. Expenses vary according to the type of business, lines handled, and operational policies, to name but a few factors. But the low supermarket rate becomes even more significant when nonfood items that are stocked by similar stores, including supers, are considered.

[2] The middle-range figures are the values at the one-quarter and three-quarter points from the array of data listed, from the smallest to the largest. Extremes in the top and bottom quarters are thus omitted.

[3] *United States v. The Great Atlantic and Pacific Tea Company*, U.S. Circuit Court of Appeals, 7th District, Docket 9221, Records and Briefs, Vol. II, p. 194.

[4] See Table 8-7.

TABLE 6-2

Operating Expenses as a Percentage of Sales for Various
Types of Retail Stores for the Year 1954.

Type of store	Expense % of sales
Department store	33.50 [a]
Drug store	27.80 [b]
Furniture store (large)	37.44 [c]
Hardware store	27.55 [d]
Meat market	20.00 [e]
Supermarket	15.80 [f]
Variety store	32.90 [g]

[a] Controllers Congress, *1954 Merchandise and Operating Results* (New York: National Retail Dry Goods Association, 1955), p. 1.

[b] *Lilly Digest* (Indianapolis: Eli Lilly & Co., 1955), p. 21.

[c] *1954 Furniture Operating Experiences* (Chicago: National Retail Furniture Association, 1955), p. 5.

[d] "1954 Retail Hardware Survey," *Hardware Retailer*, June, 1955, p. 77.

[e] *Meat Markets—Operating Results in 1954* (New York: Dun & Bradstreet, Inc., 1954), p. 2.

[f] *Facts in Food Distribution* (New York: Progressive Grocer, 1955), p. F–17.

[g] "Harvard Report on Variety Chains," *Chain Store Age*, Variety Store Managers Issue, XXXI, no. 8, August, 1955, p. 52.

Comparison of Major Expense Items by Retailers

Data in Table 6-3 present major expense breakdowns for certain types of retail stores, including supermarkets. The four most significant expense items confronting retailers, as shown by the statistics in Table 6-3 are (1) employees' salaries, (2) owners' or administrative salaries, (3) occupancy, and (4) advertising, publicity, and promotion. In almost every instance the supermarket was able, more than any other type of retailer shown, to operate at a considerably lower expense rate as a percentage of sales.)

Owner or administrative expense in supermarkets was 1.92 per cent of sales in 1954 compared with 7.7 per cent in drugstores, 5.8 per cent in variety stores, and 7.8 per cent in department stores for the year 1954. Simply, supermarkets are geared for large-volume operation, and they require a small percentage of the sales dollar for supervision. Operations are routinized, sales are largely on a self-service cash basis, and a high degree of division of labor is obtained. Efficiencies through central management in chain supermarts have been attained. Management at the store level in chains generally is paid a fixed salary plus a small percentage of sales above a set goal. Local management emphasis is on volume.

Similarly, self-service, division of labor, and large-volume operation have kept employees' salaries as a percentage of sales smaller than those paid by most types of retailers, except the small stores where the owner does most of the work personally. In the larger

TABLE 6-3

Major Operating Expenses as a Percentage of Sales for
Certain Types of Retail Outlets.

Expense	Super-market [a]	Drug store [b]	Depart-ment store [c]	Variety store [d]	Hard-ware store [e]	Meat market [f] (complete or partial self-service)
Administration	0.78 to 1.26	7.70	18.40 [g]	17.50 [g]	17.75 [g]	6.40
Employees' salaries	5.24 to 5.89	10.60	—	—	—	6.40
Occupancy	0.82 to 1.01	2.40	6.10	5.90	2.45	2.70
Advertising, promotion, publicity	2.93 to 3.07 [h]	—	4.30	0.40	1.40	0.70

[a] *Facts in Grocery Distribution* (New York: Progressive Grocer, 1958), p. F–18.

[b] *Lilly Digest* (Indianapolis: Eli Lilly & Co., 1954), p. 62.

[c] Controllers Congress, *Merchandising and Operating Results* (New York: National Retail Dry Goods Association, 1955), p. 2.

[d] "Harvard Report on Variety Stores," *Chain Store Age*, Variety Store Managers Edition, August, 1955, p. 62.

[e] "1954 Retail Hardware Survey," *Hardware Retailer*, June, 1955, p. 77.

[f] *Meat Markets—Operating Results in 1954* (New York: Dun & Bradstreet, Inc., 1954).

[g] Administration and employees' salaries are included under one classification.

[h] This includes trading stamps of approximately 2 per cent of sales. Advertising expense alone for the 1954 typical super was reported at 0.87 to 1.02 per cent of sales. Only 36 per cent of the supers offer trading stamps.

super operations, personnel departments have been established to hire, train, set job descriptions, and determine promotion, transfer, and layoff policies. Most operations especially train the check-out girls through whom contact with the public is maintained. Not only are trained check-out girls more efficient from the use of equipment and error standpoints, but the consumer receives faster service. Variety and drugstores had employees' salaries expressed as a percentage of sales of 11 and 10.6 per cent, respectively, for 1954; supermarkets have averaged between 5 and 6 per cent. With only 55 per cent of department store employees active in selling, their compensation alone in 1954 was 7 per cent of sales.[5]

The low percentage expenditure for salaries and wages has been aided further by simplifying and eliminating work. Manufacturers perform some of the retail functions. Supermarkets are one of the few retailers that require manufacturers to do this. Baby food manufacturers and biscuit bakers, to name but two, have taken on such functions as ordering, stocking shelves, keeping merchandise clean, and arranging displays. Unions oppose this practice.

The policy of self-service obviously requires the customer to take over some of the functions of the clerk. Not only has this practice been successful in grocery operation (by definition, the grocery division of a supermarket must be self-service), but the principle has spread to other departments within the supermarket. In 1950 a study by the research staff of the Super Market Institute reported 8 per cent of its members operated completely self-service stores.[6] By 1958, 57 per cent of all supermarkets were on a completely self-service basis in all major departments.[7] The meat department is now fully self-service in 88 per cent of the supermarkets, with most of the remainder semi-self-service. Only 2 per cent of the meat departments are still operated on a complete service basis. The produce department is the principal division not operated on a full self-service basis.

[5] Controllers Congress, *1954 Merchandise and Operating Results* (New York: National Retail Dry Goods Association, 1955), p. 21.
[6] *The Super Market Industry Speaks* (Chicago: Super Market Institute, 1951), p. 17.
[7] *Ibid.*, 1959, Part II, p. 9.

Occupancy or real estate cost is the third significant expense item faced by retailers. This cost as a percentage of sales also favors the supermarket type of operation. Data in Table 6-3 indicate that the typical supermarket expended 0.82 to 1.02 cents out of every sales dollar for occupancy as compared with a minimum of 2.4 cents for all other types of stores. This does not mean necessarily that supermarkets obtain cheaper dollar rental. In some cases the super has been given a rental advantage where the mart is the key store in a shopping center. However, the low percentage of the sales dollar expended for rent primarily is the result of their policy to exploit customer traffic to the fullest so that increased volume can reduce rental expense as a percentage of sales.

Advertising, publicity, and promotion for a typical supermarket shown by the data in Table 6-3 ranged from 2.93 to 3.07 per cent of the sales dollar. Of this, advertising itself ranged from 0.87 to 1.04 per cent. Studies since 1950 made by the Super Market Institute indicate that slightly under 1 per cent of every sales dollar is spent for advertising. Expenditures by media are shown by the figures in Table 6-4. The over-all expenditure of less than 1 per cent of the

TABLE 6-4 *

Advertising Expenditures by Media for the Supermarket
Industry as a Percentage of Total Dollar
Ad Expenditures for the Year 1956.

Medium	% of total expenditure
Newspaper	67.0
General promotion (door prizes, civic drives, etc.)	7.5
Circulars	6.9
Television	6.6
Radio	4.9
Display posters	3.4
Direct mail	3.1
Magazines	0.6
Total	100.0

* "Where Advertising Dollars Went in 1956," *Super Market Merchandising*, XXII, no. 11, November, 1957, p. 68.

sales dollar is primarily for newspaper ads, which commanded 67 per cent of the ad funds. Supermarts compare favorably with department stores, which spend about 2.6 per cent of the sales dollar for newspaper costs alone.[8]

However, this figure of slightly less than 1 per cent of the sales dollar does not give a true picture of supermarket advertising volume because of the cooperative advertising deals offered supers, particularly the large chains. Food manufacturers have agreed to sponsor ads and have paid the cooperating store for its portion, frequently at the national newspaper rate. The local store can arrange for the ad and pay the media at the local rate. Thus supers have not only passed on to the manufacturer part of the advertising expense but in addition have found a source of added income as a result of the difference between the national and local media rates. On the average, the local rate is 50 per cent less than the national rate on weekday newspaper ads.[9] Supermarkets feel they are entitled to this allowance inasmuch as they perform some of the advertising function. Manufacturers' cooperative advertising and advertising allowances come under the Robinson-Patman Act, which holds in substance that whatever allowances a manufacturer offers to one dealer must be proportionally available to all other comparable dealers of that product in the same competitive market and must be a bona fide allowance for advertising and not merely an additional trade discount. Cooperative advertising with all its implications has created vast problems among food manufacturers, supermarkets, and publishers.

Trading stamps have become the largest promotion item in the supermarket industry. While not all the stores issue stamps, this expenditure in a typical super averages slightly above 2 per cent of the sales dollar. Other forms of promotion, publicity, and advertising are practiced by nonstamp stores; some have contended they sell for less than stamp stores.

[8] Controllers Congress, *1954 Merchandise and Operating Results, op. cit.,* p. 2.
[9] Otto Kleppner, *Advertising Procedure* (Englewood Cliffs, N. J.: Prentice-Hall, Inc., 1950), p. 297.

Governmental agencies, universities, and business have endeavored to study this nebulous concept of trading stamp impact on
margins, prices, and restraint of trade. Factors for successful use
of stamps have been discussed before.[10] No clear-cut results are
available. Some supers have found the needed volume to use this
tool successfully and have spread fixed and semifixed costs over
larger sales. In addition, some stamp users also shifted from other
kinds of advertising or promotional effort. This cyclical promotion
tool appears to have passed its zenith at this time, however, with a
drop in its use reported for the second consecutive year. About 35
per cent of the supers used stamps in 1958 according to *Progressive
Grocer*. The failure of supers to attain needed volume increase apparently was a major factor in the end of this boom. Stamp-giving
supers have made no volume headway at the expense of the nonstamp supermarkets in the past three years, as shown by the data
in Table 6-5. The movement could be revived if one or several of
the large chains adopted their use.

TABLE 6-5 *

How Stamps Affect Supermarket Sales.

Years	Average % sales gain in stores giving stamps	Average % sales gain in stores not giving stamps
1954 vs. 1953	18	12
1955 vs. 1954	25	12
1956 vs. 1955	13	14
1957 vs. 1956	14	14
1958 vs. 1957	10	12

* *Facts in Grocery Distribution* (New York: Progressive Grocer, 1959), p.
F–11.

Functional Expense Analysis

Diversity exists in the operating statistics of member stores of the
supermarket industry owing to size of stores, size of concerns, merchandise handled, location, method of operation, and merchandising

[10] The use of trading stamps was discussed in Chapter 4.

policies. Still, operating data from surveys and studies made by the four major statistical sources in this industry—Super Market Institue Figure Exchange, *Super Market Merchandising, Progressive Grocer,* and the Harvard Study of Food Chains—are generally in accord with each other. In the postwar period, total operating expenses have been on the increase in the supermarket industry.

It is imperative to know in what areas and for what reasons expenses are increasing. This can be ascertained by two basic types of distribution cost analyses. One is the familiar examination of operating statements, in which expenses are listed and then analyzed by the nature of cost items or the object of expenditure. Reference is made to the operating statistics of selected food chains shown in Table 4-2. Expenses expressed as a percentage of sales are itemized by the nature of the cost such as payroll, real estate, and supplies. Changes in specific items over the years can be detected. (For example, data in Table 4-2 indicate that payroll, real estate costs, fixture and equipment costs, and advertising expenses in recent years have been taking a larger share of the sales dollar.)

These increases in expenses could be attributed to added functions or activities assumed by the supermarket chains. Therefore a second type of distribution cost study was undertaken in the Harvard Report, namely, an analysis of functional operations performed. In the department store field, the Controllers' Congress of the National Retail Dry Goods Association has set up five major functional divisions of expense: administration, occupancy, publicity, buying, and selling and delivery. The classification set forth in the Harvard Study of Food Chains includes the store or selling function, warehousing or storage function, transportation, and administration and general expense. These functions are of importance for food chains faced with store, warehouse, and transportation problems. An individual super may not find this breakdown of value.

Changes in these functions over the years can be detected by a study of the data in Table 6-6. A breakdown of these classifications by the specific expense items for the year 1958 is shown by the sta-

tistics in Table 6-7. Food chains have kept their storage, transportation, and general and administrative costs in line from 1950 to 1958.
In fact, efficiencies in the transportation function are shown by the
statistics, with transportation costs dropping slightly almost yearly
from 1.07 cents out of the sales dollar in 1950 to 0.91 cents in 1958.
Lower transportation costs are accounted for by fewer and larger
stores better located geographically. Warehousing costs have been
aided by better handling, modern equipment, new buildings, and
supervision. The larger sales over which to spread overhead have
benefited the ratios of general and administration expenses.

It is in conjunction with the stores, the selling function, that expenses have mounted. Store expense rose from 10.85 per cent of
the sales dollar in 1950 to 13.58 per cent in 1958, as shown by the
data in Table 6-6.

In turn, the specific store expenses that principally have accounted
for this increase were store payroll, real estate costs or occupancy,
equipment costs, advertising, and supplies. Payrolls have increased
faster than sales. This results from higher hourly wages, primarily
for the same type of work, in line with the industrial wage-rate pattern. It does not appear as though the industry has added a different
quality of labor performing new and specialized services which require a boost in wages per hour; for example, in areas such as pre-
packing meat. Real estate costs as a percentage of sales have risen
as a result of higher store construction costs, mounting interest rates,
increased real estate taxes, more elaborate stores, larger parking lots,
and higher land costs. Even when a super does not own its own
buildings, it faces increased rental charges for new locations inasmuch as the owner passes on increased costs. Similarly, new equipment not only tends to make older fixtures obsolete but costs more
than the item replaced so that depreciation charges are higher. The
sharp increase of advertising expenses is attributed primarily to
certain respondents of the survey adopting trading stamps in this
period. Other factors that have led to increased advertising costs are
higher space rates, increased use of radio and TV time, and larger

TABLE 6-6 *

Functional Expense Analysis of Selected Food Chains as a Percentage of Sales for the Years 1950 to 1958.

	1958	1957	1956	1955	1954	1953	1952	1951	1950
Gross margin	19.51	19.38	19.08	18.43	18.87	18.76	17.97	17.50	18.51
Expenses									
Store	13.58	13.22	12.85	12.30	11.83	11.51	11.01	10.80	10.85
Warehouse	1.12	1.11	1.15	1.15	1.17	1.19	1.14	1.17	1.17
Transportation	0.91	0.92	0.95	0.99	1.01	1.02	1.03	1.03	1.07
General and overhead	1.85	1.90	2.01	1.96	2.07	2.15	1.99	2.00	2.02
Total	17.46	17.15	16.96	16.40	16.08	15.87	15.17	15.00	15.11
Net operating profit	2.05	2.23	2.12	2.03	2.79	2.89	2.80	2.50	3.40

* Wilbur B. England, *Operating Results of Food Chains in 1958* (Cambridge, Mass.: Harvard Business School, Bulletin No. 156, 1959), p. 8.

TABLE 6-7 *

Itemized Expenses Classified by Functions for Selected Food Chains as a Percentage of Sales for the Year 1958.

Item	Store	Warehouse	Trans-portation	Adminis-trative and general
Payroll	6.86	0.54	0.21	1.41
Real estate cost	1.27	0.16	0.01	0.06
Equipment expense	1.10	0.09	0.16	0.11
Utilities	0.54	0.04	—	0.01
Supplies	0.91	0.01	0.05	0.09
Advertising	2.39	—	—	—
Travel	0.01	—	—	0.09
Insurance	0.16	0.02	—	0.03
Taxes	0.37	0.07	0.02	0.05
Services purchased	—	—	0.16	—
Miscellaneous	0.32	0.04	0.01	0.26
Total	13.93	0.97	0.62	2.11

(handwritten annotations: "9.02 ADD FOR TOTALS")

* Wilbur B. England, *Operating Results of Food Chains in 1958* (Cambridge, Mass.: Harvard Business School, Bulletin No. 156, 1959), p. 20.

promotional costs involved in the introduction of new stores. Furthermore, nonstamp users have intensified their promotional activities to retain their respective market shares.)

Increased costs of supplies have resulted from higher paper costs, changes in store packaging policies, and wider use of office supplies such as punch cards. As a result, supermarket food chains have been forced to increase gross margins; but this increase has not been sufficient to offset higher costs, with the result that net operating profit before taxes has tended to decrease for these chains.

Although these results are for food chains, similar results can be assumed for smaller concerns and independent supermarkets which face the same slowly rising costs of doing business. Yearly surveys conducted by the Super Market Institute indicate that the majority of members report encountering continually higher costs over the past decade.

A third type of distribution cost study, namely the manner in which the distribution effort is applied, is considered in the next section under expense control. This involves expense studies of product lines, customers, or other segments of the business and is exemplified by a study to determine net operating profit for the dairy department.

Expense Control

The supermarket industry has been faced almost since its inception with gradually rising costs of operation. Concomitant with the rise in costs has been added services furnished and activities assumed by this industry. However, in a narrow profit-margin field such as this, the trend could prove to be especially dangerous if increased costs resulted from services not desired or if no improvement in services were offered. In time the supermarket conceivably could lose its competitive position or see its profits erode if consumers believed the value added to the goods by the supers was not worth the prices charged. Marketing is dynamic in nature; nothing is so certain as change. Therefore control of operating expenses is vital.

The wide diversity among industry members makes it difficult to generalize as to policies adopted to gain effective control. However, the following practices have been instituted to some degree by members of the industry in an effort to keep expenses under control.

Expense budgeting. A budget is a plan of expected future operations. A complete budget should include anticipated sales, margins, expenses, and profits. It should serve as a guide or a control mechanism for management. A budget is not only a tool for large organizations but also a useful device for the small concern. The activity of preparing a budget is at least as important as the budget document that results because the activity itself forces formalized planning. This may be even more significant for the smaller concern, which is often less likely than a large organization to formalize its plans. An example of the budget program of one chain is shown below. This program also can be adopted with some modification by the smaller concern.

In the short run, at the most a year, an expense budget can serve as a valuable tool to supermarket management. It can point out discrepancies between actual and anticipated results, illustrate the need for adequate records, and show the information that must be

Outline of Budgeting Procedure *

Step 1: Data to be furnished to the divisions.

DATA	SOURCE
a. Last year's experience for period to be covered	Accounting department
b. Over-all tonnage goals for existing stores	General manager
c. Store expansion and renovation plans including target dates	General manager
d. Commodity price forecast	Market research department

Step 2: Preparation of divisional budgets.
  a. Each division head shall submit to the chief budget officer budget figures broken down by department and by account classifications as listed on a standard budget form. An appropriate text explaining the bases for the budget projection is to accompany the form when submitted. The budget figures, for the present, shall be on a quarterly basis. Sales, gross profit, salaries, and wages shall be further broken down by four-week periods.
  b. The chief budget officer shall review the divisional budgets, consolidate them into an over-all company budget, and submit it with adequate explanatory text to the general manager.
Step 3: Approval of budget by general manager.
  a. The general manager will review the budget and text and will indicate such modification of plans as he deems advisable.
  b. The approved budget shall be presented to the division heads at a special meeting chairmanned by the general manager.
Step 4: Evaluation of results versus plans.
  a. Each division head shall prepare and submit to the chief budget officer a review and evaluation of the division's results versus plans on a four-week and quarterly basis.
  b. The chief budget officer shall prepare a consolidated review and submit it to the general manager, who after studying it, will indicate

* Lloyd B. Tarlin, "How a Super Market Chain Started Budgeting," *Super Market Merchandising*, XXI, no. 7, July, 1955, p. 65.

what adjustments and action are to be taken to achieve the desired goals. The general manager will choose the time and means for conveying his views to the division heads.

readily available to make merchandising decisions. It can make store managers on the firing line cost-conscious. It can aid in the movement toward decentralization of management by illustrating the need for profits as well as volume. While the supermarket is geared to volume operation, top management does not appear to have entrusted sufficient responsibility to store managers.

Establishment of standards. More and more the management of a super needs guide posts by which to judge marketing efficiency. Some of the standards already developed include:

Sales per square foot of selling space
Tons of merchandise handled in warehouse operation per man-hour
Sales per employee
Transactions handled per check-out stand per hour
Labor turnover
Analysis of sales per day of week and per hour of the day
Average sale per customer
Expense per linear foot of display space
Itemized expenses expressed as a percentage of sales
Cost of handling various product lines
Sales velocity by item
Profit per item

For example, various company and industry standards are published in trade magazines and by the trade association Super Market Institute. A survey of the industry in 1957 revealed that the average sale per customer was $4.85, and average weekly sales per square foot of selling area were $3.00.[11] A study of warehouse costs disclosed that from 1947 to 1956, tons of merchandise handled per

[11] "Super Market Institute Mid-Year Gives Hard Facts on Markets," *Super Market Merchandising*, XXII, no. 1, January, 1957, p. 101.

man-hour rose from 1.06 to 1.87 tons.[12] In the 1958 study of operations conducted by the Super Market Institute, it was disclosed that sales per full-time employee equivalent averaged $41,200, or 4 per cent higher than 1957.[13] This figure is based on all employees in a company as well as the assumption that two part-time employees are equivalent to one full-time worker. Sales per man-hour were $22.97, compared with $21.66 a year earlier (Typical sales per square foot of selling area were $3.71 a week compared with $3.77 in 1957.)

Akin to the setting of standards is the problem of effective use of labor, the major expense item. Concerns have made job analyses, set up job descriptions, and developed division of labor to a high degree. Efforts have been made to reduce employee turnover.

Fixed cost-volume relationship. From its inception the supermarket has been geared to volume operation. Store managers have been rewarded by salary incentives for developing volume, with the usual arrangement being a fixed salary plus a percentage of sales above a predetermined amount. Large volume has been its basic tenet so that the multitude of fixed costs which are present can be spread over a more substantial dollar sales. The fixed costs are not reduced dollarwise, but when expressed as a percentage of a larger sales volume, they appear as a lower ratio and of lesser importance. The whole concept of profitable use of trading stamps as a promotional tool was suited for supers because it was predicated on increased volume so that fixed costs such as rent, insurance, fuel, depreciation, telephone, and other utilities could be spread over a larger volume. Simply, a super faced with a contractual rental obligation of $10,000 per year while transacting a $1,000,000 volume can reduce its rental as a percentage of sales from 1 per cent to ½ per cent if sales can be doubled. However, as vital as this principle is, emphasis also should be placed on more responsibility at the store level for expense control. This necessitates higher caliber, better educated, and more skilfully trained managers.

[12] "How to Fight Costs and Win," *Super Market Merchandising*, XXIII, no. 4, April, 1958, p. 64.
[13] *Super Market Industry Speaks, op. cit.*, 1959, p. 17.

Cost reduction. In supermarkets, reduction of expenses has been centered in six major areas. These include labor, warehouse and transportation, general operations, store department operations, back room, and construction maintenance. These divisions are more suitable for expense analysis of both large and small supermarket concerns than are the functional divisions set forth by the Harvard Study of Food Chains. Store operators who desire a comprehensive check list of 119 ways to reduce costs are referred to Appendix A.

Labor is the major expense item in a retail store. All executives in the firm must be in favor of a sound personnel program in order to obtain the greatest productivity from the employees. Every supervisory person must be sold on the idea of labor performance. Care must be taken in the selection of workers. Employees should be trained for their respective tasks. If management expects to obtain the superior profits of effective merchandising, then store managers and key personnel must be trained to be merchandisers. Whatever is expected of the workers should be transmitted in the form of work schedules, which should include a man-hour program and the payroll percentage of sales of each department. This is the result of job analysis. The desired goals of productivity should be set forth. Every effort should be expended to maintain interest and show the progress being made. The employees should be made part of a team effort. Rewards should be commensurate with performance.

The original premises of self-service in supermarket operation substantially reduced labor expense. It brought the customer "into the act" by taking over some of the functions of the clerk. Since then, self-service has spread to most departments of the super. Another factor that reduced labor expense was the requirement that manufacturers perform some of the retail functions such as ordering, stocking shelves, keeping merchandise clean, and arranging displays. Finally, supers have passed on to the customer some of the carry-out and delivery activities. For example, in many areas customers can cart their purchases home free or pay extra to have them delivered by an external delivery concern. In either instance, no entry appears in the expense records of the supermarket. The decision rests with the customer as to whether it is to be a cost to the consumer. In a department store, however, delivery appears in the store records as a cost.

Warehouse and transportation costs have been subject to intensive study to determine optimum size and layout of warehouses, order-handling systems, routing, and scheduling. The number and type of tractors and trailers, if any, must be scrutinized to obtain maximum use. Another facet open for review is the use of mechanical loaders to stock merchandise on shelves.

General operations embrace systems and devices to make the administration of the store more efficient. These range from a study of bag sizes for packing customer purchases in order to eliminate the odd sizes, to a review of insurance in force by a consulting firm.

Store department operations include systems, devices, and routines to make the operation of an individual department more efficient. In the produce department, for example, racks for display can be filled substantially quicker by the use of two hands rather than one. Or, in the meat department, specific sizes of cellophane or other wraps should be established and only those sizes should be kept on hand.

Back-room expenses include the behind-the-scenes costs. These can best be kept in hand by centering responsibility in one person and keeping that individual or a replacement for him there at all times. This assures greater productivity as well as reducing inventory shortages.

Construction and maintenance costs include expenses involved in modernization, repair, and maintenance of facilities. These range from protection of shopping carts, by assuring their proper use, to the channeling of all orders for equipment servicing through central purchasing at headquarters.

Distribution costs studies should be conducted in these six major areas of expense control to make certain maximum efficiency of operations is being obtained.

PROFIT

In the preceding section, the operating expenses of a supermarket were examined. It was shown that management in this industry faces a severe challenge from constantly rising costs that are tending to erode profits. The latter—profit—is the residue left from total sales after the goods sold and the operating expenses are taken into account. The term *profit* or *net profit* refers to earnings before income taxes. Profits before taxes are used in order to discern the operating status without having to consider the changing income-tax structure.

Trends in Net Profit

There are three major reasons for going into business, namely, altruistic purposes, desire for power, and profit. Of these, the major motive is profit. The results of yearly surveys conducted by the staff of *Super Market Merchandising* for 1947 through 1956 indicated that the average profit of the reporting supermarkets as a percentage of sales was: [14]

Year	% sales
1947	3.7
1948	3.7
1949	2.8
1950	3.4
1951	2.0
1952	2.2
1953	2.2
1954	3.0
1955	2.9
1956	2.7

Net profits expressed as a percentage of sales for the selected supermarket chains in 1956 are shown in Table 5-2 to range from a low of 1.3 per cent for Shaffer Stores Company, a Pennsylvania chain, to a high of 5.2 per cent for A. J. Bayless Markets, Incorporated, an Arizona chain.[15] For the years in the postwar period, the rate of return for the companies has ranged generally from 2 to 5 per cent

---

[14] These statistics are from the yearly surveys published in May editions, 1948 through 1951, respectively, of *Super Market Merchandising*. Statistics for 1952 through 1956 are from the yearly studies published in August editions, 1953 through 1957, respectively, of *Super Market Merchandising*.

[15] Diversity of ownership and operating policy within the industry plus non-standardized accounting practices have resulted in wide variation in the reported net profits of individual companies. The principal variation has been in the methods of reporting returns to the owners; that is, whether it be reported as salaries or profit.

of sales; statistics from these selected companies generally indicate a fluctuating but slightly decreasing earnings trend measured as a percentage of sales. However, dollar profits of the individual concerns have increased along with the sharp rise in sales in the postwar period.

The operating results of the Harvard Study of Food Chains and the yearly surveys of the Super Market Institute shown in Tables 4-2 and 6-1, respectively, indicate that in the 1950's there has been a rising expense trend, and while gross margins have tended upward, they have not kept pace with expenses; hence net profits have suffered.

Comparison of Profit with Other Types of Retailers

Profits of supermarkets have been shown to vary between 2 and 3 per cent of sales. Statistics in Table 6-8 indicate that drug, variety,

TABLE 6-8

Net Profit as a Percentage of Sales for Various Types of Retail Stores for the Year 1954.

Type of store	Net profit as a % of sales
Department store	4.20 [a]
Drug store	5.40 [b]
Furniture store (large)	1.58 [c]
Hardware store	1.90 [d]
Meat market	1.40 [e]
Supermarket	3.00 [f]
Variety store	5.32 [g]

[a] Controllers Congress, *1954 Merchandise and Operating Results* (New York: National Retail Dry Goods Association, 1955), p. 1.

[b] *Lilly Digest* (Indianapolis: Eli Lilly & Co., 1955), p. 21.

[c] *1954 Furniture Operating Experiences* (Chicago: National Retail Furniture Association, 1955), p. 5.

[d] "1954 Retail Hardware Survey," *Hardware Retailer*, June, 1955, p. 77.

[e] *Meat Markets—Operating Results in 1954* (New York: Dun & Bradstreet, Inc., 1954), p. 2.

[f] *Facts in Grocery Distribution* (New York: Progressive Grocer, 1955), p. F–17.

[g] "Harvard Report on Variety Chains," *Chain Store Age*, Variety Store Managers Issue, XXXI, no. 8, August, 1955, p. 65.

and department stores return a much larger profit percentage than the supermarket. Both variety stores and drugstores earned over 5 cents in the form of profit out of every sales dollar. Yet, this modest 2 to 3 per cent return for a super is significant when viewed against the large dollar volume of a supermarket.

Other measures of profitability, such as profits as a percentage of net worth and earnings on total assets, are considered in the following chapter.

SUMMARY

From its inception, the supermarket profit was predicated on volume operation. Low price policies, display techniques, advertising, and promotion were cornerstones for substantial sales. Expenses of supers to attain this volume have risen steadily since the 1930's, despite efforts to keep them in hand. These included the devising of policies such as self-service and simplified stock handling to reduce expenses as a percentage of a given sales volume, the developing of a large volume against which the more fixed expenses such as rent and utilities could be allocated, and the instituting of cost-reduction programs. However, store management has centered its attention on volume and has left unrealized a source of possible earnings through closer control of expenses at the local level. The net profit that has filtered down has appeared modest when expressed as a percentage of sales. While there has been a slight lowering of profit margins, the modest percentage return is significant when viewed against the large dollar volume per store.

7 | FINANCIAL FACTORS

INTRODUCTION

In the previous three chapters, internal operating procedures and policies developed by supermarket management were examined in the framework of an operating statement. Selling techniques, buying practices, establishment of margins, promotional strategy, and expense analysis and control were the major operating principles examined. It is the objective of this chapter to continue the study of internal supermarket characteristics that have led to the success of the industry, except that in this section, financial aspects are scrutinized in the framework of a balance sheet. The approach used in this chapter to study the financial characteristics was necessitated by the general failure of the supermarket industry to publish representative balance sheet statistics.

GENERAL ASSET STRUCTURE OF A SUPERMARKET

The finances required to open a modern supermarket have undergone considerable change from the days of Roy O. Dawson and Robert Otis, who started the Big Bear with $10,000.[1] Consider the case of Food Fair Stores, Incorporated, an expanding and progressive supermarket chain of 362 units as of January 31, 1959. According to Meyer Marcus, vice president, a modern suburban unit, occupying from 12,000 to 15,000 sq ft of space and grossing $1,000,000 to $1,500,000 yearly, required: $65,000, inventory; $65,000, equipment; and about $200,000, land and building.[2]

---

[1] M. M. Zimmerman, *Super Market Spectacular Exponent of Mass Distribution* (New York: Super Market Publishing Co., 1937), p. 8.

[2] "Food Fair Supermarkets," *Fortune*, Vol. XLI, no. 6, June, 1950, p. 99.

Harley V. McNamara, president of the National Tea Company, a supermarket chain of 932 units as of December 31, 1958, reported the costs of a new supermarket as follows: inventory, $58,000; fixtures and installations, $42,000; and real estate, $100,000.[3] Some of the recently opened "super duper" stores required: inventory, $100,-000 to $250,000; equipment and installation, $100,000 to $250,000; and monthly rental from $2,000 to $5,000.

A new 26,000 to 27,000-sq ft store in Houston, Texas, required: [4]

Land	$100,000
Building	350,000
Equipment	150,000
Inventory	150,000
	$750,000

Similarly, a new store in Oklahoma City, Oklahoma, on 72,800 sq ft of land, with a building of 18,000 sq ft of space, required: [5]

Land	$ 47,750
Building	140,000
Paving	20,000
Equipment	90,000
Inventory	95,000
Cash fund	30,000
	$422,750

John A. Logan, president of the National Association of Food Chains, reported the following asset items of an average supermarket in a statement to the Consumers Study Subcommittee of the Committee on Agriculture, House of Representatives, on May 7, 1957: [6]

[3] Taken from an address, "Modern Trends in Food Retailing," given before the Chicago Federated Advertising Club on October 12, 1952.

[4] M. M. Zimmerman, *The Super Market* (New York: McGraw-Hill Book Co., Inc., 1955), p. 171.

[5] *Ibid.*

[6] John A. Logan, *Progress in Food Distribution* (Washington: National Association of Food Chains, 1957), p. 20.

Building	. . . .	$192,000
Parking lot	. . . .	10,000
Leasehold improvements	. .	34,300
Land	. . . .	25,000
Sales equipment	. . . . .	87,100
Behind-the-scenes equipment	.	65,500
Inventory	. . . .	82,000

This total outlay for a modern super is a far cry from the $3,000 capital required to open an A & P unit in the 1920's or the $10,000 Big Bear in 1933.

DEVELOPMENT OF A REPRESENTATIVE SUPERMARKET BALANCE SHEET

The major assets required to open a supermarket, regardless of who owns or finances the building, have been shown to be cash, inventory, prepaid expenses, equipment, land, and building. Intangible assets in the form of good will and leasehold improvements also appear. Inasmuch as no statistics based on industry surveys as to asset and liability items have been published, a balance sheet of a representative supermarket was developed and presented in Table 7-1 along with a representative operating statement. These financial statistics were based on ratio analyses from various industry sources, particularly data submitted by certain supermarket chains which operated 6,379 stores out of total industry units of 17,024 in 1956. Other data were gleaned from statements and comments of bankers and executives in the industry, obtained through personal interview, and from speeches and trade magazines. This is the first known endeavor to depict a representative store. The estimates developed will of course vary from statistics of individual concerns because of operating policies, location, and size.

Assume that the representative super in Table 7-1 occupies a 10,-000-sq ft, single-story brick building in a suburban location. Adjacent is a lighted and paved parking lot of 40,000 sq ft—four times the store area. Using $110 yearly sales per square foot of building space as a conservative estimate, the store transacts a $1,100,000

TABLE 7-1 *

**Balance Sheet and Yearly Operating Statement of
a Representative Supermarket.**

BALANCE SHEET

Asssets		*Liabilities*	
Cash	$ 30,000	Accounts payable . . .	$ 40,000
Inventory	75,000	Accruals and notes payable	20,000
Total current assets .	105,000	Total current liabilities .	60,000
Equipment	75,000	Long-term debt	104,000
Deferred charges . . .	3,000	Net worth	164,000
Building	100,000		
Parking lot	15,000		
Land	30,000		
Total assets	$328,000	Total liabilities	$328,000

YEARLY OPERATING STATEMENT

Sales	$1,100,000	100%
Cost of sales	891,000	81
Gross margin	209,000	19
Operating expenses, fixed	66,000	6
Operating expenses, variable	110,000	10
Net profit before taxes	$ 33,000	3%

* Based on ratio analyses from various industry sources.

yearly volume. Assuming a gross margin of 19 per cent and a stable monthly inventory, yearly cost of sales will be

$$\$1,100,000 \times (100\% - 19\%) = \$891,000$$

With a turnover of 12 times per year, the average inventory in the store is

$$\$891,000 \div 12 = \$74,250$$

or, for approximate purposes, inventory is estimated at $75,000. Equipment in a store approximately equals the inventory of $75,000. Another rule of thumb employed is $3.00 of equipment for each $1.00 in weekly sales.

The ratio of inventory to total current liabilities equals from 1:1 to about 1½:1. Using a ratio of 1¼:1, current liabilities will equal

$$\$75,000 \div 1.25 = \$60,000$$

In turn, accounts payable equals about two-thirds of current liabilities, or $40,000, with the balance accruals plus current payments on indebtedness. Cash should average from one-half to equal the current liabilities, thus assuring adequate working funds. If the one-half ratio is used, cash needed will be $30,000. The current ratio in this typical balance sheet is 1¾:1, a figure in line with ratios that vary from 1¼:1 up to 2:1.

The 10,000-sq ft building, using an estimate of $10 per square foot, will cost $100,000. Land cost varies by location, but it has been estimated to be about 20 to 30 per cent of the building for suburban locations. If the 30 per cent figure is used, land cost will be $30,000. The grading, paving, and lighting of a 40,000-sq ft parking lot will cost approximately $15,000. Prepaid expenses are nominal and would be no more than $3,000.

Indebtedness can vary widely among the individual markets. Total debt to net worth tends to be heavy, especially for concerns financing real estate. Under the assumption that this firm owns its building, a figure of $1.00 of debt to $1.00 of equity capital is used. Thus net worth will be one-half of total assets of $328,000, or $164,000. Total debt will be $164,000, of which $60,000 is already accounted for by current liabilities. The balance of indebtedness will be

$$\$164,000 - \$60,000 = \$104,000$$

This $104,000 is long-term debt secured by equipment and building and is represented by both chattel and real estate mortgages.

To develop the picture further, an operating statement predicated on ratios established in Chapters 4 through 6 is presented in Table 7-1.

CURRENT ASSETS

The principal current items are cash and inventory. This highly simplified, current asset condition results from sales on a cash basis.

In addition, the amount of working capital needed for a super-market tends to be less than that for most other forms of retailing because:

1. Inventory turnover is considerably higher. Therefore less inventory is needed for a given sales volume.

2. Cash sales reduce the time for one merchandising cycle, namely, the movement from inventory, to receivables, to cash, and back to inventory. The speed of the merchandising cycle also is increased by high inventory turnover in supermarts.

3. Consigned merchandise from rack jobbers is used frequently in the nonfood area. The super then not only has no merchandising problems but also has no funds tied up in nonfood items.

4. Relatively stable sales from week to week or month to month can lower working capital needs and simplify its control. Seasonal inventories are much less of a problem than in most other forms of retailing, so that peak working capital needs are less. In addition, the predictability of sales, inventory, and working funds is simpler, so that supers can work on narrower cash requirements.

Therefore the current assets needed, compared with other forms of retailers doing the same volume, can be substantially less. A steady cash flow from sales reduces cash requirements and makes budgeting problems simpler. Thus management can center its attention on inventory and its control. A retailer is a merchandiser, and profits are made from merchandising operations—buying and selling. However, because of rising food costs and more diversified inventories, members of this industry have found it necessary to gradually increase working capital over the years.

Investment bankers who have assisted this industry in its financing problems by selling securities to the general public have indicated that working capital needs for a smaller concern should be 150 per cent of total debt and for large chains at least 125 per cent of total liabilities.[7] An examination of the balance sheets of representative industry members indicates that this ratio varies by size

---

[7] These statistics are from an address by Al Donohue, Kidder Peabody and Co., at the Twentieth Annual Meeting of the National Association of Food Chains held in Washington, D.C., on December 5, 1953.

of concern and is also a function of the number of buildings owned, the current expansion plans, and the method of financing. Colonial Stores, Incorporated, as of December 31, 1958, had a ratio of working capital to debt of 125 per cent; Fisher Brothers Company, a Cleveland chain, had a ratio of over 200 per cent on the same date; and Daitch Crystal Dairies, Incorporated, a New York chain, had working capital approximately equal to indebtedness.

EQUIPMENT NEEDS IN A SUPERMARKET

Next consider the specific equipment needed in a modern supermarket. Basically it takes as much capital to equip a store as to stock it. The substantial investment becomes apparent when the costs of specific items are considered: [8]

1 check-out stand and register	$1,775
1 double-decked dairy case	1,360
1 gondola for display	675
1 shopping cart	22
1 ice cream freezer	2,100
1 frozen food case	1,475
1 coffee grinder	375
Refrigerated display space for produce and meat, per linear foot	150
Air conditioning cost for a single store, 20,000-sq ft building	17,700
Compressor for the same size building	6,850

In a modern market with 14,200 sq ft of selling space and total space of 24,200 sq ft, the following layout specifications for meat, produce, and dairy displays were established: [9]

	Lin ft
Produce	170
Fresh meat	70
Processed meat	20
Delicatessen items	20
Floral	15
Dairy and cheese	60
Total	355

[8] "The Cost of a Supermarket," *Chain Store Age*, Grocery Executive Edition, October, 1953, p. 197.

[9] "How Three Get More for Their Construction Dollar," *Super Market Merchandising*, Vol. XXIII, no. 5, May, 1958, p. 86.

At a cost of $150 per linear foot, this equipment alone cost approximately $53,250. In addition, the market required 144 ft of frozen-food display space.

Furthermore, behind-the-scenes equipment must be considered. In a 20,000-sq ft market built in the 1950's, these expenditures necessitated (1) $1,300 for mechanical handling of merchandise, (2) $2,200 for a built-in overnight produce refrigerator, and (3) $8,500 for a built-in meat-storage room.[10] A cork cooler room in a 10,752-sq ft market built in 1958 cost $11,225.[11]

Outside equipment also must be considered. Furr's, a supermarket operation in Lubbock, Texas, paid $5,225 for neon display signs in a modern market.[12] Parking lot lights can vary from $800 to $2,500, depending on the size of lot and type of equipment. An advertising pylon or tower used to differentiate the stores of a Midwest chain cost $15,000.

Although smaller supers do not require as much in fixtures on a dollar basis, it is important to recognize the costly and specialized equipment required to operate a supermarket. In addition, the equipment needs continue to grow both in dollar cost and in absolute amounts.

LAND AND BUILDING

The direction taken by investment in assets plays a vital role in supermarket earnings. On the one hand, supers need to locate in areas where operations can be profitable. This may involve real estate commitments in order to have a place to do business. On the other hand, supers are in business to make money on merchandising, not real estate.

To erect a supermarket building is costly. Vice-President Meyer Marcus of Food Fair Stores indicated that a 12,000- to 15,000-sq ft building and land in a suburban location would cost about $200,-

---

[10] "The Cost of a Supermarket," *Chain Store Age, op. cit.*
[11] "How Three Get More for Their Construction Dollar," *Super Market Merchandising, op. cit.*
[12] *Ibid.*, p. 100.

000.[13] Carl Teutsch, architect and engineer of supermarkets in the Midwest, estimated that a 1954 one-story supermarket cost $9.00 to $10.00 a square foot plus the land.[14] He quoted the cost just prior to World War II at about $5.00 a square foot. John A. Logan, president of National Association of Food Chains, reported the average modern chain supermarket cost $25,000 for the land and $192,000 for the building.[15]

Specific building costs vary by areas. Eagle-United Supermarkets, Rock Island, Illinois, reported the following building cost figures for a 10,752-sq ft building built in 1958: [16]

General contract	$ 86,310
Steel	17,573
Gypsum roof	6,800
Floor covering	1,820
Electrical contract	37,460
Plumbing	12,230
Painting	1,202
Acoustical ceiling	5,896
Heating and air conditioning	22,500
Magic doors	3,391
Miscellaneous	2,184
Total	$197,366

H. W. Underhill, Los Angeles architect, reported the following building costs for a one-story stucco building with 27,800 sq ft of space all on one floor: [17]

Structure finish and plumbing	$204,000
Electrical work	37,000
Air conditioning	16,500
Fire sprinklers	14,250
Cooler rooms	8,200
Total	$279,950

[13] "Food Fair Supermarkets," *Fortune, op. cit.*

[14] These estimates were made in an interview on December 10, 1954. Mr. Teutsch had designed and constructed many of the buildings for the National Tea Company.

[15] John A. Logan, *Progress in Food Distribution, op. cit.*

[16] "How Three Get More for Their Construction Dollar," *Super Market Merchandising, op. cit.*, p. 101.

[17] *Ibid.*, p. 95.

The average 1957 super, as reported by the Super Market Institute, required building costs of $11.24 per square foot, exclusive of land, parking lot, coolers, and sprinklers but including air conditioning.[18] Costs were slightly lower ($9.83 per square foot) if all construction was on one floor. The industry figure for all equipment, land, and building for the year 1957 was $19.98 per square foot of building space.

INTANGIBLE ASSETS

Two intangible assets commonly appear on the records of supermarkets. One results from improvements or alterations made to property controlled by the super under lease—leasehold improvements. Such improvements become a part of the real estate and revert to the owner of the real estate at the expiration of the lease. Leasehold improvements include remodeled store fronts, electronic doors, and loading platforms. These assets are of value to the super in the conduct of its business in leased quarters, but they are subject to amortization over the period of the lease. The extent of improvement put in by a lessor is related to the rental charge, the value of the real estate, and the length of the lease.

The other intangible asset that appears is good will. This occurs in the outright purchase of a unit or group of units by another super. Selling price is predicated on earning power, not the book value of the assets. For example, one supermarket chain in the Midwest paid $100,000 for a market that constantly earned $25,000 yearly profit before taxes. Assets were carried on the sellers books, however, at $80,000. The buyer recorded on its records $80,000 in tangible assets and $20,000 in good will. The recent strong trend toward acquisition and merger that developed in this industry in the 1950's has led to the rapid appearance of this intangible asset on supermarket balance sheets. Good will can be written off to a $1.00 value at the discretion of the purchaser.

[18] From an address, "Facts About New Supers Opened in 1957," given by Curt Kornblau, Director of Research, Super Market Institute, at the annual convention in Cleveland, Ohio, in May, 1958.

LEASING OF FIXED ASSETS

Supermarkets are merchandising organizations that thrive on a large volume of fast-moving inventory. Profits result from selling merchandise—the cash-to-inventory-to-cash cycle. In order to achieve this objective in a dynamic industry, supers have been forced to pioneer new locations with modern stores that require a substantial investment in equipment.

There are two methods by which supers can obtain the necessary fixed assets needed for their operation, namely, lease or purchase. Under the lease arrangement, the fixed assets used do not appear on the balance sheet nor do the lease payments contracted for appear as a liability, even though the rental obligation over a long period of years is there. Supers, in effect, are able to have their long-term financing provided by others. Under a purchase arrangement, the fixed assets and such indebtedness as results from financing appear on the records. This financing of fixed assets also can be furnished by others or by the supermarket itself through equity capital; or the financing can be furnished jointly by others (creditors) and the operators (owners). Therefore the method of acquiring fixed assets, either leasing or purchasing, significantly affects the ratio of profits to total assets used by supermarkets and makes analyses and comparisons among firms difficult. In addition, the method of acquisition has a bearing on profits related to net worth. If the fixed assets are leased, ownership capital can be used for current operations. If fixed assets are owned and can be financed 100 per cent by creditors, the equity capital can still be used entirely for current operations. Thus the ratio of net profit to net worth will not be changed. If fixed assets are owned and a portion of these assets must be financed from equity capital, which is generally the case, then one of two things must happen. Either more equity capital is needed (in which case the ratio of net profit to net worth decreases) or creditors' funds must be obtained to finance part of current operations (in which case the ratio of net profit to net worth remains the same as in the first case).

To compare companies that (1) own fixed assets, (2) lease fixed assets, or (3) both own and lease fixed assets, the long-term lease payments should be capitalized at some rate depending on real estate market conditions in order to get a true picture of debt in relation to controlled assets. This capitalized figure can be considered as debt when making comparisons, to put all concerns on a comparable basis.

Theory of Leasing versus Owning Store Buildings

Should a supermarket invest in land and buildings? The "cheapy" supers looked for abandoned factories or warehouses to rent. But the supers followed the population shift. As supermarkets mushroomed, particularly in outlying areas, new buildings and parking lots have been required. Many of these structures are specialized as to size, arrangement, and location. Alternate uses of the property frequently are limited, which increases the risk. Although some locations have been available for rent in shopping centers and in new suburban buildings, the supermart operators frequently are required to finance buildings in new locations. Is this the best alternative use of capital?

Assume the super shown by the statistics in Table 7-1 could lease the property. Then the balance sheet of the super would be as follows:

Cash	$ 30,000	Accounts payable	$ 40,000
Inventory	75,000	Accruals and payments	20,000
Equipment	75,000	Long-term debt	31,500
Deferred charges	3,000	Net worth	91,500
Total assets	$183,000	Total liabilities	$183,000

The changes from Table 7-1 are predicated on the following assumptions: Building, land, and parking lot are eliminated from the records. Assume that the real estate of $145,000 was financed equally by the operator and an insurance company; both long-term debt and net worth would be reduced $72,500 each to $31,500 and $91,500, respectively. No change in the current position would be involved. On the reasonable assumption that the rental expense of the property to the super would be approximately the same as the building expense involved under ownership of the property (under ownership the super faces depreciation, interest, insurance, and taxes), the net profit would remain 3 per cent of sales. With the volume unchanged, the net profit would remain at $33,000.

Profit on total assets of $328,000 for the company shown in Table 7-1 would be

$$\frac{\$33,000}{\$328,000} \times 100 = 10.06\%$$

Profit on total assets of $183,000 for the same company but with the real estate leased would be

$$\frac{\$33,000}{\$183,000} \times 100 = 18.03\%$$

Simply, leasing the real estate instead of owning it requires less equity capital and results in a substantially larger profit related to total assets owned. Yet, in effect, the super is controlling $328,000 in assets although only $183,000 appear on the financial records. The lease payments could be capitalized and considered as debt and the real estate regarded as an asset in order to compare assets used.

Profit on ownership capital of $164,000 for the super in Table 7-1 that owns the building would be

$$\frac{\$33,000}{\$164,000} \times 100 = 20.12\%$$

But if the building were leased, the percentage profit on ownership capital of $91,500 would be

$$\frac{\$33,000}{\$91,500} \times 100 = 36.07\%$$

Inventory versus Real Estate

Continue this analysis in terms of an alternative of investing either in real estate or in merchandise. The representative balance sheet in Table 7-1 indicates that real estate totaled $145,000. Assume this property commands a rental equal to 1 per cent of sales of $1,100,-

000, or $11,000, per year. Furthermore, assume taxes and insurance of $1,500 and neglect depreciation and repairs. The yearly net return on this asset bearing no mortgage would be

$$\$11,000 - \$1,500 = \$9,500$$

On an investment of $145,000, this $9,500 would furnish a return of 6.6 per cent.

To make an even better percentage showing on the investment in real estate, introduce leverage. Assume the property to be mortgaged for 70 per cent of its value at 5 per cent yearly interest. The owner would tie up only 30 per cent of his equity in the property, or

$$\$145,000 \times 30\% = \$43,500$$

Interest per year on the balance would be

$$(\$145,000 - \$43,500) \times 5\% = \$5,075$$

Therefore total yearly expense would be

$$\$5,075 \text{ interest} + \$1,500 \text{ taxes and insurance} = \$6,575$$

This would leave a yearly net profit of

$$\$11,000 \text{ rental} - \$6,575 \text{ expense} = \$4,425$$

A return of $4,425 on an investment of $43,500 would be 10.2 per cent. This would leave $101,500 of the original equity capital of $145,000 still available for other purposes.

If the $145,000 capital were placed in merchandise and the property leased at a comparable rate, the added inventory of $145,000 divided by the gross margin of 81 per cent would bring sales of

$$\frac{\$145,000}{(100\% - 19\%)} = \$179,000$$

Net profit of 3 per cent on that volume would be $5,370. But inventory is turned over 12 times per year, thus offering a phenomenal advantage in favor of merchandise instead of building ownership. Or, if the minimum investment in the building of $43,500 is used as the addition to merchandise, this will result in yearly sales at a turn-over of 12 times

$$\frac{\$43,500}{(100\% - 19\%)} \times 12 = \$644,000$$

The net profit on the $644,000 volume at a 3 per cent rate would be

$$\$644,000 \times 3\% = \$19,320$$

There is thus a substantially greater profit possibility of $19,320 from merchandising versus the $4,425 earned on the building investment, with $101,500 of the original equity capital of $145,000 still available for other purposes. The $19,320 profit is equivalent to a rate of 44.4 per cent return on the $43,500 placed in merchandise.

Obviously the addition of a larger stock totaling $43,500 as as-sumed above would require a larger market or an additional market and make exact comparisons difficult. If the same market were used, conceivably turnover could drop. But generally there is a compara-tive advantage of inventory over fixed assets. While a super must have a place in which to transact business, management must real-ize that greater profits can accrue from skillful merchandising than from investment in real estate.

Leasing New Locations

The major difficulties with owning store buildings are: first, tying up capital in fixed assets; and second, using capital in a less profit-able alternative, namely, real estate activities and not merchandis-ing. Several plans have been used to finance real estate requirements with no capital needed or with funds tied up for only a short period of time.

The first is to have the building erected and financed by outside interests. The super in turn leases the premises. Private individuals who own suitable land or concerns who develop shopping centers negotiate with supermarkets. On the strength of a lease, perhaps 10 years, private sources erect the building for the supermart. Fre-quently small satellite stores are included in the plans, or the project is designed as a regional shopping center housing several supers and a department store. If the property is developed by a concern specializing in that field, it is generally sold in turn to private and institutional investors.

The second plan is to have a supermart concern purchase the land, erect the building, and then sell the property to private investors. The supermarket leases the premises over a period of 10 to 25 years, generally with an option to renew at a stipulated increased rate. Funds are tied up in the property until sold. This leaseback method has developed into a widely used vehicle for financing real estate inasmuch as it offers the merchant a "tailor-made" market, frees capital, enables rental paid to be a legitimate tax expense, and furnishes a market to the merchant over a long period of years in an inflationary era. In addition, many leases contain a negotiation clause which will permit the lessee to terminate the lease should the location prove undesirable. Most real estate departments of large chains have developed properties they desire to sell.

A modification of the leaseback method used particularly by larger chains is the organization of real estate holding affiliates. An affiliate is a corporation related to another by owning or being owned by a common management or by any other control device. The concerns involved are separate legal entities; to the owner of the property (the lessor), the supermarket operating concern (the lessee) is simply a tenant. The supermarket chains execute long-term leases with their affiliates at going market rental rates. The affiliates in turn have been able to obtain financing, sometimes up to 100 per cent of cost, by offering as security not only the properties but an assignment of the rentals under the leases. The lender in this instance bases the appraisal not on the cost of the property but on the value under terms of the lease. This value is determined by market surveys which predict expected sales volume related to the rentals to be paid under the lease. Frequently these leases require a fixed obligation plus a percentage of sales above a prearranged amount.

The use of subsidiary corporations to finance real estate properties is examined later in this chapter in the section Sources of Capital—Debt.

Lease of Equipment

The arguments advanced for leasing real estate properties also can be used as reasons for supers to lease equipment. While the rental amount of equipment has nowhere near attained the proportions of real estate leasing, there has been a movement in this direction by either the straight-lease plan or the rental-purchase agreement. The latter has the advantage in that the lessor has an option to buy the equipment at some time during the term of the lease, receiving credit against the purchase price for any rental payments made. The rental-purchase plan may meet with objections of the Internal Revenue Bureau. The key as to what constitutes a bona fide lease is the option price to the lessee-purchaser. Where this price runs considerably lower than a reasonable market value for the equipment, tax authorities may reverse the claim. Operators who contemplate leasing equipment should bear in mind the annual cost of owning equipment, which in 1958 averaged 1.38 per cent of sales.[19] These costs include all charges for taxes, insurance, interest, repairs, and depreciation.

SOURCES OF CAPITAL—DEBT

Two sources of capital in a business enterprise appear on the credit side of a balance sheet, namely, ownership funds and indebtedness. In the preceding section, Leasing of Fixed Assets, it was shown that a super can control certain assets needed for the operation of the business without legally acquiring title to them. The asset and such accompanying financing do not appear on the balance sheet. Indebtedness, considered in this section, generally is classified by length of maturity as either a short- or long-term obligation. The usual accounting practice is to regard all obligations due within one year as a short-term liability; all others are long-

[19] Wilbur B. England, *Operating Results of Food Chains in 1958* (Cambridge: Harvard Business School, Bulletin No. 156, 1959), p. 2.

term. A list of sources of capital for the supermarket industry is shown in Table 7-2.

Supermarket management must borrow on the most favorable

TABLE 7-2 *

Sources of Capital for the Supermarket Industry.

Unsecured short-term loans	Commercial banks
Unsecured long-term loans (debentures)	Commercial banks Insurance concerns Public
Secured real estate loans	Commercial banks Savings banks Building and loan associations Mortgage bankers Investment trusts Pension funds Insurance concerns Universities U.S. Government corporations Investment bankers
Secured equipment loans	Finance concerns Factors Commercial banks
Inventory loans	Suppliers Commercial banks
Invested equity capital	Private Public sale of stock Customers

* Arthur H. Richland, "How to Raise Cash and Influence Bankers," *Super Market Merchandising*, XX, no. 8, August, 1956, p. 42.

terms possible in this narrow-profit industry. To do this, it is necessary to maintain a satisfactory financial condition and operating record. In addition, management (especially of the smaller firms) should make certain that: [20]

[20] This check list is from an address, "Essential Factors in Sound Financing," given by Henry Shaffer, Shaffer Stores Co., Inc., at the 20th Annual Meeting of Food Chains in Washington, D.C., on December 5, 1953.

1. The chief officer delegates authority and spends time on policy making and its direction.

2. A good No. 2 man is in the company.

3. A financial policy man is on the staff working with the top executives.

4. The accountant has set up a good system of records including cost control measures.

5. A personnel and training director is on hand.

6. An organization chart has been set up.

Short-Term Indebtedness

Supers sell on a cash basis. Stock turns over about once a month. It would seem possible for the trade debt to be large and for creditors' money to be used to finance the inventory. However, credit terms vary from daily or weekly for some lines (such as bread and dairy products) to monthly for others (such as coffee and certain canned goods). In addition, it is imperative that supermarkets take advantage of the 2 per cent cash discount frequently offered by food product manufacturers or distributors; the operating profit as a percentage of sales has averaged only 3 per cent of sales before income taxes. Thus the shortness of the selling terms and the necessity for taking cash discounts has mitigated to some extent in the use of suppliers' funds to finance the inventory. However, the super that gets into an overstocked inventory position frequently is aided financially by a wholesaler who has some control over the inventory. Banks find it inconvenient to make loans secured by the inventory in such a situation because it is difficult to supervise and control merchandise on a shifting-stock basis. Unsecured loans are possible in the right credit environment.

Supermarkets have found bank loans, in the form of short-term notes payable, to be of significant help in financing many activities. These short-term loans have been used: (1) in the purchase of an existing store by a larger organization with large cash flow from sales so that the loan can be paid off shortly, (2) as down payment on land, (3) for the start of construction pending the raising of long-term capital, (4) for purchase of equipment, and (5) for working capital. The expanding supermarkets have been wide users of bank credit. There is a trend toward increased current indebtedness in the form of notes payable, including current payments on long-term indebtedness.

Long-Term Indebtedness

Most indebtedness contracted for by members of the supermarket industry has been of a long-term nature in the form of:

1. Long-term notes payable
2. Debentures
3. Chattel mortgages
4. Real estate mortgages

Sources of long-term borrowing are shown in Table 7-2. Insurance companies and investment bankers have been the two major lenders to the large supermarket chains. For the small operators, insurance companies have been the main source of real estate financing; commercial banks and finance companies have been the principal lenders for the purchase of equipment. One source of long-term financing available to the small supermarket concern with annual gross sales less than $2,000,000 is the Small Business Administration. This governmental agency was organized to make loans to small business if no credit is otherwise available from private sources at reasonable rates of interest. These loans, which can run for a maximum of 10 years, generally require a real estate and chattel mortgage on all capital assets of the business. From 1953 to 1957 the Small Business Administration granted 409 loans to food retailers totaling $12,855,000.[21] The main reasons for the denial of loans by the Small Business Administration were (1) the earning ability of the firm was not demonstrated and (2) the collateral was insufficient.

[21] "Government—Its Role in Financing," *Cooperative Merchandiser*, August, 1958, p. 17.

Long-term notes payable. A *note payable* is a term applied to a promissory note with reference to its maker.[22] The classification *long-term liability* refers to an obligation which will not become due within a relatively short period, usually a year. Supers have borrowed for expansion on long-term notes from institutional investors or banks. It has been a common practice for supermart concerns, particularly the chains, to borrow sizable funds from a private source such as an insurance company or pension fund. The funds obtained have been used for general corporate purposes, including additions to working capital, purchase of another concern, or expansion. Examples of promissory notes payable, outstanding as of December 31, 1958, include notes totaling $453,316 of the Evans Grocery Company with 13 supers in West Virginia, Ohio, and Kentucky, and note indebtedness of $1,375,000 owed by Fisher Brothers Company with 87 supers in the Cleveland area.

Debentures (bonds). Debentures are securities not protected by collateral or tangible assets but only by the general credit of the issuer. The underlying indenture may require certain protective measures such as the maintenance of a specified working capital ratio, limitations on the amount of any additional funded debt, and restrictions on dividends to stockholders.[23] There is no clear-cut distinction between a bond and a note other than the fact that the latter generally means a relatively short-term obligation, one maturing not more than 10 years after issuance.[24]

While this method of financing has been used sparingly by one- or few-unit operators, many of the larger supermarket concerns have sold debentures both publicly and privately. Some concerns have offered several different issues of debentures. In addition, other operators have used successfully the subordinated debenture with conversion or warrant privileges. These privileges permit the holder

[22] Eric Kohler, *Dictionary for Accountants* (New York: Prentice-Hall, Inc., 1952), p. 285.
[23] *Ibid.*, p. 136.
[24] B. A. Graham and D. L. Dodd, *Security Analysis* (New York: McGraw-Hill Book Co., Inc., 1953), p. 83.

to convert the bond to capital stock at certain specified dates and at specified prices. Certain insurance concerns have loaned on debentures totaling as little as $500,000, but they may require an operator to furnish detailed financial statistics for a period of at least 10 years. On December 31, 1958, the previously mentioned Evans Grocery Company had $84,162 outstanding in 10-year debentures issued to employees. One of the largest users of debentures is Food Fair Stores, Incorporated. As of January 1, 1959, this concern had outstanding the following long-term obligations:

3 per cent debentures due January 1, 1965	$ 5,562,000
3⅜ per cent debentures due September 1, 1974	$18,750,000
4 per cent convertible, subordinated debentures due April 1, 1979	$21,203,200

Chattel mortgages. These are mortgages on personal property—equipment in a super. Financing by chattel mortgages has been used extensively in this industry, particularly by smaller chains or supers with one store or a few outlets. The large chains in the main have generated funds for equipment through normal cash flow operations or have borrowed from banks or institutions on a note basis.

Two principles of equipment financing are: (1) A particular fixed asset should "pay for itself" during its useful life; and (2) Ownership capital should provide a portion of the required financing. The different types of equipment in a supermarket vary in their useful life, but the operators and lenders alike report the maximum financing terms should not exceed 10 years, preferably 5 to 7 years. Some progressive banks that have become familiar with the supermarket industry have shown a willingness to extend loans longer than the traditional 36 months, considered to be a rule-of-thumb maximum for equipment financing by banks.

Repayment rate for chattel mortgages can be (1) a fixed amount payable monthly or quarterly or (2) a declining rate with a rapid payoff in the early years and nominal payments toward the end.

The latter plan has become more popular since tax authorities have approved accelerated depreciation. The two approved methods of computing rapid depreciation are the "sum-of-the-years-digits" and the "declining-balance method." Equipment manufacturers and dealers have given wide publicity to the "pay-as-you-depreciate" plans.

Real estate mortgages. These are liens on land or buildings given by a borrower to the lender as security for his loan. When a mortgage constitutes the security against which bonds are issued, the lien is conveyed by what is ordinarily known as a *deed of trust.* Mortgages can be secured by a specific piece of real estate or all the real estate property.

The basic method by which a supermarket finances and owns a new location is simply to acquire the land, erect the building, and mortgage the property for about two-thirds of the total cost. On the average, for a new $200,000 location a super would tie up $70,-000 of its funds and mortgage the balance for $130,000. In some cases, mortgage money only up to one-half of land and building costs is available.

A refinement of this fundamental method of financing real estate employed by some supermarket chains is the use of a subsidiary corporation. The stock of the subsidiary is owned partially or entirely by the parent supermarket. The subsidiary issues first mortgage bonds secured by mortgages on all the properties and by assignment of the lease rentals. These bonds are legal investments for a number of institutional investors who otherwise are not interested in single property financing. This plan also has the added attraction of more diversified security behind the bonds since the security consists of a number of properties with geographical spread. Furthermore, the insurance companies, which are an important source of long-term funds for the supermarket owner, are limited in most states by law as to the amount of fee-owned real estate they can hold. This limits their capacity for direct leasebacks. Institutional investors also are limited as to the mortgages they may hold both as to amount and location. The first-mortgage bonds of a real estate subsidiary are not limited to these extents and also make available to the operator 100 per cent financing of the cost of a store.[25]

SOURCES OF CAPITAL—OWNERSHIP

Many of the growing regional chains that started as one-store units back in the 1930's entered the capital markets in the postwar period to procure funds for expansion. As a result of public sale of securities, their financial records were revealed. This was the case for many of the concerns included in Table 7-4. The equity securities sold included both preferred and common stock. The quest for equity funds for expansion has taken many forms and has been a constant problem in expansion.[26] The sale of equity securities also has broadened the base for borrowing by supermarket operators.

The sale of preferred stock, generally offering 5 and 6 per cent cumulative dividends and preferable as assets in case of liquidation, has been widely used by over 60 per cent of the larger members of the industry. In fact, two issues of preferred stock were sold by six of 37 firms studied. However, preferred-stock financing is not limited to large firms. One enterprising operator sold preferred stock to his customers in the store literally "over the counter." Not only did he obtain funds, but he more or less tied his customers to the market. Care must be taken in this kind of operation to make certain the laws governing security sales are not broken.

The larger concerns that have sold stock publicly still have managed to maintain control of the business. This is possible because, with a large and widely held stock offering, a small active management minority can control the operation. Some of the smaller concerns, perhaps fearful of losing control, have issued several forms of common stock. The public on occasion has been sold nonvoting securities.

[25] Donohue, *op. cit.*
[26] "Methods of Financing Store Construction," *Super Market Merchandising,* XIII, no. 6, June, 1946, p. 66.

PROFITS ON EQUITY CAPITAL

Net profits expressed as a percentage of sales for the supermarket industry were found in Chapter 6 to be about a modest 3 per cent of sales before taxes. Then how can this industry flourish with such a relatively low profit rate, especially since it has tended to decline in the postwar era? The analysis of sales, cost, and profit relationships at various levels of volume of the representative supermarket given in Table 7-1 furnishes the key to one of the most vital super-marketing financial principles. The results of this analysis are found in Table 7-3.

(Assume the representative supermart illustrated in Table 7-1 is a successful venture with yearly sales of $1,100,000, profits of $33,-000, ownership capital of $164,000, net profit of 3 per cent of sales, and return on ownership capital of 20.12 per cent. Statistics contained in Table 7-3 indicate what the operating results of this store would be at various volume levels. Fixed costs (basic rent, depreciation, utilities, etc.) are assumed at 6 per cent of the $1,100,000 volume, or $66,000.[27] Merchandise cost and variable operating expenses fluctuate with sales; and in Table 7-3 these items are 81 per cent and 10 per cent, respectively. The variable expenses include such items as wages, stamps, and merchandise handling. The breakeven point for this store is $733,000, at which level the sales dollar equals merchandise cost plus all operating expenses.)

Basically the supermarket has a low fixed cost and a low breakeven point as compared with those of heavy industry. These, along

---

[27] The 6 per cent fixed expense figure was established jointly with Everett Mann, C.P.A., and former professor of accounting, Emory University, afer an analysis of operations at different levels of volume for several supermarket firms. This figure involved certain assumptions in classifying expenses as either fixed or variable. Fixed expenses are not absolutely constant in a supermarket inasmuch as certain expenses listed in this category, such as utility expense, could be curtailed if the volume shrank materially. In addition, all variable expenses do not vary absolutely with sales. Discontinuities develop in certain production services; for example, an additional check-out stand may be needed but yet may not be used at maximum efficiency when added. By allowing for these factors and assumptions, the relationships established are believed accurate for use in the analysis of breakeven operations.

TABLE 7-3 *

Sales, Cost, and Profit Relationships for the Representative Supermarket at Various Levels of Volume.

Sales	Fixed cost	Cost of merchandise, 81% of sales	Variable expense, 10% of sales	Total cost	Profit or loss	Profit as a % of sales	Profit as a % of net worth
$ 100,000	$66,000	$ 81,000	$ 10,000	$ 157,000	−$57,000		
200,000	66,000	162,000	20,000	248,000	− 48,000		
300,000	66,000	243,000	30,000	339,000	− 39,000		
400,000	66,000	324,000	40,000	430,000	− 30,000		
500,000	66,000	405,000	50,000	521,000	− 21,000		
600,000	66,000	486,000	60,000	612,000	− 12,000		
700,000	66,000	567,000	70,000	703,000	− 3,000		
733,000	66,000	594,000	73,000	733,000	0	0	0
800,000	66,000	648,000	80,000	794,000	+ 6,000	0.75	3.66
900,000	66,000	729,000	90,000	885,000	+ 15,000	1.67	9.15
1,000,000	66,000	810,000	100,000	976,000	+ 24,000	2.40	14.63
1,100,000	66,000	891,000	110,000	1,067,000	+ 33,000	3.00	20.12
1,200,000	66,000	972,000	120,000	1,158,000	+ 42,000	3.50	25.61
1,300,000	66,000	1,053,000	130,000	1,249,000	+ 51,000	3.92	31.10

(Note: "Variable expense" column annotated by hand as "LABOR ONLY")

* Calculations based on relationships set forth in Table 7-1.

Handwritten marginal notes:

← OVER

```
25,000        20,000
   52             52
------        -------
 50000        40000
125060       100000
$13,000,000.00  1040000.00
```

with other factors, allow concerns to pioneer markets in new, growing locations. At the outset, the market can still be profitable if the sales result is considerably below the future expected volume or if the actual volume is considerably in error on the low side from the sales forecast. As volume at a location rises, the profit percentage increases substantially. From a breakeven point at $733,000 sales, the results in Table 7-3 show that at a $1,300,000 volume, the margin is 3.92 per cent of sales. In turn, as a competitor encroaches on the market of a store, the original super still can suffer a considerable volume decline and remain profitable.

A business with high fixed expenses, like the steel industry, desperately needs added sales. Why then has the supermarket striven for large volume per store, since its fixed expenses are low and since the net profit tends to increase at a decreasing rate? As sales rose from $800,000 to $900,000, according to the figures in Table 7-3, the profit rose from $6,000 to $15,000, an increase of 150 per cent. As sales rose from $900,000 to $1,000,000, net earnings rose from $15,-000 to $24,000, an increase of only 60 per cent.

The answer commonly advanced is that even though the profit margin is modest, it becomes a sizable dollar amount when related to a large volume. This is true as evidenced by the data in Table 7-3 for the representative super at its $1,100,000 volume. However, this is only a partial answer to the super's success. Actually, for a given market, the profit margin and the absolute dollar profit rise with an increase in sales and will continue to do so until some added fixed expense is incurred, which may result eventually because the market could outgrow its present facilities. The market shown by the data in Table 7-3 earns $33,000, or 3 per cent, at a volume of $1,100,000; but at the $1,300,000 level, profits increase to $51,000, or 3.92 per cent. Furthermore, profit expressed as a percentage of net worth rises consistently and rapidly with volume. Profit as a percentage of net worth was 20.12 per cent at the $1,100,000 level; but at the $1,-300,000 volume, the rate rose to 31.10 per cent. Profit as a percentage of net worth is further aided by the high degree of leverage in the industry and by the policy of leasing fixed assets. Herein lies the key to financial success of supermarket operation.

From the viewpoint of management and store personnel, this increase in volume, with the resulting increase in net profit percentage on sales and equity, is vital. For example, consider the data of the representative super in Table 7-1. If one additional family that spends $1,000 per year can be induced to shop at that super as a result of the promotional effort, that marginal family will reflect the following changes in operating results:

Sales	$1,101,000
Fixed cost	66,000
Cost of sales	891,800
Variable cost	110,100
Total cost	1,067,900
Net profit	33,100
Profit as a % of sales	3.01
Profit as a % of net worth	20.18

Simply, this marginal family to the store is worth 0.01 per cent increase in net profit on sales and 0.06 per cent increase in net profit on equity. The marginal family appears highly significant and can have a double-edged effect. A loss of a customer can drop profits just as the addition of one can increase return.

RESULTS OF THE ANALYSIS OF CERTAIN FINANCIAL STATEMENTS OF SUPERMARKET CHAINS

The preceding discussion has indicated the large financial requirements of a single supermarket, the risk involved in pioneering new locations, the relatively specialized type of equipment and building, and the problem of obtaining capital. These appear as deterrents to expansion. However, the industry has grown. Profits as a percentage of sales have been modest. But what have the earnings on the investment been for actual concerns?

Inasmuch as balance sheet statistics based on an industry study are not available, the financial statements of selected supermarket chains, which operated 6,379 stores out of the 17,024 units in 1956, were studied. These revealed certain common characteristics. It is not to be inferred that these results were typical of the entire industry. The findings from this study presented in Table 7-4, when related to the previous financial discussion, revealed the following data:

1. (A large rate of return on the investment was realized by the owners. For the year 1950 the highest return was that for Colonial Stores, with a net profit before taxes of 34 cents on every dollar of owner's equity. In 1956 Market Basket earned 44 per cent on its equity. In the postwar years the rates of return on ownership funds have been consistently large. A high rate of return has been reported typical of this industry but has not been regarded excessive in view of the risks involved.[28] A favorable profit showing has been held essential for expansion financed from earnings and creditor's funds.)

2. The trend has been toward larger indebtedness as compared with the net worth. In many cases studied, owners and creditors in the postwar era had almost equal funds invested. The owners tended to "trade on the equity" fully.[29] By this policy of profitably controlling and using larger resources than their own funds permitted, supermarket operators were able to get large returns on their investment. The relative stability of this type of business, food, enabled large borrowing.

3. There was a limited use of suppliers' funds to finance the inventory, although the trend is toward a heavier current debt as compared with the inventory. The increase in current debt is accounted for largely by borrowing on a short-term note basis for current expansion funds.

4. The bulk of the debt has been of a fixed nature in connection with the acquiring of new outlets, the remodeling of existing units, and the rising equipment needs.

5. There has been a trend toward financing new store buildings by many of the companies. Inventory represents less of the total assets, and a greater percentage of fixed assets to total assets has been

[28] "Methods of Financing Store Construction," *Super Market Merchandising, op. cit.*

[29] Use of borrowed funds or stock with a limited return is known as *trading on equity*. See Harry G. Guthmann and Herbert E. Dougall, *Corporate Financial Policy* (New York: Prentice-Hall, Inc., 1955), p. 99.

TABLE 7-4 *

Results of Financial Ratio Analysis of Certain Major Supermarket Chains for the Years 1950 and 1956.

Company	Inventory to current liabs.		Net profit to tangible net worth, in %		Total debt to tangible net worth		Inventory to total assets, in %	
	1950	1956	1950	1956	1950	1956	1950	1956
American Stores Co.	2.34	1.44	13.73	23.40	0.64	0.70	48.39	37.93
A. J. Bayless Markets, Inc.	—	1.42	—	40.43	—	0.70	—	44.47
Century Food Markets Co.	1.08	0.71	15.28	16.51	1.13	1.18	45.60	27.35
Colonial Stores, Inc.	1.60	1.51	34.00	32.40	0.88	1.12	44.19	44.44
Daitch Crystal Dairies, Inc.	—	1.17	—	18.42	—	1.14	—	29.93
Fisher Bros., Co.	1.63	1.76	30.13	21.66	0.56	0.48	33.00	40.16
Food Fair Stores, Inc.	1.30	1.44	32.70	36.95	1.22	1.09	29.07	27.18
Food Mart, Inc.	—	1.56	—	27.11	—	0.64	—	40.59
Grand Union Co.	1.60	1.01	30.12	28.18	0.72	1.23	50.97	33.66
Jewel Tea Co., Inc.	1.09	1.02	31.99	31.68	0.58	0.92	39.10	32.49
Kroger Co.	1.36	1.15	27.86	26.52	0.63	0.99	51.65	40.95
Lucky Stores, Inc.	1.10	0.99	26.00	34.71	0.81	0.98	32.65	31.88
Market Basket	1.52	1.22	28.00	44.09	0.53	1.53	46.98	41.87
Purity Stores, Ltd.	—	0.84	—	19.19	—	1.13	—	24.72
Safeway Stores, Inc.	0.85	1.13	25.08	27.35	1.25	1.01	37.74	38.20
Shaffer Stores Co.	2.88	0.67	7.33	14.73	0.18	1.96	42.06	32.34
Shopping Bag Food Stores	0.83	0.77	31.28	30.59	1.98	1.52	40.60	32.02
Sunrise Supermarkets Corp.	—	1.06	—	25.29	—	0.98	—	31.64
Thriftimart, Inc.	—	1.17	—	24.27	—	0.96	—	47.41
Weingarten, J., Inc.	1.86	1.39	—	20.66	—	0.79	41.38	34.83

* Calculated from data in *Moody's Industrial Manuals.*

noted. Most concerns in the postwar era had larger net asset holdings in equipment and buildings than in merchandise.

SUMMARY

In summary, a modern supermarket is not a small business. The trend has been toward larger assets per store. Even the minimum-volume supers require a sizable outlay compared with that of the economy stores of the late 1920's. Rising equipment needs and costs plus the trend toward building in outlying locations have necessitated larger investments in fixed assets. Finding suitable quarters to rent has been a problem, particularly in the postwar period. Capital for expansion has been needed and obtained from many sources including the capital markets. These issues were met when the sizable profit possibilities of the industry were discerned. However, the trend toward real estate acquisitions has militated against profits to some extent, and management must assess whether supers are in the merchandising or real estate business. Finally, once a given location is established, there is a wide latitude in volume over which a store can operate and still be profitable. However, the sales and cost structures in this industry are such that increased volume augments considerably the profit rate expressed as a percentage of sales and enhances substantially the profit rate expressed as a percentage of net worth.

8 | EARLY SUPERMARKET IMPACT ON THE FOOD STORE INDUSTRY

INTRODUCTION

The development of the supermarket industry and the factors responsible for its innovation and growth have been presented in the seven preceding chapters. It is the purpose of this and the subsequent three chapters to examine the influence that the supermarket industry has tended to exert on the food and allied industries. The approach is to

1. Study qualitatively the early supermarket impact on small combination markets and grocery stores in the Los Angeles area and the East.
2. Follow quantitatively the movement of the large food chains toward supermarket operation, with special reference to the Great Atlantic and Pacific Tea Company.
3. Measure the strong trend within the supermarket industry toward horizontal integration in the post-World War II era.
4. Measure statistically the changes in the over-all pattern of food store sales in the year 1958 as compared with that of 1929.

This chapter examines qualitatively the early supermarket impact and the movement of the large food chains toward supermarket operation. The importance of early impact is that (1) it offers a key to shifts and trends in the pattern of food store sales that were to follow, and (2) it furnishes a better understanding of the statistical analysis in which the 1958 pattern is compared with 1929.

LOS ANGELES AREA SUPERMARKETS

Supermarts conforming to our definition in this book were in operation in the late 1920's in California, particularly in Los Angeles. One source estimated the number of supermarkets in the Los Angeles area as follows: [1]

1929	.	.	.	.	.	.	.	.	.	.	25
1930	.	.	.	.	.	.	.	.	.	.	39
1931	.	.	.	.	.	.	.	.	.	.	51
1932	.	.	.	.	.	.	.	.	.	.	79
1933	.	.	.	.	.	.	.	.	.	.	103

From 1929 to 1933 the estimated volume for these stores rose from $3,500,000 to $22,000,000, an increase of nearly 600 per cent.

Another source indicated as follows:

No attention was paid to the first super market in the Los Angeles area about five years ago (1928) or the increase in the number of such markets up to nearly 250, including about 200 large "drive-ins." Returning travelers now say they are amazed at the size and beauty of the super markets in Southern California, at their attractive methods of display and their clever merchandising stunts. They are crowded all day, drawing trade from a radius of eighty blocks away and do approximately 40 per cent of the total grocery business of the territory. Leaving 30 per cent each to the chains and independents has made pretty hard going for the chain stores.[2]

A third source is quoted as follows:

One of the directing heads of a large food company recently showed *Printers Ink* some figures received from an authentic source in Los Angeles. These show that a year ago (1932) there were 160 market stores in Los Angeles, while today (1933) there are 260 such stores. It is estimated these stores are doing about 35 per cent of the food volume of Los Angeles. . . . The 500 chain stores are getting about 21½ per cent. The remaining 44½ per cent is going to about 3300 independent stores, which

---

[1] M. J. Rowaldt, "Inside Figures of a Los Angeles Super," *Progressive Grocer,* XVI, no. 1, January, 1937, p. 43.

[2] H. M. Foster, "Threat of the Supermarket," *Sales Management,* XXXII, no. 9, April 20, 1933, p. 436.

is approximately close to the volume that those independents have been
doing right along.[3]

This same source also indicated that several years earlier only 14
per cent of the food store sales had been transacted by supers, while
the small independents transacted about 44 per cent of the total food
store volume. These statistics indicate the sales these "market stores"
gained at the expense of the chain stores.

Another writer indicated the presence of 104 large drive-in "market stores," as they were called in the Los Angeles area, on January
1, 1929.[4] People drove to these outlets in such numbers that the development of these "market stores" had a depressing effect on the
chains. In an effort to join the movement, chain stores took over
some of the departments in these large drive-in markets.[5]

In summary, writers at this time were of the opinion that these
large "market stores" captured in a relatively short time a noticeable portion of the grocery and combination market sales in the Los
Angeles area. This was largely at the expense of the chains. While
other rough estimates on the depth of penetration varied, they
judged that by 1933, supermarket sales were about 35 to 40 per cent
of the available grocery store and combination market volume.

INVASION OF THE EAST BY THE "CHEAPY" SUPERMARKET

The wide publicity and uproar that accompanied the opening of
the Big Bear Market in Elizabeth, New Jersey, led independent
grocers and chains alike to recognize this menace.[6] Although the
super was considered a depression product, they sought to eradi-
cate it. But the Big Bear fought back and made headline news,

[3] C. B. Larrabee, "Grocery Manufacturers Condemn Supermarket Price Cutters," *Printers Ink*, CLXII, no. 9, March 2, 1933, p. 41.

[4] Walter Van de Kamp, "An Innovation in Retail Selling," *Magazine of Business*, July, 1929, p. 28.

[5] S. L. Brevit, "Drive-In Department Store Gaining Popularity in the West,"
Sales Management, XXX, no. 3, January 17, 1931, p. 118.

[6] M. M. Zimmerman, *Super Market Spectacular Exponent of Mass Distribution* (New York: Super Market Publishing Co., 1937), p. 27.

while Giant Tigers, Big Chiefs, and a host of other similarly named "cheapy" supers multiplied in many parts of the country.[7]

Briefly, the following tactics were used to oppose the Big Bear Market, with pressure originating from both independents and chain operators: [8]

1. A local drive was initiated to license all retail stores, with the implication of refusing to license supermarkets.

2. Parking limitations were imposed against the supers.

3. Many annoying small local ordinances were imposed against the Big Bear.

4. Union pickets had relatively free play.

5. Newspapers were coerced into refusing to carry Big Bear ads.

6. The State Retail Association attempted to push through legislation in New Jersey that would curb Big Bear and other supermarkets.

7. The Associated Manufacturers of America of Grocery Products drafted a bill to be introduced in all state legislatures against price cutting. Provisions of this bill, "An Act to Protect Intrastate Commerce Against Unfair Price Competition," included the following:

   a. The term *unfair price competition* means the advertisements or offer of an article of merchandise at or below its purchase price in the course of intrastate commerce.

   b. Unfair price competition is unlawful and violators shall be guilty of a misdemeanor and if convicted, suffer penalty.

   c. The Attorney General's duty is to prosecute in the proper state courts.

   d. Any person injured by unfair price competition which is outlawed by this act may sue and shall receive three-fold damages sustained plus costs of the suit.

But all these legal maneuvers were in vain. Supermarkets mushroomed; nationally advertised brands continued on sale in the stores; known brands of merchandise were purchased in many instances directly from the manufacturers. Even wholesalers started to sponsor

[7] *Ibid.*
[8] Foster, *op. cit.*, p. 437.

their own supermarkets or to work in close relationship with supers
on narrow cost-plus arrangements.[9]

THE SMALL INDEPENDENT GROCER VERSUS
THE "CHEAPY" SUPERMARKET

The "cheapy" supermarkets in this early period did not exist in
sufficient numbers to affect appreciably the national sales of the
small independent grocers as a group. Data for the years 1929 and
1935, as shown in Table 8-1, indicate that (1) the number of large-

TABLE 8-1 *

Statistics on the Number and Volume of Sales of Large Combination
Markets in the United States for the Years 1929 and 1935
(in thousands).

Dollar sales volume classification	1929		1935	
	Number	Sales volume	Number	Sales volume
300,000 to 499,999	58	$21,492	264	$ 97,253
500,000 to 999,999	20	13,083	100	66,915
1,000,000 and over	2	6,641	25	39,119
Total †	80	$41,216	389	$203,287

* U.S. Bureau of Census, *Census of Business, 1935, Retail Distribution Part
II*, Vol. 1, Government Printing Office, Washington, D.C., pp. 2–21.

† These figures give the closest census statistics on the number of supermarkets existing in this period. No other statistics, even from private sources, were
available. These data underestimate slightly the number of supermarkets, inasmuch as the accepted definition in this thesis includes markets with $250,000
sales volume and up.

volume combination markets increased from 80 to 389, and (2) their
sales volume rose from $41.2 million to $203.3 million. Yet this $203.3
million volume of the large combination markets was only 2 per cent
of the total food store sales of the country, which totaled $9.71 bil-
lion in 1935.[10]

In the many sections of the country where "cheapies" failed to

[9] Zimmerman, *op. cit.*, p. 29.
[10] U.S. Bureau of the Census, *1951 Statistical Supplement, Survey of Current
Business*, Government Printing Office, Washington, D.C., 1952, p. 25.

open, the battle of the chains versus the independents still waged. The widely publicized supermarket was regarded as a depression product which would soon disappear.[11] But in the areas adjacent to operating supermarkets, independent grocery stores and small combination markets suffered losses in volume. Some independents, after the advent of the supermarket, reported losses of 30 to 40 per cent of sales volume.[12] It was in these areas that grocers reviewed their operating policies.

Certain of the choices open to the independent grocers were to

1. Join the movement toward supermarket operation.
2. Control expenses closely.
3. Switch to self-service or partial self-service.
4. Improve the service and try more to please the customers.
5. Add meats and switch to combination market operation.
6. Join cooperatives or buying associations for the purchase of staples at low prices in order to compete with the supers and the chains.
7. Work with wholesalers closely on a variety of plans in order to cut distribution costs.
8. Shift the hours of operation.

In reviewing the early impact of the "cheapy" supermarket, it can be concluded that the small independent grocer lost in sales volume upon competition with a nearby supermart. Generally, the closer the independent was to the super, the greater the loss; and some "cheapy" supers drew customers from as far as 50 miles away.[13] Not only did the independents covered here lose upon competing with nearby supermarkets, but the chains which are reviewed in the next section also lost.

FOOD CHAINS VERSUS THE "CHEAPY" SUPERMARKET

To review briefly the history of the supermarkets, the chain stores were not the innovators of the supermart, according to Malcolm

[11] Foster, *op. cit.*, p. 436.
[12] Zimmerman, *op. cit.*, p. 44.
[13] *Ibid.*

P. McNair.[14] In fact they were slow in adopting its format. Chains had developed a system of economy stores located close to the customer; these stores, except for differences in color and layout, were modeled after each other. Gradually in the late 1920's chains began to add meats; some offered services such as credit and delivery, did local advertising, and maintained all-day operations. These attempts at differentiation were quickly limited by competing chains.[15] The dominant chain, the Great Atlantic and Pacific Tea Company, boasted 13 per cent of all grocery store and combination market sales in 1929.[16]

Suddenly their price advantage was stolen from them by the "cheapy" supermarket. The alacrity with which the large super chains rallied to shift operations varied among the leaders. In 1935 the Kroger Company met competition in its home town of Cincinnati from the Albers Supermarkets by operating supers under the name of Pay'n Takit. On the Pacific coast, Safeway Stores, Incorporated, closed more than 70 of the Piggly Wiggly units purchased several years previously, abandoned more than 250 of its other smaller units, and replaced them with supermarkets. First National Stores in the New England region started toward supermarket operation in 1937.

Statistics on the total number of stores of the five largest volume food chains for the years 1934 to 1940 are included in Table 8-2. Each company reduced the number of stores it operated. During the same interval the total dollar volume for these concerns increased, as shown by the statistics in Table 8-3. While the figures do not specifically indicate the number of supermarkets, they represent an over-all movement to close small economy stores and replace them with fewer but larger units of the supermarket type.

[14] Testimony given at the trial, *United States* v. *The Great Atlantic & Pacific Tea Company,* U.S. Circuit Court of Appeals, 7th district, Docket 9221, Records and Briefs, Vol. II, p. 194.

[15] T. N. Beckman and H. C. Nolen, *The Chain Store Problem* (New York: McGraw-Hill Book Co., Inc., 1938), p. 137.

[16] Sales for A & P in 1929 were $1.04 billion; grocery store and combination market sales in 1929 were $7.4 billion. See Table 8-5.

TABLE 8-2 *

Number of Stores in the Five Largest Food Chains for the Years 1934 to 1940.

	1934	1935	1936	1937	1938	1939	1940
A & P	14,716	14,610	14,446	13,058	10,671	9,021	7,073
Kroger Co.	4,352	4,250	4,212	4,212	3,992	3,958	3,727
Safeway Stores	3,228	3,330	3,370	3,327	3,227	2,967	2,671
American Stores	2,859	2,826	2,816	2,620	2,416	2,272	2,157
First National Stores	2,623	2,556	2,473	2,350	2,244	2,137	1,923

* *Moody's Industrial Manuals*, 1935, 1936, 1937, 1938, 1939, 1940, and 1941.

TABLE 8-3 *

Sales for the Five Largest Volume Food Chains for the Years 1934, 1937, and 1940 (in millions).

Company	1934	1937	1940
A & P	$820	$907	$990
Safeway Stores	242	381	399
Kroger Co.	221	242	258
American Stores	114	115	124
First National Stores	105	120	131

* *Moody's Industrial Manual*, 1941.

The remainder of this chapter is concerned with the detailed reaction of the Great Atlantic and Pacific Tea Company to the supermarket development. The general practices adopted by this industry leader have appeared to be in line with those of the other large food chains. All the food chains were confronted by the supermarket development; all followed the same common policy of eliminating small stores and opening supermarkets; they differed only in the speed of change-over. In this respect A & P tackled the problem of conversion at a rate more accelerated than that of any of the big concerns.

THE CASE OF THE GREAT ATLANTIC AND PACIFIC TEA COMPANY

In the subsequent text, an examination of A & P's reaction to the supermarket invasion is presented in detail.

Initial Attention Given Supermarkets by A & P

John A. Hartford, president of The Great Atlantic and Pacific Tea Company, testified that his attention was first brought to supermarkets by the operation of King Kullen in the East Division [17] of A & P.[18] In February, 1934, the Central Division Executive Committee minutes reported the opening of a supermarket in Columbus, Ohio, by a former A & P employee.[19]

In the New England Division between 1930 and 1934, a great many independent supermarkets were organized. These independents operated at a much lower expense rate than the A & P stores, and their lower operating costs were reflected in lower prices.[20] During 1935 the Great Bear and Giant Tiger supermarket chains were expanding in the Southern Division.

In the Central Western Division of the A & P structure, sales had fallen, and the gross profit rate was considerably higher than the gross margin of the supermarket competitors according to Division President Toolin.[21] He took John A. Hartford on a tour of Detroit in 1934 and showed him what competition had done in the way of opening supermarkets. Toolin convinced President Hartford that A & P should change its mode of operation; but others in high authority still thought the supermarket was temporary. They further believed that the outstanding operating record of the supers was obtained by selling under cost and that A & P should not sell below cost; therefore they opposed this type of operation.[22]

---

[17] In order to facilitate control of this food giant, the management divided the company into six regional operation divisions.
[18] *U.S.* v. *The Great Atlantic & Pacific Tea Co., op. cit.*, p. 194.
[19] *Ibid.*, p. 195.
[20] *Ibid.*, p. 196.
[21] *Ibid.*, p. 198.
[22] *Ibid.*

Number of Unprofitable A & P Stores in the 1930's

That the management of the world's largest food retailer was cognizant of the supermarket is evident. At first the wide-scale operations of the A & P mitigated the supermarket influence; but as the supers increased, the number of unprofitable A & P stores steadily mounted, as shown by the figures in Table 8-4. The peak number of unprofitable units in the history of the A & P was reached in 1937 when one-third, or 4,382 stores, of the 13,264 outlets were in the red. But the substantial change in operation that took place from 1937 to 1941 literally wiped out small unprofitable units.

TABLE 8-4 *

Total Number of Stores and Number of Unprofitable Units
of the A & P Co. for the Years 1933 to 1941.

Year	Number of stores	Number of unprofitable stores	% of unprofitable to total
1933	15,095	3,060	20.0
1934	14,995	3,871	25.8
1935	14,885	3,651	24.7
1936	14,697	3,467	23.6
1937	13,264	4,382	33.3
1938	10,827	2,354	21.7
1939	9,088	1,619	17.5
1940	7,143	889	12.4
1941	6,165	639	10.3

* *United States* v. *The Great Atlantic and Pacific Tea Company*, U.S. Circuit Court of Appeals, 7th district, Docket 9221, Records and Briefs, Vol. 1, p. 291.

A & P Loss in Relative Sales Position
Among the Food Stores

The economy store operation of the A & P reached its zenith in 1930, at which time the company operated 15,422 stores in the United States. Volume attained a peak of $1.049 billion, as shown by the statistics in Table 8-3. From then until the company converted to supermarket operation, the trend in volume of sales was downward. For example, the vice-president of the Eastern Division indicated that prior to 1930, A & P had a very profitable operation in the Brooklyn unit.[23] But from 1930, when supermarkets were first opened by independents, there began a steady downward trend in the competitive position which was a direct result of supermarket competition. Sales in the Brooklyn unit dropped from $39,400,000 in 1930 to $25,400,000 in 1937; during the same period profits dropped from $1,200,000 in 1930 to a $400,000 loss in 1937.

In the Central Western Division, Albers, a supermarket chain, started about 1934. After two years Albers, with only eight supermarkets, enjoyed 9.5 per cent of the food store business in Cincinnati; the A & P volume transacted by 50 stores had dwindled to 7.7 per cent of the food store sales.[24]

The statistics in Table 8-5 further evidence the loss of the A & P competitive position. These figures indicate that the sales of A & P dropped from $1,039,000,000 in 1929 to $864,000,000 in 1937, a decrease of 17 per cent; total grocery store and combination market sales in the nation decreased from $7.35 billion to $7.25 billion, a reduction of 1.4 per cent. In terms of total food store sales, which include the specialty food shops as well as the grocery stores and combination markets, the A & P loss in relative position also was pronounced.

A & P Experimental Supermarkets

One of the unsolved questions that confronted the management of this mighty food chain was the true operating costs of a supermarket. A & P had adhered to the principle of not selling merchandise at a price less than cost; and the management questioned whether the competing independent supers could actually sell merchandise at such cheap prices and still obtain a profit.

In the spring of 1935 the Central Western Division opened a supermarket in Paducah, Kentucky, and attempted to operate at a gross margin of 13 per cent and a net profit of 2 per cent.[25] Next, 14 stores were opened in Nashville, Tennessee, and offered lower

[23] *Ibid.*, p. 195.
[24] *Ibid.*
[25] *Ibid.*, Vol. VI, p. 240.

TABLE 8-5

**Total Sales of A & P, All Grocery and Combination Markets
and All Food Stores for the Years 1929 to 1943.**

Year	Number of stores *	Dollar volume * (in billions)	Total grocery and combination store sales † (in billions)	Total food store sales † (in billions)
1929	15,150	$1.04	$ 7.4	$11.0
1930	19,422	1.05	—	—
1931	15,371	0.99	—	—
1932	15,108	0.85	—	—
1933	14,818	0.80	—	—
1934	14,716	0.83	—	—
1935	14,610	0.86	6.4	8.4
1936	14,446	0.89	6.8	9.0
1937	13,058	0.86	7.3	9.7
1938	10,671	0.87	7.2	9.5
1939	9,021	0.98	7.7	10.2
1940	7,073	1.10	8.3	10.9
1941	6,042	1.35	9.6	12.6
1942	5,821	1.38	12.1	15.8
1943	5,751	1.47	13.3	17.5

* U.S. v. *Great Atlantic and Pacific Tea Company*, U.S. Circuit Court of Appeals, 7th district, Docket 9221, Records and Briefs, Vol. I, p. 322.

† U.S. Bureau of the Census, *1951 Statistical Supplement, Survey of Current Business*, Government Printing Office, Washington, D.C., 1952, p. 8.

prices than other A & P economy stores in that city on the entire line of merchandise. This division expanded experimental operations to Cincinnati where competition raged between independent Albers and Kroger's Pay'n Takit stores.

In 1935 the A & P Eastern Division experimented with 100 stores known as Baby Bears in the Pittsburgh area.[26] Prices were cut in these stores on merchandise that was directly delivered from carload lot purchases. These Baby Bears emphasized in their advertising the lowest prices in town on this carload lot merchandise.

[26] *Ibid.*, Vol. II, p. 162.

The available evidence from the testimony indicated that these experimental stores were for the most part developed independently by the separate divisions with little or no support from the central management. In 1937 the central management reviewed the situation and decided to switch to supermarket operation. Its aim was to operate each super at a gross margin of 12 per cent, expenses of 10 per cent, and a net profit of 2 per cent.[27]

A & P Joins the Supermarket Industry in 1937

The success of the divisional experimental supers, coupled with the loss of sales, profits, and competitive position in the conventional stores, finally resulted in a decision by top management to shift the operational policy. The data in Table 8-6 indicate the complete re-

TABLE 8-6 *

Statistics on Total Number of A & P Stores, Number
of Supermarkets, Total Sales and Supermarket
Sales for the Years 1936 to 1943
(sales in millions of dollars).

Year	Number of stores	Number of supers	Total dollar sales	Super sales
1936	14,446	20	$ 889	$ 00
1937	13,058	282	864	53
1938	10,671	771	866	220
1939	9,021	1,119	976	401
1940	7,073	1,396	1,099	594
1941	6,042	1,594	1,348	846
1942	5,821	1,633	1,435	934
1943	5,751	1,646	1,259	761

* *United States* v. *The Great Atlantic and Pacific Tea Company*, U.S. Circuit Court of Appeals, 7th district, Docket 9221, Records and Briefs, Vol. 1, p. 323.

versal of policy and the rapid conversion to supermarket operation that this giant food chain made within six years. At the close of 1937, A & P was already operating 282 supermarkets. Yet, President Hartford expressed concern over the pace of supermarket develop-

[27] *Ibid.*, p. 196.

ment and urged that everything possible be done to speed up the program. He suggested the advisability of having special men concentrate on the search for new locations.

In addition to concentrating on supermarket expansion, the management endeavored to ascertain whether the larger or smaller supers were more profitable. Statistics from the Central Western Division indicated that the larger type of supermarket with weekly sales of $10,000 and over had an operating expense advantage over the stores with $6,000 or less weekly volume.[28]

Data in Table 8-6 indicate that by 1941, the 1,594 units (or about 29 per cent) of all A & P stores were supermarkets; and these units, with sales of $846,000,000 accounted for 63 per cent of the total sales. However, following 1941, supermarket expansion by the A & P was handicapped because of World War II. The management reported operations were hampered by gas rationing, food rationing, and man power shortages. Furthermore, some customers switched to stores where they could establish personal relationship with the owners.

Effect of A & P Supermarket Operation on Its Gross Margin, Expense, and Profit

Once the supermarket independents became important in the food store field, the operation of the industry giant was adversely affected. From 1932 until A & P joined the supermarket operation, the average A & P store was forced to operate on a smaller gross margin in order to meet price competition. Even though expenses were reduced through close control, profits dwindled. However, after 1937 company operations improved because of its switch to supermarket activity. By 1941 the supermarket division of A & P was working on a gross margin of 12.4 per cent, an expense of 10.51 per cent, and a net profit of 1.96 per cent as indicated in Table 8-7. This was a vastly superior showing compared with the economy stores that still remained in operation in 1941. A & P gained in its relative sales posi-

[28] *Ibid.*

tion in the grocery store and combination market industry after it switched to supermarket operation; whereas A & P had only 11.7 per cent of the total grocery store and combination market sales in 1937, it increased its position to 14.1 per cent of the industry sales by 1941.[29]

SUPERMARKET ADVANTAGES FOR LARGE FOOD CHAINS

The numerous red-front A & P units scattered throughout the country were the leaders in food store retailing prior to 1930. Other large chains had a similar type of operation.[30] Then, almost simul-

TABLE 8-7 *

Operating Results of the A & P Detailed into Economy Stores and Supermarkets for the Year 1941 (sales in thousands).

	4,448 Economy stores		1,594 Supers	
	Dollar sales	% of sales	Dollar sales	% of sales
Weekly sales	$6,276	100.00	$17,336	100.00
Cost of sales	5,208	82.99	15,169	87.53
Gross margin	1,068	17.01	2,167	12.47
Expenses	966	15.39	1,820	10.51
Net profit	$ 102	1.62	$ 347	1.96

* *United States* v. *The Great A & P Tea Co.*, U.S. Circuit Court of Appeals, 7th district, Docket 9221, Records and Briefs, Vol. I, p. 323.

taneously, the A & P and its brethren had to meet the challenge of the supermarket, the NRA, the Robinson Patman Act, and chain store tax laws. The supermarket was underpricing the food chains; the NRA forced the chains to raise wages; the Robinson Patman Act

[29] Statistics to make these calculations are contained in Table 8-5. The 1937 A & P sales were $864 million, and grocery store and combination market sales were $7,300 million. In 1941 A & P sales were $1.348 billion, and grocery and combination market sales were $9.6 billion.

[30] Paul H. Nystrom, *Retail Store Operation* (New York: The Ronald Press Co., 1937), p. 466.

restricted the buying advantages of the large operators; and the progressively heavier chain store taxes levied on the number of units operated stifled large multi-unit expansion.

Actually, the supermarket type of operation adopted by the A & P and other large chains aided them to meet successfully the existing price competition. The advantages of supermarket operation stemmed from the following:

1. Fewer stores resulted in reduced chain taxes per store.

2. The total cost of opening new stores was reduced since fewer stores were opened.

3. Reduced operating costs as a percentage of sales were realized.

The principal disadvantage lay in the larger investment per store with its accompanying risk.

SUMMARY

The independent operators were the innovators of supermarkets. Unlike David versus Goliath, they tackled two adversaries, namely, the food chains and the host of small independent food store operators. The supermarket methods of merchandising and store operation proved so successful that they rapidly spread consternation among the chains and small independents. The supers captured substantial portions of the volume in the trading areas they invaded. The small independents, in the main, either became supers or gradually disappeared from the scene. The chains successfully competed by joining the supermarket movement. Chains substantially revamped operations and soon became dominant in the industry volumewise. This change-over by the chains, as evidenced in this chapter by the record of the Great Atlantic and Pacific Tea Company, was revolutionary in nature.

9 | SUPERMARKETS BECOME BIG BUSINESS— INTEGRATION

INTRODUCTION

In the preceding chapter, the initial impact of the supermarket on the field of food store retailing was presented. The reaction of both small independent merchants and giant food chains, with special emphasis on the Great Atlantic and Pacific Tea Company, was measured. Through rationing restrictions beyond its control, the supermarket showed little growth and impact during the World War II years. The only exception was the addition of nonfoods to the line in order to sustain or build volume.

This chapter measures the impact of the supermarket in the postwar era when the industry literally came of age. Food retailing became big business, not only in the sense that larger and larger stores requiring substantial investments were built in new locations, but also through a strong trend toward concentration in the hands of fewer and larger concerns.

CHAINS DOMINATE SUPERMARKET INDUSTRY

In the early 1930's all supermarts were independents. In the early 1940's chains began to make inroads. These chains were not necessarily the big food concerns of the 1920's. Shrewd and capable merchants who started with one unit built empires as exemplified by Food Fair Stores and Albers Supermarkets. By 1950, according to *Progressive Grocer,* about 37 per cent of the supermarkets with less

168

than 37 per cent of the volume were still individual operations at one location; by 1958 only 20.7 per cent of the supermarkets transacting 18.2 per cent of the industry volume were one-unit operations in an industry that now dominated all food store sales.[1] Chain stores in 1958 operated 66.6 per cent of the stores and transacted 69.1 per cent of the supermarket industry volume.[2]

INTEGRATION

The entire supermarket industry has mushroomed in the postwar era as indicated by statistics in Table 1-2; yet the chain members have outstripped the independent operators in this aura of growth. Integration has played an important role in the drive of the chains to dominate this field since they used this device more frequently than the independents. Although all chains have not grown at the same rate, the most rapidly growing concerns generally have been the principal users of integration.

Integration, which means the bringing of parts into a whole, has taken two directions, namely, horizontal and vertical combinations. In marketing parlance, horizontal or lateral integration occurs with consolidations of two or more similar concerns performing the same functions in the same stage of distribution. This occurs when one supermarket concern purchases the store or stores of another supermart firm. Vertical integration refers to the operation by a firm of the processes and functions in two or more stages of distribution or production.[3] Simply, a supermarket firm that operates its own bakery and distributes the products through its outlets is integrated vertically. Also, the supermarket concern that performs wholesale functions by operating its own warehouse is integrated vertically. Inherent in a successful combination is the reduction in expense that results from the coordination of the various parts of the integrated concern.

---

[1] See Table 1-3.
[2] *Ibid.*
[3] Paul Converse and Harvey Huegy, *The Elements of Marketing* (New York: Prentice-Hall, Inc., 1958), p. 243.

Supermarkets generally have employed both horizontal and vertical integration. The usual practice has been for the smaller concerns to integrate horizontally until they are large enough (have sufficient outlets) to assume the major part of wholesale operations. The assumption of the wholesale function is vertical integration of marketing activity. Supermarkets obtain 81 per cent of their groceries through their own central warehouses and an additional 10 per cent through retailer-owned cooperatives.[4] Supermarket chains or retail-sponsored cooperatives design and operate their wholesale integration at different levels of volume. Some need about 12 to 14 retail outlets doing from $15 million to $20 million in yearly volume to make the entire operation a success. Certain larger chains may require as many as 25 stores doing at least $30 million in sales to be serviced by the wholesale division in order to make the integration profitable.

As the concerns attain sufficient size, they can extend vertical integration by entry into certain manufacturing operations and can thus perform all the consecutive processes in food manufacture and distribution. The extent of food manufacturing performed by food chains is shown by the data in Table 9-1. In 1958 the 62 major chain supermarkets owned 326 factories that produced and shipped $1.304 billion in products. Chain-branded products of $1.304 billion at manufacturer's prices or $1.630 billion at retail prices (adjusted for a 20 per cent markup) are slightly under 10 per cent of total chain food store sales of $18.589 billion in 1958. The coffee and bakery areas are two of the most frequently entered fields. Generally a supermarket operation needs about $30 million in volume to make the vertical integration into the bakery operation profitable. Other areas invaded by supers include dairy products, mayonnaise, preserves, and confections. Certain of the larger supermarket operations are experimenting with or have entered into the meat-packing field with 22 packaging and preparing plants in operation. Food processing in the form of storing green bananas and tomatoes until they

[4] "How the Super Markets Get Their Groceries," *Super Market Industry Speaks* (Chicago: Super Market Institute, 1956), p. 14.

TABLE 9-1 *

Number of Food Manufacturing Plants Operated by 62 Major Food Chains and the Value of Shipments from These Establishments for the Years 1954 and 1958.

Kind of establishment	Number of establishments		Value of shipments (in thousands)	
	1954	1958	1954	1958
Meat packing	9	9	$ 94,500	$ 149,000
Prepared meats	11	13	38,200	78,100
Poultry dressing	2	4	3,400	7,100
Dairy products	32	41	34,700	54,800
Concentrated milk	12	12	46,800	57,200
Fluid milk	22	27	57,500	95,900
Canning and freezing	11	13	77,000	99,100
Bread and related products	126	147	289,500	379,500
Confectionery	6	7	31,000	43,200
Miscellaneous food preparation	16	14	85,700	105,300
Coffee, roasted or concentrated	38	39	316,700	234,400
Total	285	326	$1,075,000	$1,303,600

* Federal Trade Commission, *Federal Trade Commission Economic Inquiry into Food Marketing—Interim Report*, Government Printing Office, Washington, D.C., June 30, 1959.

are ripe is performed on a large scale. The ultimate in vertical integration is exemplified currently by the Great Atlantic and Pacific Tea Company with its widely known Ann Page, Jane Parker, Iona, Red Circle, Bokar, and Whitehouse lines of products.

While the statistics in Table 9-1 indicate that the supermarket industry is expanding into the meat packing area through vertical integration, a battle with the giant packers may be in the offing. The meat-packing industry, one in which there is a high degree of concentration of power in a relatively few firms, has been hamstrung by the Consent Decree of 1920. This decree resulted from action taken by the federal government under the Sherman Anti-trust Act and listed more than 100 products which the packers were not allowed to make, sell, or transport. In addition, the packers involved agreed to divest themselves of businesses considered to be unrelated to the preparation and wholesale distribution of meat products. In November, 1956, the Cudahy Packing Company filed a petition in the United States District Court in Chicago, Illinois, seeking release from certain provisions of the 1920 Decree. Two other parties to the decree, Armour and Company and Swift and Company, also filed petitions asking for similar relief. Extensive evidence demonstrating the significant changes in the distribution of food products at all levels since 1920 has been presented to the court; a decision is expected in 1961. Some of the possible areas of expansion for the meat packers include diversification into allied food products, integration through acquisition of common stock in supermarket chains, expansion into the area of frozen and prepackaged meats for the retail trade to be sold under an identifying label, and development of new operating methods.

CONCENTRATION AMONG MAJOR FOOD CHAINS

The major food chains currently dominate the supermarket and food store industries volumewise. The sales statistics of ten of these chains are recorded in Table 9-2 and show a phenomenal $10.1 billion increase between the years 1945 and 1958. The industry giant, the Great Atlantic & Pacific Tea Company, had a sales rise from $1.435 billion to $5.095 billion in this 13-year period, or an increase of 355 per cent. Food Fair Stores, Incorporated, experienced a phenomenal sales boost during this interval from $61 million to $734 million, or over 1,200 per cent.

Further evidence of this high degree of concentration in the retail food industry is indicated by the statistics in Table 9-2. Ten of the largest volume concerns with sales of $13.4 billion transacted about one-fourth of all food store sales in the country in 1958.

It is not solely in the number of stores where strength of the large chains lies. Examine the trend toward fewer and larger stores with bigger investments per location, as shown by the statistics of American Stores Company in Table 9-4. The statistics of this company exemplify the direction the large supermart chains generally have

TABLE 9-2 *

**Dollar Sales of Ten of the Largest Food Store Chains
for the Years 1945 and 1958 (in millions).**

Company †	1945	1958
Great A & P Tea Co.	$1,435	$ 5,095
Safeway Stores	615	2,225
Kroger Co.	457	1,776
American Stores Co.	224	866
National Tea Co.	107	794
Food Fair Stores	61	734
First National Stores	182	531
Colonial Stores	99	437
Grand Union Co.	55	504
Jewel Tea Co.	62	444
Total	$3,297	$13,406

* *Moody's Industrial Manuals.*
† In 1958, Winn-Dixie Stores, Inc., transacted $631 million in sales. However, consolidated sales for this firm, which is the result of a merger in 1955, are not available for the year 1945.

TABLE 9-3

**Sales of Ten Major Supermarket Chains and
Total Food Store Sales for the Years 1945
and 1958 (in millions).**

	1945	1958
Sales of 10 major supermarket chains *	$ 3,297	$13,406
Total food store sales †	19,120	53,075
10 major supermarket chains as a per cent of total food store sales	17.24%	25.26%

* See totals Table 9-2.
† *Facts in Grocery Distribution* (New York: Progressive Grocer, 1959), p. F–17.

taken to dominate the food store industry. Between 1945 and 1958, American Stores followed a policy of integration while decreasing the number of outlets from 1,954 to only 844; but in the same interval, average sales per store rose from $118,000 to almost $1,000,-000, and net income per outlet rose from $1,005 to $12,432.

FOOD CHAIN DILEMMA—ACQUIRE OR EXPIRE

In the postwar era, the supermarkets became the largest class of food stores, according to volume. In turn, the food chains as a group gained volume and numerical superiority in the supermarket industry. They were able to attain superiority over the independent supers

TABLE 9-4 *

Number of Stores, Sales per Store, and Net Income per Store for American Stores Company for the Years 1945 to 1958.

Year	Number of stores	Average sales per store (in thousands)	Net income per store
1945	1,954	$118	$ 1,005
1946	2,012	156	2,237
1947	1,921	202	3,084
1948	1,833	227	3,089
1950	1,637	254	4,119
1951	1,505	312	4,727
1952	1,408	370	3,590
1953	1,289	421	3,948
1954	1,132	533	6,597
1955	1,076	581	6,520
1956	953	687	8,745
1957	903	864	10,731
1958	844	992	12,432

* *Moody's Industrial Manual.*

as to the number of stores and volume even though they eliminated many small outlets. The food chains attained dominance by the standard procedure of (1) continuously building and opening new large units and (2) integrating horizontally through the acquisition of going concerns. The Federal Trade Commission reported that 151 companies during the years 1953 to 1958 opened new stores and acquired existing outlets which had sales of $3.908 billion and $1.2999 billion, respectively, for the year 1958.[5]

[5] Federal Trade Commission, *Federal Trade Commission Economic Inquiry Into Food Marketing—Interim Report,* Government Printing Office, Washington, D.C., June 30, 1959.

Further evidence of the extent of acquisitions is shown by the data in Table 9-5. In the years 1949 to 1958, 83 supermarket concerns acquired 315 operating companies which owned 2,238 stores that transacted $1.916 billion in annual sales at the time of acquisition. The merger movement trend continues to increase. The year 1958 was the most active year for mergers, both as to the number of companies active in acquiring outlets and as to the sales of the stores purchased at the time of acquisition.

Among the food chains themselves, however, significant shifts had been taking place in the pattern of sales. Statistics in Table 9-2 indicate remarkable growth for all major members of the industry; but all concerns did not expand at the same rate. The fast-moving, medium-sized chains appear to have made inroads in the relative position volumewise at the expense of the giants in the industry and the small-chain operators.

In order to assess this development in supermarket chain sales, it is necessary (1) to measure changes in relative volume among the large, medium, and small chains; (2) to summarize recent acquisitions and mergers; (3) to examine the underlying forces behind the merger movement; and (4) to indicate the impact on food store distribution.[6]

Changes in Relative Position Among Food Chains by Size

Only for the purpose of showing approximate size are the food chains grouped into three classifications by volume. This grouping includes large concerns with sales of $1 billion or more, medium-sized chains with sales from $100 million to $999 million, and small companies with sales of less than $100 million as of the year 1957. This classification need not be sacrosanct in that large and small concerns bordering on the $100 million and $999 million boundaries have been active in mergers and could be considered for the purposes of analysis in the medium-sized class.

---

[6] The author first presented these ideas in an article, "Food Chain Dilemma—Acquire or Expire," which appeared in the *Journal of Retailing*, XXXIV, no. 4, Winter, 1958–1959, p. 216.

TABLE 9-5 *

Number and Volume of Food Stores That Were Acquired
by Food Chains for the Years 1949 to 1958.

Year of acquisition	Number of acquiring companies	Number of concerns acquired	Number of stores acquired as a result of the merger	Annual sales of stores purchased at time of acquisition (in thousands)
1949	6	6	72	$ 66,180
1950	5	5	5	3,889
1951	10	12	69	27,829
1952	5	10	273	67,343
1953	11	12	71	86,617
1954	17	20	70	60,580
1955	23	48	455	434,166
1956	36	70	439	397,325
1957	34	54	363	322,520
1958	38	78	421	450,003
Total	83 †	315	2,238	$1,916,452

* Federal Trade Commission, *Federal Trade Commission Economic Inquiry Into Food Marketing—Interim Report,* Government Printing Office, Washington, D.C., June 30, 1959.

† This total represents the number of concerns that made acquisitions; it is not based on a column total inasmuch as some companies made acquisitions in more than one year.

The individual leader in the food chain field, by far, continues to be the Great Atlantic and Pacific Tea Company, which in 1957 transacted 27.44 per cent of all chain grocery and combination store sales, as shown by the statistics in Table 9-6. Yet, the A & P together with Safeway Stores suffered a loss in relative industry position among the food chains in recent years. Although they followed the standard practice of eliminating smaller stores and opening larger units, they were inactive in the merger movement with one notable exception, namely, Safeway's expansion in the Des Moines, Iowa, market.[7]

[7] *The Merger Movement in Retail Food Distribution* (Chicago: National Association of Retail Grocers, 1959), p. 15.

This does not mean, however, that these concerns are losing their share of total food store volume. For example, A & P had 9.1 per cent of the total food store sales in 1951 and 10.1 per cent in 1958.[8]

TABLE 9-6

Chain Grocery Store Sales Classified by Volume,
Expressed in Dollars and as a Percentage of Total Chain
Grocery Sales for the Years 1951 and 1957.

	1951		1957	
Number of outlets	*Millions of dollars*	*% of total*	*Millions of dollars*	*% of total*
Chains with $1 billion and over sales in 1957 * Great Atlantic & Pacific Tea Co.	$ 3,393	31.66	$ 4,769	27.44
Safeway Stores, Inc.	1,455	13.58	2,117	12.18
Kroger Co.	997	9.30	1,674	9.63
Subtotal	5,845	54.54	8,560	49.25
Chains with $100–999 million sales in 1957 †	2,922	27.26	6,267	36.06
Chains with sales less than $100 million in 1957 ‡	1,951	18.20	2,552	14.69
Totals §	$10,718	100.00	$17,379	100.00

* Compiled from statistics published in the Federal Trade Commission report entitled *Federal Trade Commission Economic Inquiry Into Food Marketing—Interim Report*, Government Printing Office, Washington, D.C., June 30, 1959.
† *Ibid.*
‡ Calculated by subtracting total chain food store sales of $100 million or more volume from total industry sales.
§ U.S. Bureau of the Census, *Statistical Abstract of the U.S.*, Government Printing Office, Washington, D.C., 1959, p. 834.

The other member of the billion-dollar volume classification, The Kroger Company, improved its relative position through opening new stores and the merger route. These three members of the billion-dollar classification group acquired 179 stores transacting $240 million in annual sales during the period 1955 to 1958.[9]

[8] Federal Trade Commission, *op. cit.*
[9] *The Merger Movement in Retail Food Distribution, op. cit.*

The greatest increase in volume from 1951 to 1957 was made by the medium-sized group of stores in the $100 million to $999 million volume class. In 1957 these stores commanded 36.06 per cent of the chain food sales as compared with only 27.26 per cent in 1951. Mergers and acquisitions were responsible primarily for this gain. This segment of chain food stores acquired 1,092 outlets transacting $1.220 billion in annual sales during the period of 1955 to 1958.[10]

The small chains of less than $100 million in annual volume have suffered a significant loss in relative position in recent years. They have dropped in volume from 18.20 per cent to 14.69 per cent of chain grocery and combination store sales. It was on this group, multi-unit operators of less than 11 stores and single-unit concerns, that the medium-sized chains made their raids. These inroads resulted even though the chains of $100 million sales or less in turn made acquisition among the smaller supermarket companies; these acquisitions included 392 stores that transacted $443 million in annual sales during the period 1955 to 1958.[11]

Acquisitions

The numerical record of mergers compiled by ten of the major supermarket chains for the years 1949 to 1958 is summarized in Table 9-7. All but the Great Atlantic and Pacific Tea Company have participated to varying degrees in this movement; the most active concerns in the merger movement have been the National Tea Company, Winn Dixie Stores, Incorporated, the Kroger Company, and the Grand Union Company.

Specifically, what acquisitions have the major supermarket concerns made? What marketing areas have they invaded? The A & P, the major operator among the food chains as to volume and number of outlets, has added no new stores through merger or acquisition in recent years. Safeway Stores, Incorporated, the second largest operation, has been a relatively minor factor nationally in the merger movement, with its only major acquisition activity in the Des

10 *Ibid.*
11 *Ibid.*

TABLE 9-7

Number and Volume of Food Stores That Were Acquired by
Ten Major Food Chains for the Years 1949 to 1958.

Name of company	Number of acquisitions	Number of of stores acquired	Annual sales of stores purchased at time of acquisition (in thousands)
American Stores Co.	5	93	$ 34,442
Colonial Stores, Inc.	10	99	121,906
Food Fair Stores, Inc.	6	67	107,731
Grand Union Co.	15	128	128,417
Jewel Tea Co., Inc.	2	43	56,234
Kroger Co.	5	130	174,064
Lucky Stores, Inc.	4	56	72,612
National Tea Co.	24	485	251,612
Safeway Stores, Inc.	25	67	33,016
Winn-Dixie Stores, Inc.	11	306	221,070
Total	107	1,474	$1,201,104

* Federal Trade Commission, *Federal Trade Commission Economic Inquiry
Into Food Marketing—Interim Report,* Government Printing Office, Washington,
D.C., June 30, 1959.

Moines, Iowa, market. Kroger, on the other hand, has been on a
constant program of acquisition. It recently acquired control of the
26 Henke & Pillot Stores of Houston, Texas, and the 25-unit Krambo
Food Stores, Incorporated of Wisconsin. Whereas Henke & Pillot
Stores were in an entirely new marketing area, the other merger put
Krambo and Kroger in direct competition with each other for more
intensive market coverage. Then, in 1958, Kroger acquired the 44
stores of Wyatt and Evans Food Stores in Texas. On April 6, 1959,
however, the Federal Trade Commission charged the Kroger Company with illegally acquiring since 1928 more than 40 corporations
and their 1,900 stores. The commission charged the acquisitions vio-
lated the antimerger laws in that they may result in a substantial
lessening of competition or a tendency toward monopoly in the
processing, manufacturing, purchasing, and distributing of grocery
products and in the sale of merchandise in retail grocery stores.

In the classification of chains with annual sales of $100 million to $999 million, the following changes occurred: Colonial Stores, Incorporated, captured the 73 stores of Albers Super Markets, Incorporated, of Ohio and 14 units of Stop and Shop Enterprise of Indiana. Food Fair Stores, Incorporated, after experiencing remarkable growth in the postwar era, added 16 Carl's Markets, Incorporated, of Florida and four stores of Budget Markets, Incorporated. American Stores Company purchased the 92-unit chain of the Market Basket Corporation of New York. Grand Union Company acquired 31 Carrolls' Limited Stores and certain Food Fair Stores in Washington, D.C.; Shirley Food Stores and certain Stop and Shop outlets in New Haven, Connecticut; six Food Center Supermarkets in New York; and two Value Markets and three Tanner Stores in Miami. Jewel Tea Company added 41 stores of Eisner Grocery Company of Champaign, Illinois.

The greatest forager of the medium-sized chains was the National Tea Company, which acquired C. F. Smith Stores Company, Northwest Piggly Wiggly Company, George T. Smith's Market Basket, Incorporated, Dale Supermarkets, 28 Food Center Stores in St. Louis, Missouri; 28 Capital Stores, Incorporated, of Baton Rouge, Louisiana; Ashton's Supermarket of Gulfport, Mississippi; and H. A. Smith Markets, Incorporated, and Montag's Supermarket Chain of Memphis, Tennessee. The most recent additions of National Tea Company include the Maker's Food Chain of Michigan and seven stores in Peoria, Illinois, from Illinois Valley Stores; seven units of Devan's Food Stores, Mobile, Alabama; nine Logan's Supermarkets of Nashville; and 85 Council Oak Stores in Minnesota and Iowa. Other recent additions include stores in Colorado, Michigan, Iowa, and Illinois.

In addition, National Tea Company may become part of a new major international company in the industry. George Weston, Limited, a Canadian biscuit manufacturer, controls Loblaw Groceterias Company, Limited, one of Canada's largest grocery chains. In turn, Loblaw Groceterias' assets include 56 per cent of the stock of Loblaw, Incorporated, and 33 per cent interest of National Tea Company. Both of the last two are classed as medium-sized chains. The George Weston group, which has been built in recent years, also has cast covetous glances at certain Safeway Stores. On March 31, 1959, the National Tea Company was charged by the Federal Trade Commission with illegally acquiring stores in violation of the Clayton Act's antimerger section and with unfair competition and business practices in violation of the Federal Trade Commission Act.

Two of the medium-sized group, Dixie Home Stores and Winn-Lovett Company, merged into the Winn-Dixie Stores, Incorporated, a chain of some 447 stores. Prior to the merger, Winn-Lovett Company had acquired eight Jitney Jungle Stores of Alabama and Edins Food Stores of Columbia, South Carolina. In 1956, Winn-Dixie acquired 24 stores in North Carolina from Ketner-Milner Stores, Incorporated, and 42 stores of H. G. Hill Stores, Incorporated, in the New Orleans area.

Perhaps the most revolutionary merger of the medium-sized chains was the formation in 1955 of ACF-Wrigley Stores, Incorporated. In this, ACF-Brill Motors Company and the 92 Wrigley Stores of Detroit, Michigan, were the principals. Also included in this and subsequent development were the 20-odd Big Bear Markets of Michigan, Incorporated, 33 Humpty Dumpty Stores of Oklahoma, 13 Foodtown Stores, Incorporated, and 10 Fred Rapp, Incorporated, stores of St. Louis, Missouri. This new company of about 177 stores is reported planning additional acquisitions and openings.

Mergers have taken place in the classification of chains with less than $100 million yearly volume, but these have been of substantially less importance volumewise in the industry as shown by the statistics in Table 9-6. Perhaps one of the most significant of these was the growth of Lucky Stores, Incorporated, from a 40-odd unit chain into a 96-unit operation as of December 31, 1956, through merger of Cardinal Stores, Incorporated, Serv-U-Meat Markets, and Dolly Madison International Foods, Limited. In this class, the trend is toward larger operation by the individual chain.

Underlying Forces Behind the Movement

While there are many evident causes for this merger movement, the following are advanced as the major reasons for this growing concentration in the food chain industry.

1. The food chains are the major factor volumewise in the supermarket industry, which in turn dominates retail food store distribution. The general supermarket movement has been characterized by an aggressive attitude by management toward growth. The supermarket industry has been one to adapt operations to meet the needs and requirements of the consumer. "Non progredi est regredi" (not to go forward is to go backward) or expand or die is the keynote.

2. Profits before taxes as a percentage of tangible net worth among food chains in the post-World War II era have been excellent. For example, Dixie Home Stores and Big Bear Markets of Michigan, Incorporated, have earned in some years as much as 50 cents on every dollar of owner's equity. In 1956, Food Fair Stores earned 39 per cent and Market Basket, Incorporated, earned 36 per cent on tangible net worth. Reinvestment in merchandising activity is necessary to continue this high level of earnings.

3. New locations constantly are being pioneered. However, as these are harder to find, management has turned to acquisition of existing locations. It is easier to estimate and evaluate the potential of a going operation than a new location.

4. The problems are fewer in acquiring existing locations than in pioneering new stores. There is no time delay in start-up expense, no financing of real estate and building, and less waiting for the location to pay off profitably.

5. The larger concerns are able to spread the risk of failure over a wider geographical area by acquiring outlets in new regions. This, plus the stability of the industry (food sales), has enabled many chains to enter the capital markets to "trade on equity." The ability to borrow more easily and cheaply because of size and diversified locations has benefited the larger firms. The rates paid for capital have been less substantial than the profits that accrued from the

use of these funds. Many of the firms studied in the postwar period have had consistently more creditors' funds than owners' funds in the business.

6. The larger firms have more marketable securities to exchange for the shares of the smaller companies than do those concerns under $100 million annual volume. This has given the larger concerns an advantage in acquisition through stock exchange.

7. A number of food chains were started in the 1930's by individuals as single-unit operations, many of which were supermarkets. These ventures have grown into multi-unit operations. Management now is nearing retirement and is selling out to larger operators.

8. Many of the local operators have found it difficult to secure outside capital and have been forced to rely to a large extent on retained earnings for expansion. The present tax rate reduces the amount available for reinvestment, especially since the cost of pioneering new locations has increased substantially. This has placed the independent at some disadvantage.

9. The estate tax also has influenced the merger movement. The small, family firms in which the owners have a large share of their wealth in the supermarket operation have been facing the prospect in recent years of paying the estate tax. The possibility that payment of this tax may jeopardize the financial stability of the firm and injure the heirs of the owner are factors that contribute to the mergers.[12]

10. Independents find it difficult to expand into shopping centers. The big insurance companies that do the bulk of the financing of the centers demand as tenants under long-term rental contracts the big regional and national chain outlets. The independent, in most instances, is prohibited by economic fact from expanding into shopping centers. The centers are changing the retail pattern of the United States.[13]

[12] *Ibid.*

[13] Testimony of Earl W. Kintner, Chairman, Federal Trade Commission, before a Subcommittee of the Select Committee on Small Business, United States Senate, Eighty-sixth Congress, First Session, July 2, 1959. These hearings are published as *Mergers and Unfair Competition in Food Marketing,* Government Printing Office, Washington, D.C., 1960.

11. There are economies of large-scale operation in certain instances. Better utilization of warehouses, transportation equipment, and manufacturing facilities have been advanced as reasons for acquisitions. One of the supermarket successes has been in spreading fixed costs over a large volume. Large units can integrate vertically more easily. Certain buying and selling advantages accrue to the large-scale operator; for example, the Thursday newspaper advertising cost can be spread over more stores.

Trends in Mergers and Conclusions

This trend toward concentration among the food chains is a manifestation of a general trend in the economy—the big absorbing the small. The largest member of the food chain industry has had frequent bouts with the Department of Justice as to the size and scope of its operations. Safeway Stores, Incorporated, operating in 24 states and commanding from 12 to 13 per cent of the chain food store volume, likewise has been aware of the A & P versus the government. But the framework of operation and the advantages of integration and growth are such that the lesser lights in the industry will continue to gain on the top few. In the not-too-far future the data indicate definite trends toward fewer and larger food chains. Not only will the medium-sized concern capture the small but they will also join forces with other medium-sized chains. The expansion to new regions, such as the move of Kroger Company to the Southwest, will be continued. In fact, large international chains such as the aforementioned George Weston, Limited, organization, are more than a remote possibility. The main limiting factor appears to be fear of government interference.

As chains grow larger and outlets for investment of funds are needed, more emphasis may be placed on vertical integration. There seems to be a parallel between size of food chain and degree of emphasis on manufacturing operations. If vertical integration is followed, more products of the Ann Page or Jane Parker variety can be expected, although some of the actual manufacturing may be done by regular food manufacturers. This leads to what can be called "chain labels" as distinct from private labels or nationally advertised brands. "Chain labels" supported by strong advertising and promotion can make it more difficult for the national brands to gain shelf space. Brand competition will become keener with more emphasis placed on advertising and promotion.

Faced with large capital requirements and competition from large chains with diversified locations, the individual entrepreneur will find it more difficult to enter the food business successfully. There is a trend toward fewer and larger food stores in the economy.

The death knell of the service and limited-function wholesaler has been sounded for many years; yet, they continue to exist. However, increased concentration in the food chain industry, with emphasis on buying and shipping direct from the manufacturer to chain stores or warehouses, could affect adversely wholesalers' operations.

As a corollary to the above, important contracts may tend to be made to a great extent at chain branches or headquarters. This would make the position of many manufacturers' salesmen come under review in this battle for survival. Some salesmen possibly could be eliminated, or their functions could be changed to those of setting up displays and other merchandising activities, or both possibilities could occur.

In the past 25 years, developments in food store retailing have been almost revolutionary. How much further these changes will go depends primarily on governmental policy in curbing mergers. The economic forces in food chain distribution are marshaled in favor of bigness.

VOLUNTARY CHAIN GROWTH

Faced with the integration threat of the food chains in the postwar period, many independent supermarket operators have joined the voluntary chain movement. Voluntary chains are of two types, namely: (1) wholesale grocers sponsoring voluntary retail groups and (2) retailer-owned food cooperatives jointly owning the wholesale activity.[14] Both types have shown substantial growth in the post-

---

[14] The activities of the voluntary chains are discussed in Chapter 5.

war period, as shown by the statistics in Table 9-8. While the data show wholesale sales of the two types of cooperatives, the statistics can be adjusted to retail figures by applying an approximate 20 per cent markup. Wholesale data are furnished inasmuch as this is one of the most feasible methods of collecting statistics to assess the importance of the numerous independent retail operators throughout the country.

TABLE 9-8 *

Wholesale Sales of Certain Voluntary Food
Chain Groups in the United States for the
Years 1948, 1954, and 1958 (in millions).

Type	1948	1954	1958
Wholesale-sponsored †	$746	$1,444	$2,096
Retailer-owned food cooperatives ‡	543	1,211	2,030

* Federal Trade Commission, *Federal Trade Commission Economic Inquiry Into Food Marketing—Interim Report,* Government Printing Office, Washington, D.C., June 30, 1959.

† Includes the data for 146 wholesale grocers sponsoring voluntary retail groups for each of the years.

‡ Includes the data for 141 retailer-owned food cooperatives for each of the years.

These voluntary groups not only have become powerful buying forces, but in addition, they are growing more and more important as manufacturers. In 1958 the voluntary chain wholesalers that participated in the Federal Trade Commission study reported operating 57 manufacturing plants that shipped $65.7 million in products.[15] The plants operated primarily in the coffee roasting, dairy products, baking, and canning areas.

SUMMARY

In the postwar era, the supermarket industry literally came of age. Volumewise, the supermarkets became the largest group of food retailers. In turn, the independent supermarkets that started and dominated the industry were surpassed by the chain supers, both as to number of stores

[15] Federal Trade Commission, *op. cit.*

and volume. The industry has become one of bigness—not only as to size of stores—but as to concentration among its members. The industry has followed a standard practice of closing small units and opening new and large locations in order to maintain relative competitive position. Except for the two largest concerns, A & P and Safeway Stores, the industry members have been on a shopping spree of gobbling up going concerns. As a result, the fast-moving, medium-sized chains have acquired a host of new outlets through merger and acquisition. The smaller chains in turn have been acquiring numerically the even smaller operators. The forces within the industry are marshaled toward bigness, with the only major deterrent being the action of the federal government through the Federal Trade Commission and the Department of Justice. Legal action has been taken by the government against certain of the major industry members for both horizontal and vertical integration. More legal action against the major concerns now active in mergers can be anticipated in the near future.

This move toward bigness is a result of many factors. Basically, management in this industry has been characterized by an aggressive spirit. The earnings of the industry have been excellent, and a source for reinvestment in merchandising activities is necessary to continue this high level of earnings. New locations are more and more difficult to find, and it is easier to estimate and evaluate the potential of a going operation than a new location.

In addition, the larger firms have more marketable securities to exchange for the shares of the smaller companies. Next, management of many supermarkets that were started in the 1930's is nearing retirement and is selling out to the larger operators. Finally, there are economies of large-scale operation in certain instances that benefit the large supermarket chains.

This trend toward concentration among the supermarket members is a manifestation of a general trend in the economy—the big absorbing the small. Faced with large capital requirements and competition from large chains with diversified locations, the individual entrepreneur will find it more difficult to enter the food business successfully. The trend toward fewer and larger food stores in the economy will continue.

10 | CHANGES IN THE NUMBER OF FOOD STORES AND THEIR SALES VOLUME

INTRODUCTION

The preceding chapter examined the movement of the large food chains toward domination of the supermarket industry in the postwar era. Integration policies and practices of the large food chains were examined. The purpose of this and the following chapter is to discern changes in the pattern of food store sales between 1929 and 1958. To do this, it is necessary to examine data at three points in time—1929, 1954, and 1958.

The year 1929 was selected because (1) for all practical purposes, supermarkets were nonexistent at the time, and (2) it was a year for which the Bureau of Census published Retail Distribution Statistics. The year 1954 was included because it was the closest year to date for which Retail Trade Statistics were given by the Bureau of the Census. The changes that are measured statistically at these points in time are shifts in the absolute and relative positions. These include:

1. Number of different types of food stores
2. Dollar sales of different types of food stores
3. Sales of the major product lines transacted by different types of food stores

The first two issues are examined in the remainder of this chapter.

188

Product-line sales by type of food store outlet are analyzed in Chapter 11.

CHANGES IN THE NUMBER OF FOOD STORES

The era of the "roaring twenties" was also the heyday of specialty food stores. This is evidenced by data in Table 10-1 which indicate

TABLE 10-1

Number of Food Stores in the United States by Type of Store for the Years 1929, 1954, and 1958.

Type	1929 stores [*]	1954 stores [†]	1958 stores [‡]
Grocery stores (without meat)	191,876	000 [§]	72,300
Combination markets	115,549	279,440	188,700
Meat and seafood markets	49,865	27,354	22,500
Fruit and vegetable markets	22,904	13,136	12,000
Confectionery stores	63,265	20,507	20,000
Bakery product stores	12,013	19,034	18,500
Delicatessen stores	11,166	8,132	8,000
Other food stores	15,253	13,777	15,000
Country general store	104,089	17,701	16,000
Total	585,980	399,081	373,000

[*] U.S. Bureau of the Census, *Retail Distribution Part I,* Vol. 1, Government Printing Office, Washington, D.C., 1933, p. 47.

[†] U.S. Bureau of the Census, Retail Trade, *Summary Statistics,* Vol 1, Government Printing Office, Washington, D.C., 1957, p. 2–3.

[‡] *Facts in Grocery Distribution* (New York: Progressive Grocer, 1959), p. F–5.

[§] Grocery stores without meat were not classified separately in the 1954 census and are contained in the combination markets classification.

the large number of stores (62.8 per cent) handling specific food lines. However, the trend toward the combination of at least the grocery and meat departments was under way. In the year 1929, 115,549 grocery stores handled meat and were thus in the combination market class. These represented 19.8 per cent of all food stores. The major industry class was the neighborhood grocery store without meat, representing about one-third of all food stores.

While not classified as a food store by the Bureau of the Census, the country general store did approximately 60 per cent of its volume in food products in 1929. Therefore it is included in the study.

By 1958 the major shifts in the number of food stores can be summed as follows:

1. The most startling change was the passing of the country general store. The decline by more than 88,000 units from a total of 104,089 was a decrease of 85 per cent.

2. The next significant shift was the sharp increase in the number of combination markets (the classification for supermarkets). These increased by 73,151 units to become the dominant member of the food store group. Supermarkets, which numbered 20,413 in 1958, accounted for 27 per cent of the increase in the combination market class.

3. The group of grocery stores without meat lost its major relative and absolute status. However, an undisclosed number of this class added meats and became combination markets. This changeover was also true of the meat market, which added groceries and joined the combination movement. The exact number of both types that shifted to combination operation is not known. But grocery stores without meat and meat markets as specialty stores decreased numerically between 1929 and 1958 by 146,941 units; combination markets increased numerically only 73,151 units in this 29-year period, and a growing number of these were new supers under chain ownership. Therefore a substantial number of limited-line stores under individual ownership permanently closed their doors.

4. Of the specialty food group members, the produce stores, delicatessens, meat markets, and confectionery outlets suffered losses in numerical position. Only the bakery product stores improved their numerical status.

5. Supermarkets, classified under combination stores in Table 10-1, for all purposes were nonexistent in 1929. As of 1958 their total was estimated at 20,413, a mere 5.5 per cent of all the food stores and 10.8 per cent of all the combination markets. Numerically the dominant class of food stores in 1958 comprised the nonsuper combination markets with an estimated 168,287 units or about 45 per

cent of all food stores in the country as compared with the supermarkets, which represented only 5.5 per cent of all food stores. However, a true appraisal of the supermarket movement is not obtainable from an examination of the number of supermarkets alone. Their basic operating practice of developing a large volume of sales per store must be considered along with their relatively insignificant but growing numerical status.

6. There had been a trend toward fewer small combination markets. This movement had been quite pronounced in the past decade. The combination market class numerically declined from 223,662 units in 1948 to 188,700 outlets in 1958.[1] The supermarket made impressive numerical gains in this decade, as shown by the statistics in Table 1-2. However, the superette, a combination market that transacts a yearly volume of possibly several hundred thousand dollars, had become an important factor in the food store group during this period. Superettes, which numbered 59,700 units in 1958, had been growing in numerical importance along with the supermarket to the detriment of the small combination market with yearly sales under $75,000.[2]

CHANGES IN THE SALES BY TYPE OF FOOD STORE

Total food store industry sales, including statistics for the country general store, increased from $12.589 billion in 1929 to $50.263 billion in 1958, as shown by the statistics in Table 10-2. This gain of 400 per cent in food store sales included a rise in price plus an improvement in over-all tonnage. But all membership classes by type of store did not experience the same relative growth. The statistics on the distribution of sales by type of store, shown in Table 10-2, indicate the following salient changes:

1. Grocery stores without meat commanded 28 per cent of all food store sales in 1929. By 1948 this group had slipped to 13 per cent of

---

[1] U.S. Bureau of the Census, *Retail Trade-General Statistics,* Part I, Vol. 1, Government Printing Office, Washington, D.C., 1952, p. 104.

[2] *Facts in Grocery Distribution* (New York: Progressive Grocer, 1959), p. F–9.

TABLE 10-2

Food Store Sales in the United States by
Type of Store for the Years
1929, 1954, and 1958.

Type	1929 sales (in millions) *	1954 sales (in millions) †	1958 sales (in millions) ‡
Grocery store (without meat)	$ 3,449	$ 000 §	$ 000 §
Combination markets	3,904	34,421	44,547
Meat and seafood markets	1,337	2,128	
Fruit and vegetable markets	308	485	
Confectionery stores	572	568	
Bakery product stores	201	862	
Delicatessen stores	195	480	
Country general store	1,622	707	
Other food stores	1,001	818	5,716 ¶
Total	$12,589	$40,469	$50,263

* U.S. Bureau of the Census, *Retail Trade-General Statistics,* Part I, Vol. 1, Government Printing Office, Washington, D.C., 1952, p. 104.

† U.S. Bureau of the Census, *Statistical Abstract of the United States,* Government Printing Office, Washington, D.C., 1959, p. 840.

‡ *Ibid.,* p. 833.

§ Grocery stores without meat were not classified separately in the 1954 census or in the 1958 estimates. Statistics for this group are contained in combination markets.

¶ For 1958 the other food stores classification contains all food stores with the exception of combination markets. The data were not reported separately and are grouped as specialty food stores.

all food store sales, and the trend continued downward.[3] By 1958 this class had only 72,300 stores, compared with 154,277 outlets in 1948, and the volume was considered under $4 billion. The Bureau of the Census no longer considers it essential to report this dwindling group.

2. Combination markets were last reported separately in 1948, at which time they had captured almost 66 per cent of all food store

[3] In 1948 there were 154,277 grocery stores without meat that transacted $4.027 billion in sales. Combination markets of that year numbered 223,662 units and transacted sales of $20.743 billion. These data are from the U.S. Bureau of the Census, *Retail Trade-General Statistics, Part I,* Vol. 1, Government Printing Office, Washington, D.C., 1952, p. 104.

sales, compared with 31 per cent in 1929. Combination store sales in 1958 were estimated to transact at least $40 billion of the total grocery and combination classification volume of $44.547 billion or over 80 per cent of all food store sales, as shown by the statistics in Table 10-2.

3. The supermarket group is contained in the combination market classification in Table 10-2. This division had sales of $28.7 billion in 1958 and had become the major factor in both the combination market class and the food store industry. From 1929 to 1958 the supermarket classification raised its share of food store sales from zero to 57.1 per cent. Not only had the supermarket made vast inroads in the volume of food store sales, but the superettes also had captured $11.85 billion of the food store sales in 1958.[4] The small grocery and combination stores as a group in 1958 numbered 195,400 outlets and yet transacted a mere $3.75 billion in food store sales.[5] The small combination markets (nonsupermarket combination stores with sales under $75,000 per year) suffered a severe loss in relative industry position between 1929 and 1958.

4. Sales of food products by the country general store had fallen to an insignificant amount of total food store sales.

5. Among the specialty food store group, the only one to show significant progress and improve its relative industry position was the bakery products group.

CONCLUSIONS ON CHANGES IN THE NUMBER OF FOOD STORES AND THEIR SALES VOLUME

If the preceding analysis is viewed in its broadest aspects, three major features stand out:

1. The passing of the country general store as a significant medium for the sale of food products.

2. The attainment of major status by the combination market in the food store industry coupled with a noticeable loss in relative

---

[4] *Facts in Grocery Distribution, op. cit.*
[5] *Ibid.*

position by the single-line stores.[6] (The supermarket was the major exponent of multiline operation in the food group.)

3. The successful combating of the trend toward multiline operation by the bakery shops.

These three aspects are reviewed in the following section to establish the major underlying forces that brought about these changes and to discern what role, if any, the supermarket played.

Passing of the Country General Store

The country general store, which at one time held an important place in the retailing pattern, dwindled to a position of insignificance. As late as 1929, 12.7 per cent of the food store sales were transacted by this type of outlet; by 1954 sales were reduced to 1.7 per cent. This decline can be traced to both internal and external factors. A list of the important internal failings includes: [7]

1. Lack of capacity to buy in quantity
2. Small size of stores preventing specialization
3. Unskilled buying because of wide lines handled
4. Incomplete assortments
5. Inadequate records

Externally, the most important factors have been: [8]

1. The farm-to-city movement
2. Improved roads and transportation
3. Increased importance of fashion merchandise
4. Development of rural mail delivery

Most of the internal factors could be lumped under one heading—poor management. To this can be added changes in the buying

[6] A single- or limited-line store is used here to indicate a food store in which the sale of one type of merchandise, such as bakery products, groceries, or confections, predominates. These are distinguished from the multiline outlets, exemplified by the combination market which handles groceries and meat plus any number of other lines. The supermarket is perhaps the best example of an exponent of multiline operation among the food store group.

[7] C. F. Phillips and D. J. Duncan, *Marketing Principles and Methods* (Chicago: Richard D. Irwin, 1956), p. 159.

[8] *Ibid.*, p. 177.

habits of the rural people plus their ability to travel great distances to shop. Supermarkets have attracted farm and rural patronage.[9] The ability of the super to operate as a low-cost marketer of food and its ability to merchandise farm produce have earned the respect and support of many of the farm folks.[10] Although the number of supers in rural areas is small, the trend has been toward locating in these rural and small communities. The location of many new supers on or adjacent to arterial highways has attracted rural trade. These data indicate that the supermarket development added to the decline of the general store; but in view of other factors, the specific influence of the supermarket cannot be assessed.

Rise of the Combination Market and the Decline of the Limited-Line Food Store

In 1931 the trend toward competition among different types of retailers in selling the same commodity was indicated. Malcolm P. McNair wrote:

It is an era of scrambled merchandising. Grocery stores sell cigarettes; drug stores sell grocery products; and tobacco stores sell razor blades. Grocery stores are on the way to becoming food department stores.[11]

The theory that limited-line stores move toward multiline operation and then back again in a cyclical nature has been advanced.[12] However, after World War I, there was a pronounced trend of grocery stores to widen their lines; this continued on a larger scale, with impetus given by the success of the supermarket.[13]

[9] B. A. Durrant, "Why Go After the Small Town Market," *Chain Store Age,* Grocery Executive Edition, April, 1945, p. 171.

[10] L. L. Clovis, "What the Farmer Expects from the Operator," *Super Market Merchandising,* XII, no. 11, November, 1947, p. 81.

[11] Malcolm P. McNair, "Trends in Large-Scale Retailing," *Harvard Business Review,* X, no. 1, Fall, 1932, p. 31.

[12] Paul D. Converse and Harvey W. Huegy, *The Elements of Marketing* (5th ed.; New York: Prentice-Hall, Inc., 1952), p. 399.

[13] "50 Years—1888 to 1938," *Printers Ink,* Vol. 184, no. 4, July 28, 1938, p. 309.

Specifically, the causes of intertype competition among retailers were: [14]

1. The large pool of overhead or common costs
2. Interrelated demand among several products
3. Changing consumer shopping habits
4. Development of new products; improvement and standardization of old ones

The economic consequences of such a movement had important effects on the structure of retail trade and on the economy at large. Ostensibly, improvement was realized in the market position of the multiline distributor at the expense of the limited-line dealer. There were possible shifts in the relative importance of price competition and nonprice competition in various lines. There was encouragement of further legal restrictions.[15]

This pattern of scrambled merchandising is exemplified by the record of the food store industry. The 1920's were largely an era of specialty stores that handled limited-line merchandise. However, the trend toward multiline operation had started with the growth of the combination market. By 1958 the combination market had gained major status in the food store industry—both numerically and as to volume—at the expense of all limited-line stores except bake shops. The movement was given impetus by conversion to combination markets of many limited-line outlets. The combination market movement was one manner in which the small merchant could attempt to combat the spectre of the supermarket.

The reasons for this were two: (1) The small combination mart generally was able to reduce substantially the costs of products purchased.[16] (2) The small combination market alert to new trends also could reduce operating expenses. The nonsuper combination market was able to reduce purchase costs largely through the media of buying associations or cooperatives. Many wholesalers sponsored dealer

[14] Richard N. Alt, "Competition Among Types of Retailers in Selling the Same Commodity," *Journal of Marketing*, XIV, no. 3, January, 1948, p. 442.

[15] *Ibid.*, p. 446.

[16] Robert Mueller, "Detroit Dealers Thrive on Modern Plan," *Progressive Grocer*, XXIX, no. 2, February, 1950, p. 40.

plans.[17] The methods varied, but usually they enabled the small merchant to purchase grocery products at a small percentage above the cost to the buying association plus a percentage for cartage to the store.

The reduction in the operating expenses for the small combination market enabled many of them to compete with the supers insofar as expense as a percentage of sales is considered. Lower operating expenses were effected through adoption of self-service, displays, and reduced credit and delivery.[18] The owner of the small combination market of 1958 generally was considered to have more knowledge of how to run a store than did his counterpart in the 1920's. He was able to observe the supermarket techniques, and buying associations furnished valuable service on operations to its members.

Despite the fact that the nonsuper combination markets were able to lower both the cost of goods purchased and expenses, they appeared at a disadvantage in the intraclass struggle with the supermarket. The latter opponent generally had facilities and resources to adopt operating practices more in line with the changing desires of the shoppers. The super was able to exploit more fully than the nonsuper combination market the customer attractions of one-stop shopping, new suburban locations, diversified lines of merchandise, and other buying preferences.

Position of the Bakery Shops

The bakery products outlets successfully challenged the trend toward scrambled merchandise and the desire for one-stop shopping. The bakery stores were at the same time the beneficiary and the victim of cross-currents in the economy. On the one hand, people reduced their per capita consumption of bakery products in favor of other types of food.[19] On the other, the population grew numeri-

---

[17] R. D. Tousley, "Reducing Distribution Costs in the Grocery Field," *Journal of Marketing*, XII, no. 4, April, 1948, p. 40.

[18] Godfrey Lebhar, "Self-Service Marches On," *Chain Store Age*, Grocery Executive Edition, September, 1952, p. 67.

[19] Charles Slater, "Statistical History of the Baking Industry," *Baking Industry*, Vol. 97, no. 1219, April 12, 1952, p. 264.

cally. In addition, a decided change in the past twenty years reflected the consumer's demand for convenience in the preparation of meals; this brought about a decided shift to store-bought bakery products.[20] Yet, above all, consumers demanded freshness in their bakery products; and freshness was associated with purchase near the point of manufacture—the bake shop. This single-line type of food store actually improved its industry position in regard to sales. However, this group is not removed from supermarket competition inasmuch as many members of the latter have attained sufficient size to open their own bake shops and compete on both a price and quality basis.

SUMMARY

In 1929 supermarkets were for practical purposes nonexistent. By 1958 this member of the food store industry claimed only 5 per cent of all food stores but 57.1 per cent of all food store sales. The supermarket became a highly successful exponent of scrambled merchandising to the detriment of the limited-line retail food merchant. The only limited-line store to improve its relative industry position in this 29-year period was the bakery products store. While the latter was subject to cross-currents in the economy, these stores succeeded in satisfying consumer demand by emphasizing freshness of their products as well as offering convenience in the serving of meals. The small combination market has followed the supermarket's technique of multiline operation, but as a class it has not been able to withstand the competition offered by the supermarket industry, which has more resources at its command.

[20] *Ibid.*, p. 47.

11 CHANGES IN THE SALES OF MAJOR PRODUCT LINES BY TYPES OF FOOD STORE OUTLETS

INTRODUCTION

This chapter continues the analysis of changes in the food store sales pattern between 1929 and 1958. In the preceding chapter, significant changes in number and sales of different types of food stores were discerned. The purpose of this chapter is to examine shifts in the sales of certain major product lines transacted by different types of food stores.

Analysis is made at the same points in time—1929, 1954, and 1958 —and for the same reasons advanced in Chapter 10. The major product classes selected for study include:

1. Meat, poultry, and seafood
2. Fresh fruit and vegetables or produce
3. Confections
4. Bakery products
5. Canned goods, grocery items
6. Nonfood lines

SALES OF MAJOR PRODUCT CLASSES IN SUPERMARKETS

The 1958 supermarket handled 5,600 separate items.[1] These can be grouped primarily by departments under eight major headings. Three separate studies recently were completed which measure the relative importance of various product classes; these findings, expressed as a percentage of sales, are shown in Table 11-1. Individual

TABLE 11-1

Results of Three Recent Studies on the Percentage of Sales of Major Product Classes Transacted by Supermarkets.

Product class	Food Town * study, %	Super Valu † study, %	Food chain ‡ survey, %
Meats	28.11	22.42	25.10
Dairy products	8.61	11.51	10.30
Bakery products	2.67	5.76	4.30
Frozen foods	4.14	4.78	4.50
Confections	1.48	1.85	1.60
Produce	12.76	8.79	9.90
Grocery items	38.01	37.14	36.10
Nonfoods	4.22	7.75	8.20
	100.00	100.00	100.00

* "The Food Town Study," *Progressive Grocer*, XXXV, no. 1, January, 1955, p. 49.

† "How an Average Customer Spends Her Super Market Dollars—Super Valu Markets," *Facts in Grocery Distribution* (New York: Progressive Grocer, 1959), p. F–20.

‡ "What Do Food Chain Stores Sell," *Chain Store Age*, Grocer Executive Edition, July, 1959, p. 47.

markets may have product statistics that vary from these data as a result of size, finances, facilities, location, competitive factors, and policy. But approximately 25 per cent of a supermarket's sales is in meat, 10 per cent each in produce and dairy, 4 to 5 per cent in frozen

[1] *Facts in Grocery Distribution* (New York: Progressive Grocer, 1959), p. F–3.

Changes in Sales of Major Product Lines

foods, about 4 to 5 per cent in bakery products (exclusive (
aged cookies and crackers), and from 4 to 9 per cent in nonfood
lines. Confections, which average between 1 and 2 per cent of sales,
normally are considered part of the grocery line, but this class is
recorded separately since the impact of the super on confectionery
stores is assessed later in this chapter.

A breakdown of sales of the multitude of grocery products is given
in Table 11-2. The gross margin percentage for these grocery items

TABLE 11-2 *

**How an Average Customer Spends Her Supermarket
Dollars for Grocery Products and the Percentage
of Gross Margin on Sales of These Items.**

Product group	% total supermarket sales	% gross margin of sales
Beverages	5.42	12.1
Household and laundry supplies	2.59	28.3
Vegetables, canned	2.48	21.4
Cookies and crackers	2.20	25.3
Paper products	2.11	23.4
Soaps and detergents	2.01	10.5
Fruit, canned	1.82	21.6
Baking needs, flour	1.45	16.5
Breakfast foods	1.44	18.1
Soups	1.41	15.0
Baking, batter mixes	1.36	17.5
Fish, canned	1.09	19.4
Jams, jellies, and spreads	1.04	23.6
Sugar	1.04	8.0
Snack and party foods	1.01	23.9
Baby foods	0.99	14.1
Juices, canned	0.86	19.4
Pet foods	0.70	20.2
Salad dressings, mayonnaise	0.68	15.5
Shortening	0.66	9.7
Condiments, sauces	0.56	18.4
Pickles, olives, relishes	0.55	26.7

Table 11-2 (*Continued*)

Desserts	0.54	16.7
Prepared foods, canned	0.42	20.8
Salt, seasonings, spices	0.39	24.6
Milk, canned and dry	0.38	13.5
Macaroni products, dry	0.36	18.8
Meat, canned	0.31	21.0
Fruits, dried	0.30	22.1
Vegetables, dried	0.25	25.4
Syrups and molasses	0.23	17.9
Chinese foods	0.16	24.3
Diet foods	0.15	27.0
Pet supplies	0.02	29.8
Misc. grocery items	0.16	25.9
Total grocery products	37.14	18.2
Total all others	62.86	
	100.00	

* *Facts in Grocery Distribution* (New York: Progressive Grocer, 1959), p. F–20.

also is included. Again, individual markets may have sales that vary from these findings inasmuch as this industry is so diverse. In the wide range of products handled by a super, the importance of beverages, household and laundry supplies, paper products, and soaps and detergents is apparent.

SALES OF MEAT PRODUCTS, POULTRY, AND SEAFOOD BY TYPE OF FOOD STORE

(This category includes the sale of all fresh meat, poultry, fresh fish, and other fresh seafoods, plus meat provisions such as cured hams, bacon, and sausage.)

In 1929 the meat market, a limited line store, was the principal outlet for meat and related products, as shown by the statistics in Table 11-3. By 1954 total food store sales of meat in the United States soared to more than $10 billion. The rise was due in part to an increase in population and to a higher per capita consumption of meat products—from 139 lb in 1929 to 164 lb of meat per inhabitant

TABLE 11-3

Estimated Meat, Poultry, and Seafood Sales by Major Type of Food Store Outlet for the Years 1929 and 1954.

	1929		1954	
Type of store	*Sales* * *(in billions)*	*% total*	*Sales* † *(in billions)*	*% total*
Meat markets	$1,245	54.4	$ 2,128	19.9
Nonsuper combination markets	1,045	45.6	4,547 ‡	42.6
Supermarkets	0	0.0	3,995 ‡	37.5
Total	$2,290 §	100.0	$10,670 §	100.0

* U.S. Bureau of the Census, *Retail Distribution—Food Retailing*, No. R-83, Government Printing Office, Washington, D.C., 1934, p. 82.

† U.S. Bureau of the Census, *Retail Trade*, No. R-2-2, Government Printing Office, Washington, D.C., 1957, pp. 2–333.

‡ Total grocery and combination market sales of meat products for 1954 were estimated at $8.542 billion in *What the Public Spends for Grocery Store Products* (New York: Topics Publishing Co.). Supermarket sales for 1954 were estimated at $15.980 billion in Table 1-2. On the assumption that 25 per cent of a supermarket's sales are in meat products, supermart sales of meat in 1954 were estimated at $3.995 billion. Nonsuper combination market sales of meat are the difference between total grocery and combination market sales of meat and the meat sales of supermarkets.

§ These totals do not include the sale of meat products in other food stores such as country general stores and delicatessens. Sales through these channels are considered relatively insignificant.

in 1954.[2] In addition, the wholesale price index for meat products (1947 to 1949 equals 100) rose from 48.1 in 1929 to 91.5 in 1954.[3] Among the stores, the nonsuper combination market became the major retailer of meat, followed closely by the supermarket, which made substantial progress during this period, rising from negligible sales of meat in 1929 to 37.5 per cent in 1954.

[2] Data on meat consumption are found in Table 3-2.

[3] Changes in the wholesale price of meat are considered generally to indicate changes in the same direction in the retail price of meat. Statistics are from the U.S. Department of Commerce, reported in "Meat and Dairy Products," *Standard and Poor's Industrial Surveys*, Section 3, October, 1959, p. 4. This same source reported that consumption of meat per capita rose 3.7 per cent between 1954 and 1958 and that the wholesale price index for meat products rose 18 per cent, or from 91.5 to 107.9, during this same four-year interval.

In the years 1954 to 1958, further shifts in the pattern of meat sales resulted, to the detriment of the limited-line stores and the smaller combination markets. Statistics of the approximate 1958 sale of meat products by major food stores were: [4]

Meat markets	$2.128 billion
Nonsuper combination markets	$4.917 billion
Supermarkets	$7.175 billion

The supermarket became the dominant factor in the sale of meat products, grossing more than 50 per cent of the volume. Small meat markets and combination markets seemed destined to becoming the new "Vanishing American."

SALES OF FRESH FRUIT AND VEGETABLES BY TYPE OF FOOD STORE

(This category includes all items classed by the Census as fresh fruits and vegetables. It does not contain frozen or canned produce.)

For the year 1929 the "big three" in the sale of fresh fruit and vegetables among the major food stores, as indicated in Table 11-4, were: grocery stores without meat (claiming 32.5 per cent of total U.S. fresh fruit and vegetable sales), nonsuper combination markets (34.8 per cent), and fruit and vegetable stores (22 per cent). The country general store also was significant, with about 11 per cent of the produce sales by major food outlets for fruits and vegetables.

In the 25 year interval, produce sales among the food stores increased to over $4 billion. The price level rose; the population in-

---

[4] The 1954 meat market had average sales of $77,700 per outlet. In 1958 this same market would have its sales raised to $94,600 as a result of a 3.7 per cent increase in the per capita consumption of meat and an 18 per cent rise in the price index of meat products. However, by 1958 there was a decrease in the number of units to 22,500 which, when multiplied by the new average sales per store, gave the $2.128 billion estimate for meat markets.

Total grocery and combination market sales of meat products in 1958 were estimated by the Topics Publishing Company in its yearly study at $12.092 billion. Supermarket sales in 1958 were $28.7 billion, of which 25 per cent were estimated to be in meat products. Thus supermarket sales of meat products were estimated at $7.175 billion. Nonsuper combination market sales of meat products is the difference between total grocery and combination market sales of meat and supermarket sales of meat.

TABLE 11-4

Estimated Fresh Fruit and Vegetable Sales by Major Type of
Food Store Outlet for the Years 1929 and 1954.

	1929		1954	
Type of store	Sales [a] (in millions)	% total	Sales (in millions)	% total
Fruit and vegetable	$ 285	22.0	$ 485 [b]	10.8
Grocery stores without meat	421	32.5	000 [c]	—
Nonsuper combination markets	451	34.8	2,416 [d]	53.7
Supermarkets	0	0	1,598 [d]	35.5
Country general store	139	10.7	— [e]	—
Total	$1,296 [f]	100.0	$4,499 [f]	100.0

[a] U.S. Bureau of the Census, *Retail Distribution—Food Retailing,* No. R-83, Government Printing Office, Washington, D.C., 1934, p. 82.

[b] U.S. Bureau of the Census, *Retail Trade,* No. R-2-2, Government Printing Office, Washington, D.C., 1957, pp. 2–333.

[c] This class has become relatively insignificant, and the data are included under nonsuper combination markets by the Bureau of the Census.

[d] Total grocery and combination market sales of produce for 1954 were estimated at $4.014 billion in *What the Public Spends for Grocery Store Products* (New York: Topics Publishing Co.). Supermarket sales for 1954 were estimated at $15.980 billion in Table 1-2. On the assumption that 10 per cent of a supermarket's sales are in produce, supermarket sales of fruit and vegetables in 1954 were estimated at $1.598 billion. Nonsuper combination market and grocery store sales of produce are the difference between total grocery and combination market sales of produce and the produce sales of supermarkets.

[e] This type of outlet became relatively insignificant in the sale of produce by 1954, with sales estimated well below $100 million.

[f] These totals do not include the sale of fresh fruits and vegetables in other food stores such as delicatessens. Sales through these other channels are considered relatively insignificant.

creased; but most significantly, changes took place in the dietary habits. There was a shift from consumption of bulky, lower-cost produce of the potato type to greater consumption of the higher cost leafy green vegetables and citrus fruits.

The 1954 sales pattern of produce differed substantially from that of 1929. The country general store became almost extinct. Grocery stores without meat had lower fresh fruit and vegetable sales than those of 1929 and had become insignificant in this area.[5] Both non-super combination markets and supermarts gained substantially in absolute and relative positions in the sale of produce during this 25-year era.

In the years 1954 to 1958, further shifts in the pattern of produce sales resulted, to the detriment of the limited-line stores and the smaller combination markets. Statistics on the approximate 1958 sale of produce by the three major food stores were: [6]

Fruit and vegetable stores	$ 510 million
Grocery stores and nonsuper combination markets	$2,020 million
Supermarkets	$2,870 million

The supermarket has become the dominant factor in the sale of fresh fruit and vegetables with more than 50 per cent of the volume. Small fruit and vegetable markets, grocery stores without meat, and small combination markets are suffering substantially from the stepped-up activities of the supermarket in the merchandising of produce in the past few years.

[5] In 1948 there were 154,277 grocery stores without meat that transacted $346 million in sales of produce. These data are from the U.S. Bureau of the Census, *Retail Trade—General Statistics, Part I*, Vol. 1, Government Printing Office, Washington, D.C., 1952, p. 104. By 1954 the number of grocery stores without meat dwindled to an estimated 119,000 units, according to *Progressive Grocer*.

[6] The 1954 fresh fruit and vegetable market had an average sales volume of $37,000. In 1958 this same market would have its sales raised to $42,500 as a result of a 15 per cent increase in the value of produce consumed at retail prices during this four-year interval, as reported by Topics Publishing Company in its annual reports on *What the Public Spends for Grocery Store Products*. However, by 1958 there was a decrease in the number of units to 12,000 which, when multiplied by the new average sales per store, gave the $510 million estimate for fruit and vegetable markets.

Total grocery and combination market sales of produce in 1958 were estimated by the Topics Publishing Company in its yearly study at $4,890 million. Supermarket sales in 1958 were $28.7 billion, of which 10 per cent were estimated to be in produce. Thus supermarket sales of fresh fruits and vegetables were estimated at $2,870 million. Nonsuper combination market and grocery store sales of produce are the difference between total grocery and combination market sales of produce and supermarket sales of fresh fruits and vegetables.

SALES OF CONFECTIONERY PRODUCTS
BY TYPE OF FOOD STORE

(Included in the category of confectionery products are bar candy, gum, packaged confections, bulk candy, candy specialties, and nuts.)

Although candy and confections can be bought in many types of retail establishments, the custom of the 1920's was to buy them largely in the little neighborhood candy store. In 1929 confectionery stores transacted 67 per cent of all confectionery sales in the food store group and 45 per cent of the total $512 million sales retailed by both food and nonfood outlets.[7] The nonfood trio of restaurants, drugstores, and variety shops also was significant in the retailing of confections.

But from 1929 to 1954 many changes in the marketing of confections resulted in taking more and more of the candy sales away from the specialty confectionery store. The confectionery group suffered a 68 per cent reduction in the number of outlets in 1954, compared with the number in 1929.[8] Dietary changes over the 25-year interim influenced the purchase of confectionery products; per capita consumption increased only from 15.7 to 16.1 lb between 1929 and 1954.[9] Retail dollar sales rose with the growth of population and with an increase in the average price of confections from 20.5 cents to 37.5 cents per pound during this same interval.[10] There was, however, an important change in the type of confections produced, namely, a shift to the branded, prepackaged candy bar. These nickel and dime bars together with gum and related items were regarded as convenience goods and were given wide distribution in a variety of new outlets. Vending machines became large sellers of confections. Theaters discovered additional revenue from the sale of con-

[7] U.S. Bureau of the Census, *Retail Distribution—Food Retailing*, No. R-83, Government Printing Office, Washington, D.C., 1934, pp. 82–86.

[8] See Table 10-1.

[9] U.S. Department of Commerce, *Confectionery Sales and Distribution*, Government Printing Office, Washington, D.C., 1957, p. 49.

[10] *Ibid.*

fections. The small candy store next to the theater became a rare phenomenon.

By 1954 three new outlets for confections, namely, vending machines, theaters, and supermarkets, transacted a total volume larger than the confectionery store, as shown by the data in Table 11-5.

TABLE 11-5

Sales of Confections by Certain Major Retail Outlets for the Years 1929 and 1954.

Outlet	1929 * (in millions)	1954 (in millions)
Confectionery stores	$230	$568 †
Grocery stores and nonsuper combination markets	87	177 ‡
Supermarkets	—	240 ‡
Vending machines	—	165 §
Theaters	—	160 ¶

* U.S. Bureau of the Census, *Retail Distribution—Food Retailing*, No. R-83, Government Printing Office, Washington, D.C., 1934, pp. 82–86.

† U.S. Bureau of the Census, *Retail Trade*, No. R-2-2, Government Printing Office, Washington, D.C., 1957, pp. 2–333.

‡ 1954 supermarket sales were $15,980 billion, as shown by data in Table 1-2. On the assumption that 1.5 per cent of a super's sales are in confections, the 1954 figure for supermarket sales is $240 million. Total grocery and combination market sales were $417 in 1954, according to the Topics Publishing Company. Therefore grocery store and nonsuper combination market sales are $417 million less $240 million supermarket sales, or $177 million.

§ U.S. Bureau of the Census, *Retail Trade Summary Statistics*, Government Printing Office, Washington, D.C., 1957, pp. 1–6.

¶ U.S. Bureau of the Census, *Retail Trade-Selected Service Trades*, Government Printing Office, Washington, D.C., 1957, p. 16.

Since 1954, both supermarkets and vending machines have increased their relative market shares, as have the theaters, which have been aided by the expansion to outdoor movies; yet, the confectionery store group decreased numerically by more than 500 units according to estimates by *Progressive Grocer*. Supermarkets merchandise candies at the check-out counter where they utilize little display space and are ideal as an impulse purchase; supers sell candies in volume at a narrow gross margin and on a low price basis. If a statistic of

1.5 per cent is used to represent candy sales in a supermarket as a percentage of total super volume, the 1958 supermarket industry sold over $400 million in confections and is closing in rapidly on the confectionery store.

SALES OF BAKERY PRODUCTS BY TYPE OF FOOD STORE

(This category of bakery products includes bread, bread products, pastries, doughnuts, and related items. It does not contain crackers, packaged cookies, and pretzels.)

The principal outlet for the $614 million food store volume of bakery products in 1929 was the neighborhood bake shop (with 31.4 per cent of U.S. sales of baked goods), followed closely by the combination markets (30.7 per cent) and grocery stores without meat (26.2 per cent). These statistics are found in Table 11-6. The figures do not separately list house-to-house sales of bakery products; these are estimated to have been negligible during this period (well under 5 per cent of the total bakery product sales in food stores) although their importance to the industry in recent years has increased.[11]

During the interval between 1929 and the 1950's, there was a decided shift from baking at home to the purchase of store products.[12] This was attributed to women's demand for greater convenience in the preparation and serving of food. This change in buying habits, the population increase, and the rise in the price level of bakery products more than compensated for the decrease in per capita consumption of bakery goods.[13] Major food store sales of bakery products, reported in Table 11-7, increased substantially in this period. However, the bake shops were able to prosper and had sales rocket-

[11] This estimate was made in an interview on March 1, 1954, by Charles Slater, Research Economist, Bakery Industry Study conducted at Northwestern University.

[12] Charles Slater, "Statistical History of the Baking Industry," *Baking Industry*, Vol. 97, no. 1219, April 12, 1952, p. 266.

[13] *Ibid.*

TABLE 11-6

Estimated Bakery Product Sales by Major Type of
Food Store Outlet for the Years 1929 and 1954.

| | 1929 | | 1954 | |
| | Sales *a* | | Sales | |
Type of store	(in millions)	% total	(in millions)	% total
Bakery products	$170	31.4	$ 862 *b*	29.6
Grocery without meat	142	26.2	000 *c*	
Nonsuper combination markets	166	30.7	1,343 *d*	45.9
Supermarkets	0	0	719 *d*	24.5
Country general store	63	11.7	000 *e*	—
	$541 *f*	100.0	$2,924 *f*	100.0

a U.S. Bureau of the Census, *Retail Distribution—Food Retailing,* No. R-83, Government Printing Office, Washington, D.C., 1934, p. 86.

b U.S. Bureau of the Census, *Retail Trade,* No. R-2-2, Government Printing Office, Washington, D.C., 1957, pp. 2–333.

c This class has become relatively insignificant, and therefore the data are included under nonsuper combination markets by the Bureau of the Census.

d Total grocery and combination markets sales of bakery products for 1954 were estimated at $2.062 billion in *What the Public Spends for Grocery Store Products* (New York: Topics Publishing Co.). Supermarket sales for 1954 were estimated at $15.980 billion in Table 1-2. On the assumption that 4.5 per cent of a supermarket's sales are in bakery goods, supermarket sales of bakery items in 1954 were estimated at $719 million. Nonsuper combination market and grocery store sales of bakery products are the difference between total grocery and combination market sales of baked goods and the bakery sales of supermarkets.

e This type of outlet became relatively insignificant in the sale of bakery items by 1954 with sales estimated well below $100 million.

f These totals do not include the sale of bakery products in other food stores such as delicatessens and home delivery. Sales through these other channels are considered relatively small.

ing to $862 million. The supermarket by 1954 also became a major factor in this field by capturing 26.5 per cent of the volume for baked goods. Country stores, grocery stores without meat, and the small combination markets appear to have suffered substantially because of the supermarket.

In the years 1954 to 1958, further shifts in the pattern of sales for bakery products resulted, to the detriment of the smaller combination markets and even to some extent in the relative position of the limited-line bake shops. Statistics on the approximate 1958 sale of bakery goods by the three major food stores were: [14]

Bakery shops	$ 981 million
Grocery stores and nonsuper combination markets.	$1,120 million
Supermarkets	$1,292 million

The supermarket became the dominant factor in the sale of baked goods in 1958 with approximately 38 per cent of the volume transacted by the major outlets. Supermarkets intensified activities in this area inasmuch as a growing number of chains reached sufficient size to manufacture and market their own packaged bakery products. These items were sold under the chain brand as a good value in terms of price, size, and quality, and thus attracted shoppers. This policy of merchandising by stressing good value of the frequently purchased baked goods has overcome to some extent the desire on the part of the consumer to purchase oven-fresh products at or near the point of manufacture. Thus baked goods form an integral part of marketing strategy by a super and offer an important source of profit to the integrated firm of proper size. Supermarket activities in this area also have intensified competition with the large bakery manufacturers who market packaged goods regionally or nationally.

[14] The 1954 bake shop had an average sales volume of $45,000. In 1958 this same market would have its sales raised to $53,000 by an 18 per cent increase in the value of bakery products consumed at retail prices during this four year interval as reported by Topics Publishing Company in its annual reports on *What the Public Spends for Grocery Store Products.* However, by 1958 there was a decrease in the number of units to 18,500 which, when multiplied by the new average sales per store, gave the $981 million estimate for bakery product stores.

Total grocery and combination market sales of bakery products in 1958 were estimated by the Topic Publishing Company in its yearly study at $2.412 billion. Supermarket sales in 1958 were $28.7 billion, of which 4.5 per cent were estimated to be in baked goods. Thus supermarket sales of bakery products were estimated at $1.292 billion. Nonsuper combination market and grocery store sales of baked goods are the difference between total grocery and combination market sales of bakery products and supermarket sales of baked goods.

SALES OF CANNED GOODS AND GROCERY ITEMS
BY GROCERY STORES AND COMBINATION MARKETS

The term *grocery items* has been used as a catch-all classification. Its definition has been complicated and subject to change by the wide assortment of food and nonfood lines added by the grocery stores and combination markets. The items listed in this classification are found in Table 11-2.

A variety of retail stores today handles canned goods and grocery items. However, only the major outlets for the years 1929 and 1958 are contained in the data of Table 11-7. In 1929 the grocery stores without meat were the major retailers of canned goods and grocery items. From then until 1958, the grocery store without meat suffered

TABLE 11-7

Sales of Grocery Product Items by Major Food
Store Outlets for the Years 1929 and 1958.

	1929		1958	
Type of outlet	*Sales* * *(in billions)*	*% total*	*Sales* † *(in billions)*	*% total*
Grocery stores without meat	$2.853	54.9	000 ‡	—
Nonsuper combination markets	2.347	45.1	$ 6.531	37.9
Supermarkets	0	0	10.659	62.1
Total	$5.200	100.0	$17.190	100.0

* U.S. Bureau of the Census, *Retail Distribution—Food Retailing*, No. R-83, Government Printing Office, Washington, D.C., p. 82.

† Total grocery and combination market sales of grocery items for 1958 were estimated at $17.190 billion in *What the Public Spends for Grocery Store Products* (New York: Topics Publishing Co.). Supermarket sales for 1958 were estimated at $28.7 billion in Table 1-2. From Table 11-2, grocery items are represented as 37.14 per cent of total supermarket sales. This percentage applied to total supermarket sales furnished the $10.659 billion estimate for supermarkets. Nonsuper combination market and grocery store sales of grocery items are the difference between total sales of $17.190 billion and supermarket sales of $10.659 billion.

‡ This class has become relatively insignificant as to volume, and the data are included under nonsuper combination markets by the Bureau of the Census.

a severe loss, in relative numbers and volume, to both the nonsuper combination market and the supermarket. Again, the shift in buying habits, price competition from more efficient marketers of food, and the ability of the large multiline outlet to spread overhead costs over a wider line enabled supermarkets to attain major status in this area.

SALES OF NONFOOD PRODUCTS IN GROCERY STORES AND COMBINATION MARKETS

Nonfood products in grocery stores and combination markets do not include food or food products for consumption. But the classification also excludes commonly carried items such as soap, cleanser, household supplies, and paper products.

Growth of Nonfoods in Supers

Supermarkets were not the innovators of the sale of nonfood merchandise among the food stores. In the 1920's some combination markets handled nonfoods before the supers were in existence. H. C. Bohack in 1929 operated a chain of 512 service grocery stores which sold razor blades, drug items, and even automobile tires.[15] However, the tendency to scramble merchandise among the grocery stores and combination markets in the 1920's was not common. In fact, the 1929 retail census did not have a separate category for nonfoods.

The early supermarkets concentrated on merchandising food products. During World War II, supers added nonfoods in order to supplement their reduced lines of food items. In 1949 nonfood items continued to be no novelty to supermarkets, but health and beauty aids were the only major items universally stocked.[16] Since then, sales of nonfoods have increased steadily in supermarkets through broadening the product line until they have currently reached about 5 per cent of total sales.[17] The middle half of the companies report-

[15] "Diversified Lines Give Bohack Chain $60,000 Yearly Unit Sales," *Sales Management*, XXIX, no. 10, March 8, 1930, p. 441.
[16] Curt Kornblau, *Facts and Figures About Non-Foods in Super Markets* (Chicago: Super Market Institute, 1959), p. 1.
[17] *Ibid.*, p. 4.

ing volume statistics to the Super Market Institute in 1958 achieved nonfood sales between 3 and 8 per cent of their total sales. While there is no clear-cut pattern in the proportion of nonfood sales to total sales according to volume groups, the largest companies with sales of more than $50 million average the highest nonfood sales; these were reported at 6.3 per cent of total volume. One of the major exponents of nonfoods among the giants is Grand Union Company which in recent years has opened a series of combined supermarkets and junior department stores under the same roof.

The two principal nonfood lines generally carried by supermarkets, however, are health and beauty aids and housewares. Statistics on the major nonfood lines carried by supermarkets in 1958 are shown in Table 11-8 along with the relative percentage of supers carrying these products. In addition, the major source of supply for each of the 21 classifications is listed. The method of procurement differs widely for the various kinds of products.

Much diversity exists among individual operators as to the extent of nonfood lines carried. In order to conform with supermarket operating techniques, normally merchandise must: [18]

1. Have rapid turnover.
2. Require little space.
3. Need no technical selling or readily lend itself to self-service.
4. Have no high-styling of goods.
5. Lend itself to simplified purchasing and reordering, since the supermarket operator is not normally an expert in the wide line of nonfoods.

For the smaller concerns, the rack jobber has simplified the problem of merchandising items that do not conform strictly to the above prerequisites. Larger companies are becoming strong advocates of separate nonfood departments. Approximately 27 per cent of all supermarkets have a separate department with at least one full-time employee in charge; the majority of supers with separate depart-

[18] Milton Alexander, "Where We Stand in Non-Food Merchandising," *Progressive Grocer*, XXXI, no. 10, October, 1952, p. 197.

TABLE 11-8 *

Estimated Percentages of Supermarkets That Handle Nonfood Lines
Together with Major Source of Supply for the Year 1958.

	% super markets handling	Typical number of items	% Major source of supply		
			Rack jobber	Whole-saler	Manu-facturer
Health and beauty aids	98	325	52	31	17
Housewares	87	200	78	16	6
Women's hosiery	81	10	48	25	27
Stationery	74	25	48	34	18
Children's books	73	35	55	29	16
Magazines (general line)	71	75	55	42	3
Glassware	69	40	43	20	37
Baby needs	68	25	47	34	19
Toys	66	75	80	13	7
Men's socks	64	10	59	21	20
Pet supplies	63	50	73	20	7
Phonograph records	62	75	87	9	4
Hardware	58	75	73	22	5
Garden supplies	58	25	24	43	33
Children's socks	55	10	63	19	18
Underwear	47	12	60	20	20
Photographic supplies	37	10	42	50	8
Greeting cards	35	150	56	18	26
Notions and sundries	33	50	60	30	10
Other soft goods	33	35	61	19	20
Electrical appliances	11	20	31	54	15

* Curt Kornblau, *Facts and Figures About Non-Foods in Super Markets* (Chicago: Super Market Institute, 1959), p. 6.

ments are larger concerns.[19] The titles given to the nonfood specialist include nonfood buyer, nonfood supervisor, and director of nonfood division.

[19] Curt Kornblau, *op. cit.*, p. 7.

Impact of Nonfoods in Supers

Generally the supermarket exploited nonfoods ahead of small grocery stores and combination markets. Therefore the sales penetration by the supermart in nonfoods has been at the expense of other than food store retailers. The success of the supermarket in these areas resulted in the grocery store and small combination market imitating the supers in an effort to increase sales and profits. Data in Table 11-9 indicate the extent to which all grocery stores and

TABLE 11-9 *

Sales of Nonfood Items in Grocery Stores and
Combination Markets, in Dollars and as a Percentage
of Total Consumption for the Year 1958.

Product	Sales (in millions)	% total domestic consumption †
Tobacco products	$1,774	29
Packaged medications	220	23
Health aids	80	26
Oral hygiene products	182	48
Hair products	171	40
Shaving products	84	38
Cosmetics and lotions	52	16
Other toiletries	34	26
Greeting cards	10	3
Magazines and newspapers	60	3
Toys	21	1
Phonograph records	50	12
Housewares	265	—

* *What the Public Spends for Grocery Store Products* (New York: Topics Publishing Co., 1959).

† Total domestic consumption includes all consumption, even at the farm level, or by institutions, restaurants, or government, at the value of retail store prices.

combination markets, including supers, have invaded the nonfood field. Tobacco products and certain health and beauty aids almost universally are distributed through grocery and combination stores.

However, the activities of the small merchant are dwarfed by the supermarket with its large and diversified assortment of nonfoods.

Specific merchandising practices of supermarkets in the nonfood area and the extent of penetration in some lines can be assessed. The Toilet Goods Association reported in 1957 that supermarkets had captured 20.3 per cent of the retail business in toilet goods.[20] Drugstores still were the main outlet, with 28.6 per cent of the sales; but the supermarket has been making inroads on this lead. Furthermore, these figures are distorted since they include high-priced perfume normally not handled in supers. Margins for toilet goods in supers range from 25 to 40 per cent, with an average of about 30 per cent, and turnover ranges from 12 to 25 times per year. Total 1957 sales of toilet goods in supers were $600 million.

Dollarwise, apparel has taken over the No. 3 position in non-food supermarket sales; the most important item is nylon hosiery.[21] The markup for apparel averages from 30 per cent to 35 per cent. The bulk of the merchandise is sold on impulse and is priced at $1.00 or less. Purchases are made largely from the manufacturer, and many of the items are branded and presold through advertising. In 1957 supermarkets sold $240 million in women's hosiery, or 33 per cent of total industry sales of $720 million.[22] More than 85 per cent of the larger supers carry hosiery, which sells on impulse; hosiery is conveniently displayed, attractively packaged, requires a small amount of floor space, and turns over rapidly (up to 25 times per year). With regard to complete lines of apparel, few stores have attained the position of Grand Union, which has at least three specialized apparel buyers and in some stores has up to 14,000 sq ft of space devoted to nonfoods, mostly clothing. The new Grand Union stores for the most part are junior department stores along with the food departments.

The 1957 retail sale of cigarettes was about $3 billion; of this

20 *Supermarket News*, May 5, 1958, p. 54.
21 *Ibid.*, March 10, 1958, p. 58.
22 *Ibid.*, March 31, 1958, p. 36.

total, 60 per cent, or $1.8 billion, was sold in supers.[23] Cigarettes are ideal for supermarkets since they have a turnover of as high as 52 times per year, require small display space, and need little advertising or promotion since they are presold by the manufacturer and sell in volume by the carton. Disadvantages of cigarettes are that pilferage is high, markup is low, and recently so many lines are needed that increased display space is required. However, supermarket operators have found cigarettes an ideal product to attract both men and women shoppers.

Housewares, including pots, kitchen gadgets, and brooms and mops, in 1957 had supermarket sales of $385 million, whereas in 1951 they amounted to only $16.5 million.[24] Houseware retailing is considered specialized merchandising, and many operators are willing to use service jobbers and pay slightly higher prices to get service and consigned merchandise.

Hardware items carried by supers range from 125 to 950 items.[25] These mainly include convenience goods purchased primarily by women, such as batteries, light bulbs, extension cords, paint, brushes, and small tools. These items, which carry from 25 to 40 per cent margin, have been growing in importance each year since 1950; however, they are still a relatively small portion of industry sales.

Phonograph records sold by supers in 1957 totaled $40 million or 10 per cent of the total industry sales of $400 million.[26] Records are handled primarily through rack jobbers. On the average, only 5 sq ft of space is needed for display, the records carry a 35 per cent margin, and turnover of as high as 30 times per year has been experienced. Pilferage has been low. The main difficulty is that a recording may be a hit one day and not sell the next. That is why rack jobbers are the major supplier in this field.

Toy sales in 1957 were $1.25 billion nationally, of which supermarkets transacted 2 per cent or $25 million.[27] Supermarkets were

[23] *Ibid.*, April 14, 1958, p. 52.
[24] *Ibid.*, April 21, 1958, p. 34.
[25] *Ibid.*, May 26, 1958, p. 80.
[26] *Ibid.*, June 2, 1958, p. 50.
[27] *Ibid.*, July 14, 1958, p. 42.

well behind variety stores and department stores, which transacted about 24 and 23 per cent, respectively, of toy sales. Supers have on the average devoted less than 5 sq ft of display space to toys. This display space is expanded slightly at Christmas time when half of the volume is attained. The best sellers are plastic items selling under $1.00, with the most important price line being 39 cents. On the average a super carries approximately 75 items procured primarily through rack jobbers. Whereas the sale of toys has experienced steady growth, supers have not merchandised toys effectively; and this line remains a small item in total supermarket sales and total industry sales of toys.

Cameras and sports equipment are stocked by relatively few supermarkets; only the biggest department store type of super offers a selection in these categories.[28] The reasons for this include low turnover, high price, seasonal sales, and need for many items to make a complete line. Only two photographic items provide an exception; these are film and flash bulbs, which enjoy from 33 to 40 per cent margins, require little display space at the check-out counter, and are ideal for impulse purchases.

Most supers have stayed clear of appliances.[29] Those that have succeeded in this area have done so with small items such as radios, toasters, and blenders, which sell for under $50. The reasons for not handling this type of merchandise are (1) too much display space is needed, (2) a large number of items must be carried, (3) the appliances are bulky to display, (4) discount houses offer strong competition and (5) prices are too high to qualify as an impulse item. For the same reasons, few supers have been successful with power lawn mowers, auto accessories, and large garden items.

SUMMARY

The supermarket has become the dominant factor in every division of food store retailing. The super reigns supreme over limited-line stores in

---

[28] *Ibid.*, July 21, 1958, p. 30.
[29] *Ibid.*, July 28, 1958, p. 37.

such areas as fresh fruits and vegetables, bakery products, fresh meats, sea food, and grocery items. Supermarkets currently gross more than 50 per cent of the retail food store sales of meat, produce, and grocery items. Even the delicatessens have felt the impact of the supermarket, which has opened delicatessen departments in neighborhoods where products of that nature are sold readily. Supers are the major retail channel for such diverse items as cigarettes, ice cream, canned fruit, bread, soap, and bananas.

In the nonfoods area, the supermarket, with its scrambled merchandising techniques, has become a nightmare to other retailers such as drugstores, variety shops, and department stores. The supermarket industry yearly continues to invade new areas in an effort to exploit customer traffic to the fullest. Products that are attractively packaged, require small display space, are relatively inexpensive, are purchased on impulse, carry good margins, experience a high turnover, and are subject to frequent purchase have become "must items" for the supermarket. The trend toward wider lines of nonfoods continues unabated, especially by the larger supers. Approximately 27 per cent of the supers now have separate nonfoods departments under the management of a nonfoods specialist who merchandises such items as apparel, toys, books, household supplies, phonograph records, and health and beauty aids. Currently about 5 per cent of a supermarket's sales are in nonfood lines; but the expansion in nonfoods is expected to grow over the years as the stores become larger.

12 | MANAGERIAL POLICY
AND PERSPECTIVE

INTRODUCTION

The preceding eleven chapters traced the development of the supermarket industry, examined external factors and internal policies that influenced its growth, and measured the impact of the supermarket movement on the food store industry. This final chapter sets forth industry trends and conclusions of this study written from a managerial viewpoint. The major topics to be considered are the dynamic nature of the industry, the position of the supermarket in its growth cycle, the trend toward "bigness," organizational concepts, the science of decision making in management, the use of research, the relationship of profit to volume, fixed expense and promotion, merchandising policies, store operations, financing growth, deterrents to progress, and the illusiveness of good will. The purpose of these discussions is to facilitate the making of present and future policy and decisions.

DYNAMIC NATURE OF THE SUPERMARKET

Management must realize that change is the cornerstone on which a successful supermarket operation is based. If management stops its quest for a better way of merchandising food and related products in line with the desires of the consumer, then growth will cease and the supermarket will become just another mature retailer.

The record of this industry is one of astute and capable management. No other segment of retailing has demonstrated greater dynamism in the past 30 years. The super, a marketing innovation, came into national prominence because it pursued an unusual practice with regard to the sale of food store products. It featured large volume, narrow margins, and reduced expenses through self-service and a variety of other economies. In a period of depression it established itself as a low-cost marketer of food as compared with existing food store retailers, and it passed on some of its savings in lower prices to the consumer.

Once the movement started amidst much controversial publicity, it continued its dynamic policy of constant change. With the rise in national income, supers switched from the "cheapy" form to a better-equipped, better-located and better-housed type of market. During World War II when food rationing was in effect, the supermarkets added nonfoods.

Supers continued to capture more of the business in older, densely populated areas where the price appeal was important. But in the postwar period, they followed the trend to the suburbs and stressed locations in these new areas where purchasing power was higher and opportunity for growth was greater. These new units featured such customer services as parking facilities, air conditioning, music, and rest rooms.

When the trend toward one-stop shopping developed, supers exploited this preference to the fullest with their wide lines of merchandise. As new products were introduced, supers in general had more facilities to handle them than the small grocer or combination market. The postwar trend of supermarkets was to build larger stores to handle greater varieties of stock.

These changes increased both gross margins and expenses of the supermarket. Margins were forced upward because there was a tendency to expand into wide lines, including nonfoods, which earned a higher markup than grocery items. Gross margins also increased as a result of higher expenses because of the trend to "trade up" the store and to increase customer services. In addition to the rise in expenses attributed to improving customer shopping facilities, there was an increase in the percentage of sales expended for salaries and wages.

The supermarket management attempted to combat this rise in wages with an increase in self-service. The wider use of self-service was in line with the wishes of the customers; and the trend towards complete self-service continues to grow.

Chain brands, manufacturing and food processing activities, and prepackaging are more recent areas of investigation by management. And the future offers promise for additional change for more effective and efficient marketing that ranges from electronic checkout stands to spirally designed stores.

More than any other type of food store, the super has adapted its operations and policies to meet changes in consumer buying habits. Management has been aware of economic trends and has shaped operations accordingly. The small stores frequently had neither the finances nor the business acumen to profit by the changing times. The ability of management generally to experiment, to adapt, and to take advantage of the circumstances must be continued if this industry is to grow in the future. Management of a specific supermart operation that lacks vision in setting forth its objectives and also the means and the ability to attain these objectives will cause that concern to become just another mature retailer.

POSITION IN ITS GROWTH CYCLE

The record of the supermarket industry is a story of growth. Normally an industry passes through four phases in its pattern of development or growth cycle. These stages include (1) the period of experimentation, (2) the period of rapid growth into the social fabric, (3) the period when growth continues but at a diminishing rate, and (4) the period of maturity or stability.

The supermarket, an innovation, invaded a mature or relatively stable business—the sale of food for home consumption—which is more or less geared to population growth. And in a short span of 30 years it revolutionized the food business and related industries. Currently the supermarket transacts about 65 per cent of grocery and combination market sales and 57 per cent of all food stores sales. While the industry currently continues to grow and command a larger share of the market, the rate of growth—not the absolute amount—tends to decrease. This would place the supermarket in the third stage of its asymptotic growth, but at no time to date has this industry evidenced maturity.

Underlying reasons for past and future growth are found in (1) operating practices and techniques, (2) the favorable economic and social climate in which to operate, (3) the basic philosophy of management, and (4) the composition of the industry. The operating techniques developed by management stand as a monument to retailing. The external factors of new developments from research, suburbia, and prosperity show no evidence of basic change in the immediate future. The original philosophy of management to seek a better way to market food and related products has remained in effect throughout. Like the New York Yankess in baseball, management has never stopped winning and will continue under the spirit of "success breeds success." Many grass-root operators—pioneers and innovators who were imbued with the desire to create and who fought their way to the top—are still with the industry. Many of these have developed large, even gigantic, operations. Others who have since joined the movement, including many chains, learned there is no such term as "status quo" in this field. Those who could not stand the pace any longer have left the industry. Inasmuch as there are advantages to large-scale operation in this field, it is no problem to sell an operation profitably to a larger competitor. This trend of "acquire or expire" will continue.

Chains have now come to dominate the supermarket industry; and yet no one concern ranks supreme. Competition prevails everywhere. The major battle is no longer a struggle among segments of the food distribution area; rather, it is an intra-industry battle among supermarkets. The small markets and limited-line stores are caught in the cross fire of supermarket operators who vie among themselves for new products, locations, and ideas to secure some marketing advantage. Intensive competition has kept and will continue to keep the industry alert. The growth in the foreseeable future will continue independently of the increase in population and in personal disposable income. The industry will continue in phase three of the growth cycle in the era of the "sizzling sixties."

While the industry as a whole is in phase three of the growth cycle, all members are not necessarily in this stage. All concerns are not experiencing the same rate of growth; some individual companies evidence maturity. Managements of individual concerns should assess their past rate of progress, set forth objectives, and plan for the future to attain these goals whatever they may be. In recent years, chains with 100 to 1,000 units as a class experienced the greatest absolute and relative growth. Concerns with one or a limited number of stores will continue to experience a more fluctuating pattern of development since the opening of one new super influences operations significantly. But the small members of the industry are not growing at the accelerated rate of the medium-sized chains and are becoming the more stable members of the industry. This also is the case of the largest industry members who must watch expansion closely, not for lack of resources, markets, facilities, and ability but for fear of governmental interference.

SUPERMARKET TREND TOWARD "BIGNESS"

The supermarket industry today is basically one of big business. Management must realize that forces within the industry no longer favor "large" but "larger" scale operation. This trend toward "bigness" reflects the investment in each store and the size of the concern that owns and operates the markets.

The "cheapy" supermarket investment was at a minimum. These stores rented abandoned buildings and used flimsy fixtures. Since then the investment in a supermarket has spiraled, particularly in the postwar period because of the trends toward (1) larger stores, (2) larger inventories, (3) more and better equipment, and (4) holdings in real estate. Larger stores are needed to handle the increased lines of merchandise and enable better display. Larger inventories reflect the growing lines handled including nonfoods and the host of convenience food products. Additional equipment is required to handle frozen foods, self-service meats, and food preparation and processing. Many pioneer locations require the erection of buildings and the development of parking lots. Since rented facilities are not always available, supers erect many of their own buildings or arrange for financing them in this postwar era of expansion. Today a modern supermarket requires a substantial investment at one location. The degree of risk inherent in pioneering a new location with a substantial investment limits entry into the industry to the large operator. And the long-range trend continues toward larger and better equipped markets with wider lines of merchandise.

Whereas the supermarket was an innovation of independent merchants, the industry received its main impetus when the chains joined the movement. By 1958 the local, regional, and national chains dominated the supermarket field with 67 per cent of the stores and 69 per cent of the sales. And these chains continue to capture more of the volume and to operate the larger markets. These trends will continue in the near future.

Management must realize that the industry has certain definite advantages for the big operator. In financing, supers have used retained profits as an important source of funds for expansion; yet, outside capital to a large degree also has been needed. The larger concerns have been able to acquire capital (sell stock or debentures) on a more advantageous arrangement since the degree of risk inherent in pioneering a new location or withstanding the inroads of an encroacher in a given market can be minimized by geographical diversification of the outlets. "Bigness" also has certain operational advantages in such areas as buying, warehousing, advertising, and promotion. The low, fixed expense of a supermarket accentuates territorial encroachment by the diversified large enterprise. Furthermore, horizontal and vertical integration practices benefit the larger concerns. When chains acquire a sufficient number of outlets as a result of horizontal expansion, they find it advantageous to integrate vertically by assuming some of the wholesale activities. Horizontal integration as a result of acquiring existing markets of smaller competitors furnishes the needed outlets rapidly and eliminates the risk and the increased costs of an untried location. After a chain attains a sufficient number of outlets, additional vertical integration is feasible by entry into manufacturing and food-processing activities. The chains are able to incorporate their own branded products in their marketing strategy in this highly competitive field where price and value are vital; and the manufactured products also can become an important source of profits to firms of the proper size in terms of retail volume.

The wave of horizontal integration that has taken place in recent years primarily through acquisitions is creating a growing class of medium-sized chains that wield a potent force in buying and selling operations. Furthermore, these medium-sized chains have branched out into manufacturing and food-processing activities that range from coffee to store fixtures. Manufacturers of food products, even the national advertisers with widely known brands, are finding growing competition with chain brands arising from vertical integration; and this trend is expected to continue.

The largest member of the industry, the Great Atlantic and Pacific Tea Company, for years was singled out by the federal government for antitrust action as a result of its broad line of manufactured products and its 4,500 plus outlets. Two other major concerns, the Kroger Company and the National Tea Company, recently have been charged with violation of the antimerger law resulting from extensive acquisitions. In the Kroger compaint, the Federal Trade Commission charged that 20 per cent of the supermarket concerns now transact 72 per cent of the sales. While these actions may deter the largest members of the industry from aggressive expansion, the smaller members (but large in their own right) continue on their merry pace of integration, both horizontal and vertical. The extent to which this industry becomes one of large-size chains depends solely on the policing action of the federal government.

Future possibilities for this industry that make for "bigness" are mergers of supermarkets with appliance, variety, drug, and department stores. This would enable expansion through mergers without running afoul of the antimonopoly provisions of the Clayton Act. Possibly, supermarket chains could be merged with discount houses.

Or the pattern established by the Grand Union Company in developing its Grand-Way stores may offer expansion in the junior department store area. All these developments point toward "bigness."

Individual company management must think in terms of "bigness." This must be inherent in its policy and perspective. Management must cope with these trends toward horizontal and vertical integration and all the ramifications of reorganization. It can join the movement in its own manner or sell out at the best possible price. It is difficult to swim upstream or fight against statistical odds favoring the opposition. Forces are marshaled in favor of "bigness," both in size of stores and size of concerns.

ORGANIZATION CONCEPTS

Management has come more and more to realize that "bigness" leads to complications in the operation of a supermarket. This fact of life requires that an organization—a team—be developed to achieve with the minimum of effort the goals of the enterprise, which, whatever they may be, are set forth by top management. Everyone in authority must know, endorse, and be imbued with these objectives. Otherwise friction, confusion, and disagreement can render ineffective the organization and operation of the business.

Top management of a large-scale operation must set forth the major functions of the business required to achieve the desired goals. For example, the selling operation is a major function in a supermarket; the number of individuals in the chain of command depends upon the size and scope of the concern. The chain of command for a large supermarket company runs from the president to the vice-president in charge of operations. Then it passes to the district managers and finally to the store managers from their respective district supervisors. In turn, the department managers in a super are responsible to the store manager, and the crews report to the department managers. Throughout, this organization must center responsibility with certain individuals; and it is imperative to give these individuals the specific authority that goes with their assigned responsibility and to make compensation accordingly. A staff of experts is required to offer technical information and assistance to the managers and other executives in the line operation. These staff members—experts in such areas as research and development, merchandising, personnel, advertising, promotion, and home economics—facilitate the work of the line executives. Finally a committee of major executives from both staff and line departments (or an outside management-consulting firm) should evaluate the organization to assure proper operation. Every supermarket organization should be subject to frequent review.

There has been a trend in the past decade in the supermarket industry toward this type of line-and-staff organization and away from the functional kind in which, for example, the store produce department managers in a division are responsible to a district or headquarters specialized produce manager. This suggested basic pattern of line-and-staff organization has been used successfully by large organizations. It centers the responsibility in the store, and it enables the market to operate under a line authority as a team effort. The supermarket is a big business, and management must have an organization geared for big business. The organization chart should be made available to all personnel so that enterprising employees can see avenues for advancement.

SCIENCE OF DECISION MAKING IN MANAGEMENT

Management problems of any business become more complex as the enterprise becomes larger and more diversified. Supermarket management faces added difficulties in decision making which result from the wide geographical dispersement of its operating units: that is, stores, warehouses, processing plants, and factories. Furthermore, the logistics problems of handling a large physical volume of bulky, diversified merchandise which is sold on a narrow margin of profit become exceedingly complex. This is no industry of apron-stringed men with strong backs. Supermarket concerns require capable management personnel who are able to make proper decisions at all levels of the organization. Decentralized management is essential.⟩

Decisions basically fall into three categories, namely: (1) policy, (2) operating, and (3) crisis.[1] Policy decisions as to the broad objectives of the concern, such as extent of integration or general product line, are set forth by the board of directors. Lesser policy decisions involving personnel or purchasing are made by the key executives in the concern. Operating decisions relating to the daily activities of the company, such as the purchase of a particular product or the pricing of an item, should be made by store managers and department heads to allow for maximum flexibility in taking advantage of local conditions. Crisis decisions are those made on the spur of the moment to solve an immediate problem without regard to existing policy or due to the lack of policy. These can be made at any level of management, but normally they appear at the operational level. Too often the danger of crisis decisions made to solve particular problems lies in the fact that they become company policy.⟩

Local management is confronted with the problem of making more and better operating decisions. These decisions should be predicated on a rational, systematic basis rather than on intuition or experience-based judgment alone. The process of decision making is not a substitute for judgment but is a systematic approach to the solution of problems. For the purposes of analysis, the elements of decision making can be reduced to:

1. Finding the problem
2. Analyzing the problem
3. Developing alternative solutions
4. Selecting the best solution
5. Making the decision effective

For example, consider two supermarkets in the same chain in adjacent trading areas. One store purchases perishables from local

[1] These categories were suggested by Dr. Robert Carney, Associate Professor of Management, Georgia Institute of Technology.

farmers and the other from the central warehouse. Friction exists between the two store managers, and there is resentment toward the division manager on the part of the one store manager who follows orders and purchases from the central warehouse. *Problem Found.*

The problem can be defined as (1) misinterpretation of policy by either or both local managers, (2) obedience to formal policy by one manager and disregard for it by the other, or (3) failure to include all stores in the policy. Next, in order to develop a solution, an analysis must be made as to what caused these two different practices to exist in the first place. Management must know where to find sufficient information; it must have the ability to draw together data and set forth the necessary assumptions. *Analysis* Otherwise a sufficient number of alternatives will not be set forth, and the analysis will be made in too narrow a framework. The analysis must assess the information accurately by assigning the correct weights to the data. For example, if vine-ripened produce in season is demanded by the vast majority of customers of one store and this feature is known to differentiate the particular market and attract customers, then this factor that favors the practice of buying locally may outweigh many minor points favoring central purchasing. *Alternative Solutions*

As one solution to this dilemma in produce buying, management could inform all local managers to follow policy as set forth. A second choice would be to have formal policy followed except in special circumstances. Or, if the policy regarding outside purchasing is too rigid and needs to be made flexible, a third solution would be to permit decision making at the operating level. *Solution*

Circumstances in each case would determine what the specific solution to the problem should be. It is essential in good decision making that the solution not be made in a vacuum without regard for the human element. The goals of the individuals who will be affected by the choices must be considered. It is also necessary to anticipate the reaction of those affected by the solution selected because, in the final analysis, decisions will be ineffectual unless accepted by those who are to carry them out. Other factors to *Making decision effective.*

be considered are the cost, time, personnel, skill, equipment, and resources with which to do the job.⟩

The above problem could have evolved from lack of company over-all policy on outside buying, or it could have resulted from a crisis decision made by a division manager or store manager. This crisis decision may have become a precedent for the one store to follow. Management must organize and operate the concern so as to require the fewest number of crises decisions. Yet, policy should not be so rigid that store managers are prevented from making sound decisions affecting the operation of their respective stores.

USE OF RESEARCH

The small food store operator knows his customers; he can survey his domain daily, ascertain his requirements, and make his decisions on first-hand information.⟨Supermarket management is more removed from the customer. The business is larger and more complex, the operation is more widespread and diversified, and competition among the markets is rampant. These factors indicate the growing need in a supermarket for research to furnish reliable data to management for decision making.⟩

Research activities in a supermarket are directed toward marketing or merchandising functions and operating practices. Frequently the marketing and operating activities in a supermarket are difficult to separate.⟨By definition, marketing research is the gathering, recording, and analyzing of all facts about problems relating to the transfer and sale of goods and services from producer to consumer.[2] Operations research is the prediction and comparison of the values, effectiveness, and costs of a set of proposed alternative courses of action involving man-machine systems.[3]⟩Operations research uses a model of the action that has been developed analytically by a logical and, when feasible, mathematical methodology, the values for

[2] Harper W. Boyd and Ralph Westfall, *Marketing Research* (Homewood, Illinois: Richard D. Irwin, Inc., 1956), p. 4.

[3] Joseph McCloskey and Florence Trefethen, *Operations Research for Management* (Baltimore: The Johns Hopkins Press, 1954), p. xxiii.

which are derived from past actions or designed operational experiments. While operations research normally has a broad connotation and overlaps the area of marketing research, the technique is used in supermarkets more narrowly to denote logistic problems in the physical movement of merchandise in performing buying, selling, warehousing, delivery, and handling functions.

Marketing research applicable to the supermarket industry includes activities pertaining to (1) markets, (2) products, (3) motivation, (4) internal sales analysis, and (5) advertising and display. Market research includes a study of the characteristics of the customers and their purchasing habits. It also embraces the detailed research needed for new store locations. Prior to sinking a substantial investment in a new outlet or contracting to make rental payments over a long period of years, management must make exhaustive studies of the past, present, and future possibilities of the location. Only too frequently markets have been opened in unsuitable areas. This practice is abetted by promoters who are willing to make deals and concessions to put the land into use and by supermarket operators who are willing to take on an outlet with low, fixed expenses so that a competitor won't get it, even though the location is questionable. Product research measures consumer preference for brands, types of products, packaging, size, and other physical attributes. Motivation studies measure why people buy a particular product or patronize a certain market. The store image in the minds of the customers can be depicted along with psychological attitudes held by consumers as to color and style of markets. Sales analysis furnishes information on the movement of particular products as well as profitability of departments and product lines. Advertising and display research measure the effectiveness of the types and kinds of strategy employed.

Of all the research designs available to perform the various marketing research studies, the experimental method offers supermarket management the most unusual opportunity to collect data as to permit clear and unconfused conclusions as to the correctness of an hypothesis which involves cause-and-effect relationships. The data obtained from experimentation can furnish management vital information for decision making. Supermarket concerns possibly have the best facilities of any business for conducting experimental research in the area of social science. Only those industries engaged in the physical sciences appear more favorably situated to conduct experiments. Supermarket management can use experimentation to check advertising effectiveness, display techniques, product preferences, pricing strategy, and packaging. Even small concerns can use the various experimental methods such as the before-after, the before-after-with-control group, and the after-only-with-control group designs. For example, the operator of only one store can measure for one week the sale of potatoes in the traditional package, introduce a new packaging method for the following week, hold all other factors unchanged, and measure the difference in sales. Consumer panels which can serve as a valuable adjunct to the buying committees should not be restricted to the large companies. To facilitate experimentation, concerns should designate certain stores for the purpose of conducting experimental tests. Necessary facilities for conducting tests can be maintained permanently.

Opportunities for the successful use of operations research exist in supermarkets in the physical movement of goods in all areas. There is only a specific amount of shelf space in a given market; each new item purchased takes its place only at the expense of some other product. Operations research can furnish quantitative aids in determining what to buy and how much to buy. This technique also can facilitate the warehousing and delivery of groceries. For example, one concern revamped its entire delivery system so that selectors at the warehouse loaded the trailers daily, drivers delivered them at night during periods of little traffic, and store managers assigned the correct number of grocery clerks to be available for unloading and stocking shelves on a predetermined morning. Operations research also can be of value in the area of selling by increasing efficiency of personnel in stocking shelves and operating check-out stands. For some concerns, it has led to the establishment of standards by departments for man-hours expended in relation to sales.

Produce and meat departments, for example, need not necessarily have the same ratio of sales to man-hours.

These illustrations indicate the types of opportunities that are available in a supermarket for operations research. The principal contribution of this technique is that it presents to management alternative opportunities or courses of action in quantitative terms. Management can use these data in making decisions.

Product research of the technical type involved in producing an item that will accomplish certain results has been passed on to the manufacturer by the supermarket industry. Expenditures of this type thus do not appear as a cost to the supermarket in performing its functions. Competition for shelf space has been so intense that food manufacturers have been forced to develop a multitude of new and improved products which are marketed in cooperation with supermarket concerns. This research involved in the creation of form utility rightfully belongs to the manufacturer. But, as the supermarket industry becomes more integrated and active in manufacturing, management may have to face the problem of product development and not depend so much on the research accomplishments of other manufacturers as it has in the past. Some compromise has appeared in which supermarkets and food manufacturers have engaged in joint research efforts.

In summary, the larger members of this industry have tended to do most of the research in the areas of marketing and operations. The total amount spent as a percentage of sales has appeared negligible for the industry as a whole. Management of some concerns has rationalized its position on limited research by contending that this activity is not needed, inasmuch as operations are flexible and the market is in constant contact with the consumer. Or, under the guise of research, management has used casual observation to substantiate ideas or concepts. Casual observation is not scientific in its approach because it is not objective, subject to accurate measurement, or conducted exhaustively. Managements of individual concerns must assess the benefits derived from true research versus the cost involved because of the narrow profit margin on which they operate. Money properly spent on research can more than pay for itself in economies of operation and better merchandising.

RELATIONSHIP OF PROFIT TO VOLUME, FIXED EXPENSE, AND PROMOTION

A supermarket is geared by management to transact a large volume on a narrow margin of profit. The industry has flourished even with a relatively low profit margin expressed as a percentage of sales since this rate can reflect a sizable dollar profit when related to a large volume. This concept has been expounded by management throughout as a basic financial tenet.

But, this truism is only a partial answer to the super's financial success. The factor of large variable costs and expenses, or of low, fixed expenses estimated at 6 to 7 per cent of sales, must also be considered as a factor in the profit picture. The low fixed expense of a supermarket and the ability of fixed expense to remain constant over a fairly wide range in sales accentuate the ability of a concern with territorial diversification to invade a new area. Stores for a particular location are planned to transact a certain predetermined present and future volume. The design is such, however, that a super can still operate profitably even though a considerable variation in actual volume from planned sales occurs. The absence of a large fixed expense is a beneficial factor for a store in which sales fail to materialize. On the other hand, the fact that the fixed expense remains constant, even with a considerable increase in sales over normal anticipated volume, benefits the volume-building market. Instead of the 2 to 3 per cent profit before taxes, some stores have earned 5 per cent on sales as a result of a high level of volume. Even though the investment in a new super is sizable, the fact that fixed expenses are low relative to sales is an added inducement to new territory invasion.

For an industry faced with this relationship of profit to volume and to fixed expense, the additional or marginal customer is of considerable importance. The marginal family that spends $1,000 to $1,500 per year in a super must be obtained and retained. The marginal family reflects a sizable increase in profits, both as a percentage of sales and of net worth for a supermarket operating at the normal volume for which it was designed. For example, if local management of a typical super operating at normal volume can induce an additional hundred families to shop regularly at the market, an increase in profits of 1 per cent as a percentage of sales for that market is possible. Retention of the consumer is vital since a loss of a customer can reduce profits just as the addition of one can increase return. This is why trading stamps and other promotional devices have met with such wide adoption by the industry. In the near future, increased competition will make for even wider use of promotional devices. Management easily could consider funds spent on continuous promotion as a short-term capital investment on which earnings now and in the very near future are possible. Some of the best creative brainpower should be devoted to the development of new promotion ideas.

The prize of profits is held out to all supermarket competitors in a trading area as a significant reward for attracting these marginal families. Unfortunately, most promotion tends to be transitory in effect. Other operators mimic the successful concern. Thus it is a constant race among the competitors to attract the customers. And while the profit prize may not be fully attained by any one market, the manager who doesn't advertise and promote to gain consumer patronage will be left literally "in the dust," with the remaining competitors still in the lead. As more supers are opened, the marginal families continue to be drawn away from the existing markets and detract from their earnings. However, new markets should be opened only after careful research has been performed to forecast the success of the venture. Yet, the wide range of volume over which a given market can operate and still be profitable is a lure to opening new outlets and will continue to make for highly competitive conditions. There is no lessening of it; the conclusion is that competition among the supermarket members will be more intensive in the years immediately ahead.

MERCHANDISING POLICIES

Executives in retail concerns basically must be merchandisers. This is especially true for all levels of supermarket management. All store personnel must realize they are part of a merchandising team. Their economic justification for employment is that the store in which they work adds value to the merchandise sold. Basically, a supermarket buys 81 cents worth of merchandise from its suppliers which it sells for $1.00 to its customers. Whether a consumer will pay this 19-cent differential is a direct function of the merchandising skill of the store management and the efforts of all employees.

The term *merchandising* was defined in this text as the practice of making certain that the products sold meet the needs and desires of the customers; at the same time the goods must be presented effectively. In the main, supermarkets have been effective merchandisers of food products. On a more limited scale, supers have been moderately successful in merchandising nonfoods. At the local level, skillful tactics in merchandising nonfoods have not always been demonstrated.

Supermarket executives merchandise when they screen the 100 to 200 new products presented weekly for their inspection and decide which ones will sell. Powerful buying committees have been established to help make the selection process more rational and free from personal prejudice. In cases of doubt, the marketing research techniques of test stores or consumer panels have been used. This selection of merchandise by management constitutes a major factor in determining the success of the venture. In an endeavor to please the consumer further, management has increased the number of lines handled almost yearly in the postwar era. The wide line of products in turn has forced manufacturers into a continuous battle both to attain and then retain shelf space.

Food manufacturers have become highly cognizant of product policy. They have developed through research a broad line of convenience goods and other new items such as pot pies, TV dinners, and instant hot cereals. The near future of food manufacturers depends on producing new convenience goods which meet the needs of the consuming public. In turn, these and related products must be pulled through the channels as a result of extensive advertising and promotion. As new and really improved products continue to come out of the research laboratories and into the markets, producers will of necessity need to cooperate with the supermarket operators to develop merchandising strategy that will move the goods. These new items are the life blood for the dynamic supermarket which strives for added volume and greater profit while retaining its basic competitive position in a trading area.

The use of chain brands as a part of merchandising strategy has been on the increase in recent years. Wider use of chain brands will continue as stronger and larger supermarket chains dominate more of the industry. The increased use of chain brands in canned goods, for example, will in time lower over-all margins on these items. Manufacturers may be forced to innovate pricing systems in which staples as price leaders compete with chain brands. The bulk of the profit will be earned by the manufacturer in new food specialties that the supermarket will not find suitable to manufacture. But the supermarket industry will become more powerful as it branches out into untried areas such as private branding in prepackaged meats. The pendulum of customer satisfaction that once favored the manufacturer is now swinging wider and wider over the area of the supermarket industry.

In the nonfoods area, the trend will continue toward increased sales of these products. The rapid growth of separate nonfood departments under a nonfoods specialist coupled with the building of larger stores able to handle more products pretells the story. While nonfood sales currently are about 5 per cent of total sales of a supermarket, this percentage can easily be doubled in the near future by adding general lines of merchandise. However, supermarkets must learn to do a more effective job of merchandising nonfoods. This includes better product plans and control of inventories. In addition, pricing policies more in line with those of food products must be employed; and merchandising techniques for the sale of seasonal products must be developed. Inasmuch as there is a strong organizational trend toward separate nonfood departments under a specialist, these merchandising prerequisites can be attained.

Merchandising also includes the effective presentation of goods to the consumer. The produce manager who trims the decay from the lettuce to make the head more salable is merchandising as is the manager who marks sale prices on all badly dented cans and places them in a cart near the check-out stand. Displays that create impulse sales also are part of the merchandising function. Supermarkets have been the innovator and proponent of self-service and impulse selling. As a result of mass display, which psychologically tends to make people buy, the supers have found an unusually prolific source of unplanned purchases. However, wider use of experimental research must be adopted in order to gain maximum benefit from display. For example, before-and-after studies should be used more widely to measure the impact of a particular display arrangement. Also, psychological tests of the consumer should be made to approach more scientifically the subject of display.

The display practices of the supers in turn have forced manufacturers to revamp their merchandising policies and to adopt better packaging, branding, and display practices. As supermart chains become more powerful through integration, manufacturers may be forced to establish tailor-made displays, promotions, and deals for different kinds and classes of stores. In turn, representatives of the manufacturers will be better merchandisers and devote less time to being only salesmen.

STORE OPERATIONS

Management must realize that the economic justification for a supermarket lies in the time, place, and ownership utility (or usefulness) the store gives the merchandise it sells. This measure of value imparted to the goods is measured by the gross margin. However, in order to perform its economic function, a super must have physical facilities and personnel with which to operate. These areas of store operations are growing in importance and complexity with the size of the markets and the unionization movement.

Management currently faces the problem of furnishing individual stores more and more selling space and larger parking facilities. One solution for additional selling space is better control of inventory and ordering procedures through use of electronic computers so that less storage is needed at the store. Also, processing activities conceivably could be centralized in many concerns; this would furnish additional display facilities. Thus, within limitations, management can remodel and offer a market some additional selling space. However, the added space from relocating processing activities in most instances will not offer sufficient space, and the markets will have to be relocated in the same area if possible in the near future. This change in location will have strong repercussions on the financial community holding mortgages on present supermarket properties that lack sufficient facilities. Furthermore, management must design new stores with an eye on costs, present and future requirements, and flexibility in the use of space. The importance of planning space requirements is exemplified in a recent study of 100 markets that were built in the year 1940.[4] Only 23 markets operate unchanged, whereas 26 were abandoned and 51 required major remodeling.

Another operating feature that may reward a chain organization with patronage loyalty is chain differentiation. With the trend toward fewer and larger concerns in this industry, the chains should take on more of an individualized appearance as to color, design of store fixtures, arrangement, and outside appearance. This familiarity will wed customers to the entire chain and not just one store.

As markets become larger and require greater investment, better management at the local level is required constantly. There has been an organizational trend in the industry in the past decade for each store to be under a general manager who is responsible for operations at the store level. Department managers report to him and not some central specialized supervisor. Store managers must

---

[4] "NAFC Looks into the Future," *Super Market Merchandising*, XIX, no. 12, December, 1955, p. 61.

be trained to be business executives with administrative prowess; they must be merchandisers, advertisers, and publicists as well. Executive development programs for middle management in decision making and case study are a must if this industry is to be successful in operating larger stores with greater varieties of merchandise in the future. Some companies have taken steps in this direction by sending key personnel to universities that offer programs in executive development; others have developed short-term clinics for their personnel. The Super Market Institute's program of executive training has drawn favorable response, but more positive action must be taken in this entire area of development and management training.

Many concerns have attracted young, capable future leaders, but the industry as a whole apparently has failed to draw its share of junior executives in competition with industry generally and department, drug, and variety stores in particular. Universities hear little about the supermarket industry. Supers have not made themselves competitive in search for the top talent needed because of the growing size of markets and the intense competition facing the stores. This does not mean to imply that hard work and long hours should be played down, but the rewards to management could be accentuated in salary, bonus, stock options, insurance, and retirement. Organization charts clearly showing paths for promotion should be publicized; opportunities for training programs and executive development must be made available.

No big business can operate without effective personnel. Workers are a vital part of the operation in a supermarket. Those who have daily contact with the public, from the grocery clerks stocking shelves to the check-out personnel, form a part of the store image. Supers should be a good place in which to work as well as to shop. Individuals must be trained, motivated, and made part of the store team to make them efficient. In this era of high labor costs, the supermarket stands today as a monument for all retailers and industry alike to envy. The supermarket and self-service are synonymous, and yet, 6 to 7 per cent of the sales dollar expended on labor is a substantially larger percentage of the sales dollar than that paid out by the pioneers in the field. Added services have been offered the consumer in "traded up" markets that necessitate additional personnel expenditures, but management must watch this expense so that the super does not lose its "claim to fame." Increased expense for personnel must be matched with increased output from the worker; and management must furnish the equipment and facilities for increased efficiency. Rising expenses generally will continue to be a constant threat for management, which must counter with increased productivity from the worker, more efficient methods and equipment, complete self-service, better use of resources, and the elimination of unnecessary frills.

FINANCING GROWTH

The aggressive expansion plans pursued by management in this industry have made financing a major issue. Dynamic growth over a protracted period of time cannot occur without adequate funds. Management has acquired assets to operate the business through (1) reinvesting of earnings, (2) selling of equity securities, (3) borrowing, and (4) leasing. All four methods are used widely.

Operations of the members of this industry in the main have been profitable. While the earnings as a percentage of the sales dollar have been a modest 2 to 3 per cent before taxes, profits on equity capital have appeared excellent. Over the years management has plowed back earnings into the business to finance growth and improvements. Dividend policies have been conservative, even for companies with widely held common stocks. Since the industry is expected to grow, no major change in this dividend policy for the industry appears imminent. Management of individual concerns must realize, however, that if growth diminishes, stockholders will insist on larger dividends.

Many of the supermarket chains that dominate the industry have sold equity securities in the capital markets. The investment attitude of the public toward the industry in general and specific concerns in particular is important if the industry is to obtain equity funds

advantageously. Many investors are attracted to growth equities.
The retail food business in itself is relatively stable and noncyclical.
It faces gradual growth as the population rises; and it is influenced
only slightly by changes in per capita family income. This also is
the case of the electric power industry whose members generally
have attained a high investment status for their equity securities as
a result of the monopoly feature in their services. Supermarkets, the
principal segment of the food store group, face strong competition
in the market place. They have countered with aggressive practices
that have imparted growth characteristics to their division of the
food store group. But, as a class, supermarket shares are not likely
to attain in the near future the status of a utility equity because of
this turmoil in the market. On the other hand, the supermarket concerns lack the growth aura of companies in the fields of chemicals,
missiles, and electronics. Stocks of these concerns traditionally sell
at a high multiple of earnings and considerably above their net tangible book value per share. Equity financing for supermarkets generally will continue more on the basis of good-grade industrial concerns. The financial community is aware that the supermarket is not
completely immune to recessions. Competitive pressures can force
concerns to pass on to the customers reductions in the cost of merchandise. These pressures, coupled with the trend toward handling
merchandise with higher margins, can squeeze gross profit in a
period of economic turbulence, such as during a steel strike. Since
the cost of handling food in a supermarket is tied more to the tonnage handled than to revenue, expenses in a recession can increase
relative to sales and squeeze net profit. In addition, the growing
trend toward more luxury items can make dollar sales more volatile.

Many individual members of the supermarket industry, primarily
the medium-sized chains, have experienced remarkable sales and
earnings growth resulting, in part, from acquisitions. The financial
community has recognized these features and has placed a premium
price on the common stocks of these concerns more in line with
those of other growth equities. The very largest concerns, ham-

strung by possible antitrust legislation, tend to have their common stocks sell on a more conservative basis. The small concerns or supers with one store are for the most part dependent on local financing for expansion. As a result of the risk involved in a limited number of outlets and the relatively small number of possible shares outstanding, the small companies will find it difficult to attract equity funds in the national capital markets and will depend upon the ingenuity of management to obtain equity funds locally.

Supermarket management must borrow on the most favorable terms possible in this narrow-profit industry. To do this, it will be necessary to maintain a satisfactory financial condition and operating record. Furthermore, management (especially of the smaller firms) should make certain that capable younger executives are available in the organization to take over the reins. This has been a weakness in many of the smaller firms and in part has contributed to the increase of mergers in the industry. Supermarkets have borrowed extensively for working funds, for expansion, equipment financing, and real estate acquisitions. It is not unusual for debt to be equal to net worth. There appears to be no letup in the need for funds in the immediate future; thus debt will remain heavy.

Management of supermarkets has been astute in its method of controlling assets through lease. While a concern is liable for lease payments over an extended period of years, the company actually uses assets that are financed over a long term by others. Supers have been forced to pioneer new locations with modern stores that require a substantial investment in equipment. Under the lease arrangement, the fixed assets used do not appear on the balance sheet, nor do the lease payments contracted for over a period of years appear as a liability. Inasmuch as supermarts are merchandising organizations that thrive on a large volume of fast-moving merchandise, the lease has proved an essential element in expansion. With growing need for cash to finance larger inventories and modernization, the lease method will be more essential in the future, especially during periods of tight money and high interest rates.

DETERRENTS TO SUPERMARKET GROWTH

Management must recognize certain limiting internal and external forces that restrict the supermarket growth; some concerns are particularly vulnerable.

Consider the first limitation, namely, the distribution cost cycle. According to Malcolm P. McNair:

> It seems to be characteristic of new types of distributive enterprises that in the first state of their development they gain a foothold primarily by means of low prices. In the second stage they "trade up" the quality of the merchandise carried, and in the third stage they compete by offering services. Companies in this third stage, unless they are managed with exceptional ability, not uncommonly encounter an increasing cost of doing business, a rising ratio of fixed investments to total investments and a decline in the rate of return on capital.[5]

At the time this concept was advanced, the large food chains had made substantial sales gains in the food store industry. But they had entered the third stage of the cycle, and their rate of growth was decreasing. The analysis in this text indicates that although the supermarket industry is relatively young in years and has shown considerable growth, it also appears to have entered the third stage of the distribution cost cycle. To date, supermarkets have operated in a progressive manner; they have demonstrated ability to experiment, to adapt, and to take advantage of changing trends. This has had a direct bearing on their development; but in this third stage, management must operate with exceptional ability if this industry is to continue expansion. There is the ever-increasing problem of attracting young men to this field who are managerial timber. Future skilled executives must be developed for an industry in the third stage of the distribution cost cycle. Currently, the competitive situation confronting the supermarkets, coupled with the basic nature and composition of the industry, indicate vigorous administration

---

[5] Malcolm P. McNair, *Expenses and Profits in the Chain Grocery Business* (Cambridge: Harvard Business School, Bureau of Business Research, 1931, Bulletin No. 84), p. 21.

in the near future. Those individual concerns under ineffective management in this third stage of the cost cycle will continue in the doldrums until management changes or the company expires.

Another limitation to the growth of this industry is that the small food stores cannot be completely eliminated. They fall by the wayside at a remarkable rate, and this trend will continue. But, owners of many small food stores are not aware always of their costs; they live in the rear of the premises, and perhaps the husband is employed elsewhere during the day. The everlasting hope for gain and independence keeps many small stores in business.

Machine vending, certain limited-line stores that are well entrenched, and the superette also will prevent the supermarket from completely dominating the food store industry. Strategically located superettes handling limited brands of convenience items will continue to play a role in food store sales. They have copied the techniques that made the supermarts low-cost operators. Many operate at an expense rate that compares favorably with that of a super. Membership in buying associations or cooperatives enables them to lower the cost of merchandise purchased and to realize other advantages such as cooperative advertising. These endeavors of the superette have tended to reduce the price advantage of the supermarket.

In time the pattern of food store retailing probably will be one in which the majority of the so-called convenience items needed for supplemental shopping will be handled by superettes or by machine vending. A small core of limited-line stores will handle special products. Small combination markets will become relatively insignificant volumewise. Strategically located supermarkets will dominate their respective trading areas as well as the food store industry. Gigantic supers, merchandising a wide line of junior department store products as well as foods, will be the core store dominating large shopping centers.

Another deterrent to extensive growth is the limitation of size of supermarkets. All stores cannot be gigantic operations since some consumers prefer the personal touch and friendly attitude on the part of the store personnel that cannot be obtained easily in a mammoth operation. Personalized management can lead to more community acceptance of the store, particularly if it is a member of a large chain.

In 1958 the supermarket transacted 57 per cent of total food store sales. Eventually the super will encounter market saturation at possibly 80 per cent of total food store volume. When this condition occurs, progress will be limited to population growth unless supermarket activities are channeled into other fields of retailing, wholesaling, food processing, and manufacture. With the vast distribution system that members of this industry have attained as the foundation, supers can invade these other areas successfully. Unless the government intervenes, this appears to be the future pattern.

The adaptable supermarket has added an increasing number of nonfood lines. This movement has been one of the industry's recent developments to increase sales. Here, too, there are limitations, but these have not been reached. The supermarkets' successful sales of these nonfood lines have forced drug, variety, and department stores to review their selling techniques. All three of these competitors in the nonfoods area are boosting the number of their outlets, embarking on modernization programs, and opening branches in the suburbs and in shopping centers. They have adopted self-service or simplified selling and have copied the display techniques of supermarkets. The chain members in these areas have been growing in size through horizontal and vertical integration. For example, many drug chains now produce pharmaceuticals, toiletries, and ice cream; many process films. At the retail level, these drug chains have broadened their product lines to include glassware, books, hardware, toys, jewelry, foodstuffs, and appliances. Where local regulations permit, packaged liquor has been dispensed. Department stores, with their new satellite units in outlying shopping centers, also handle increased lines of baked goods, frozen foods, and convenience food products such as completely prepared dinners for the busy shopper. Variety stores have broadened their lines in the impulse soft-goods area. The trend toward scrambled merchandising among all types of large retailers continues on the increase. In the near future there will be more stress on food items of the convenience type by the drug, department, and variety stores. Trends are under way to make all three of these resemble the supermarket more closely.

THE ILLUSIVENESS OF GOOD WILL

The supermarket is constantly in the public eye inasmuch as food shopping is done frequently. It is imperative that supermarket management recognize the importance of the good will that establishes a patronage attachment for trading at a particular store. No fundamental differences exist among supermarkets as to basic products, prices, and values, inasmuch as this field is so highly competitive. Any manager who believes that the only prerequisite for success is to provide good merchandise values at competitive prices is in error. Management must fashion a store image that is favorable in the eyes of the general public in order to gain a patronage following.

Store differentiation can be due in part to appearance, facilities, advertising, promotional devices, or special merchandising techniques, all of which have been stressed in this chapter. These are all part of the store's personality. But there is some illusive factor in the store image that is difficult to measure; generalizations about it are difficult to make because of the diverse nature of the industry and community differences. In the main, this illusive feature in good will for an individual concern and for the industry as well is a function of management's attitude toward the consumers, the suppliers, the employees, the governmental authorities, and the community in which it operates. How well management meets the expectations of these interests will be reflected in part in the store image and in the success of the venture. These preconceived standards of behavior on the part of the different groups are not necessarily in harmony with each other, nor are they always of the same importance to the welfare of the supermarket concern.

The supermarket is not an eleemosynary institution; it is operated primarily for the profit of the owners. But its operations are influenced by the public's attitude toward it. What has supermarket management done to generate a favorable image in the minds of these interest groups?

To the American consumer, the supermarket has lowered food costs and raised the plane of living. It has given the customer what is wanted at a lower cost. These are its most noteworthy achievements from the viewpoint of the consumer. Individual concerns that have not been completely consumer-oriented have suffered in the battle for survival in this competitive industry. While there are limits in placating the customers, conditions in this industry dictate that management must consider foremost in its decisions the wants and desires of the consumer so that it can return a satisfactory profit to the stockholders.

Supermarket management has shifted the balance of power away from the food manufacturer and in the direction of the retailer. As a result of this countervailing power, supers have tended to relegate the wholesaler more or less to a status of delivery agent for the manufacturer who performs the selling function but who cannot handle physical distribution of the merchandise as economically as the wholesaler. Manufacturers have been forced to give ground in all quarters. Their entire selling program has undergone change for the better by lowering distribution costs. Supermarket management must realize, however, that the functions of the manufacturers still are vital to the success of this industry despite all its integration practices. Many consumers prefer the national brands. Management must continue to work cooperatively with the suppliers in an endeavor to merchandise on a profitable basis all the products the consumer desires. Unless fair dealings exist between the supers and the manufacturers, new-product development will be retarded, and the supers will lose their "life blood" or added source of profit resulting from new items.

Management's relations with employees affect the store image. In order to attract and keep desirable personnel, management must offer workers steady employment, opportunities for training and advancement, satisfactory working conditions and hours, fringe benefits, and a competitive wage. These are all subject to differences in opinion between management and employees, but the differences should be resolved without resort to strikes so as not to engender bitterness that may be expressed by store personnel in daily contact with the customers. The relatively pleasant employee-employer relations that have characterized this industry must be maintained, and the markets must continue to function under a team effort.

Decisions of supermarket management that affect relationships with the community and the government should be summed up in the phrase, "Supermarkets Are Responsible Citizens." Obviously a supermarket cannot devote 100 sq ft of space for a charity cookie sale, but management must stay in tune with the expectations of the community. These differ by location, and management on the proper occasions should make its sidewalks available for charity drives, put signs in the windows for relief funds, and assist in blood banks and cancer drives. How active managers are in civic affairs will depend on the community attitude. Management must know what is expected of the market to make it a responsible citizen.

Still another problem of community relationships is the advisability of continuing a policy of "scrambled merchandising" which is detrimental to many limited-line stores and small combination markets near it. Similarly, other community members in the nonfood areas feel the impact of the supermarket. Management's drive to sell general merchandise that is easily displayed, attractively packaged, inexpensively priced, and impulsively purchased has been to the detriment of department, drug, variety, and hardware stores, to name but a few. While the battle of the market place occurs daily and no retailer has the assurance of guaranteed profits, the victorious supermarket should not disdain its rivals. An old saying should be remembered: "Don't rub salt into the wound."

To paraphrase from a childhood game, the supermarket currently is "King of the Hill." How long it remains on top is a function of the industry's skill in keeping a favorable image in the eyes of the general public whose wants must be served so that the cash register will continue to ring up larger profits. For the individual firm, success in this highly competitive industry will depend primarily upon management's ability to think creatively so as to be a leader in judging the wants and whims of the consumer. And if a competitor gains some marketing superiority, success will hinge further on management's ability to recognize quickly any disadvantage and to take action accordingly.

APPENDIX A

119 COST-CUTTING IDEAS

Management is confronted with the Herculean task of controlling, and if possible reducing, expenses of operation if the supermarket is to perform its merchandising activity at a profit. Recognizing this need, the magazine *Super Market Merchandising* devoted the majority of its April, 1958, issue to the problem of "How to Fight Costs and Win." One article from this section, "119 Cost-cutting Ideas," contained a reference list of pragmatic suggestions which appear to be of extreme value to the supermarket operator who faces the task of expense control at the firing line. This check list is classified according to operations, labor, warehouse and transportation, construction and maintenance, store departments, and back room.

Operations

1. Accident costs can be reduced by equipping each store with a small flash camera. Kept at a handy location, pictures of each customer accident can be taken immediately. Experience demonstrates that customers will not file exaggerated claims if they know a photo has been taken.

2. A certain degree of shrinkage can be controlled in the area of the direct vendor. A good policy is to instruct all vendors not to put merchandise on shelves, or mix merchandise with any stock on hand until the person in charge of the department has checked in the merchandise. When a vendor leaves, he must have any outgoing packages checked to see that no merchandise is carried out that is unaccounted for.

3. Have stores send in weekly cash reports instead of daily reports. This should save a lot of time for store managers as well as for bookkeepers.

4. Proper use of self-insurance applied to such things as collision, plate glass, holdups, and even fires, boilers, and cargos can save you considerable money. Explore its possibilities with qualified insurance agents or others who have had experience with it.

5. Every time you create a new form, you increase clerical costs because each piece of paper has to be handled by many people. Take time out to review the use of your forms and simplify them. It is a good idea to have a trial run of 60 to 90 days on every form that you introduce be-

fore making it a permanent part of the business. You may decide after two months that some of these forms are worthless, and you can save on further clerical expense.

6. To save paper work on price reduction reports, make use of pilot stores. Here you can get information that you can apply to all your other stores.

7. By sorting the checks yourself, you can reduce the bank's charges. This calls for putting the checks of one type in an envelope.

8. There is something in the Draft Plan to bring money in fast from your neighborhood transfer banks to the banks used by the main headquarters disbursement bank. The bank informs headquarters of the total deposits to be made the next day. The money is made available at the headquarters disbursement bank. The bank informs headquarters of the total of drafts. This plan will lower the daily balance in the neighborhood banks, but the extra charge may be worth it, since it makes so much ready cash available at headquarters.

9. You can reduce charges on customer checks by sending them directly to the main depository bank rather than depositing them in the local transfer bank.

10. Are you sure it's worth the cost and effort to list every customer check on a separate tabulation, just in case checks are stolen? A study of this may reveal that you are recovering very little money over a long period of time. You may be burdening your managers with useless and time-consuming work.

11. If you are a small company, it may pay you to hire an engineering service to reduce your insurance rates. The bigger companies use their own men for this purpose.

12. Don't rely on a building alarm for warehouse control. Either have an ADT system or tie your alarm in with the local police department.

13. Pay store employees in cash. They prefer it. And you can save on the bank charges, which can go as high as 10 cents on each payroll check. This method is being used by a national chain, particularly in the bigger stores, where there is a full-time cashier on hand to help the manager. It is worth investigating to establish the proper procedures for preparing the payroll journals.

14. Study the advantages of leasing equipment, particularly equipment that becomes obsolete fast, such as: air conditioners, sprinklers, supervisors' cars, incinerators, tabulating machines, delivery equipment.

15. Have clerks keep a daily inventory check on standard items. It will save the buyer's time.

16. Keep paperwork where it belongs—in the central office. It costs less per hour there. Even weekly payrolls can be done more efficiently at headquarters.

17. Turn out copies (up to 10,000) of reports, bulletins, etc., by xerography. Equipment for this quick, inexpensive process is made up of three pieces: camera, copier, and fuser. It cuts out second typing from original copy to stencils and eliminates second proofreading.

18. Use newsprint or cheap wrapping paper in handling glassware, rather than the much more expensive kraft paper bags.

19. Check to see whether your company should be paying local taxes as a single corporate unit rather than as separate stores. You may be under unnecessary assessment.

20. Set up a salvage department to make daily or weekly pickups of waste and damaged goods from the stores. It's all good for resale.

21. Put up reminders to your checkers to look into the bottom shelf of the shopping cart.

22. If your managers are paying cash for store-door deliveries, it may be wise to relieve them of this burden. Over the month, the "cash payouts" can amount to hundreds.

23. To cut public liability insurance costs, it may be wiser to pay small claims yourself.

24. Use the "miscellaneous" key of your cash register to ring up tax on registers that have no tax key.

25. Have all store managers submit ideas for cost control before going ahead on them. Cost controls can become big expenses in themselves, especially if store managers start keeping detailed records without asking which ones the head office may require.

26. Stamp "paid by cash" clearly on the face of merchandise vouchers. In that way, if the voucher is lost or stolen, no one will be able to redeem it again.

27. Keep an alphabetical check list handy in each store of people known to be phony-check passers.

28. Don't keep stock on odd-sized bags that you seldom use. Store bag supplies in a place where they won't be damaged in any way.

Labor

29. Try using a job assignment card that outlines employees' duties by days. In this way the employee gets definite assignments and does not waste time each day waiting for his next assignment.

30. You can cut down on telephone expenses by following these rules: Don't allow employees to send or receive calls during working hours

(emergency calls excepted); equip only one phone with a dial; use a buzzer system for signaling; calls should be brief and to the point; install pay phones; do not tie up office personnel with details that can be handled by supervisors; check phone bills carefully.

31. Compute employee tax deductions in payroll work in a single tax table combining FICA and withholdings. You can obtain combined withholding tables from companies that supply accountants.

32. Want to reduce costs of inventory taking? One company starts inventory at 7 A.M. on a Monday morning, using regular store help on a quarterly basis. An administrative staff member is sent in to help the store crew. This gives both crew and administrators a better understanding of the store problems and leads to new suggestions for improving operations.

33. You can increase productivity in checking orders if, when using two-man teams, the first half of the items on the invoice are placed on one side of a four-wheel selector truck and the other half on the other side.

34. Check unemployment compensation claims periodically. You may be paying tax on dead claims.

35. List special prices alphabetically at the cash registers to help checkers with sale merchandise.

36. Cut down on unnecessary phone calls by having a central place for locating supervisors after the switchboard is closed. One company has each supervisor give his schedule to one key store in his district.

37. Use guide pictures to help clerks stock departments in new markets. Place photos of segments of top departments in other stores on shelves where you want the merchandise. Then send sufficient opening inventories to fill shelves. You'll save stocking time, layout time, and inventory time.

38. Have the company nurse make spot checks at the homes of men who are absent because of illness. Usually the man is really sick and will appreciate a call from the nurse. If not, a friendly talk with his boss will usually keep him from playing sick another time. Also, the calls will discourage other employees from trying the same ruse. If your company has no regular nurse, you can have your personnel office check with employees' doctors.

39. Check time cards regularly for employees who are late three or more times in a month. Have supervisors talk over with these men ways in which they can avoid being late.

40. Check previous employment records of all job applicants before you hire them, to make sure they are trustworthy. Some companies em-

ploy an investigation service to check prospective cashiers, managers, and others who will be handling large amounts of money.

41. When you fire an employee, keep a record in your central personnel office of your reasons for firing and of his social security number. Check this list whenever you hire a new man. This is particularly important where store managers hire their own personnel. A man who has been fired from one of your stores for dishonesty may look for work in another store in your chain.

42. Careful records of reasons for separating employees can lower your payments for unemployment compensation in many states. The amount you have to pay to the state for unemployment compensation usually is determined by the number of valid claims filed by former employees of yours. Thus, if you can show that you fired employees for reasons which were their own fault, such as dishonesty, your unemployment compensation payments will be lower. Many employers issue written warnings to workers and have the workers initial them, before they fire them. Then if you have to fire the workers, the warnings prove that you did so for good and just cause.

43. Punch employees' time cards each time you issue laundry to them, to make sure they return it. Issue laundry according to a regular schedule—so many fresh uniforms, aprons, towels, etc., for each classification of worker per week. Check all laundry against delivery sheets before the driver arrives.

44. To cut down on accidents, have store managers or department heads fill out an accident report each time a mishap occurs. In addition to having them fill in details of the accident, have them tell how the accident could have been prevented and what has been done to keep it from happening again.

45. Kroger appoints an employee in each store to serve as "Safety Promoter" for one or two months. Working under direction of the store manager, the "Safety Promoter" inspects the store and its equipment daily to remove safety hazards. At the end of his tour of duty, the job passes to another employee. Albers uses a similar system. A "Mr. Super Safety" or "Miss Super Safety" reports daily to the manager on safety conditions in each store.

46. Schedule part-time help only when and where it's really needed. Don't have part-timers standing around with time on their hands in off hours.

47. Set up a system of department numbers on pay checks so that checks for each department can easily be told apart from the others.

48. An easy way to eliminate extra help and overtime problems in

also pictures, shelf-guides, etc.

stocking new markets is this technique: Soon after the market has had its floors and shelving installed, and electricians, carpenters, and decorators are finished with their work, set your stocking crews to work. Let them work from master plans, filling in first one front-faced row of items and later depositing the balance on each line. As a gondola or section of shelving is completely stocked, huge sheets of clear plastic are draped over it to seal it off from the dust and dirt resulting from unfinished work. When the store is ready for opening, the covers are removed to reveal gleaming, dust-free stocks.

Warehousing and Transportation

49. For additional security measures, use seals on trucks making grocery deliveries to stores.

50. Unload and tally in small units when you check warehouse deliveries into the store. That way, if a difference shows up between the store receiver's count and the truck driver's billing count, you won't have to retally the whole load to find where the trouble is. Here's how to do it: Unload in lots, say, of 20 pieces. Mark the twentieth piece. Enter a "20" on your tally sheet. Any difference in count will show up immediately within the group of 20 pieces and can be cleared up in a few minutes.

51. When you order carload shipments from suppliers, specify the track over which it should be shipped to reach your spur of the railway. This will eliminate possible delays through misrouting. Some companies have a special warehouse assistant to study rail and trucking tariffs and routings.

52. An electronic scale in the dispatcher's office to register axle loads of outgoing trucks can save on traffic fines. If the axle load exceeds legal limits, the dispatcher can head off the truck and direct it to a dock for unloading before it gets out on the road.

53. To cut paper work in warehouse receiving, install a tape recorder in your warehouse tabulating office with a microphone at the receiving dock. As merchandise arrives, a clerk dictates receiving into the microphone. Another clerk in the tabulating department transcribes the receivings from the tape recorder. If the receiving dock and tabulating office are too far apart for a direct cable connection, a telephone with a special attachment may be used for dictating into the tape recorder. Transcribing the receivings on continuous forms further speeds the operation.

54. Some warehouses install two-way radios on lift trucks to maintain constant contact with the warehouse office. The radios eliminate a lot of delay and wear and tear on warehouse supervisors.

55. Have delivery truck drivers phone the warehouse dispatcher's

office from the gate for instructions on where to deliver their load. This system helps avoid delivery delays and traffic snarls.

56. To head off misrouting of orders going to different offices, use different-color mailing envelopes for each order destination.

57. Hold on to the cardboard cartons in which warehouse merchandise comes to the store. Then send them back for use a second time.

58. In warehouse orders, list items in any given line of goods in the same sequence as they turn up in the orders left by the service salesman.

59. Send pallets to local distributors who do not already use them. And encourage them to send palletized deliveries to your warehouse. If you sell the pallets at or near cost, your savings in warehouse efficiency will make up any loss many times over.

60. Price-mark as much of your merchandise as you can in the warehouse. This saves the time it takes for clerks in the stores to look up prices. It is recommended particularly for nonfoods.

61. Carry portable conveyors under trailers of your trucks. This avoids the necessity of having a complete conveyor system in small stores.

62. Use nets to separate orders for individual stores in your delivery trucks. They allow better use of space than rigid dividers.

63. Use hub mileage meters on trailers of delivery trucks. Tractors and trailers seldom travel the same distances, so you need separate mileage meters to tell you when the trailers should be serviced.

64. One chain has a store unloading system that cuts down time of unloading each truck from a half-hour to 5 minutes. The company's new markets are coming equipped with compartments exactly matching in size the standard 35-ft trailer. The compartments are tilted slightly, and the trailer backs into its "twin" compartment. Gravity pulls its merchandise down the slope on conveyor belts and pallets.

65. In warehouse receiving you can get increased labor productivity by separating the palletizing operation from the storing operation. By doing this and by providing the palletizing crew with pallet jacks, four-wheel trucks, or skids, you can reduce the number of men on the job by one-third.

66. One man working alone in palletizing groceries and moving the loaded pallet out of the car is nearly 38 per cent more productive per man-hour than a two-man team. You can gain economies by one man, providing you leave the car in the dock long enough and the one man does not have to unload extremely heavy merchandise.

Construction and Maintenance

67. Laundry bills can be cut down by following these procedures: Assign a responsible employee to head up laundry handling in the markets. Have employees sign a record form every time a uniform is issued. Have employees use partly soiled coats for messy work and change to clean uniforms once the work is completed.

68. To cut utility expenses, assign one person to oil all motors, as specified by the manufacturer; keep motors clean and drive belts tight; replace used bulbs; turn off lights when not in use; check filters in air conditioners and replace or clean when necessary; check burners in the heating units to see that they are firing properly; check water lines and water heaters against leaks.

69. Investigate whether or not capacitators can be installed as a means of cutting power cost, despite their rather high initial cost.

70. To protect shopping carts against breakdowns, observe the following rules: Don't use shopping carts in place of heavy-duty trucks. Don't use shopping carts for carry-out service. Make sure that the carts are properly maintained. For special jobs use special equipment.

71. Put in a clock thermostat control if you have air conditioning. It will shut the units off when your stores are not open.

72. Put up prominent notices in all stores, telling your employees not to throw water on fires starting in electrical equipment.

73. Post a notice near your garbage disposal machine, telling what should not be thrown in.

74. Channel all orders for equipment servicing through central purchasing at headquarters. These people have the service contacts and can get better prices than the store manager.

75. Check scales to see that they're properly calibrated. Make frequent test weights. Each overage costs money; each underweight can cost you a paying customer.

76. Keep up-to-date telephone numbers of your company's maintenance office or service firm posted conveniently. This keeps store personnel from putting off a maintenance call.

77. One way to keep down shopping cart losses is to point out what each one costs. Most shoppers value the carts at less than $5.00 each and are amazed to learn that they cost up to $50. They think twice before inadvertently stealing something that expensive. You can offer to sell carts to customers; put a price tag on them.

78. Cost-saving construction technique: Concrete wall panels are precast on the floor of the warehouse and tilted up into place by a crane.

Then reinforced concrete columns are poured between the wall panels.

79. Flexible plastic strips along the hinged edge of doors prevent crushed kiddies' fingers, which could mean expensive damage suits against you.

80. Establish a regular schedule for using a light meter to check intensity of light from the lamps in your stores, and for cleaning and replacing lamps.

81. Attach pull cords to light bulbs so that it won't be necessary to throw the main switch in order to turn off lights in individual areas of the store.

82. Throughout the day make frequent temperature checks on refrigeration equipment. Catch any defects before they get a chance to pile up spoiled goods. Know the defrost cycles of each piece of machinery, so that your temperature report will be a valid one. Make sure compressors are kept clean. Dirt makes extra wattage necessary.

83. Put up a complete diagram of the plumbing and electrical layout in each store, with "X marks the spot" indications for all the sewer clean-outs and fuse boxes.

84. A stainless steel moulding on each side of the gasket on walk-in freezer doors in stores will keep the gasket from pulling loose.

85. Make scale models of new stores before the real thing goes into the works. This way you can avoid "hindsight blues" over layout.

Store Departments

86. To handle quarters of beef you will save considerable labor time if you cut into wholesale pieces, trim, and then put into the cooler. That is faster than putting them into the cooler in quarters and then cutting them into wholesale cuts later.

87. When handling cartons of meat, cut the tops off, place in cooler, and work from the cartons. That proves at least 70 per cent faster than unpacking the cartons and hanging or shelving them in the cooler.

88. Decide what specific sizes of cellophane or other wraps you need, and keep only those sizes on hand. Where you can use second-quality paper instead of first (cheese, for example), do so. Cut down on overlap in sealing packages.

89. Use silver polish instead of steel wool to take price markings off cellophane-wrapped items in meat and delicatessen departments. It won't tear the wrapping.

90. Cut down on power-saw accidents by putting decals on the saws reading, "Turn off main switch before opening."

91. To avoid duplicate payment and to get greater efficiency in trans-

shipment, print and staple labels to crates of produce from local farmers.

92. In filling produce racks, two hands are better than one. The USDA estimates that 4 to 5 man-hours weekly can be saved if an employee takes items in both hands and places them simultaneously on the display. In a test, the two-handed technique reduced display filling time by as much as 14 to 38 per cent.

93. To cut unloading time, use a production-line setup in your back room. One man calls off items as they arrive, while a second checks them with the order sheet. The third man splits the case, and the fourth opens it on the conveyor, exposing tops of two layers of merchandise containers. Two more men stamp prices, and the goods are ready for the store shelves.

94. File special display signs under item headings and use them again when these items come up for another special; this saves you the cost of printing new signs each time.

95. Carton openers have a tendency to disappear like rabbits. You can cut down on carton-opener losses by selling them to clerks at wholesale prices.

96. Keep weekly records of produce "throw-outs" by items or poundage, or both. With a comparison record of waste to sales, you can correct your ordering.

97. You can facilitate deliveries on sale items by splitting them up— half in the week before the actual sale and half during the sale time.

98. Check your use of boards and trays and cellophane in meat-packaging departments. By using materials just 1 inch less in width, you can save.

99. Instruct meat department heads to inspect and weigh all products carefully upon receiving. You can cut down on short weights and poor quality this way.

100. Place elastic bands around chicken parts and fresh-cut whole birds before packaging to keep loose parts from tearing the wrapper.

101. Tie beef rib roasts and all kinds of rolled roasts with butcher's twine before wrapping, to prevent damage to the package from inside.

102. Place the sharp, bony side of pork loin roasts against the cardboard in the package, and use rubber bands around the outside to safeguard against tearing.

Back Room

103. Assign one man to the back room and do not allow him to leave this room unless someone replaces him.

104. Do not permit anybody to take anything out of the store through

the back door without a signed transfer or charge note, to be checked by the person assigned to the back room.

105. Do not permit a delivery man to take anything into the front of the store without permission of the back-room man. No boxes, bags, or other containers should leave the store without being checked thoroughly.

106. Give strict warning, just once, to any delivery man who is found to have taken something through the back door without first being checked. If there are any further violations, ask that another man take over his route.

107. Do not permit employees to take anything out of the store unless they go through the check-out stands. Never permit them to leave by the back entrance. See to it that all their purchases are paid for at the time they leave the store and never before.

108. Make frequent checks to see that back doors are locked.

109. Set a fixed time for deliveries, except in case of emergency. After the set time for deliveries, the manager should collect all keys to the back room and should not permit anyone to open these doors without his consent.

110. Check delivery man, particularly when he collects the empty bottles.

111. Lock in night stockers and cleaning crews for your stores.

112. Locate your receiving office for all merchandise in the back room.

113. Make it your store policy to limit access to the back room to authorized personnel only.

114. Keep a running record of "ins and outs." Check this record periodically by physical inventory.

115. If you have an outside service for protection against pilferage, extend it to surveillance of back-room operation.

116. Do not permit any open cases or damaged merchandise to be stored in the back room.

117. Do not permit employees to change clothes in the warehouse or back room, but see to it that they go to the employees' locker room.

118. When you notice that back-room losses are getting excessively large, hold a staff meeting and direct the attention of personnel to the fact that if the losses are traced to pilferage, they will come under the heading of stealing—with corresponding punishment.

119. Put two separate locks on the back-room door: one a daytime lock, and one a nighttime lock.

BIBLIOGRAPHY

The author owes a debt of gratitude to the editors, contributors, and staff writers of the magazines *Super Market Merchandising, Progressive Grocer,* and *Chain Store Age,* Grocery Executive and Supermarket Editions. Articles that appeared in these publications over the years have traced the creative thinking of the leaders of this industry. The yearly reports over the past decade of the Super Market Institute, *The Super Market Industry Speaks,* and of the *Progressive Grocer, Facts in Grocery Distribution,* also were of value. Statistics issued by the Topics Publishing Company in *What the Public Spends for Grocery Store Products* were essential in the analysis.

An alphabetized list of all sources of information used in this text is given below. Inasmuch as the footnotes were given in detail, only the names and publishers of the various periodicals are submitted here.

Advertising Agency, Moore Publishing Co., Inc., 48 W. 38th St., New York 18, N. Y.

Applebaum, William, and Moulton, Richard. *An Exploration into Reasons Why Supermarkets Add and Discontinue Items.* New York: McCall Corp., 1956.

Baking Industry. Clissold Publishing Co., 105 W. Adams St., Chicago 3, Ill.

Barker, Clare W., Anderson, Ira D., Butterworth, J. Donald. *Principles of Retailing.* New York: McGraw-Hill Book Co., Inc., 1956.

Barron's, Barron's Publishing Co., 50 Broadway, New York 4, N. Y.

Beckman, Theodore, and Nolen, H. C. *The Chain Store Problem.* New York: McGraw-Hill Book Co., Inc., 1938.

Boyd, Harper W., and Westfall, Ralph. *Marketing Research.* Homewood, Illinois: Richard D. Irwin, Inc., 1956.

Bureau of Agricultural Economics, U.S. Department of Agriculture, *Consumption of Food in the U.S.,* Agriculture Handbook No. 62, Government Printing Office, Washington, D.C., October, 1955.

Business Week. McGraw-Hill Publishing Co., Inc., 330 W. 42 St., New York 36, N. Y.

Chain Store Age, Grocery Executive Edition, Lebhar-Friedman Publications, Inc., 2 Park Ave., New York 16, N. Y.

Controllers Congress. *1954 Merchandise and Operating Results.* New York: National Retail Dry Goods Association, 1955.

Converse, Paul D., and Huegy, Harvey W. *The Elements of Marketing.* New York: Prentice-Hall, Inc., 1956.

Cooperative Merchandiser, Cooperative Food Distributors of America, 141 W. Jackson Blvd., Chicago 4, Ill.

Donohue, Al. An address given by this executive of Kidder Peabody and Company at the 20th Annual Meeting of the National Association of Food Chains in Washington, D.C., on December 5, 1953.

Edison Electric Institute, Edison Electric Institute, 750 Third Ave., New York 17, N. Y.

Electrical Merchandising, McGraw-Hill Publishing Co., Inc., 330 W. 42 St., New York 36, N. Y.

England, Wilbur B. *Operating Results of Food Chains in 1958.* Cambridge: Harvard Business School, Bulletin No. 156, 1959.

Facts in Grocery Distribution. New York: Progressive Grocer, 1950 to 1959.

Federal Trade Commission. *Chain Stores, Final Report on the Chain Store Investigation,* submitted to 74th Congress, 1st session. Senate Document 4. Government Printing Office, Washington, D.C., Dec. 14, 1934.

Federal Trade Commission. *Federal Trade Commission Economic Inquiry into Food Marketing—Interim Report,* Government Printing Office, Washington, D.C., June 30, 1959.

Food Business, Putman Publishing Co., 111 E. Delaware Pl., Chicago 11, Ill.

Food Field Reporter, Topics Publishing Co., 708 Third Ave., New York 17, N. Y.

Food Mart News, 333 N. Michigan Ave., Chicago 1, Ill.

Food Topics, Food Publications, Inc., 708 Third Ave., New York 17, N. Y.

Forbes, Forbes, Inc., 70 Fifth Ave., New York 11, N. Y.

Fortune, Time, Inc., 9 Rockefeller Plaza, New York 20, N. Y.

Frozen Food Industry. Philadelphia: Curtis Publishing Co., 1954.

Goodwin, Arthur E. *Markets Public and Private.* Seattle: Montgomery Printing Co., 1939.

Graham, Benjamin, and Dodd, David. *Security Analysis.* New York: McGraw-Hill Book Co., Inc., 1953.

Grimes, Don R. An interview with the assistant to the president, IGA, on July 10, 1957 at Chicago, Ill.

Guthmann, Harry G., and Dougall, Herbert E. *Corporate Financial Policy.* New York: Prentice-Hall, Inc., 1955.

Hardware Retailer, National Retail Hardware Association, 964 N. Pennsylvania Ave., Indianapolis 4, Ind.

Haring, Albert, and Yoder, Wallace O. *Trading Stamp Practice and Pricing Policy.* Bloomington: Indiana University, 1958.

Harvard Business Review, Soldiers' Field, Boston 63, Mass.

Hayward, Walter, and White, Percival. *Chain Stores.* New York: McGraw-Hill Book Co., Inc., 1922.

Here's How We Shop for Our Big Grocery Order. New York: Batten, Barton, Durstine & Osborne, 1949.

Home Testing Institute, Inc., *McCall's Food and Grocery Products Purchase Diary Study.* New York: McCall Corp., 1956.

IGA Grocergram, Independent Grocers' Alliance of America, 131 S. Wabash Ave., Chicago 3, Ill.

International Super Marketing, Red and White Corp., 300 W. Washington St., Chicago 6, Ill.

Journal of Marketing, Marketing Association, 27 E. Monroe St., Chicago 3, Ill.

Journal of Retailing, New York University School of Retailing, Washington Square, New York 3, N. Y.

Kintner, Earl W. Testimony given by the chairman of the Federal Trade Commission before a Subcommittee of the Select Committee on Small Business, United States Senate, 86th Congress, 1st session, July 2, 1959. These hearings are published as *Mergers and Unfair Competition in Food Marketing,* Government Printing Office, Washington, D.C., 1960.

Kleppner, Otto. *Advertising Procedure.* Englewood Cliffs, N. J.: Prentice-Hall, Inc., 1950.

Kohler, Eric. *Dictionary for Accountants.* New York: Prentice-Hall, Inc., 1952.

Kornblau, Curt. An address, "Facts about New Supers Opened in 1957," given by the Director of Research, Super Market Institute, at the annual convention in Cleveland, Ohio, in May, 1958.

Kornblau, Curt. *Facts and Figures About Non-Foods in Super Markets.* Chicago: Super Market Institute, 1959.

Kuznets, Simon. *Shares of Upper Income Groups in Income and Savings.* New York: National Bureau of Economic Research, Inc., 1953.

Lilly Digest, Eli Lilly and Company, Indianapolis, Ind., 1955.

Logan, John A. *Progress in Food Distribution.* Washington: National Association of Food Chains, 1957.

Market of the Sixties. New York: Time, Inc., 1960.

Mattei, G. L. A letter written by the district manager, William J. Burns International Detective Agency, to the Super Market Institute on January 22, 1958.

Maynard, Harold, and Beckman, Theodore. *Principles of Marketing.* New York: The Ronald Press Co., 1952.

McNamara, Harley V. An address, "Modern Trends in Food Retailing," given by the President of National Tea Company before the Chicago Federated Advertising Club on October 12, 1952.

Meat and Dairy Products, Standard and Poor's Industry Surveys, 1959. New York: Standard and Poor's Corp.

Meat Markets—Operating Results in 1954. New York: Dun & Bradstreet, Inc., 1954.

Merger Movement in Retail Food Distribution. Chicago: National Association of Retail Grocers, 1959.

Moody's Industrial Manual. New York: Moody's Investor Service.

Myers, Herman L., and Scott, Forrest. *The Rise of the Super Market.* U.S. Department of Agriculture, Bureau of Agricultural Economics, MTS-103. Government Printing Office, Washington, D.C., December, 1951.

McCloskey, Joseph, and Trefethen, Florence. *Operations Research for Management.* Baltimore: The Johns Hopkins Press, 1954.

McNair, Malcolm P. *Expenses and Profits in the Chain Grocery Business.* Cambridge: Harvard Business School, Bureau of Business Research, 1931.

Nargus Bulletin, National Association of Retail Grocers, 360 N. Michigan Ave., Chicago 1, Ill.

Nielsen Researcher, A. C. Nielsen Company, 2101 Howard St., Chicago, Ill.

1954 Furniture Operating Experiences. Chicago: National Retail Furniture Association, 1955.

1954 Operating Statistics. New York: American National Retail Jewelers Association, 1955.

1958 Survey of Super Market Shoppers, Their Buying Habits and Attitudes. Cincinnati: Burgoyne Grocery and Drug Index, Inc., 1959.

Nugent, William C. An address given November 12, 1957, to the Grocery Manufacturers of America, Inc., at New York, N. Y.

Nugent, William C. An address presented at the United States Wholesale Grocers' Convention, April 21, 1957, St. Louis, Mo.

Nystrom, Paul H. *Economics of Retailing.* New York: The Ronald Press Co., 1936.

Nystrom, Paul H. *Retail Store Operation*. New York: The Ronald Press Co., 1937.

Peckham, J. O. *Planning Your Marketing Operations for 1959*. Chicago: A. C. Nielsen Company, 1959.

Phillips, Charles F., and Duncan, Delbert J. *Marketing Principles and Methods*. Homewood, Illinois: Richard D. Irwin, 1956.

Printers' Ink, Printers' Ink Publishing Co., 205 E. 42nd St., New York 17, N. Y.

Progressive Grocer, Butterick Co., Inc., 161 Sixth Ave., New York 13, N. Y.

Sales Management, Sales Management, Inc., 386 Fourth Ave., New York 16, N. Y.

Shaffer, Henry. An address, "Essential Factors in Sound Financing," given by this executive of Shaffer Stores Co., at the 20th Annual Meeting of Food Chains in Washington, D.C., on December 5, 1953.

Standard Ratios for Retailing. New York: Dun & Bradstreet, Inc., 1936.

Super Market Industry Speaks. Chicago: Super Market Institute, 1949 to 1959.

Super Market Merchandising. Super Market Publishing Co., Inc., 67 W. 44th St., New York 36, N. Y.

Super Market News, Fairchild Publications, Inc., 7 E. 12th St., New York 3, N. Y.

Supermarket News Food Industries Financial Manual. New York: Fairchild Publications, Inc., 1957.

Super Markets in the United States. Philadelphia: Curtis Publishing Co., 1954.

Tarrant, Christ. An interview with the secretary, Grocerland Co-operative, Inc., in Chicago, Illinois, on June 20, 1957.

U.S. Bureau of the Census, *Census of Business, 1954,* Bulletin R-2-2, Government Printing Office, Washington, D.C., 1957.

U.S. Bureau of the Census, *1951 Supplement, Survey of Current Business,* Government Printing Office, Washington, D.C., 1959.

U.S. Bureau of the Census, *Census of Business, Retail Distribution, Part I.,* vol. 1, Government Printing Office, Washington, D.C., 1933.

U.S. Bureau of the Census, *Census of Business, Retail Trade, Parts I and II,* vols. 1 and 2, Government Printing Office, Washington, D. C., 1952.

U.S. Bureau of the Census, *Census of Business, Retail Trade,* No. R-2-2, Government Printing Office, Washington, D.C., 1957.

U.S. Bureau of the Census, *Census of Business, Selected Service Trades,* Government Printing Office, Washington, D.C., 1957.

U.S. Bureau of the Census, *Census of Business, Retail Trade Summary Statistics,* vol. 1, Government Printing Office, Washington, D.C., 1957.

U.S. Bureau of the Census, *Current Population Reports,* Government Printing Office, Washington, D.C., 1958.

U.S. Bureau of the Census, *Food Retailing—Retail Distribution,* M-93, Government Printing Office, Washington, D.C., 1934.

U.S. Bureau of the Census, *Number of Inhabitants, U.S. Summary 1950 Census of Population,* Government Printing Office, Washington, D.C., 1952.

U.S. Bureau of the Census, *Sixteenth Census of the U.S., 1940 Population,* vol. 1, Government Printing Office, Washington, D.C., 1942.

U.S. Bureau of the Census, *Statistical Abstract of the United States,* Government Printing Office, Washington, D.C., 1959.

U.S. Bureau of Labor Statistics, *Monthly Labor Review,* Government Printing Office, Washington, D.C., 1933.

U.S. Department of Commerce, *Confectionery Sales and Distribution.* Government Printing Office, Washington, D.C., 1957.

U.S. Department of Commerce, *Distribution Cost Studies Number 1, Louisville Grocery Survey, Part IIIA,* Government Printing Office, Washington, D.C., 1932.

United States v. *The Great A & P Tea Company.* U.S. Circuit Court of Appeals, 7th district, Docket 9221, Records & Briefs, vols. I and II.

Variety Store Merchandiser, Variety Store Merchandiser Publications, 419 Fourth Ave., New York 16, N. Y.

Voluntary and Cooperative Groups Magazine, Cook Publications, 114 E. 32 St., New York 16, N. Y.

What the Public Spends for Grocery Store Products. New York: Food Topics Publishing Co., 1950 to 1959.

Weiss, E. B. *Winning Chain Store Distribution for New Products.* New York: Doyle, Dane, Bernbach, Inc., 1956.

Zimmerman, M. M. *The Super Market.* New York: McGraw-Hill Book Co., Inc., 1955.

Zimmerman, M. M. *Super Market—Its Growth and Future.* New York: Super Market Merchandising Publishing Co., 1948.

Zimmerman, M. M. *Super Market Spectacular Exponent of Mass Distribution.* New York: Super Market Publishing Co., 1937.

INDEX

Below them, out there around the old Plaza, the city drummed through its work, with a lazy, soothing rumble. Nearer at hand, Chinatown sent up the vague murmur of the life of the Orient. In the direction of the Mexican quarter, the bell of the cathedral knolled at intervals. The sky was without a cloud and the afternoon was warm.

Coudy brought Travis out upon the balcony to show her the points of interest in and around the Plaza.

"There's the Stevenson memorial ship in the center, see; and right there where the flagstaff is, General Baker made the funeral oration over the body of Terry. Right opposite where that pawn-shop is, is where the overland stages used to start in '49. And every other building that fronts on the Plaza, even this one we're in now, used to be a gambling house in bonanza times; and see, over yonder is the Morgue and the City Prison."

Beyond these the city tumbled raggedly down to meet the bay in a confused, vague mass of roofs, cornices, cupolas and chimneys, blurred and indistinct. Then came the bay. Beyond was the Contra Costa shore, a vast streak of purple against the sky. The eye followed its skyline westward till it climbed, climbed, climbed up a long slope that suddenly leaped heavenward with the crest of Tamalpais, purple and still, looking always to the sunset like a great watching Sphinx. Then, farther on, the slope seemed to break like the breaking of an advancing billow, and go tumbling, crumbling downward to meet the Golden Gate—the narrow inlet of green tide-water with its flanking Presidio. But farther than this the eye was stayed, farther

than this there was nothing, nothing but a vast illimitable plain of green—the open Pacific. But at
this hour the color of the scene was its greatest
charm. It glowed with all the somber radiance of
a cathedral. As the afternoon waned, the west
burned down to a dull red glow that overlaid the
blue of the bay with a sheen of ruddy gold. The
foothills of the opposite shore, Diablo, and at last
even Tamalpais, resolved themselves to the velvet
gray of the sky. The sky and land and the city's
huddled roofs were one. Only the sheen of dull
gold remained, piercing the single vast mass of purple like the blade of a golden sword.

"There's a ship!" said Travis, in a low tone.

A four-master was dropping quietly through the
Golden Gate, swimming on that sheen of gold, a
mere shadow. In a few moments her bows were
shut from sight by the old fort at the Gate. Then
her stern vanished, then the main-mast. She was
gone. By midnight she would be out of sight of
land, rolling on the swell of the lonely ocean under the moon's white eye.

They turned back into the room, and a great, fat
Chinaman brought them tea on Coudy's order.
But, besides tea, he brought dried almonds, pickled
watermelon rinds, candied quince and "China
nuts."

Travis cut the cheese into cubes with Coudy's
penknife, and arranged the cubes in geometric figures upon the crackers. "I wonder if this green,
pasty stuff is good," she asked.

They found that it was, but so sweet that it
made their tea taste bitter. The watermelon rinds
were flat to their Western palates, but the dried

almonds were a great success. Then Coudy promptly got the hiccoughs from drinking his tea too fast, and fretted up and down the room like a chicken with the pip till Travis grew weak and faint with laughter.

"Oh, well," he exclaimed, aggrievedly—"laugh, that's right! I don't laugh. It isn't such fun when you've got 'em yourself—'hulp.'"

"Come along, and don't be so absurd. It is getting late. I wonder," said Travis, as they skirted the Plaza going down to Kearney street, "I wonder if we are talked out. I never remember to have had a better time than I've had to-day," she said as Coudy put her on the cable car. "Goodbye, Coudy; haven't we had the jolliest day that ever was?"

"Couldn't have been better," he answered. "Good-bye, Travis!"—From "Blix."

ADVENTURES OF THE 'FORTY-NINERS

By William Lewis Manly

WE found the little mule stopped by a still higher precipice or perpendicular rise of fully ten feet. Our hearts sank within us and we said that we should return to our friends as we went away, with our knapsacks on our backs, and the hope grew very small. The little mule was nipping some straw blades of grass and as we came in sight she looked around to us and then up the steep rocks before her with such a knowing, intelligent look of confidence that it gave us new courage. It was a strange, wild place. The north wall of the canon leaned far over the channel, overhanging considerably, while the south wall sloped back about the same, making the walls nearly parallel, and like a huge crevice descending into the mountain from above in a sloping direction.

We decided to try to get the confident little mule over this obstruction. Gathering all the loose rocks we could, we piled them up against the south wall, beginning some distance below, putting up all those in the bed of the stream and throwing down others from narrow shelves above, we built a sort of inclined plane along the walls, gradually rising till we were nearly as high as the crest of the fall. Here was a narrow shelf scarcely four inches wide, and a space of from twelve to fifteen feet to cross to reach the level of the crest. It was all I could do to cross this space, and there was no foundation to enable us to widen it so as to make a path for an animal. It was a forlorn hope, but we made the most of it. We unpacked the mule, and getting all our ropes together, made a leading line of it. Then we loosened and threw down all the projecting points of rocks we could above the narrow shelf, and every piece that was likely to come loose in the shelf itself. We fastened the leading line to her and with one above and one below, we thought we could help her to keep her balance, and if she did not make a misstep on that narrow way, she might get over safely. Without a moment's hesitation, the brave animal tried the pass. Carefully and steadily she went along, selecting a place before putting down a foot, and when she came to the narrow ledge leaned gently on the rope, never making a sudden start or

jump, but cautiously as a cat, moved slowly along.
There was now no turning back for her. She must
cross this narrow place over which I had to creep
on hand and knees, or be dashed down fifty feet to
certain death. When the worst place was reached
she stopped and hesitated, looking back as well as
she could. I was ahead with the rope, and called
encouragingly to her and talked to her a little.
Rogers wanted to get all ready, and "holler" at
her as loud as he could and frighten her across, but
I thought the best way was to talk to her gently and
let her move steadily.

I tell you, friends, it was a trying moment. It
seemed to be weighed down with all the trials and
hardships of many months. It seemed to be the
time when helpless women and innocent children
hung on the trembling balance between life and
death. Our own lives we could have saved by going
back, and sometimes it seemed as if we would perhaps save ourselves the additional sorrow of finding
them all dead to do so at once. I was so nearly in
despair that I could not help bursting into tears,
and I was ashamed of the weakness. Finally Rogers said, "Come, Lewis," and I gently pulled the
rope, calling the little animal to make a trial. She
smelled all around and looked over every inch of
the strong ledge, then took one careful step after
another over the dangerous place. Looking back I
saw Rogers with a very large stone in his hand,
ready to "holler" and perhaps kill the poor beast
if she stopped. But she crept along, trusting to the
rope to balance, till she was half-way across, then
another step or two, when, calculating the distance
closely, she made a spring and landed on a smooth

bit of sloping rock below, that led up to the highest crest of the precipice, and safely climbed to the top, safe and sound above the falls. The mule had no shoes, and it was wonderful how her little hoofs clung to the smooth rock. We felt relieved. We would push on and carry food to the people; we would get them through some way; there could be no more hopeless moment than the one just passed, and we would save them all.

Out of Death Valley we surely were. To Rogers and I the case seemed hopeful, for we had confidence in the road and believed all would have power to weather difficulties, but the poor women—it is hard to say what complaints and sorrows were not theirs. They seemed to think they stood at death's door, and would as soon enter as to take up a farther march over the black, desolate mountains and dry plains before them, which they considered only a dreary vestibule to the dark door after all. They even had an idea that the road was longer than we told them, and they never could live to march so far over the sandy, rocky roads. The first day nearly satisfied them that it was no use to try. Rogers and I counted up the camps we ought to reach each day, and in this way we could pretty nearly convince them of the time that would be consumed in the trip. We encouraged them in every way we could; told them we had better get along a little every day and make ourselves a little nearer the promised land, and the very exercise would soon make them stronger and able to make a full day's march.

The route was first along the foot of the high peak, over bare rocks, and we soon turned south somewhat so as to enter the cañon leading down to the falls. The bottom of this was thick with broken rock, and the oxen limped and picked out soft places about as bad as the women did. A pair of moccasins would not last long in such rocks and we hoped to get out of them very soon. Rogers and I hurried along, assisting Arcane and his party as much as we could, while Bennett stayed behind and assisted the women as much as possible, taking their arms, and by this means they also reached camp an hour behind the rest.

A kettle of hot, steaming soup, and blankets all spread out on which to rest, was the work Rogers and I had done to prepare for them, and they sank down on the beds completely exhausted. The children cried some, but were soon pacified, and were contented to lie still. A good supper of hot soup made them feel much better all around.

The first thing Bennett and Arcane did was to look around to see the situation at the falls, and see if the obstacle was enough to stop our progress, or if we must turn back and look for a better way. They were in some doubt about it, but concluded to try and get the animals over rather than to take the time to seek another pass, which might take a week of time. We men all went down to the foot of the precipice, and threw out all the large rocks, then piled up all the sand we could scrape together with the shovel, till we had quite a pile of material that would tend to break a fall. We arranged everything possible for a forced passage in the morning, and the animals found a few willows to browse and a few bunches of grass here and there, which gave them a little food, while the spring supplied them with enough water to keep them from suffering from thirst.

Early in the morning, we took our soup hastily and with ropes lowered our luggage over the small precipice, then the children, and finally all the ropes were combined to make a single strong one about thirty feet long. They urged one of the oxen up to the edge of the falls, put the rope around his horns, and threw down the end to me, whom they had stationed below. I was told to pull hard when he started so that he might not light on his head and break his neck. We felt this was a desperate undertaking, and we fully expected to lose some of our animals, but our case was critical and we must take some chances. Bennett stood on one side of the ox and Arcane on the other, while big Rogers was placed in the rear to give a Tennessee boost when the word was given. "Now for it," said Bennett, and as I braced out on the rope those above gave a push and the ox came over sprawling, but landed safely, cut only a little by some angular stones in the sand pile. "Good enough," said some one, and I threw the rope back for another ox. "We'll get 'em all over safely," said Arcane, "if Lewis, down there, will keep them from getting their necks broken." Lewis pulled hard every time, and not a neck was broken. The sand pile was renewed every time, and made as high and soft as possible, and very soon all our animals were below the falls. The little mule gave a jump when they pushed her and landed squarely on her feet all right. With the exception of one or two slight cuts, which bled some, the oxen were all right and we began loading them at once.

Bennett and Arcane assisted their wives down along the little narrow ledge which we used in getting up, keeping their faces toward the rocky wall, and feeling carefully for every footstep. Thus they worked along and landed safely by the time we had the animals ready for a march. We had passed without disaster the obstacle we most feared, and started down the rough cañon, hope revived, and we felt we should get through.—From "Death Valley in '49."

HOW SANTA CLAUS CAME TO SIMPSON'S BAR

By Bret Harte

IT was one o'clock, and yet he had only gained Rattlesnake Creek. For in that time Jovita had rehearsed to him all her imperfections and practiced all her vices. Thrice had she stumbled; twice had she thrown her Roman nose up in a straight line with the reins, and, resisting bit and spurs, struck out madly across the country. Twice had she reared, and, rearing, fallen backward; and twice had the agile Dick, unharmed, regained his seat before she found her vicious legs again. And a mile beyond them, at the foot of a long hill, was Rattlesnake Creek. Dick, knowing that here was the crucial test of his ability to perform his enterprise, set his teeth grimly, put his knees well into her flanks, and changed his defensive tactics to brisk aggression. Bullied and maddened, Jovita began the ascent of the hill. Here the artful Richard pretended to hold her in with ostentatious objurgation and well-feigned cries of alarm. It is unnecessary to add that Jovita instantly ran away. Nor need I state the time made in the descent; it is written in the chronicles of Simpson's Bar. Enough that in another moment, as it seemed to Dick, she was splashing on the overflowed banks of Rattlesnake Creek. As Dick expected, the momentum she had acquired carried her beyond the point of balking, and, holding her well together for a mighty leap, they dashed into the middle of the swiftly flowing current. A few moments of kicking, wading and swimming, and Dick drew a long breath on the opposite bank.

The road from Rattlesnake Creek to Red Mountain was tolerably level. Either the plunge in Rattlesnake Creek had dampened her baleful fire, or the art which led to it had shown her the superior wickedness of her rider, for Jovita no longer wasted her surplus energy in wanton conceits. Once she bucked, but it was from force of habit; once she shied, but it was from a new, freshly painted meeting-house at the crossing of the county road. Hollows, ditches, gravelly deposits, patches of freshly springing grasses, flew from beneath her rattling hoofs. She began to smell unpleasantly, once or twice she coughed slightly, but there was no abatement of her strength or speed. By two o'clock he had passed Red Mountain and began the descent to the plains. Ten minutes later the driver of the fast Pioneer coach was overtaken and passed by a "man on a Pinto hoss"—an event sufficiently notable for remark. At half-past two Dick rose in his stirrups with a great shout. Stars were glittering through the rifted clouds and, beyond him, out of the plain rose two spires, a flagstaff, and a straggling line of black objects. Dick jingled his spurs and swung his riata, Jovita bounded forward, and in another moment they swept into Tuttleville, and drew up before the wooden piazza of ''The Hotel of All Nations.''

What transpired that night at Tuttleville is not strictly a part of this record. Briefly, I may state, however, that after Jovita had been handed over to a sleepy hostler, whom she at once kicked into unpleasant unconsciousness, Dick sallied forth with the barkeeper for a tour of the sleeping town. It was three o'clock before this pleasantry was over, and with a small water-proof bag of India rubber strapped on his shoulders Dick returned to the hotel. And then he sprang to the saddle and dashed down the lonely street and out into the lonelier plain, where presently the lights, the black line of houses, the spires and the flagstaff sank into the earth behind him again and were lost in the distance.

The storm had cleared away, the air was brisk and cold, the outlines of adjacent landmarks were distinct, but it was half-past four before Dick reached the meeting-house and the crossing of the road. To avoid the rising grade, he had taken a longer and more circuitous road, in whose viscid mud Jovita sank fetlock deep at every bound. It was a poor preparation for a steady ascent of five miles more; but Jovita, gathering her legs under her, took it with her usual blind, unreasoning fury, and a half hour later reached the long level that led to Rattlesnake Creek.   Another half hour would bring him to the creek.   He threw the reins lightly over the neck of the mare, chirruped to her and began to sing.

Suddenly Jovita shied with a bound that would have unseated a less practiced rider.   Hanging to her rein was a figure that had leaped from the bank, and at the same time from the road before her arose a shadowy horse and rider.

"Throw up your hands!" commanded the second apparition, with an oath.

Dick felt the mare tremble, quiver, and apparently sink under him.   He knew what it meant and was prepared.

"Stand aside, Jack Simpson. I know you, you thief! Let me pass on——"

He did not finish the sentence.   Jovita rose straight in the air with a terrific bound, throwing the figure from her bit with a single shake of her vicious head, and charged with deadly malevolence down on the impediment before her.   An oath, a pistol shot, and horse and highwayman rolled over in the road, and the next moment Jovita was a hundred yards away.   But the good right arm of her rider, shattered by a bullet, dropped helplessly at his side.

Without slacking his speed he shifted the reins to his left hand.   But a few moments later he was obliged to halt and tighten the saddle-girths that had slipped in the onset.   This, in his crippled condition, took some time.   He had no fear of pursuit, but looking up he saw that the eastern stars were already paling, and that the distant peaks had lost their ghostly whiteness, and now stood out blackly against a lighter sky. Day was upon him. Then completely absorbed in a single idea, he forgot the pain of his wound, and, mounting again, dashed on toward Rattlesnake Creek. But now Jovita's breath came by broken gasps, Dick reeled in the saddle, and brighter and brighter grew the sky.

Ride, Richard; run Jovita; linger, O day!

For the last few rods there was a roaring in his ears. Was it exhaustion from loss of blood, or what? He was dazed and giddy as he swept down the hill and did not recognize his surroundings. Had he taken the wrong road, or was this Rattlesnake Creek?

It was. But the brawling creek he had swam a few hours before had risen, more than doubled its volume, and now rolled a swift and restless river between him and Rattlesnake Hill. For the first time that night Richard's heart sank within him. The river, the mountain, the quickening east, swam before his eyes. He shut them to recover his self-control. In that brief interval, by some fantastic mental process, the little room at Simpson's Bar and the figures of the sleeping father and son rose upon him. He opened his eyes wildly, cast off his coat, pistol, boots and saddle, bound his precious pack tightly to his shoulders, grasped the bare flanks of Jovita with his bared knees, and with a shout dashed into the yellow water. A cry rose from the opposite bank as the head of a man and horse struggled for a few moments against the battling current, and then were swept away amid uprooted trees and whirling driftwood.

———

9

The Old Man started and awoke. The fire on the hearth was dead, the candle in the outer room flickering in its socket, and somebody was rapping on the door. He opened it, but fell back with a cry before the dripping, half-naked figure that reeled before the doorpost.

"Dick?"

"Hush. Is he awake yet?"

"No! but, Dick."

"Dry up, you old fool. Get me some whisky, quick."

The Old Man flew and returned with an empty bottle.

Dick would have sworn that his strength was not equal to the occasion. He staggered, caught at the handle of the door, and motioned to the Old Man.

"Thar's suthin' in my pack fer Johnny. Take it off. I can't."

The Old Man unstrapped the pack, and laid it before the exhausted man.

"Open it, quick."

He did so with trembling fingers. It contained only a few poor toys—cheap and barbaric enough, goodness knows, but bright with paint and tinsel. One of them was broken; another, I fear, was irretrievably ruined by water, and on the third—ah me, there was a cruel spot.

"It don't look like much, that's a fact," said Dick ruefully. "But it's the best we could do. Take 'em, Old Man, and put 'em in his stocking, and tell him—tell him, you know—hold me, Old Man." The Old Man caught at the sinking figure. "Tell him," said Dick, with a weak little laugh—"tell him Sandy Claus has come."

And even so, bedraggled, ragged, unshaved and
unshorn, with one arm hanging helplessly at his
side, Santa Claus came to Simpson's Bar and fell
fainting on the first threshold. The Christmas
dawn came slowly after, touching the remoter
peaks with the rosy warmth of ineffable love. And
it looked so tenderly on Simpson's Bar that the
whole mountain, as if caught in a generous action,
blushed to the skies.—From "Tales of the Argonauts."

THE PEARLS OF LORETA

By Gertrude Atherton

THE fog lay thick on the bay at dawn next
morning. The white waves hid the blue, muf-
fled the roar of the surf. Now and again a whale
threw a volume of spray high in the air, a geyser
from a phantom sea. Above the white sands strag-
gled the white town, ghostly, prophetic.

De la Vega, a dark sombrero pulled over his
eyes, a dark serape enveloping his tall figure, rode,
unattended and watchful, out of the town. Not
until he reached the narrow road through the brush
forest beyond did he give his horse rein. The indo-
lence of the Californian was no longer in his car-

riage; it looked alert and muscular; recklessness accentuated the sternness of his face.

As he rode, the fog receded slowly. He left the chaparral and rode by green marshes cut with sloughs and stained with vivid patches of orange. The frogs in the tules chanted their hoarse matins. Through brush-covered plains once more, with sparsely wooded hills in the distance, and again the tules, the marsh, the patches of orange. He rode through a field of mustard; the pale yellow petals brushed his dark face, the delicate green leaves won his eyes from the hot glare of the ascending sun, the slender stalks, rebounding, smote his horse's flanks. He climbed hills to avoid the wide marshes, and descended into willow groves and fields of daisies. Before noon he was in the San Juan Mountains, thick with sturdy oaks, bending their heads before the madroño, that belle of the forest, with her robes of scarlet and her crown of bronze. The yellow lilies clung to her skirts, and the buckeye flung his flowers at her feet. The last redwoods were there, piercing the blue air with their thin, inflexible arms, gray as a dusty band of friars. Out by the willows, whereunder crept the sluggish river, then between the hills curving about the valley of San Juan Bautista.

At no time is California so beautiful as in the month of June. De la Vega's wild spirit and savage purpose were dormant for the moment as he rode down the valley toward the mission. The hills were like gold, like mammoth fawns veiled with violet mist, like rich, tan velvet. Afar, bare blue steeps were pink in their chasms, brown on their spurs. The dark yellow fields were as if thick with gold-dust; the pale mustard was a waving yellow sea. Not a tree marred the smooth hills. The earth sent forth a perfume of its own. Below the plateau from which rose the white walls of the mission was a wide field of bright green corn rising against the blue sky.

The padres in their brown hooded robes came out upon the long corridor of the mission and welcomed the traveler. Their lands had gone from them, their mission was crumbling, but the spirit of hospitality lingered there still. They laid meat and fruit and drink on a table beneath the arches, and sat about him and asked him eagerly for the news of the day. Was it true that the United States of America were at war with Mexico, or about to be? True that their beloved flag might fall, and the stars and stripes of an insolent invader rise above the fort of Monterey?

De la Vega recounted the meager and conflicting rumors which had reached California, but, not being a prophet, could not tell them that they would be the first to see the red-white-and-blue fluttering on the mountain before them. He refused to rest more than an hour, but mounted the fresh horse the padres gave him and went his way, riding hard and relentlessly, like all Californians.

He sped onward, through the long, hot day, leaving the hills for the marshes and a long stretch of ugly country, traversing the beautiful San Antonio Valley in the night, reaching the Mission of San Miguel at dawn, resting there for a few hours. That night he slept at a hospitable ranch-house in the park-like valley of Paso des Robles, a grim, silent figure amongst gay-hearted people who de-

lighted to welcome him. The early morning found
him among the chrome hills; and at the Mission of
San Luis Obispo the good padres gave him breakfast. The little valley, round as a well, its bare
hills red and brown, gray and pink, violet and
black from fire, sloping steeply from a dizzy
height, impressed him with a sense of being pris-
oned in an enchanted vale where no message of the
outer world could come, and he hastened on his
way.

Absorbed as he was, he felt the beauty he fled
past. A line of golden hills lay against sharp blue
peaks. A towering mass of gray rocks had been
cut and lashed by wind and water, earthquake and
fire, into the semblance of a massive castle, still
warlike in its ruin. He slept for a few hours that
night in the Mission of Santa Ynes, and was high
in the Santa Barbara Mountains at the next noon.
For brief whiles he forgot his journey's purpose as
his horse climbed slowly up the steep trails, knock-
ing the loose stones down a thousand feet and more
upon a roof of tree-tops which looked like stunted
brush. Those gigantic masses of immense stones,
each wearing a semblance to the face of man or
beast; those awful chasms and stupendous heights,
densely wooded, bare, and many-hued, rising above,
beyond, peak upon peak, cutting through the visible
atmosphere—was there no end? He turned in his
saddle and looked over low peaks and cañons, rivers and abysms, black peaks smiting the fiery blue,
far, far, to the dim azure mountains on the horizon.

"Mother of God!" he thought; "no wonder California still shakes! I would I could have stood
upon a star and beheld the awful throes of this

country's birth.'' And then his horse reared between the sharp spurs and galloped on.

He avoided the Mission of Santa Barbara, resting at a rancho outside the town. In the morning,
supplied as usual with a fresh horse, he fled onward, with the ocean at his right, its splendid roar
in his ears. The cliffs towered high above him; he
saw no man's face for hours together; but his
thoughts companioned him, savage and sinister
shapes whirling about the figure of a woman. On,
on, sleeping at ranchos or missions, meeting hospitality everywhere, avoiding Los Angeles, keeping
close to the ponderous ocean, he left civilization behind him at last, and with an Indian guide entered
upon that desert of mountain-tops, Baja, California.

Rapid traveling was not possible here. There
were no valleys worthy the name. The sharp peaks,
multiplying mile after mile, were like the teeth of
gigantic rakes, black and bare. A wilderness of
mountain-tops, desolate as eternity, arid, parched,
baked by the awful heat, the silence never broken
by the cry of a bird, a hut rarely breaking the barren monotony, only an infrequent spring to save
from death. It was almost impossible to get food
or fresh horses. Many a night De la Vega and his
stoical guide slept beneath a cactus, or in the mock-
ing bed of a creek. The mustangs he managed to
lasso were almost unridable, and would have
bucked to death any but a California. Sometimes
he lived on cactus fruit and the dried meat he had
brought with him; occasionally he shot a rabbit.
Again he had but the flesh of the rattlesnake

roasted over coals. But honey-dew was on the leaves.

He avoided the beaten trail, and cut his way through naked bushes spiked with thorns, and through groves of cacti miles in length. When the thick fog rolled up from the ocean he had to sit inactive on the rocks, or lose his way. A furious storm dashed him against a bowlder, breaking his mustang's leg; then a torrent, rising like a tidal wave, thundered down the gulch, and, catching him on its crest, flung him upon a tree of thorns. When dawn came he found his guide dead. He cursed his luck, and went on.

Lassoing another mustang, he pushed on, having a general idea of the direction he should take. It was a week before he reached Loreta, a week of loneliness, hunger, thirst and torrid monotony. A week, too, of thought and bitterness of spirit. In spite of his love, which never cooled, and his courage, which never quailed, Nature, in her guise of foul and crooked hag, mocked at earthly happiness, at human hope, at youth and passion.

If he had not spent his life in the saddle, he would have been worn out when he finally reached Loreta, late one night. As it was, he slept in a hut until the following afternoon. Then he took a long swim in the bay, and, later, sauntered through the town.

The forlorn little city was hardly more than a collection of Indians' huts about a church in a sandy waste. No longer the capital, even the barracks were toppling. When De la Vega entered the mission, not a white man but the padre and his assistant was in it; the building was thronged with

Indian worshipers. The mission, although the first built in California, was in a fair state of preservation. The Stations in their battered frames were mellow and distinct. The gold still gleamed in the vestments of the padre.

For a few moments De la Vega dared not raise his eyes to the Lady of Loreta, standing aloft in the dull blaze of adamantine candles. When he did, he rose suddenly from his knees and left the mission. The pearls were there.

It took him but a short time to gain the confidence of the priest and the little population. He offered no explanation for his coming, beyond the curiosity of a traveler. The padre gave him a room in the mission, and spent every hour he could spare with the brilliant stranger. At night he thanked God for the sudden oasis in his life's desolation. The Indians soon grew accustomed to the lonely figure wandering about the sand plains, or kneeling for hours together before the altar in the church. And whom their padre trusted was to them as sacred and impersonal as the wooden saints of their religion.—From ''The Splendid Idle Forties.''

THE OVERLAND FLYER

By Charles Keeler

TO-TOO! to-too! Ka-ding, ka-dong!
      Down the mole comes the flyer
      A-zipping along,—
Smoke clouds panting and hissing of steam,
Rattling of rails and a sudden scream!

The iron dragon snorts up to the station,
The proudest beast in the wide creation;
Fed on fire it puffs and blows,
Cyclops-eyed like a fiend it glows.

We kiss our hands to the friends by the Bay,
On the dragon's tail we are whisked away,
And faster we whiz by the glistening shore—
Towns spin past as we ride with a roar.

Now the iron throat is gasping astrain,
As the beast up the mountain is dragging his train.
O where are you taking us, monster of steel?
Out in the darkness the pine-trees reel!

Over the desert we swing and fly,
Towns and prairies are flashing by;
When, lo! to your castle you plunge in the night,—
The great walls tower in ghostly light.

Does a princess live in that tall black tower?
Are all of the people here under your power?
I never was certain that dragons were true
Till I got on your tail and rode with you!

                —From "Elfin Songs of Sunland."

[All copyright privileges are retained by the author.]

A BREEZE FROM THE WOODS

By W. C. Bartlett

ONE learns to distinguish the sounds of this
multitudinous life in the woods, after a few
days, with great facility. The bark of the coyote

becomes as familiar as that of a house dog. But there is the solitary chirp of a bird at midnight, never heard after daylight, of which beyond this we know nothing. We know better from whence come the cries, as of a lost child at night, far up the mountain. The magpies and the jays hop round the tent for crumbs; and a coon helped himself from the sugar box one day in our absence. He was welcome, though a question more nice than wise was raised as to whether, on that occasion, his hands and nose were clean. There is danger of knowing too much. It is better not to know a multitude of small things which are like nettles to the soul. What strangely morbid people are those who can suggest more unpleasant things in half an hour than one ought to hear in a lifetime! Did I care, before the question was raised, whether the coon's nose was clean or otherwise? Now there is a lurking suspicion that it was not. If you offer your friend wine, is it necessary to tell him that barefooted peasants trampled out the grapes? Is honeycomb any the sweeter for a confession that a bee was also ground to pulp between the teeth? We covet retentive memories. But more trash is laid up than most people know what to do with. There is great peace and blessedness in the art of forgetfulness. The memory of one sweet, patient soul is better than a record of a thousand selfish lives.

It was a fine conceit, and womanly withal, which wove a basket out of plantain rods and clover, and brought it into camp filled with wild strawberries. Thanks, too, that the faintest tints of carnation are beginning to touch cheeks that were so pallid a fortnight ago. Every spring bursting from the

hillside is a fountain of youth, although none have
yet smoothed out certain crow tracks. The madro-
no, the most brilliant of the forest trees, sheds its
outer bark every season; when the outer rind curls
up and falls off, the renewed tree has a shaft polished like jasper or emerald. When humanity begins to wilt, what a pity that the cuticle does not
peel as a sign of rejuvenation!

There is a sense of relief in getting lost now and
then in the impenetrable fastnesses of the woods;
and a shade of novelty in the thought that no foot-
fall has been heard in some of these dells and jungles for a thousand years. It is not so easy a matter to get lost after all. The bark of every forest
tree will show which is the north side, and a bright
cambric needle dropped gently upon a dipper of
water is a compass of unerring accuracy. A scrap
of old newspaper serves as a connecting link with
the world beyond. The pyramids were probably
the first newspapers—a clumsy but rather permanent edition.

But let us hope that the musician is born who
will yet come to the woods and take down all the
bird songs. What a splendid baritone the horned
owl has! Who has written the music of the orioles
and thrushes? Who goes to these bird operas at
four o'clock in the morning? There is room for
one fresh, original music book, the whole of which
can be written at a few sittings upon a log just
where the forests are shaded off into copses and
islands of verdure beyond.—From "A Breeze from
the Woods."

SOUTHERN CALIFORNIA BEFORE THE BOOM

By Theodore Van Dyke

FROM 1870 to 1875 Southern California was passing out of the control of the large land-owners, nearly all of whom were raising cattle, horses and sheep to the exclusion of everything else, and into the control of the general farmer and fruit-grower. These were mainly small owners of what had been public land. Some of the great ranchos, or Mexican grants, which embraced the greater part of what was then considered good land, had been opened by the owners to settlement. But most of the large owners were unwilling to injure their stock-range by admitting scattering farmers; so that the great majority of the new settlers were upon the outlying tracts of public land around the edges of the large ranchos, and in the small pockets and valleys of the surrounding hills. In 1875 their number was considerable; but their work was a combination of laziness, imitation of Mexican methods, and general shiftlessness, the bad effects of which were increased by ignorance of the peculiarities of California.

Almost every attempt of this class to make a dollar from the soil was thwarted by these causes. Nevertheless there was an attraction about the soft climate of winter and the dry, cool sea-breeze of summer, in the long line of sunny days with nights made for soundest sleep, and in the absence of storms, high winds and other climatic discomforts, that made people stay, however unsuccessful, and steadily brought more to stay with them. It was a grand play-country, and one could get along with less than in any other part of the United States and still be respectable and fat. But everywhere there was a broad smile when some enthusiastic new-comer said that it would some day be the richest part of the United States outside the great cities.

Descending one day in the fall of 1875 from a hunt among the foothills of one of the great mountain ranges of Southern California, my companion and I came into a little valley or pocket where one of the long slopes of a great valley broke into the hills. It contained some sixty acres of dark soil along the bed of a little creek, with some reddish land sloping toward the hill on one side. The bottom-land looked as if with judicious coaxing it might be induced to raise a bean or possibly a cabbage; but nothing could seem more hopeless than any attempt to raise anything on the land that sloped toward the hills.

The most conspicuous thing about the place, or "ranche," as all such places were then called, was a group of some two hundred beehives set upon low stands on a bit of rising ground at the base of the hill. Around some of them a few bees were lazily crawling, but the greater number of hives were silent. Near by was the "honey-house," also deserted, except where a few bees were exploring the keyhole and the chinks in the sides, lured by the smell of honey that still lingered within. Near by a pile of poles half hidden in decayed straw betrayed some symptoms of having once been intended for a stable. A little farther on we came to the "ranche house." It was of the regulation pat-

tern of the granger's house of that time—a mere
shell of rough lumber mounted upon stilts, full in
the sun, with its only window on the side from
which in summer the breeze is certain never to
come. Under a huge live oak behind the house
hung a box with a door and back of wire screen,
through which was dimly visible a long strip of
desiccated bacon rind with the butt-ends of departed slices standing along its inner surface, yellow and gray with time—a melancholy stub-book
of past prosperity. All round the house were fragments of honey-boxes, masses of dead bees and
moth cocoons, broken glass, empty tin cans, rabbit skins and empty tobacco sacks, while the outside
of the house was adorned with nails full hung with
an assortment of almost everything from a plow-
clevis to a weather-beaten wild-cat skin.

A lank dog drew himself with considerable effort from under the house at our approach, gave a
perfunctory bark, and hastily retreated to the
shade he had unwisely left. As we rounded the
corner of the house the sound of dragging feet
came from within, then a stream of tobacco juice
cleared the soapbox that served for a door-stoop,
and in another second a bushy head, ragged whisk-
ers and frowsy mustache came slowly into view
round the door post.

"Morning," drawled the owner of the head,
propping himself with care against the door-post,
and smiling as in my friend he recognized an old
acquaintance.

"Come in," he added, as he shuffled himself inside, hooked one foot within one of the legs of a
three-legged stool and gave it a lazy jerk into the

middle of the floor, while with the other foot he kicked an empty nail-keg toward my companion.

"Take a seat," he continued, as, with a minimum of exertion that he had evidently studied out with long practice, he half slid and half tumbled upon a rough cot in one corner.

The solar heat of the autumn day upon the thin roof was increased by a fire in an open fireplace, where a flapjack suitable for a cannon wad was sputtering in a frying-pan.

"We'll have some dinner directly, said the owner of the frying-pan with a dubious glance at the half of a rabbit that lay on the table awaiting its turn in the frying-pan.

"Can't stop, thank you," said my companion, who had taken a hasty review of the larder. "How are the bees doing?"

"Fine! I ain't lost over two-thirds of mine. Some of my neighbors have lost about all of theirs. Last winter the rain was too light and the feed short, and they robbed the bees too close. I didn't have to rob mine. They were so hungry they robbed each other and saved me the trouble," said the granger.

"You raise good fruit here, I suppose?" I remarked, quite innocently.

"The bluejays and linnets think so; I never had a chance to sample any of it myself."

"That land along the creek looks like good garden land," said my friend; "you raise good vegetables there, of course."

"I've laid down lots of them. I never raised any yet."

"But you certainly raise your own potatoes?"

"No; the squirrels raise them for me."

"And don't you have any garden at all?"

"Had one, one year, but the chickens got away with it."

"I don't see any chickens around here now."

"Of course not. The wild cats got away with them by the time they had finished the garden."

"Did you ever try the raisin-grape here?"

"Planted some once, but the rabbits eat off the buds as fast as they came out."

"Well, you get even on the rabbits, don't you?" said my friend with a wink at me that showed that he was drawing out the man for amusement.

"The rabbits don't owe my anything," replied the man. "I would have been busted long ago without them. But they are getting so scarce now that I have to go three or four hundred yards from the house to get one. It's a cold day when I have to split a rabbit to make two meals out of. The outlook for grub is getting really serious," with an anxious look at the half of a rabbit.

"And didn't any of the vines grow at all?" asked my friend.

"Well, a few did, but the deer closed them out in the fall."

"And can't you get even on the deer? That's the way I do."

"Too much resemblance to work, tramping over these hills."

"But wine grapes ought to do well, and deer don't bother them much."

"Quails!" replied the man with a sigh.

"I should think this would make a good hog ranche," continued my friend.

10

"Splendid. I've got several dozen; they don't require any care here at all; I haven't had to look after mine for three years. But I know they are safe; a grizzly bear couldn't catch them in the chaparral, and no man would ever try it."

"Why didn't you fence them in?" I asked.

"What! and buy feed for 'em? Stranger, if it's a fair question, may I inquire where you were raised?"

"You ought to raise corn on that land over there," said my friend.

"See those crows sitting in the sycamores? Tried it once. They are waiting for me to try it again. I'm waiting for them to die of disappointment."

"Why don't you try alfalfa? Crows don't pull that up."

"Had just that brilliant idea myself once. It only cost me a hundred dollars, though; that's the cheapest experience I've had here."

"Why, what was the matter?"

"Gophers," sighed the man.

"Have you tried grain?"

"Did you ever strike a darned fool here yet that didn't? I put in forty acres once. The header-man, threshing-machine-man and the warehouse-man in town all did well on it."

"And how did you come out?"

"Only lost some three hundred dollars."

"Why, that wasn't so bad," I remarked.

"Oh, no; it might have been a heap worse; I got out cheap. One of my neighbors lost his ranche by his crop."

"I suppose, then, that hay or something you could harvest with your own work would be bet-

ter,'' said I, as soon as I had discovered the point
of the last answer.

''That's exactly what I thought; so I sowed it to
barley for hay the next year. There was hardly
any rain, and I had to pull it up by the roots to get
any hay.''

''Why didn't you let your horse harvest it himself?'' said my friend, seeing that I was floored by
the last answer.

''Before it got big enough I had to give him
away to keep from buying feed for him. The
sheepmen used up all the grass within ten miles.''

''How long have you been here?''

''Something like six thousand.''

''I asked how long you had been here.''

''Well, I tell you some six thousand. Don't you
know yet how to measure time in this country?''

''Oh, yes, I take. But what have you done with
it all?''

''Well, there's nearly five hundred dollars of it
in that orchard,'' said the rancher, pointing to a
few rows of dead sticks in various stages of decay.

''What is the matter with them?''

''Cattle broke them all down rubbing against
them. You may notice that good rubbing posts are
scarce in this country.''

''Why didn't you fence them in?''

''Did, but a fire came up the cañon one day and
took it.''

''Your oranges don't seem very thrifty,'' continued my friend, pointing to some sorrowful-look-
ing trees, of which one-half were brown and the
rest a yellowish green.

"I let them all go; it's too much trouble to manage an irritating ditch."

"A what?" I asked.

"He means an irrigating ditch," suggested my companion.

"No, I mean exactly what I said," said the granger—"an irritating ditch—the irritatingest thing on earth. When you get ready to use it you find that a gopher has made a hole in the dam and let out all the water. You get the hole fixed and the dam filled again, and then you find a dozen gopher holes in the ditch. Each one of them will let out all the water, and you can't find the worst ones until you have turned in the water. Then by the time you get the ditch fixed another gopher has made a hole in the dam, and when you get that stopped there are some more gopher holes in the ditch. By the time you have it fixed it's dinner time, and by the time you are done smoking and get rested and ready for work it's so near night that you think it's better to wait till next day. If the gophers haven't got away with it again by that time you are in luck, and even if they haven't, the sides of the ditch are so dry that half the water is lost by seepage and evaporation, and by the time you have coaxed it around a dozen trees you wish you had never been born, especially when you reflect that you have got to go over the whole program again in about three days more or the ground will bake as hard as a petrified brick."

"Then what do you live on, if you don't raise anything?" asked my friend.

"Credit. Haven't you been here long enough to learn that trick?"

"I exhausted mine some time ago."

"What are you doing, then?" asked the granger with more interest than he had yet shown.

"Poising."

"Poising? What's that?"

"Did you ever see a hawk poising—hanging still in the air watching for something to drop on? That's my business at present."

"Well, as long as you can keep afloat on wind I would advise you not to drop on anything in this country."

"I suppose you might be induced to sell?"

"Well—yes—I—might. I have made enough out of it, and would be willing to let some one else have a show. There is nothing small about me."

"And then what would you do?"

"Go to work for somebody that had a ranche. In two years I would own it."

"Yes, and he would turn around and work for you and get it back in another two years."

"Not much. I would be too smart to run another ranche in this country. I would unload it on some tenderfoot."

"Then you would return to the East, I suppose," I remarked.

"Not a bit of it," replied the granger with an air of intense disgust. I like Southern California too well for my own good. She is a tricky damsel, first-rate to flirt with, but of no account as a business partner. But I love her in spite of her tricks, and not even the archangel's trump can ever raise my bones from her soil."

Emerging from the canyon in which lay the "ranche" of the bachelor granger, our way lay for miles over a dreary stretch of gray sand, half covered with a thin and sorry-looking gray brush about knee-high. Scarcely a lobe even of cactus relieved the monotonous gray of the sand and brush. Scarcely a sign of life relieved the hot glare of the vast expanse of desert save an occasional hare sitting in the exasperating shade of some little low bush just thick enough to stop all the breeze and just thin enough to let through the last beam of the midday sun. Each hare looked weary and mad, yet wore withal a look of mild resignation akin to that of the granger we had just left. Nowhere within sight was there for him any means of support, and yet it was evident that, like the granger, he did not wish to leave the country. It was from these two fixtures that I had my first conception of living on climate.

The man who for an instant would have dreamed of anyone living on this desert would have been deemed insane, and at that time probably would have been so. I could have bought thousands of acres of it for a song, but neither my companion nor I would have paid the land office fees to preempt the whole of it. And the oldest residents of the whole country were the most pronounced of all in their opinion that it was utterly worthless for any purpose and for all time.

Many a reader will take most of the above for a very weak attempt to be funny. But it is written in sober earnest, and does not describe one-half of the difficulties that then beset every man who departed from raising livestock and tried to coax a dollar or even worry a living out of the soil; except in a few places around Los Angeles, where some money was made by sending a few oranges to the limited market of San Francisco. So universal were the troubles of the common farmer and fruit-grower that most of them were chronic grumblers, taking a positive satisfaction in relating their experience. Everywhere one could hear people tell more harrowing tales than the one above; and they would tell it with genuine gusto, and apparently with more satisfaction before a stranger than when alone. Many an hour's amusement the writer has had from sea coast to mountain top, drawing out the unfortunate by questions which he soon learned to frame. Yet with all their troubles they were all like the bachelor granger and the hare. They were all mad and sad, but none of them wanted to leave the country. Although nearly every place in the land was for sale, it was not to get money with which to leave the country, but to repeat the same folly somewhere on another place that seemed to have better conditions.

As long as production was subject to so many drawbacks there was no prospect of a boom, and nobody thought of any. But in the next ten years the land underwent a change which was probably the most rapid and radical that the world has ever seen.—From "Millionaires of a Day."

THE LURE OF THE TRAIL

By Stewart Edward White

THE trail's call depends not at all on your common sense. You know you are a fool for answering it; and yet you go. The comforts of

civilization, to put the case on its lowest plane, are
not lightly to be renounced; the ease of having
your physical labor done for you; the joy of cultivated minds, of theaters, of books, of participation
in the world's progress; these you leave behind you.
And in exchange you enter a life where there is
much long, hard work of the hands—work that is
really hard and long, so that no man paid to labor
would consider it for a moment; you undertake to
eat simply, to endure much, to lie on the rack of
anxiety; you voluntarily place yourself where cold,
wet, hunger, thirst, heat, monotony, danger and
many discomforts will wait upon you daily. A
thousand times in the course of a woods life even
the stoutest hearted will tell himself softly—very
softly—if he is really stout-hearted, so that others
may not be annoyed—that if ever the fates permit
him to extricate himself he will never venture
again.

These times come when long continuance has
worn on the spirit. You beat all day to windward
against the tide toward what should be but an
hour's sail; the sea is high and the spray cold;
there are sunken rocks, and food there is none;
chill, gray evening draws dangerously near, and
there is a foot of water in the bilge. You have
swallowed your tongue twenty times on the alkali;
and the sun is melting hot, and the dust dry and
pervasive; and there is no water, and for all your
effort the relative distances seem to remain the
same for days.

You have carried a pack until your every muscle
is strung white-hot; the woods are breathless; the
black flies swarm persistently and bite until your

face is covered with blood. You have struggled through clogging snow until each time you raise your snowshoe you feel as though some one had stabbed a little sharp knife into your groin; it has come to be night; the mercury is away below zero, and with aching fingers you are to prepare a camp which is only an anticipation of many more such camps in the ensuing days. For a week it has rained, so that you, pushing through the dripping brush, are soaked and sodden and comfortless, and the bushes have become horrible to your shrinking goose-flesh. Or you are just plain tired out, not from a single day's fatigue, but from the gradual exhaustion of a long hike. Then in your secret soul you utter these sentiments:

"You are a fool. This is not fun. There is no real reason why you should do this. If you ever get out of here you will stick right home where common sense flourishes, my son!"

Then after a time you do get out, and are thankful. But in three months you will have proved in your own experience the following axiom—I should call it the widest truth the wilderness has to teach:

"In memory the pleasures of a camping trip strengthen with time, and the disagreeables weaken."

I don't care how hard an experience you have had, nor how little of the pleasant has been mingled with it, in three months your general impression of that trip will be good. You will look back on the hard times with a certain fondness of recollection.

I remember one trip I took in the early spring following a long drive on the Pine River. It rained steadily for six days. We were soaked to the skin all the time, ate standing up in the driving downpour, and slept wet. So cold was it that each morning our blankets were so full of frost that they crackled stiffly when we turned out. Dispassionately I can appraise that as about the worst I ever got into. Yet as an impression the Pine River trip seems to me a most enjoyable one.

So after you have been home for a little while the call begins to make itself heard. At first it is very gentle. But little by little a restlessness seizes hold of you. You do not know exactly what is the matter; you are aware merely that your customary life has lost savor, that you are doing things more or less perfunctorily, and that you are a little more irritable than your naturally evil disposition.

And gradually it is borne in on you exactly what is the matter. Then say you to yourself:

"My son, you know better. You are no tenderfoot. You have had too long an experience to admit of any glamour of indefiniteness about this thing. No use bluffing. You know exactly how hard you will have to work, and how much tribulation you are going to get into, and how hungry and wet and cold and tired and generally frazzled out you are going to be. You've been there enough times, so it's pretty clearly impressed on you. You go into this thing with your eyes open. You know what you're in for. You're pretty well off right here, and you'd be a fool to go."

"That's right," says yourself to you. "You're dead right about it, old man. Do you know where we can get another mule-pack?"—From "The Mountains."

BEN FRANKLIN

By James C. Adams

IT is with pleasure that I dwell upon this part of
my story, and I would fain distinguish it with
living words. In all the after-course of my career,
I could look back upon it with peculiar satisfaction; and rarely, in the following years, did I pat
the shaggy coat of my noble Ben but I recurred to
my fatiguing and solitary vigils in the Mariposa
cañon, my combat with the monster grizzly, my
entry in her den, and seizure of her offspring. The
whole adventure is impressed upon my memory as
if it had occurred but yesterday.

No sooner was the dam dead than I turned towards the den, and determined to enter it without
delay. Approaching its mouth, accordingly, I
knelt, and tried to peer in; but all was dark, silent
and ominous. What dangers might lurk in that
mysterious gloom it was impossible to tell; nor
was it without a tremor that I prepared to explore
its depths. I trembled for a moment at the thought
of another old bear in the den; but on second
thought I assured myself of the folly of such an
idea; for an occurrence of this kind would have
been against all experience. But in such a situation a man imagines many things, and fears much
at which he afterward laughs; and therefore
though there was really no difficulty to anticipate,
I carefully loaded my rifle and pistol, and carried
my arms as if the next instant I was to be called
upon to fight for life. Being thus prepared, I took
from my pocket a small torch made of pine splin-

ters, lighted it, and placing my rifle in the mouth of the den, with the torch in my left and the pistol in my right hand, I dropped upon my knees and began to crawl in.

The entrance consisted of a rough hole, three feet wide and four feet high. It extended inward nearly horizontally, and almost without a turn, for six feet, where there was a chamber six or eight feet in diameter and five feet high, giving me room to rise upon my knees, but not to stand up—and its entire floor was thickly carpeted with leaves and grass. On the first look, I could see no animals, and felt grievously disappointed; but, as I crawled around, there was a rustling in the leaves; and, bending down with my torch, I discovered two beautiful little cubs, which could not have been over a week old, as their eyes, which open in eight or ten days, were still closed. I took the little sprawlers, one after the other, by the nape of the neck, lifted them up to the light and found them very lively. They were both males; a circumstance which gave me reason to presume there might be a third cub, for it is frequent that a litter consists of three, and I looked carefully; but no other was to be found. I concluded, therefore, that if there had been a third, the dam had devoured it —a thing she often, and, if a cub dies, or be deformed, always does. Satisfying myself that there were no others, I took the two, and, placing them in my bosom, between my buckskin and woolen shirt, once more emerged into daylight.

The possession of the prizes delighted me so much that I almost danced my way down through the bushes and over the uneven ground to the spot where my mule had been left; but, upon arriving there, it gave me great concern to find that she was gone. At first, I thought surely she had been stolen; but, as my bag of dried venison remained undisturbed upon the tree, and much more as the tracks of a panther were to be seen in the neighborhood, I became convinced that she had been attacked by my disturber of the previous night and had broken away. Indeed, upon further examination, I found her track, leading off through the chaparral; and, following it over a hill and through another cañon, at length found her grazing in a grassy valley. She seemed much frightened at first upon seeing me, but when I called her "Betz," she stopped, turned around, looked, and then came up, apparently glad to meet me again. Her haunches bore several deep and fresh scratches, which were still more convincing evidences to my mind that the panther had sprung upon her, but that she had broken loose and escaped.

Mounting the mule, I returned to the dead bear, and, cutting her up, packed a portion of her meat; the remainder I left in the mouth of the den; and, turning my face out of the ravine, I proceeded in excellent spirits, bearing the cubs still in my bosom, toward the camp of my companions. Upon reaching there, shortly after dark, I showed Solon what I had accomplished; and, placing the cubs before him, chose one for my own and presented him with the other. He thought that this was more than his share; but I insisted upon his receiving it, and he did so with a thankful heart. He asked me the story of the capture, and I told it, from the moment of my leaving camp to my return. He won-

dered much at my patient watching in the juniper
bushes, and said he would not have done it, but
still he wished he had been with me—and thus we
went on talking, till the dying embers admonished
us of the lateness of the hour. Before retiring,
Solon christened his cub General Jackson; I remarked that General Jackson was a great man in
his way, but I would call my bear Ben Franklin—
a greater name. Such was the manner that, in one
and the same day, I captured and christened my
noble Ben.

.   .   .   .

The condition of my poor Ben, as he lay panting
on the sand of the San Joaquin plains, unable to
follow me any further, and looking up affection-
ately, but despairingly, from the midst of his pain,
in my face, grieved me to the heart, and gave me
great uneasiness. He was my favorite; I could
well have spared any other animal rather than
Ben; and I feared he would die. I reproached
myself for having brought no water along, but as
the fault could not be helped by reproaches, I
hastily split some pieces of board from my wagon,
and erecting a frame and throwing a large blanket
over it, so as to make shade, left Ben and Rambler
there, and then I drove on with the intention of
procuring water and returning more speedily than
Drury, who had no interests at stake, would be disposed to do. In the course of four or five miles I
met Drury with his bag of water; and hastily
handing him the reins, with directions to drive on,
I mounted the horse and galloped back to where
Ben lay suffering. It was dark when I reached
him, and to all appearances he had not moved from

the position in which I left him. He had life
enough, however, to express his gratitude, and
drank several quarts of water with avidity. I
then endeavored to coax him along, and he took a
few steps; but neither flattery nor blows could induce him to move far.

Seeing that it was impossible to get him along,
I again let him lie, and rode ahead for the wagon,
which I found at the side of a spring. The mules
and horses were turned out to graze, and Drury
was lying asleep at the fire, which he had hastily
kindled. I roused him and ordered him to assist
in hitching up the wagon again, to go back for
Ben. He obeyed, and we soon unloaded the heav-
iest of our articles, and, leaving them at the spring,
drove back. As the country, however, was new to
us and the night dark, we by some means or other
missed the way, and could see no signs of what we
sought. We looked about all night till daylight,
but there was no Ben in sight. I at last sent
Drury in one direction and myself took another, by
which means we succeeded in a few hours in finding the trail, and finally discovered the bear lying
under his blanket. We gave him water again, but
still he could not walk, and we had to place him in
the wagon—which could not be done without some
difficulty, as by that time he would weigh in the
neighborhood of four hundred pounds. When at
last we did get him in, partly by our own strength
and partly by his assistance, we drove on to the
spring and camped.

On account of the bear's condition, we were compelled to remain two days at this spring, during
which time I doctored him. My treatment met

with success, and we soon got him on his legs again. In the meanwhile, as his feet continued sore, I made moccasins, as I had done on the Humboldt plains, and poured bear's oil in them—which was an excellent salve for the blisters. The moccasins were bound tightly to the feet, and a muzzle was put over the nose, to prevent him from tearing them off. They worked well and on the third day after reaching the spring we hitched up again and drove on to the edge of Tulare Lake.—From "The Adventures of James Capen Adams."

THE MARIPOSA LILY

By Ina Coolbrith

INSECT or blossom? Fragile, fairy thing,
  Poised upon slender tip, and quivering
    To flight! a flower of the fields of air;
    A jeweled moth; a butterfly, with rare
And tender tints upon his downy wing
    A moment resting in our happy sight;
    A flower held captive by a thread so slight
Its petal-wings of broidered gossamer
Are light as the wind, with every wind astir,
    Wafting sweet odor, faint and exquisite,
O dainty nursling of the field and sky,
    What fairer thing looks up to heaven's blue
      And drinks the noontide sun, the dawning's
        dew?
Thou wingéd bloom! thou blossom—butterfly!

    —From "Songs From the Golden Gate."

THIRST OF THE DONNER PARTY

By C. T. McGlashan

ON the sixth day of September they reached a meadow in a valley called "Twenty Wells," as there were that number of wells of various sizes, from six inches to several feet in diameter. The water in these wells rose even with the surface of the ground, and when it was drawn out the wells soon refilled. The water was cold and pure, and peculiarly welcome after the saline plains and alkaline pools they had just passed. Wells similar to these were found during the entire journey of the following day, and the country through which they were passing abounded in luxuriant grass. Reaching the confines of the Salt Lake Desert, which lies southwest of the lake, they laid in, as they supposed, an ample supply of water and grass. This desert has been represented by Bridger and Vasquez as being only about fifty miles wide. Instead, for a distance of seventy-five miles there was neither water nor grass, but everywhere a dreary, desolate, alkaline waste. Verily, it was

"A region of drought, where no river glides,
Nor rippling brook with osiered sides;
Where sedgy pool, nor bubbling fount,
Nor tree, nor cloud, nor misty mount
Appears to refresh the aching eye,
But the barren earth and the burning sky,
And the blank horizon round and round
Spread, void of living sight or sound."

When the company had been on the desert two nights and one day, Mr. Reed volunteered to go for-

11

ward, and, if possible, to discover water. His hired teamsters were attending to his teams and wagons during his absence. At a distance of perhaps twenty miles he found the desired water, and hastened to return to the train. Meantime there was intense suffering in the party. Cattle were giving out and lying down helplessly on the burning sand, or, frenzied with thirst, were straying away into the desert. Having made preparations for only fifty miles of desert, several persons came near perishing of thirst, and cattle were utterly powerless to draw the heavy wagons. Reed was gone some twenty hours. During this time his teamsters had done the wisest thing possible, unhitched the oxen and started to drive them ahead until water was reached. It was their intention, of course, to return and get the three wagons and the family, which they had necessarily abandoned on the desert. Reed passed his teamsters during the night, and hastened to the relief of his deserted family. One of his teamster's horses gave out before morning and lay down, and while the man's companions were attempting to raise him, the oxen, rendered unmanageable by their great thirst, disappeared in the desert. There were eighteen of these oxen. It is probable they scented water, and with the instincts of their nature started out to search for it. They never were found, and Reed and his family, consisting of nine persons, were left destitute in the midst of the desert, eight hundred miles from California. Near morning, entirely ignorant of the calamity which had befallen him in the loss of his cattle, he reached his family. All day long they looked and waited in vain for the returning teamsters. All the rest of the company had driven ahead, and the majority had reached water. Toward night the situation grew desperate. The scanty supply of water left with the family was almost gone, and another day on the desert would mean death to all he held dear. Their only way left was to set out on foot. He took his youngest child in his arms, and the family started to walk the twenty miles. During this dreadful night some of the younger children became so exhausted that, regardless of scoldings or encouragements, they lay down on the bleak sands. Even rest, however, seemed denied the little sufferers, for a chilling wind began sweeping over the desert, and despite their weariness and anguish, they were forced to move forward. At one time during the night the horror of the situation was changed to intense fright. Through the darkness came a swift-rushing animal, which Reed soon recognized as one of his young steers. It was crazed and frenzied with thirst, and for some moments seemed bent upon dashing into the frightened group. Finally, however, it plunged madly away into the night, and was seen no more. Reed suspected the calamity which had prevented the return of the teamsters, but at that moment, the imminent peril surrounding his wife and children banished all thoughts of worrying about anything but their present situation. God knows what would have become of them if they had not, soon after daylight, discovered the wagon of Jacob Donner. They were received kindly by his family, and conveyed to where the other members of the party were camped. For six or eight days the entire company remained at this spot. Every effort was made to find Reed's lost cattle. Almost every man ing this search. The desert mirage disclosed against directions. This task was attended with both difficulty and danger; for when the sun shone, the atmosphere appeared to distort and magnify objects so that at the distance of a mile every stone or bush would appear the size of an ox. Several of the men came near dying for want of water during this search. The desert mirage disclosed against the horizon, clear, distinct and perfectly outlined rocks, mountain peaks and tempting lakelets. Each jagged cliff, or pointed rock, or sharply-curved hilltop, hung suspended in air as perfect and complete as if photographed on the sky. Deceived, deluded by these mirages, in spite of their better judgment, several members of the company were led far out into the pathless depths of the desert.

The outlook for Reed was gloomy enough. One cow and one ox were the only stock he had remaining. The company were getting exceedingly impatient over the long delay, yet be it said to their honor, they encamped on the western verge of the desert until every hope of finding Reed's cattle was abandoned. Finally, F. W. Graves and Patrick Breen each lent an ox to Mr. Reed, and by yoking up his remaining cow and ox, he had two yoke of cattle. "Cacheing," or concealing such of his property on the desert, as could not be placed in one wagon, he hitched the two yoke of cattle to this wagon and proceeded on the journey.—From "History of the Donner Party."

STARVATION OF THE DONNER PARTY

By C. T. McGlashan

IN the very complete account of this trip, which is kindly furnished by Mary Graves, are many interesting particulars concerning the suffering of these days. "Our only chance for camp-fire for the night," she says, "was to hunt a dead tree of some description, and set fire to it. The hemlock being the best and generally much the largest timber, it was our custom to select the driest we could find without leaving our course. When the fire would reach the top of the tree, the falling limbs would fall around us and bury themselves in the snow, but we heeded them not. Sometimes the falling, blazing limbs would brush our clothes, but they never hit us; that would have been too lucky a hit. We would sit or lie on the snow, and rest our weary frames. We would sleep, only to dream of something nice to eat, and awake again to disappointment. Such was our sad fate! Even the reindeer's wretched lot was not worse! 'His dinner and his bed were snow, and supper he had not.' Our fare was the same! We would strike fire by means of the flint-lock gun which we had with us. This had to be carried by turns, as it was considered the only hope left us in case we might find game which we could kill. We traveled over a ridge of mountains, and then descended a deep cañon, where one could scarcely see the bottom. Down, down we would go, or rather slide, for it is very slavish work going down hill, and in many cases we were compelled to slide on our shoes

as sleds. On reaching the bottom we would plunge
into the snow, so that it was difficult getting out,
with the shoes tied to our feet, our packs lashed to
our backs, and ourselves head and ears under the
snow. But we managed to get out some way, and
one by one reached the bottom of the cañon. When
this was accomplished we had to ascend a hill as
steep as the one we had descended. We would
drive the toes of our shoes into the loose snow, to
make a sort of step, and one by one, as if ascending
stair-steps, we climbed up. It took us an entire
day to reach the top of the mountain. Each time
we attained the summit of a mountain, we hoped
we should be able to see something like a valley,
but each time came disappointment, for far ahead
was always another and higher mountain. We
found some springs, or, as we called them, wells,
from five to twenty feet under ground, as you
might say, for they were under the snow on which
we walked. The water was so warm that it melted
the snow, and from some of these springs were
large streams of running water. We crossed numbers of these streams on bridges of snow, which
would sometimes form upon a blade of grass hanging over the water; and from as small a foundation
would grow a bridge from ten to twenty-five feet
high, and from a foot and a half to three feet
across the top. It would make you dizzy to look
down at the water and it was with much difficulty
we could place our clumsy ox-bow snow-shoes one
ahead of the other without falling. Our feet had
been frozen and thawed so many times that they
were bleeding and sore. When we stopped at
night we would take off our shoes, which by this

time were so badly rotted by constant wetting in snow, that there was very little left of them. In the morning we would push our shoes on, bruising and numbing the feet so badly that they would ache and ache with walking and the cold, until night would come again. Oh! the pain! it seemed to make the pangs of hunger more excruciating.''

Thus the party traveled on day after day, until absolute starvation again stared them in the face. The snow had gradually grown less deep, until it finally disappeared or lay only in patches. Their strength was well-nigh exhausted, when one day Mary Graves says: "Some one called out, 'Here are tracks!' Some one asked, 'What kind of tracks—human?'' 'Yes, human!' Can anyone imagine the joy these footprints gave us? We ran as fast as our strength would carry us.''

Turning a chaparral point, they came in full view of an Indian rancheria. The uncivilized savages were amazed. Never had they seen such forlorn, wretched, pitiable human beings as the tattered, disheveled, skeleton creatures who stood stretching out their arms for assistance. At first they all ran and hid, but soon they returned to the aid of these dying wretches. It is said that the Indian women and children cried, and wailed with grief at the affecting spectacle of starved men and wo-men. Such food as they had was speedily offered. It was bread made of acorns. This was eagerly eaten. It was at least a substitute for food. Every person in the rancheria, from the toddling papooses to the aged chief, endeavored to aid them.

After what had recently happened, could anything be more touching than these acts of kindness of the Indians?

After briefly resting, they pressed forward. The Indians accompanied them and even led them, and constantly supplied them with food. With food? No, it was not such food as their weakened, debilitated systems craved. The acorn bread was not sufficient to sustain lives already so attenuated by repeated starvations. All that the starved experience in the way of pain and torture before they die had been experienced by these people at least four different times. To their horror, they now discovered that despite the acorn bread they must die of hunger and exhaustion a fifth and last time. So sick and weak did they become that they were compelled to lie down and rest every hundred yards. Finally, after being with the Indians seven days, they lay down, and felt that they never should have strength to take another step. Before them, in all its beauty and loveliness, spread the broad valley of the Sacramento. Behind them were the ever-pleading faces of their starving dear ones. Yet neither hope nor affection could give them further strength. They were dying in full view of the long-desired haven of rest.—From "The History of the Donner Party."

A SONG OF AUTUMN

By Henry Meade Bland

'TIS old autumn, the musician,
　　Who, with pipe and tabor, weaves
The sweet music lovers sigh for
　　In the falling of the leaves.

I have heard his distant anthem
　　Go a-sighing through the trees
Like the far-off shouts of children,
　　Or the hum of swarming bees.

When he plays the leaflets flutter
　　On the boughs that hold them fast;
Or they scurry through the forest
　　Or they spin before the blast.

And they frolic and they gambol,
　　And they cling to autumn's gown
As the children to the Piper's
　　In the famous Hamelin Town.

Then they rustle and they hurry
　　To a canyon dark and deep;
And the Piper, dear old autumn,
　　Pipes till he is fast asleep.

　　　　　　　　—From "Poems."

SAN GABRIEL VALLEY

By Theodore Van Dyke

BUT to see at its best the loveliest part of Southern California, as improved, one must descend into its great valley of San Gabriel. The Sierra Madre Mountains that form its northern wall rise with a sudden sweep much higher above the valley than most of the great mountains of our country rise above the land at their feet, lifting one at once into a different climate and to a country where primeval wildness still reigns supreme. Few parts of the United States are less known and less traversed than these great hills; yet they look down upon the very garden of all California. Away up there the mountain trout flashes undisturbed in the hissing brook, and the call of the mountain quail rings from the shady glen where the grizzly bear yet dozes away the day, secure as in the olden time. From the bristling points where the lilac and manzanita light up the dark hue of the surrounding chaparral the deer yet looks down upon the plain from which the antelope has long since been driven; while on the lofty ridges that lie in such clear outline against the distant sky the mountain sheep still lingers, safe in its inaccessible home.

But a few years ago this valley of San Gabriel was a long open stretch of wavy slopes and low rolling hills, in winter robed in velvety green and spangled with myriads of flowers all strange to Eastern eyes, in summer brown with sun-dried grass, or silvery gray where light rippled over the wild oats. Here and there stood groves of huge

live oaks, beneath whose broad time-bowed heads
thousands of cattle stamped away the noons of
summer. Around the old mission, whose bells have
rung over the valley for a century, a few houses
were grouped; but beyond this there was scarcely
a sign of man's work except the far-off speck of a
herdsman looming in the mirage, or the white walls
of the old Spanish ranch house glimmering afar
through the hazy sunshine in which the silent land
lay always sleeping.

The old bells of the mission still clang in brazen
discord as before, and the midnight yelp of the
coyote may yet be heard as he comes in from the
outlying hills to inspect the new breeds of chickens
that civilization has brought in; a few scattered
live oaks still nod to each other in memory of the
past, and along the low hills far off in the south
the light still plays upon the waving wild oats; but
nearly all else has changed as no other part of the
world has ever changed. Nearly all is now covered
with a luxuriant growth of vegetation the most diverse, yet all of it foreign to the soil. Side by side
are the products of two zones, reaching the highest
stages of perfection, yet none of them natives of this
coast. Immense vineyards of the tenderest grapes
of Southern Spain, or Italy, yielding five or six
tons to the acre, lie by the side of fields of wheat,
whose heads and berry far excel in size and full-
ness the finest ever seen in the famed fields of Minnesota or Dakota. Here the barley gives often a
return that no northern land can equal, and by its
side the orange tree outdoes its race in the farthest
South, and keeps its fruit in perfection when those
of other lands have failed.

Gay cottages now line the roads where the hare so recently cantered along the dusty cattle trail; and villages lie brightly green with a wealth of foliage where the roaring wings of myriads of quail shook the air above impenetrable jungles of cactus. Houses furnished in all the styles of modern decorative art rise in all directions, embowered in roses, geraniums, heliotropes and lilies that bloom the long year 'round and reach a size that makes them hard to recognize as old friends. Among them rise the banana, the palm, the aloe, the rubber tree, and the pampas grass with its tall, feathery plumes. Perhaps the camphor tree and a dozen other foreign woods are scattered around them, while the lawns shine with grasses unknown in other parts of the United States. The broad head and drooping arms of the Mexican pepper tree fill along the road the sunny openings that the stately shaft of the Australian eucalyptus has failed to shade; and on every hand, instead of homely fences, are hedges of Monterey cypress, lime, pomegranate, arbor vitae, or acacia. Here and there one sees the guava, the Japanese persimmon, Japanese plum, or some similar exotic, cultivated, like the olive and quince and lemon, for pleasure more than profit; but grapes and oranges are the principal products. Yet there are groves of English walnuts almost rivaling in size the great orange orchards; and orchards of prunes, nectarines, apricots, plums, pears, peaches and apples that are little behind in size or productiveness. The deep green of the alfalfa may here and there contrast with the lighter green of the grape, but vineyards of enormous

size, some a mile square, make all beside them look
small.—From "Southern California."

THE POET'S WEALTH

BY RICHARD REALF

WHO says the poet's lot is hard?
　　Who says it is with misery rife?
Who pities the deluded bard
　　That dreams away his life?
Go thou and give thy sympathy
　　Unto the crowd of common men;
The poet needs it not, for he
　　Hath joys beyond our ken.

Yea, he hath many a broad domain
　　Which thou, O man, hath never seen.
Where never comes the pelting rain
　　Or stormy winter keen.
There ever balmy is the air,
　　And ever smiling are the skies,
For beauty ever blossoms there—
　　Beauty that never dies.

There sportive fancy loves to roam
　　And cull the sweets from every flower,
While meditation builds her home
　　Beneath some forest bower;
There, too, the poet converse holds
　　With spirits of the long ago,
And dim futurity unfolds
　　Secrets for him to know.

Then say not that in wretchedness
　　The poet spends his weary days,
Say not that hunger and distress
　　Are guerdon for his lays;
But rather say that lack of gold
　　Unto the bard is greatest bliss,
And say, he is not earth-controlled
　　Whilst owning wealth like this.

　　　　　　　　　　　—From "Poems."

ASCENT OF MT. RAINIER

By Ada Woodruff Anderson

THE summer day breaks early in the Puget
Sound country. It was not yet four by Stratton's watch when he stepped from his tent and
stood analyzing the weather, but all the sky overhead was changing to yellow, and directly, while
he looked, to streaks of flame. The heights, towering a thousand feet on the opposite side of the
gorge, were burnished copper, and Rainier, walling
the top of the cañon, warmed to amethyst and rose.
Its crest, at an altitude of nearly fifteen thousand
feet, was hardly seven miles distant.

But the great forest that hemmed in the small
open where the camp was pitched still gloomed in
shadow, and the air was sharp with the near breath
of the glacier and snowfield. Stratton saw that
Mose had left his blanket, gone already to bring
up the horses, and the close report of a gun told
that Kingsley was off in search of the early bird.
Then Samantha came from the other tent and stir-

[From "The Heart of the Red Firs," by Ada Woodruff
　　Anderson. Copyright, 1908, by Little, Brown & Co.]

red the smouldering fire. She added a dry hemlock bough, watching the roused flames fasten on the resinous wood.

"Good morning, Psyche," he said.

She lifted her glance, nodding. She had a mouth like a Cupid's bow and the short upper lip twitched with enforced gravity before the shaft sped. "Ef you hed er wife, I 'low she'd get er new name 'bout every day, an' mebbe twicet. Land, it 'ud keep her busy rememberin' who she was."

An hour later the little cavalcade formed in line, with Kingsley leading on his big white horse, followed by Samantha, whose clear piping voice rose in alternate upbraiding or admonition, for she rode the indifferent Ginger. Mose, mounted on Yelm, Jim's piebald pony, crowded the cayuse with the two pack animals; then came Louise and the teacher, while Stratton closed the rear.

The trail became more and more precipitous, switch-backing across the face of a spur, taking the edge of a cliff, breaking into sharp pitches to a rushing ford. Trunks, logs, netlike boughs, shelving rock crowded close. The head of the Nisqually and its glacier were not far off. Then they turned up its beautiful tributary, the Paradise. Over the stream Eagle Peak, the first of the Tatoosh Mountains, lifted a tremendous front, and boulders hurled from it, blocked the limpid current, creating innumerable cascades. The air was flooded with drifting spray, and the wet, luxuriant earth, reflecting the sun, filled the gorge with playing color.

Then finally they trailed out of the heavy timber into the parks of Paradise. A succession of em-

erald slopes opened before them, broken by clumps
of amabilis fir and mountain hemlock; where a
higher top rose out of a shapely mass it became a
cathedral spire. Sometimes the way wound through
an area of blooming heliotrope or asters; banks of
gorgeous snapdragon or flaming Indian paintbrush
gave color, like landscape gardening, to whole hillsides. Then behind them, pinnacle on pinnacle,
closed the Tatoosh range; a last sharp ascent and
they were on that small and lofty plateau, at an altitude of five thousand feet, since called The Camp
of Clouds, with the splendor of the great summit
almost overhead.

The tents were pitched; horses picketed. It was
hardly mid-afternoon. "By this time tomorrow,"
said Kingsley, "if this weather stays with us, we
shall have made and I hope passed Gibraltar."

Stratton, lounging on a blanket, looked up to the
black cliff, which, rising sheer fifteen hundred feet,
stood like a mighty fortress against the whiteness
of the dome. "I hope so," he answered, "but,
Captain, I never saw anything look so tremendous-
ly like work."

Louise rested on a grassy knob, her hands clasped
loosely on her knee, inspiration in her lifted face.
She hardly heard her husband's remark, or the
other's man reply, but Alice started from her place
beside her. "Phil," she said, "take me with you.
You can't understand what it means to me, to be
so near, to see the summit shining there, and go no
farther. I'm very strong, Phil, and clear-headed.
I'm not afraid of things. I—oh, you don't understand, but the mountains seem to beckon."

Kingsley walked a restless turn. "I do understand," he said. "I feel it myself. But we don't know what we are going through, and we can't be sure of the weather an hour ahead; clouds are manufactured right here at a moment's notice. But wait, don't tease, and we'll compromise. I'm going off now to reconnoiter. I believe the most feasible start is from that ridge across this valley of the Paradise, but I want to be sure. There'll be no time to waste in doubling back for fresh starts to-morrow. And Mose has been up that way; he says, with care we can use the horses as far as the old snow. A glacier cuts in there, probably the source of the Cowlitz, and he thinks we should be able to reach it in a couple of hours. I'll take you that far—to the glacier."

At this Mose started from his recumbent position on the earth. He threw out his arms in protest. "No, no, Mees," he said, "It ees bes' you doan' go dare. Sacré, no."

"I'm not afraid," she answered, smiling, "and if I'm a trouble, I'll turn back. I promise."

"You doan' be some tro'ble, Mees," he said, quickly. "No, no, it ees dat Tyee Sahgalee ees goin' be mad. Mebbe he ees mek dis mountain burn an' break an' fall down. Monjee, monjee, Mees, you can't ride quick 'nough away."

She laughed, shaking her head. "I don't believe that, Mose," she said, "and you won't, after we have been there. Tyee Sahgalee don't care how many of us go creeping up there any more than we care about the ants and spiders that crawl to the cabin door."

The horses were brought and presently they were
12

trailing up the pathless slopes in the wake of the piebald pony; fording countless streams, leaping them, sinking in pitfalls through treacherous banks of bloom. When, switch-backing up a loftly rise, Alice ventured to look down, all the colored breadth of Paradise Park unfolded like a map, and the dome gathered majesty at every turn. They gained a shoulder, rounded a curve, and before them stretched the levels of a plateau carpeted with snow. Then, as they moved across this field, mountain on mountain opened, shading to blue distance. Through a gap, out of a woolly cloud, shone the opal crown of Adams, and presently, far off St. Helens rose like a floating berg on an uptossed sea.

They dismounted at the foot of a knob flanked by loose rock. The red stain of old snow was under their feet, and beyond the spur shone the clean, blue-green edge of the glacier. "We are higher than the treeline, now," said Philip, "and above the clouds."

She drew a breath of delight, lifting her glance to the near dome. "And it looks as though we could reach the summit in fifteen or twenty minutes. Oh, Phil, come, let's go."

Kingsley laughed. "We haven't climbed nine thousand feet; the hardest third of the ascent is above us. Don't you remember, the only two men who ever made that summit were half a day in just passing Gibraltar? We may find it no longer passable."

While his look rested on the grim fortress a thin cloud rose like smoke from its base. It covered the cliff swiftly and trailed across the dome. "Out of nothing, without notice," and he shook his head; "that's what I've heard."

He turned. Stratton was busy searching for a safe hitching-place for his horse; he never stood well. But Mose had stepped nearer Kingsley. The boy's shoulders were inclined forward, and his eyes, in that instant, were those of a crouching animal about to spring.

"Well, Mose," he said carelessly, "your Tyec Sahgalee is hiding his face. I suppose you think we've come far enough. But we'll show him."

He moved on with Alice up the knob, and Stratton joined them. But presently Mose stalked by, leading the way to the glacier. His face had the gray look of fear, but his lips were set in the thin line that gave him an older, sinister touch, the shadow of cruelty.

He moved swiftly and surely. He did not once look back. He gave no direction or warning. They followed, slipping and stumbling through the moraine, and gaining the ragged brow of the knob found themselves suddenly on the brink of a mighty precipice. Far, far down, the infant Cowlitz sprang into life and struggled out between stupendous columns and needles. Locked in the opposite pinnacled cliffs shone the sheer, blue-seamed front of the glacier, and the throes that gave the river birth resounded through the gorge.

Stratton uncoiled the spare lariat he carried, and taking an end, with Philip closing, and the girl between, drew slowly along the rim. Mose, curving far ahead, came out on the slippery incline of the glacier. Finally he stopped under a great upheaval of ice and, resting against a block, waited, with his back turned to them and his face lifted to the clouding dome.

Behind them another cloud formed over the Tatoosh Mountains, driving fast to meet the advancing column from Gibraltar; and, in a little while, when they had come out on the ice and made slow headway up the tilting surface from the abyss, mist lifted swiftly, flooding, giving immensity to the darkening gorge. Kingsley walked a trifle in advance of Alice, with Stratton abreast of him. Suddenly Mose's tracks, on a recent light snowfall which had offered foothold, swerved, and both men stopped. They were on the brink of a narrow, deep, incredibly deep, crevasse.

Alice moved back, shivering. She looked, a mute question trembling on her lips, at Mose. But he continued to stand, oblivious, with his eyes fixed, expectantly, on the clouding dome.

"See here," called Philip, "see here; next time you let us know." Then his glance returned to the crevasse. "Reminds me of a tremendous white watermelon," he said, "with just one thin, clean slice gone."

"Yes?" questioned Stratton, smiling. "It strikes me differently. I thought right away of some curious metal, with just enough taken, by some nice process, to shape a gigantic blade."

"A blade, yes," said Alice, "for the hand of Tyee Sahgalee."

Stratton's eyes met hers amusedly. He wondered if she was capable of superstition. "Even then," he said, "it is only a surface impression, lost the moment you look down. It's an ice-crevasse; nothing else." He turned to Kingsley, who

was already studying the glacier ahead. "Of course this will not delay us tomorrow, Captain, but it is time, now, to turn back."

"In a moment. There's a streak on there that bothers me. Looks like a more serious break. I want to see it at closer range. Wait here; I won't be fifteen minutes."

He moved back impetuously, and, giving himself short headway, took the crevasse in a leap. Showers of loosened ice clinked down from the rim. Most of the particles struck the sides that closed in twenty feet below, and rebounding dropped again and sent back faint echoes from the last level of the abyss.

Stratton stood watching Philip up the glacier, but presently Alice drew away from the crevasse and turned to look back down the gorge. The sun no longer shone. All that brilliant vista of opal peak and amethyst spur, shading to blue distance, was curtained in closing sheets of mist. There a great crag loomed an instant and was gone. Here an uptossed pile of ice blocks flashed a sudden prismatic light and grew dim. Then they themselves were wrapped in a noiseless, drenching cloud.

At the same moment she was startled by Stratton's brief note of surprise and felt behind her a sudden jar. She turned. Mose was hurled sprawling at her feet, and, clutching her skirt, was up instantly, panting, with quivering nostril, eyes ablaze. Then, in the recoil, Stratton reeled on the brink of the crevasse, recovered, stumbled on breaking crust, and went down.

She stood for an interminable moment, waiting, listening, numbed body and mind. Then she was

conscious that Mose was going, and she went after him a few steps, calling his name. But his receding shape drifted faster and faster. a fading shadow in the mist. She turned back, lifting her voice in a great cry to Philip. And she was answered from the abyss.

She dropped to her knees and crept close to look down. Stratton was there, where the pale, green walls narrowed. He rested wedge-like, caught at the armpits. He looked up and saw her. "Be careful," he said, "I am all right."

Instantly the executive in her arose. "I have the lariat," she said.

"Fasten it to the ice where Mose stood," he called. "I can work along that far."

He remembered that the rope was new and strong, one he himself had selected as a reserve in picketing his own spirited horse. The question was whether the ice would take his weight. He worked carefully, laboriously, along by shoulder and elbow, his body swinging from the waist, starting a rain of ice at every move. At last, where the wall crumbled, leaving a ledge, he was able to draw himself to his knees. He cut foothold with his knife, and other niches higher up for his hands, and pulled himself erect on the slippery shelf.

Beyond him the chasm widened between sheer walls, and it was in this shaft that the lowered rope hung. It swung for a moment, like a failing pendulum, and each oscillation, though he stood alert, missed his reach a little more. The girl, peering into the abyss, understood, and again disappeared. The line was drawn up, and presently it dropped almost at his shoulder. He caught the

end and, looking up, met her eyes over the rim. "That's better," he said.

"Wait—one moment," she called and was gone once more. She did not return this time, but her voice came to him, "Now, now, all ready."

The lariat tightened. It creaked, ground on the edge of the chasm; ice chips fell ceaselessly. He swung out. He was a big fellow, heavy. Would the support hold? Would Mose, his fury cooled, be neutral? Why, yes, surely the boy was even setting himself to ease the strain. He could feel an unmistakable give and pull above on the rope, as he climbed, hand over hand.

He gained the top. He reached a palm around a slight pinnacle, for a final grasp on the line, and pulled himself slowly out on the surface of the glacier. He was a strong man physically, a man of steady nerve, one accustomed to take risks with Nature, as in those times a man of the Northwest must, but what he saw in that brief pause sent a shiver through him. He closed his eyes like one brought suddenly into intense light.

The rope was fastened, as he had directed, to a thick column in the upheaval, but it stretched diagonally to the projection on the brink of the crevasse. And it was Alice, not Mose, who steadied it, throwing her weight on it, twisting it on her hands, digging her heels in a shallow cleft, straining back to ease the pressure on the knob. Suppose the support had given way; suppose he had dragged her—this brave girl, all life, charm, loveliness—down to destruction. It was horrible to think of. Horrible!

He pulled himself together and got to his feet.

He did not speak to her then; he could not. But he put his hand to his mouth and lifted his voice in a great hail. Kingsley responded, but his "Hello," came faintly, through billows of mist. The calls were repeated. "We cannot wait," Stratton said. "We must follow that rascal's tracks down, while they last, to the horses."

"What made Mose do it?" she asked. "Oh, what made him?"

"Why, just Indian, I suppose; or say he was an instrument, self-appointed, of his Tyee Sahgalee. But he shall be punished."

They made the rocky knob and finally, out of obscurity, she caught Colonel's familiar neigh. The call shrilled again, inquiring, peremptory. But when they came to the end of the moraine, where they had left the horses, they found them gone.

The neigh was repeated once more, coming back faintly, from far across the snowfield. "Mr. Stratton," she cried, "what has happened? Where is Mose going?"

"Over the mountains to the Palouse plains, I haven't a doubt," and the blade flashed again in his eyes. "It's the first thing a half-breed does, and they always drive stolen horses over there; it is impossible to find them among those big, feeding bands of the Yakimas. He will stampede the rest in the valley, and Yelm Jim will probably meet him somewhere below the springs and help him take them through the Pass."

She stood for a moment with her head high, lips set, looking with storming eyes into the mist. Then, "There isn't any time to waste," she said. "We must take him this side of the springs." And she began to trail the horses on across the snow.

It was twilight and they were descending the final pitch into the park when Kingsley at last overtook them. The camp-fire, which Samantha had kindled with infinite difficulty on the plateau, burned like a beacon in the gloom. "You should have seen that second crevasse," he said. "It was tremendous. No way over, no way around; I tramped both directions to see. We've simply got to choose another route to-morrow. But what became of the horses?"

"Mose took them." It was Alice who answered. "He took Colonel. But I shall find him. I've got to find him if I have to walk every step of the way over the mountains and through the Palouse. You know how much Paul thinks of his horse, Philip. Oh, I can never face him; I can never tell him— the truth."

Camp was broken hurriedly, each of the men taking the necessary shoulder pack, and leaving the bulk of the outfit to be sent for when they should find horses. They pushed quickly down from the snow, which became rain in the woods. And Alice led the way. She studied the trail continually, separating the tracks of the ponies, where they struck the path down the valley, from the deeper, water-filled impressions of the American horses. She set Stratton a pace, and kept it almost to the ford of the Paradise. Then suddenly she stopped an instant, listening, and ran on along the bank to an old log foot-crossing. There on the end of the bridge, sheltered by a trailing cedar, were her bridle and

saddle, and picketed on a grassy knoll under some
alders she saw the black.

"Oh," she said, and took his head in her arms,
"you beauty! You heart's desire! But I knew—
I knew Mose couldn't take you; I knew it."

Stratton stood for a moment watching her.
"So," he said, "so the rascal was white enough to
leave your horse. He brought him this far with
the others to avoid pursuit last night."

Alice looked off a thoughtful moment, through
the dripping trees. "I knew his white conscience
would get to upbraiding him," she said. "But I
can't help feeling glad he chose Coloned for the
compromise."

Stratton laughed. "I hope it will upbraid him
some more," he said, "and induce him to leave my
horse."

Suddenly he stopped, and the black also halted,
tossing his mane, and shrilling his ready, challenging neigh. There, moving out of the stream, up the
opposite bank, was a riderless horse. It was Sir
Donald.

Stratton whistled a soft, imperative note. The
chestnut wheeled. The man repeated the call, and
the horse trotted gently back into the channel. He
halted once more on a gravel bar, his head high,
ears alert, then came on across to his master.

"So," said Stratton, slowly. "So, Donald, you
showed the rascal your little trick. You see, Miss
Hunter, it was as I thought. Mose chose the best
horse. But he never mounted him. In his hurry
he laid his hand on the bit, and Sir Donald never
allows that; he was trained that way."

With this he vaulted into the saddle and led the

way over from bar to bar. He returned bringing
the black, and while the others made the crossing
Alice waited, seating herself on a rock in the sun,
and lifting her face to the upper cañon. Presently
the clouds parted like a rent veil on the mountain.
Once more Gibraltar menaced and the summit
shone in splendor.

"After all," she said, when Stratton rejoined
her, "I can't blame Mose for that belief. I felt it
myself, for a moment, there on the glacier. It was
the steps of the Great White Throne. You can't
understand."

He bent and offered his hand to mount her on
her horse, her sister having kept the black, and she
sprang lightly up. "Then," she said, while he adjusted the stirrup, "you see no excuse for Mose?"

"No," and his face hardened. "No, I only see
the half-breed threw me into that crevasse. He
took me off guard. And he left us miles from anywhere, on that unknown mountain, in a storm,
without horses. His motives do not count."

Sir Donald started, trailing after the black. The
little company filed slowly down to the mineral
springs. And there, in the open, unpicketed, ready
for the long trail, they found the other horses
quietly feeding in company with Ginger and the
pack animals.

While Samantha made a fire and prepared the
coffee the two men caught and picketed the herd,
reserving the few horses necessary for a hurried
trip back to the plateau for the outfit. And it was
Alice, who, going for a drink from her favorite
well, discovered Mose. He was lying semi-conscious
on the wet earth, and over his black brows, branded

with the tip of an iron shoe, Sir Donald had set his mark.

The teacher dipped her handkerchief in the basin and bathed the hurt. She went to ask Stratton's flask of him, and mixed the boy a draught, and, a little later, when the young man followed her to the spring, he found Mose able to recognize him. He stood silent a moment watching him with hard eyes, and the boy met the look steadily; his muscles stiffened as they had that day at school, when he braced himself to Laramie's blow. Stratton's lip curled in disgust. After all, he could not punish the fellow, down, helpless like that. He swung on his heel.

"Wait," said Alice, "it was just as you thought. The scheme to steal the horses was Yelm Jim's; he was to meet him at the branch to the Pass and help drive them over the mountains to the Palouse plains. But he meant to leave Colonel; he only brought him as far as the Paradise to avoid being overtaken. And that trouble at the crevasse was unpremediated. He was terribly frightened by the gathering storm. He believed it was a judgment coming on us all, and he took the opportunity to— use you—for a propitiation. Afterwards, in the night, he crept back up the valley far enough to see the camp-fire, and you, safe—and keeping watch on the plateau."

There was another brief silence. Stratton stood, still hard, uncompromising, frowning down at the boy. "Be merciful," she said. "Think; you were not hurt; you have Sir Donald, unharmed. Be generous. Some time—who knows?— you yourself may ask it."

"No," he flashed. "No. I live my life; I do as I please. I ask nothing of anyone. And in the end —I take what I deserve. That is my creed. The boy must be punished."

He turned away, but she followed. In her earnestness she laid her hand on his sleeve. "He has been punished," she said. "Look. He will carry Sir Donald's brand all his life. He's just a boy, Mr. Stratton. He left home angry, outraged, and Yelm Jim took the opportunity to make him his tool. But he has good in him, I know. Remember, too, he saved my life. And I need him; I'll be responsible for him."

Her eyes were raised to Stratton eloquent with appeal; the hand on his arm trembled. "You need him; he saved your life." He paused and the hardness went out of his face. "And you saved mine— you saved mine; I do not forget that. And perhaps you were right just now; sometimes I may ask that mercy. I may ask it of—you."

Her hand fell from his sleeve; she drew back a step. "I will be ready," she said slowly, "if you are good to Mose." She looked back at the boy. He was watching her. His lip quivered and his eyes filled with unaccustomed tears. "I'll be responsible for him," she repeated. "I'm going to make him white."—From "The Heart of the Red Firs."

TO THE PIONEERS THAT REMAIN

By A. J. Waterhouse

I HAVE no word to speak their praise,
    Theirs was the deed; the guerdon ours,
The wilderness and weary days
    Were theirs alone; for us the flowers.
They sowed the seed that we might reap;
    Ours is the fruitage of their years.
And now, behold, they drop to sleep,
    And we have naught for them save tears.

The flag, whose luster none may mar,
    The brightest thing that loves the air,
See you our California's star
    Amidst the rest? They set it there. ·
What wonder that it droops to-day,
    The while another folds his hands,
And silent, floats away, away,
    From golden sands to golden sands.

So they go out. A little while
    And none shall answer to the call.
Still shall the great world weep or smile,
    But they shall be all silent—all.
Still shall the life tides ebb and flow
    And mark the rhythm of the years,
And they no more shall heed or know,
    Forgotten cares and hopes and fears.

When they are gone; when o'er one's clay
  Our tears of long farewell shall fall,
We'll pay our tribute then and say:
  "He was the last, the last of all.
Ah, they were stalwart men," we'll sigh,
  "The future's promise on each brow."
So shall we whisper then, but I—
  I pay that tribute here and now.

—From "Some Homely Little Songs."

THE LOVE MASTER

By Jack London

WHEEDON SCOTT had set himself to the task of redeeming White Fang—or rather, of redeeming mankind from the wrong it had done White Fang. It was a matter of principle and conscience. He felt that the ill done White Fang was a debt incurred by man and that it must be paid. So he went out of his way to be especially kind to the Fighting Wolf. Each day he made it a point to pet and caress White Fang, and to do it at length.

At first suspicious and hostile, White Fang grew to like this petting. But there was one thing that he never outgrew—his growling. Growl he would, from the moment the petting began till it ended. But it was a growl with a new note in it. A stranger could not hear this note, and to such a stranger the growling of White Fang was an exhibition of primordial savagery, nerve-racking and blood-curdling. But White Fang's throat had become harsh-fibred from the making of ferocious sounds through the many years since his first little rasp of anger in the lair of his cubhood, and he could not soften the sounds of his throat now to express the gentleness he felt. Nevertheless, Wheedon Scott's ear and sympathy were fine enough to catch the new note all but drowned in the fierceness—the note that was the faintest hint of a croon of content and that none but he could hear.

As the days went by, the evolution of *like* into *love* was accelerated. White Fang himself began to grow aware of it, though in his consciousness he knew not what love was. It manifested itself to him as a void in his being—a hungry, aching, yearning void that clamored to be filled. It was a pain and an unrest; and it received easement only by the touch of the new god's presence. At such times love was joy to him—a wild, keen-thrilling satisfaction. But when away from his god, the pain and the unrest returned; the void in him sprung up and pressed against him with its emptiness, and the hunger gnawed and gnawed unceasingly.

White Fang was in the process of finding himself. In spite of the maturity of his years and of the savage rigidity of the mould that had formed him, his nature was undergoing an expansion. There was a burgeoning within him of strange feelings and unwonted impulses. His old code of conduct was changing. In the past he had liked comfort and surcease from pain, disliked discomfort and pain, and he had adjusted his actions accordingly. But now it was different. Because of this new feeling within him, he ofttimes elected pain and discomfort for the sake of his god. Thus, in the early morning, instead of roaming and foraging, or lying in a sheltered nook, he would wait for hours on the cheerless cabin-stoop for a sight of his god's face. At night when the god returned home, White Fang would leave the warm sleeping place he had burrowed in the snow in order to receive the friendly snap of the fingers and friendly word of greeting. Meat, even meat itself, he would forego to be with his god, to receive a caress from him or to accompany him down into the town.

Like had been replaced by love. And love was the plummet dropped down into the deeps of him where like had never gone. And, responsive, out of his deeps had come the new thing—love. That which was given unto him did he return. This was a god indeed, a love-god, a warm and radiant god, in whose light White Fang's nature expanded as a flower expands under the sun.

But White Fang was not demonstrative. He was too old, too firmly moulded, to become adept at expressing himself in new ways. He was too self-possessed, too strongly poised in his own isolation. Too long had he cultivated reticence, aloofness, and moroseness. He had never barked in his life, and he could not now learn to bark a welcome when his god approached. He was never in the way, never extravagant nor foolish in the expression of his love. He never ran to meet his god. He waited at a distance; but he always waited, was always there. His love partook of the nature of worship, dumb, inarticulate, a silent adoration. Only by the steady regard of his eyes did he express his love, and by

13

the unceasing following with his eyes of his god's
every movement.   Also, at times, when his god
looked at him and spoke to him, he Betrayed an
awkward self-consciousness, caused by the struggle
of his love and his physical inability to express it.

He learned to adjust himself in many ways to
his new mode of life.   It was borne in upon him
that he must let his master's dogs alone.   Yet his
dominant nature asserted itself, and he had first to
thrash them into an acknowledgment of his superiority and leadership.   This accomplished, he
had little trouble with them.   They gave trail to
him when he came and went or walked among them,
and when he asserted his will they obeyed.

In the same way, he came to tolerate Matt—as a
possession of his master.   His master rarely fed
him.   Matt did that; it was his business; yet White
Fang divined that it was his master's food he ate
and that it was his master who thus fed him vicari-
ously.   Matt it was who tried to put him into the
harness and make him haul sled with the other
dogs, but Matt failed.   It was not until Wheedon
Scott put the harness on White Fang and worked
him, that he understood.   He took it as his master's
will that Matt should drive him, and work him just
as he drove and worked his master's other dogs.

Different from the Mackenzie toboggans were the
Klondike sleds with runners under them, and different was the method of driving the dogs.   There
was no fan-formation of the team.   And here, in
the Klondike, the leader was indeed the leader.
The wisest as well as the strongest dog was the
leader, and the team obeyed him and feared him.
That White Fang should quickly gain the post was

inevitable. He could not be satisfied with less, as Matt learned after much trouble and inconvenience. White Fang picked out the post for himself, and Matt backed his judgment with strong language after the experiment had been tried. But, though he worked in the sled in the day, White Fang did not forego the guarding of his master's property in the night. Thus he was on duty all the time, ever vigilant and faithful, the most valuable of all the dogs.

"Makin' free to spit out what's in me," Matt said one day, "I beg to state that you was a wise guy, all right, when you paid the price you did for that dog. You clean swindled Beauty Smith on top of pushin' his face in with your fist."

A recrudescence of anger glinted in Wheedon Scott's gray eyes, and he muttered savagely, "The beast!"

In the late spring a great trouble came to White Fang. Without warning the love-master disappeared. There had been warning, but White Fang was unversed in such things and did not understand the packing of a grip. He remembered afterward that the packing had preceded the master's disappearance; but at the time he suspected nothing. That night he waited for his master to return. At midnight the chill winds that blew drove him to shelter at the rear of the cabin. There he drowsed, only half asleep, his ears keyed for the first sound of the familiar step. But, at two in the morning, his anxiety drove him out to the cold front stoop, where he crouched and waited.

But no master came. In the morning the door opened and Matt stepped outside. White Fang gazed at him wistfully. There was no common speech by which he might learn what he wanted to know. The days came and went, but never the master. White Fang, who had never known sickness in his life, became sick. He became so sick that Matt was obliged to bring him inside the cabin. Also, in writing to his employer, Matt devoted a postscript to White Fang.

Wheedon Scott reading the letter, down in Circle City, came upon the following:

"That wolf won't work. Won't eat. Ain't got no spunk left. All the dogs is licking him. Wants to know what has become of you, and I don't know how to tell him. Mebbe he is going to die."

It was as Matt had said. White Fang had ceased eating; lost heart, and allowed every dog of the team to thrash him. In the cabin he lay on the floor near the stove, without interest in food, in Matt, nor in life. Matt might talk gently to him, might swear at him, it was all the same; he never did more than turn his dull eyes upon the man, then drop his head back to its customary position on his forepaws.

And then, one night, Matt, reading to himself with moving lips and mumbled sounds, was startled by a low whine from White Fang. He had got upon his feet, his ears cocked toward the door, and he was listening intently. A moment later, Matt heard a footstep. The door opened, and Wheedon Scott stepped in. The two men shook hands. Then Scott looked around the room.

"Where's the wolf?" he asked.

Then he discovered him standing where he had been lying, near the stove. He had not rushed forward after the manner of other dogs. He stood watching and waiting.

"Holy smoke!" Matt exclaimed. "Look at him wag his tail!"

Wheedon Scott strode half across the room toward him, at the same time calling him. White Fang came to him, not with a great bound, yet quickly. He was awkward from self-consciousness, but as he drew near his eyes took on a strange expression. Something, an incommunicable vastness of feeling, rose up into his eyes and shone forth.

"He never looked at me that way all the time you was gone," Matt commented.

Wheedon Scott did not hear. He was squatting down on his heels, face to face with White Fang, and petting him—rubbing at the roots of his ears, making long, caressing strokes down the neck to the shoulders, tapping the spine gently with the balls of his fingers. And White Fang was growling responsively, the crooning note of the growl more pronounced than ever.

But that was not all. What of his joy, the great love in him, ever surging and struggling to express itself, succeeded in finding a new mode of expression. He suddenly thrust his head forward and nudged his way in between his master's arm and body. And here, confined, hidden from view, all except his ears, no longer growling, he continued to nudge and snuggle.

The two men looked at each other. Scott's eyes were shining.

"Gosh!" said Matt in an awe-stricken voice.

A moment later, when he had recovered himself,

he said, "I always insisted that wolf was a dog. Look at 'm!''

With the return of the love-master, White Fang's recovery was rapid. Two nights and a day he spent in the cabin. Then he sallied forth. The sled-dogs had forgotten his prowess. They remembered only the latest, which was his sickness and weakness. At the sight of him as he came out of the cabin, they sprang upon him.

"Talk about your rough houses," Matt murmured gleefully, standing in the doorway and looking on.

White Fang did not need any encouragement. The return of the love-master was enough. Life was flowing through him again, splendid and indomitable. He fought from sheer joy, finding it an expression of much that he felt and that otherwise was without speech. There could be but one ending. The team dispersed in ignominious defeat, and it was not until after dark that the dogs came sneaking back, one by one, by meekness and humility signifying their fealty to White Fang.

Having learned to snuggle, White Fang was guilty of it often. It was the final word. He could not go beyond it. The one thing of which he had always been particularly jealous was his head. He had always disliked to have it touched. It was the wild in him, the fear of hurt and of the trap, that had given rise to the panicky impulses to avoid contacts. It was the mandate of his instinct that his head must be free. And now, with the love-master, his snuggling was the deliberate act of putting himself into a position of hopeless helplessness. It was an expression of perfect confidence, of absolute self-surrender, as though he said: "I put myself into thy hands. Work thou thy will with me."

One night, not long after the return, Scott and Matt sat at a game of cribbage preliminary to going to bed. "Fifteen-two, fifteen-four an' a pair makes six," Matt was pegging up, when there was an outcry and sound of snarling without. They looked at each other as they started to rise to their feet.

"The wolf's nailed somebody," Matt said.

A wild scream of fear and anguish hastened them.

"Bring a light!" Scott shouted, as he sprang outside. Matt followed with the lamp, and by its light they saw a man lying on his back in the snow. His arms were folded, one above the other, across his face and throat. Thus he was trying to shield himself from White Fang's teeth. And there was need for it. White Fang was in a rage, wickedly making his attack on the most vulnerable spot. From shoulder to wrist of the crossed arms, the coat sleeve, blue flannel shirt and undershirt were ripped in rags, while the arms themselves were terribly slashed and streaming blood.

All this the two men saw in the first instant. The next instant Wheedon Scott had White Fang by the throat and was dragging him clear. White Fang struggled and snarled, but made no attempt to bite, while he quickly quieted down at a sharp word from his master.

Matt helped the man to his feet. As he arose he lowered his crossed arms, exposing the bestial face of Beauty Smith. The dog-musher let go of him precipitately, with action similar to that of a man who had picked up live fire. Beauty Smith blinked in the lamplight and looked about him. He caught sight of White Fang and terror rushed into his face.

At the same moment Matt noticed two objects lying in the snow. He held the lamp close to them, indicating them with his toe for his employer's benefit—a steel dog chain and a stout club.

Wheedon Scott saw and nodded. Not a word was spoken. The dog-musher laid his hand on Beauty Smith's shoulder and faced him to the right about. No word needed to be spoken. Beauty Smith started.

In the meantime the love-master was patting White Fang and talking to him.

"Tried to steal you, eh? And you wouldn't have it! Well, well he made a mistake, didn't he?"

"Must 'a thought he had hold of seventeen devils," the dog-musher sniggered.

White Fang, still wrought up and bristling, growled and growled, the hair slowly lying down, the crooning note remote and dim, but growing in his throat.—From "White Fang."

FATHER SALVIERDERRA'S FAITH

By Helen Hunt Jackson

IT was longer than the Señora had thought it would be before Father Salvierderra arrived. The old man had grown feeble during the year that she had not seen him, and it was a very short day's journey that he could make now without too great fatigue. It was not only his body that had failed. He had lost heart; and the miles which would have been nothing to him had he walked in the companionship of hopeful and happy thoughts stretched out wearily as he brooded over sad memories and still sadder anticipations—the down-fall of the Missions, the loss of their fair estate, and the growing power of the ungodly in the land. The final decision of the United States Government in regard to the Mission lands had been a severe blow to him. He had devoutly believed that ultimate restoration of these great estates to the church was inevitable. In the long vigils which he always kept when at home at the Franciscan Monastery in Santa Barbara, kneeling on the stone pavement in the church, and praying ceaselessly from midnight till dawn, he had often had visions vouchsafed him of a new dispensation, in which the Mission establishments should be reinstated in all their old splendor and prosperity, and their Indian converts again numbered by tens of thousands.

Long after every one knew that this was impossible, he would narrate these visions with the faith of an old Bible seer, and declare that they must come true and that it was a sin to despond. But as year after year he journeyed up and down the country, seeing, at Mission after Mission, the buildings crumbled into ruin, the lands all taken, sold, resold, and settled by greedy speculators, the Indian converts disappearing, driven back to their original wildernesses, the last trace of the noble work of his order being rapidly swept away, his courage faltered, his faith died out. Changes in the manners and customs of his order itself, also, were giving him deep pain. He was a Franciscan of the same type as Francis of Assisi. To wear a shoe in place of a sandal, to take money in a purse for a journey, above all to lay aside the gray gown and cowl for any sort of secular garment, seemed to him wicked. To own comfortable clothes while there were others suffering for want of them—and there were always such—seemed to him a sin for which one might, not undeservedly, be smitten with sudden and terrible punishment. In vain the Brothers again and again supplied him with a warm cloak; he gave it away to the first beggar he met; and as for food, the refactory would have been bare, and the whole brotherhood starving, if supplies had not been carefully hidden and locked, so that Father Salvierderra could not give them away. He was fast becoming that most tragic yet often sublime sight, a man who has survived, not only his own time, but the ideas and ideals of it. Earth holds no sharper loneliness; the bitterness of exile, the anguish of friendlessness, at their utmost, are in it; and yet it is so much greater than they that even they seem small part of it.

It was with thoughts such as these that Father Salvierderra drew near the home of the Señora Moreno late in the afternoon of one of those midsummer days of which Southern California has so many in spring. The almonds had bloomed and the blossoms had fallen; the apricots also, and the peaches and pears; on all the orchards of these fruits had come a filmy tint of green, so light it was hardly a shadow on the gray. The willows were vivid light green, and the orange groves dark and glossy like laurel. The billowy hills on either

side the valley were covered with verdure and bloom
—myriads of low blossoming plants, so close to the
earth that their tints lapped and over-lapped on
each other, and on the green of the grass, as feathers in fine plumage overlap each and blend into
a changeful color.

The countless curves, hollows, and crests of the
coast-hills in Southern California heighten these
chameleon effects of the spring verdure; they are
like nothing in nature except the glitter of a brilliant lizard in the sun or the irridescent sheen of a
peacock's neck.

Father Salvierderra paused many times to gaze
at the beautiful picture. Flowers were always dear
to the Franciscans. Saint Francis himself permitted all decorations which could be made of flowers.
He classed them with his brothers and sisters, the
sun, moon and stars—all members of the sacred
choir praising god.

It was melancholy to see how, after each one of
these pauses, each fresh drinking in of the beauty
of the landscape and the balmy air, the old man resumed his slow pace, with a long sigh and his eyes
cast down. The fairer this beautiful land, the sadder to know it lost to the church—alien hands reap-
ing its fulness, establishing new customs, new laws.
All the way down the coast from Santa Barbara
he had seen, at every stopping place, new tokens of
the settling up of the country—farms opening,
towns growing; the Americans pouring in, at all
points, to reap the advantages of their new possessions. It was this which had made his journey
heavy-hearted, and made him feel, in approaching
the Señora's, as if he were coming to one of the last

sure strongholds of the Catholic faith left in the
country.

When he was within two miles of the house he
struck off from the highway into a narrow path
that he recollected led by a short cut through the
hills, and saved nearly a third of the distance. It
was more than a year since he had trod this path,
and as he found it growing fainter and fainter, and
more and more overgrown with the wild mustard,
he said to himself, "I think no one can have passed
through here this year."

As he proceeded he found the mustard thicker
and thicker. The wild mustard in Southern California is like that spoken of in the New Testament,
in the branches of which the birds of the air may
rest. Coming up out of the earth, so slender a stem
that dozens can find a starting point in an inch, it
darts up, a slender straight shoot, five, ten, twenty
feet, with hundreds of fine, feathery branches lock-
ing and interlocking with all the other hundreds
around it, till it is an inextricable network, like lace.
Then it brusts into bloom still finer, more feathery
and lace-like. The stems are so infinitesimally
small, and of so dark a green, that at a short distance they do not show, and the cloud of blossoms
seem floating in the air; at times it looks like golden
dust with a clear blue sky behind it; as it is often
seen, it looks like a golden snowstorm. The plant
is a tyrant and a nuisance—the enemy of the farmer; it takes riotous possession of a whole field in a
season; once in, never out; for one plant this year,
a million next; but it is impossible to wish that the
land were freed from it. Its gold is as distinct a
value to the eye as the nugget gold is in the pocket.

Father Salvierderra soon found himself in a veritable thicket of these delicate branches, high above his head, and so interlaced that he could make headway only by slowly and patiently disentangling them, as one would disentangle a skein of silk. It was a fantastic sort of dilemma, and not unpleasing. Except that the Father was in haste to reach his journey's end, he would have enjoyed threading his way through the golden meshes. Suddenly he heard faint notes of singing. He paused, listened. It was the voice of a woman. It was slowly drawing nearer, apparently from the direction in which he was going. At intervals it ceased abruptly, then began again, as if by a sudden but brief interruption, like that made by question and answer. Then, peering ahead through the mustard blossoms, he saw them waving and bending, and heard sounds as if they were being broken. Evidently some one entering on the path from the opposite end had been caught in the fragrant thicket as he was. The notes grew clearer, though still low and sweet as the twilight notes of the thrush; the mustard branches waved more and more violently; light steps were now to be heard. Father Salvierderra stood still as one in a dream, his eyes straining forward into the golden mist of blossoms.

"Ramona!" exclaimed the Father, his thin cheeks flushing with pleasure. "The blessed child." And as he spoke, her face came in sight set in a swaying frame of the branches, as she parted them lightly to right and left with her hands, and half crept, half danced through the loophole thus made. Ramona's beauty was of the sort to be best enhanced by the waving gold which now framed her face. She had just enough of olive tint in her complexion to under-lie and enrich it without making it swarthy. Her hair was like her Indian mother's, heavy and black, but her eyes were like her father's, steel blue. Only those who came very near to Ramona knew, however, that her eyes were blue, for the heavy, black eyebrows and long, black lashes so shaded and shadowed them that they looked black as night. At the same instant that Father Salvierderra first caught sight of her face Ramona also saw him, and crying out joyfully, "Ah, Father, I knew you would come by this path, and something told me you were near!" she sprang forward, and sank on her knees before him, bowing her head for his blessing. In silence he laid his hand on her brow. It would not have been easy for him to speak to her at that first moment. She had looked to the devout old monk, as she sprang through the cloud of golden flowers, the sun falling on her bared head, her cheeks flushed, her eyes shining, more like an apparition of an angle or saint than like the flesh-and-blood maiden whom he had carried in his arms when she was a babe.— From "Ramona."

"TWO BITS"

BY SHARLOTT M. HALL

WHERE the shimmering sands of the desert
    beat
  In waves to the foothills' rugged line,
And cat-claw and cactus and brown mesquite
  Elbow the cedar and mountain pine;
Under the dip of a wind-swept hill,
  Like a little gray hawk Ft. Whipple clung;
The fort was a pen of peeled pine logs,
  And forty troopers the army strong.

At the very gates when the darkness fell,
  Prowling Mohave and Yavapai
Signaled with shrill coyote yell,
  Or mocked the night owl's piercing cry;
Till once when the guard turned shuddering
  For a trace in the east of the welcome dawn,
Spent, wounded, a courier reeled to his feet—
  "Apaches—rising—Wingate—warn!"

"And half the troop at the Date Creek Camp!"
  The captain muttered, "Those devils heard!"
White-lipped he called for a volunteer
  To ride Two Bits and carry the word:
"Alone—it's a game of hide and seek;
  One man may win where ten would fail;"
Himself the saddle and cinches set
  And headed Two Bits for the Verde trail.

Two Bits! How his still eyes woke to the chase!
  The bravest soul of them all was he;
Hero of many a hard-won race,
  With a hundred scars for his pedigree;
Wary of ambush and keen of trail,
  Old in wisdom of march and fray,
And the grizzled veteran seemed to know
  The lives that hung on his hoofs that day.

"A week—God speed you and make it less!
  Ride by night from the river on;"
Caps were swung in a silent cheer,
  A quick salute and the word was gone
Sunrise, threading the Point of Rocks;
  Dusk in the cañons dark and grim—
Where, coiled like a flung thread 'round the cliffs,
  The trail crawls up to the frowning Rim.

A pebble turned, a spark out-struck
  From steel-shod hoof on the treacherous flint—
Ears wait, eyes strain, in the rocks above,
  For the faintest whisper, the farthest glint;
But shod with silence and robed with night
  They pass untracked, and mile by mile
The hills divide for the flying fleet,
  And the stars lean low to guide the while.

Never a plumed quail hid her nest
  With the stealthiest care a mother may,
As crouched at dawn in the chaparral
  These two whom a heart beat might betray;

So hiding and riding night by night;
    Four days and the end of the riding near;
The fort just hid in the distant hills—
    But hist! A whisper, a breath of fear!

They wheel and turn—too late! Ping! Ping!
    From their very feet a fiery jet;
A lurch, a plunge, and the brave old horse
    Leaped out with his broad breast torn and wet.
Ping! Thud! on his neck the rider swayed;
    (Ten thousand deaths if he reeled and fell!)
Behind, exultant, the painted horde
    Swooped down like a skirmish line from Hell.

Not yet! Not yet! Those ringing hoofs
    Have scarred their triumph on many a course;
And the desperate, blood-trailed chase swept on,
    Apache sinews 'gainst wounded horse;
Hour crowding hour till the yells died back,
    Till the pat of the moccasined feet was gone,
And dumb to heeding of foe or fear
    The rider dropped but the horse kept on.

Stiff and stumbling and spent and sore,
    Plodding the rough miles doggedly,
Till the daybreak bugles of Wingate rang
    And a faint neigh answered the reveille;
Wide swung the gate; a wounded horse—
    Red-dabbled pouches and riding gear—
A shout, a hurry, a quick-flung word—
    And Boots and Saddles rang sharp and clear.

14

Like a stern commander the old horse turned
  As the troop filed out, and straight at the head
He guided them back on that weary trail
  Till he fell by his fallen rider, dead;
But the man and the message saved! and he
  Whose brave heart carried the double load—
With his last trust kept and his last race won
  They buried him there on the Wingate road.

—From "Out West Magazine."

["Two Bits," an old racer, was, in his day, the fastest
and the longest-winded horse in Arizona. He belonged at
the time to Lieut. Chas. Curtis (now Capt. Curtis, at the
University of Wisconsin), who built the first stockade on
the present site of Ft. Whipple, A. T. The episode is
true, even to the old horse leading the soldiers back to
his fallen rider. The man lived; but "Two Bits" died of
his wounds, and is buried under a heap of stones beside
the overland road a few miles west of Ft. Wingate, N. M.
The ride was about 250 miles.—Ed.]

FERNS AND FERNERIES

By Belle Sumner Angier

BEFORE planting your out-of-door retreat for
ferns, if you may not go into the hills and
study your plan from Nature at least put yourself
in the right mental attitude by reading some of
the beautiful stories of wild woods life such as are
written by Burroughs, or Mabie, or Van Dyke, and
I am sure your results will be far more satisfactory.

Now as to how, and where, and what to plant.
When it is considered that of the adiantum alone
there are over eighty species and that of the three
great divisions of the fern family there are hun-

dreds of forms known as decorative plants, it would seem that a choice might be difficult, but in California for out-of-door planting the selection of ferns for a fernery may be summed up in this way: Avoid so-called hardy Northern ferns, because they do not like our dry air and have too long a period of sleep. On the contrary, seek for the fern of tropical or warm countries and help them adapt themselves to our conditions.

Now all ferns like about the same treatment in a general sort of way—leaf-mold, loam and silver sand. There it is in a nutshell, but, as you know from observing the habits of our native ferns, some seek shallow soil under the rocks, some like a little clay, some grow on the edge of the water, while others like to be well drained. In building a rockery for ferns, a north side is all right, but there must be some light, as, while the direct rays burn, yet the fern must have warmth. Avoid sour or heavy soil. Plenty of good loam, then your rocks, selected, if possible, with an eye to their artistic and picturesque arrangement; then, after building them together, scatter your mixture of loam and leaf-mold about in the crevices, and place your ferns. Wind is not desirable any more than sun, and, of course, frost must be provided against.

The Japanese fern-balls, so much used on this coast, are of the Japanese climbing fern, and are gathered from the trees and wound about balls of moss. No one in this country has been really successful in imitating the Japanese in making these balls. Sometimes the Japs get overeager to get their balls to market and do not let them lie dormant long enough, and then the florist who imports them has many complaints registered about the poor foliage of the ball. They should properly be allowed to remain dormant from October to January each year, and in this way can be used for three or four years successfully. When received here they are dormant, and require about six weeks of sprinkling to bring them to perfection.

I have seen our native ferns used after the same manner by taking the roots, carefully washing from them all the sand, then binding on the exterior of an ''olla,'' or Mexican porous water-jar. Use a black thread to bind with, and do not be sparing of the roots. The natural seepage of the water through the porous jar will soon start the delicate green and your cool drink will taste all the fresher and cooler for the suggestive surroundings.—From ''The Garden Book of California.''

THE WHEAT

By FRANK NORRIS

AN hour after daylight the next morning the work was resumed. After breakfast Vanamee, riding one horse and leading the others, had returned to the line of ploughs together with the other drivers. Now he was busy harnessing the team. At the division blacksmith shop—temporarily put up—he had been obliged to wait while one of his lead horses was shod, and he had thus been delayed quite five minutes. Nearly all the other teams were harnessed, the drivers on their seats, waiting for the foreman's signal.

"All ready here?" inquired the foreman, driving up to Vanamee's team in his buggy.

"All ready, sir," answered Vanamee, buckling the last strap.

He climbed to his seat, shaking out the reins and, turning about, looked back along the line, then all around him at the landscape inundated with the brilliant glow of the early morning.

The day was fine. Since the first rain of the season there had been no other. Now the sky was without a cloud, pale blue, delicate luminous, scintillating with morning. The great brown earth turned a huge flank to it, exhaling the moisture of the early dew. The atmosphere, washed clean of dust and mist, was translucent as crystal. Far off to the east the hills on the other side of Broderson Creek stood out against the pallid saffron of the horizon as flat and as sharply outlined as if pasted on the sky. The campanile of the ancient Mission of San Juan seemed as fine as frost work. All about between the horizons the carpet of the land unrolled itself to infinity. But now it was no longer parched with heat, cracked and warped by a merciless sun, powdered with dust. The rain had done its work; not a clod that was not swollen with fertility, not a fissure that did not exhale the sense of fecundity. One could not take a dozen steps upon the ranches without the brusque sensation that under foot the land was alive—roused at last from its sleep, palpitating with the desire of reproduction.

The plows, thirty-five in number, each drawn by its team of ten, stretched in an interminable line, nearly a quarter of a mile in length, behind

and ahead of Vanamee. They were arranged, as
it were, *en echelon,* not in file—not one directly behind the other, but each succeeding plow its own
width farther in the field than the one in front of
it. Each of these plows held five shears, so that
when the entire company was in motion, one hundred and seventy-five furrows were made at the
same instant. At a distance the plows resembled
a great column of field artillery. Each driver was
in his place, his glance alternating between his
horses and the foreman nearest at hand. Other
foremen, in their buggies or buckboards, were at
intervals along the line, like battery lieutenants.
Annixter himself, on horseback, in boots and campaign hat, a cigar in his teeth, overlooked the
scene.

The division superintendent, on the opposite
side of the line, galloped past to a position at the
head. For a long moment there was a silence. A
sense of preparedness ran from end to end of the
column. All things were ready, each man in his
place. The day's work was about to begin.

Suddenly from a distance at the head of the line
came the shrill trilling of a whistle. At once the
foreman nearest Vanamee repeated it, at the same
time turning down the line and waving one arm.
The signal was repeated, whistle answering whistle,
till the sounds lost themselves in the distance. At
once the line of plows lost its immobility, moving
forward, getting slowly under way, the horses
straining in the traces. A prolonged movement
rippled from team to team, disengaging in its passage a multitude of sounds—the click of buckles,
the creak of straining leather, the subdued clash of

machinery, the cracking of whips, the deep breathing of nearly four hundred horses, the abrupt commands and cries of the drivers, and last of all the prolonged, soothing murmur of the thick, brown earth turning steadily from the multitude of advancing shears.

The ploughing thus commenced continued. The sun rose higher. Steadily the hundred iron hands kneaded and furrowed and stroked the brown, humid earth, the hundred iron teeth bit deep into the Titan's flesh. Perched on his seat, the moist living reins slipping and tugging in his hands, Vanamee, in the midst of this steady confusion of constantly varying sensation, sight interrupted by sound, sound mingling with sight, on this swaying, vibrating seat, quivering with the prolonged thrill of the earth, lapsed to a sort of pleasing numbness, in a sense hypnotized by the weaving maze of things in which he found himself involved. To keep his team at an even, regular gait, maintaining the precise interval, to run his furrows as closely as possible to those already made by the plow in front—this for the moment was the entire sum of his duties.

The ploughing, now in full swing, enveloped him in a vague, slow-moving whirl of things. Underneath him was the jarring, jolting, trembling machine; not a clod was turned, not an obstacle encountered, that he did not receive the swift impression of it through all his body; the very friction of the damp soil, sliding incessantly from the shiny surface of the shears, seemed to reproduce itself in his finger tips and along the back of his head. He heard the horse hoofs by the myriads crushing

down easily, deeply into the loam; the prolonged
clinking of trace-chains; the working of the smooth,
brown flanks in the harness; the clatter of wooden
hames; the champing of bits; the click of iron shoes
against the pebbles; the brittle stubble of the surface ground crackling and snapping as the furrows turned; the sonorous, steady breaths wrenched
from the deep-laboring chests, strap-bound, shining
with sweat, and all along the line the voices of the
men talking to the horses. Everywhere there were
visions of glossy brown backs, straining, heaving,
swollen with muscle; harness streaked with specks
of froth; broad, cup-shaped hoofs heavy with
brown loam; men's faces red with tan; blue over-
alls spotted with axle grease; muscled hands, the
knuckles whitened in their grip on the reins, and
through it all the ammoniacal smell of the horses,
the bitter reek of perspiration of beasts and men,
the aroma of warm leather, the scent of dead stubble—and, stronger and more penetrating than everything else, the heavy, enervating odor of the up-
turned, living earth.

At intervals, from the tops of one of the rare,
low swells of the land, Vanamee overlooked a
wider horizon. On the other divisions of Quien
Sabe the same work was in progress. Occasionally
he could see another column of plows in an adjoin-
ing division—sometimes so close at hand that the
subdued murmur of its movements reached his ear;
sometimes so distant that it resolved itself into a
long, brown streak upon the gray of the ground.
Farther off to the west on the Osterman ranch
other columns came and went, and once, from the
crest of the highest swell on his division, Vanamee

caught a distant glimpse of the Broderson ranch. There, too, moving specks indicated that the plowing was under way. And farther away still, far off there beyond the fine line of the horizons over the curve of the globe, the shoulder of the earth, he knew were other ranches, and beyond these others, and beyond these still others, the immensities multiplying to infinity.

Everywhere throughout the great San Joaquin, unseen and unheard, a thousand plows up-stirred the lands, tens of thousands of shears clutched deep into the warm, moist earth.

From time to time the gang in which Vanamee worked halted on the signal from foreman or overseer. The horses came to a standstill, the vague clamor of the work lapsed away. Then the minutes passed. The whole work hung suspended. All up and down the line one demanded what had happened. The division superintendent galloped past, perplexed and anxious. For the moment one of the plows was out of order, a bolt had slipped, a lever refused to work, or a machine had become immobilized in heavy ground, or a horse had lamed himself. Once, even, toward noon, an entire plow was taken out of line, so out of gear that a messenger had to be sent to the division forge to summon the machinist.

At half-past twelve Vanamee and the rest of the drivers ate their lunch in the field, the tin buckets having been distributed to them that morning after breakfast. But in the evening the routine of the previous day was repeated, and Vanamee, unharnessing his team, riding one horse and leading the others, returned to the division barns and bunk-house.

*   *   *   *   *   *   *   *

The brown earth, smooth, unbroken, was a limit-less, mud-colored ocean. The silence was profound. Then, at length, Annixter's searching eye made out a blur on the horizon to the northward; the blur concentrated itself to a speck; the speck grew by steady degrees to a spot, slowly moving, a note of dull color, barely darker than the land, but an inky black silhouette as it topped a low rise of ground and stood for a moment outlined against the pale blue of the sky. Annixter turned his horse from the road and rode across the ranch land to meet this new object of interest. There were horses in the column. At first glance it appeared as if there were nothing else—a riderless squadron tramping steadily over the up-turned plowed land of the ranch. But it drew nearer. The horses were in lines, six-abreast, harnessed to machines. The noise increased; defined itself. There was a shout or two; occasionally a horse blew through his nostrils with a prolonged, vibrating snort. The click and click of metal work was incessant, the machines throwing off a continual rattle of wheels and cogs and clashing springs. The column approached nearer; was close at hand. The noises mingled to a subdued uproar, a bewildering confusion; the impact of innumerable hoofs was a veritable rumble. Machine after machine appeared, and Annixter, drawing to one side, remained for nearly ten minutes watching and interested, while, like an array of chariots—clattering, jostling, creaking, clashing an interminable procession, machine succeeding machine, six-horse team succeeding six-horse team—bustling, hurried—Magnus Derrick's thirty-three grain drills, each with its eight hoes, went clamoring past, like an advance of military, seeding the ten thousand acres of the great ranch.

When the drills had passed, Annixter turned and rode back to the Lower road, over the land now thick with seed. Now there was nothing to do but wait, while the seed silently germinated; nothing to do but watch for the wheat to come up.

*　　*　　*　　*　　*　　*　　*　　*

Now it was almost day. The east glowed opalescent. All about him Annixter saw the land inundated with light. But there was a change. Overnight something had occurred. In his perturbation the change seemed to him, at first, elusive, almost fanciful, unreal. But now, as the light spread he looked again at the gigantic scroll of ranch lands unrolled before him from edge to edge of the horizon. The change was not fanciful. The change was real. The earth was no longer bare. The land was no longer barren—no longer empty, no longer dull brown. All at once Annixter shouted aloud.

There it was, the Wheat, the Wheat! The little seed, long planted, germinating in the deep, dark furrows of the soil, straining, swelling, suddenly in one night had come upward to the light. The wheat had come up. It was there before him, around him, everywhere, illimitable, immeasurable. The winter brownness of the ground was overlaid with a little shimmer of green. The promise of the sowing was being fulfilled. The earth, the loyal mother, who never failed, who never disappointed, was keeping her faith again. Once more the strength of nations was renewed. Once more the force of the world was revivified.

*   *   *   *   *   *   *   *

The California summer lay blanketwise and smothering over all the land. The hills, bone-dry, were browned and parched. The grasses and wild-oats, sear and yellow, snapped like glass filaments under foot. The roads, the bordering fences, even the lower leaves and branches of the trees, were thick and gray with dust. All color had been burned from the landscape, except in the irrigated patches, that in the waste of brown and dull yellow glowed like oases.

The wheat, close now to maturity, had turned from pale yellow to golden yellow and from that to brown. Like a gigantic carpet it spread itself over all the land. There was nothing else to be seen but the limitless sea of wheat as far as the eye could reach; dry, rustling, crisp and harsh in the rare breaths of hot winds out of the southeast—and now the harvesting begins.

The sprocket adjusted, the engineer called up the gang and the men took their places. The fireman stoked vigorously, the two sack-sewers resumed their posts on the sacking platform, putting on the goggles that kept the chaff from their eyes. The separator-man and head-man gripped their levers.

The harvester, shooting a column of thick smoke straight upward, vibrating to the top of the stack, hissed, clanked, and lurched forward. Instantly motion sprang to life in all its component parts;

the header knives, cutting a thirty-six foot swath,
gnashed like teeth; beltings slid and moved like
smooth-flowing streams; the separator whirred; the
agitator jarred and crashed; cylinders, augers,
fans, seeders and elevators, drapers and chaff-car-
riers clattered, rumbled, buzzed and clanged. The
steam hissed and rasped; the ground reverberated
a hollow note, and the thousands upon thousands
of wheat stalks, sliced and slashed in the clashing
shears of the header, rattled like dry rushes in a
hurricane, as they fell inward and were caught up
by an endless belt, to disappear into the bowels of
the vast brute that devoured them.

Without an instant's pause, a thick rivulet of
wheat rolled and dashed tumultuous into the sack.
In half a minute—sometimes in twenty seconds—the
sack was full, was passed over to the second sewer,
the mouth reeved up and the sack dumped out upon
the ground, to be picked up by the wagons and
hauled to the railroad.

All that shrieking, bellowing machinery, all that
gigantic organism, all the months of labor, the
plowing, the planting, the prayers for rain, the
years of preparation, the heartaches, the anxiety,
the foresight, all the whole business of the ranch,
the work of the horses, of steam, of men and boys,
looked to this spot—the grain chute from the harvester into the sacks. Its volume was the index of
failure or success, of riches or poverty. At this
point the labor of the rancher ended. Here at the
lip of the chute, he parted company with his grain,
and from here the wheat streamed forth to feed the
world. The yawning mouths of the sacks might
well stand for the unnumbered mouths of the peo-

ple, all agape for food; and here, into these sacks, at first so lean, so flaccid, attenuated like starved stomachs, rushed the living stream of food, insistent, interminable, filling the empty, fattening the shriveled, making it sleek and heavy and solid.— From ''The Octopus.''

NIGHTTIME IN CALIFORNIA

By A. J. Waterhouse

NIGHTTIME in California. There's nothing like it found,
Though to and fro you come and go and journey earth around.
The skies are like a crystal sea, with islands made of stars;
The moon's a fairy ship that sails among its shoals and bars;
And on that sea I sit and look, and wonder where it ends;
If I shall sail its phantom wave, and where the journey tends,
And if—in vain I wonder; let's change the solemn theme,
For the nights of California were made for man to dream.

Nighttime in California. The cricket's note is heard,
And now, perhaps, the twitter of a drowsy, dreaming bird.

An oar is plashing yonder; the wakeful frogs re-
    ply.
The breeze is chanting in the trees a ghostly lul-
    laby.
The moon has touched with silver the peaceful,
    sleeping world,
And in the weary soul of man the flag of sorrow's
    furled.
'Tis a time for smiles and music; 'tis a time for
    love divine,
For the nights of California are Heav'n this side
    the line.

Nighttime in California.   Elsewhere men only
    guess
At the glory of the evenings that are perfect—
    nothing less;
But here the nights, returning, are the wondrous
    gifts of God—
As if the days were maidens fair with golden slip-
    pers shod.
There is no cloud to hide the sky; the universe is
    ours,
And the starlight likes to look and laugh in Cupid-
    haunted bowers.
Oh, the restful, peaceful evenings! In them my
    soul delights,
For God loved California when He gaves to her
    her nights.

—From "Some Homely Little Songs."

A SON OF COPPER SIN

By Herman Whitaker

WITHIN his bull's-hide tepee, old Iz-le-roy lay
and fed his little fire, stick by stick.   He
was sick, very sick—sick with the sickness which is
made up of equal parts of hunger, old age, fever
and despair.   Just one week before his tribe had
headed up for Winnipegoos, where the whitefish
may be had for the taking and the moose winter
in their yards.   But a sick man may not travel the
long trail, so Iz-le-roy had remained at White
Man's Lake.   And Batiste, his son, stayed also.
Not that it was expected of him, for, according to
forest law, the man who cannot hunt had better
die; but Batiste had talked with the gentle priest
of Ellice, and had chosen to depart from the custom of his fathers.

And things had gone badly, very badly, since
the tribe had marched.   North, south, east and
west, the round of the plains, and through the leaf-
less woods, the boy had hunted without as much as
a jack-rabbit falling to his gun.   For two days no
food had passed their lips, and now he was gone
forth to do that which Iz-le-roy had almost rather
die than have him do—ask aid of the settlers.

"Yea, my son," the old warrior had faltered,
"these be they that stole the prairies of our fathers.   Yet it may be that Big Laugh, best of an evil
brood, will give us of his store of flour and bacon."

So, after placing a plentiful stock of wood close

[By permission of Messrs. Harper & Brothers.]

to the old man's hand, Batiste had closed the tepee flap and laced it. At the end of an hour's fast walking, during which the northern sky grew dark with the threat of still more cruel weather, he sighted through the drift a spurting column of smoke.

The smoke marked the cabin of John Sterling, and also his present occupation. Within, John sat and fired the stove, while Avis, his daughter, set out the breakfast dishes, and his wife turned the sizzling bacon in the pan.

"I declare," exclaimed the woman, pausing, knife in hand, "if that bread ain't froze solid!"

"Cold last night," commented Sterling. "Put it in the oven, Mary."

As she stooped to obey, the door quietly opened and Batiste slipped in. His moose moccasins made no noise, and he was standing close beside her when she straightened. She jumped and gasped:

"Lor' 'a' mercy! How you do scare one! Why don't you knock?"

Batiste stared. It was the custom of his tribe thus to enter a house—a custom established before jails were built or locks invented. His eye therefore roamed questioningly from one to another until Sterling asked:

"What d' want, young fellow?"

Batiste pointed to the frying-pan. "Ba-kin!" he muttered. "The ba-kin of Big Laugh, I want. Iz-le-roy sick, plenty sick. Him want flour, him want ba-kin."

The thought of his father's need flashed into his mind, and, realizing the impossibility of expressing himself in English, he broke into a voluble stream

15

of Cree, punctuating its rolling gutterals with energetic signs. While he was speaking, Avis ceased rattling her dishes.

"He looks awfully hungry, dad," she whispered as Batiste finished.

Now, though Sterling was a large-souled, generous man, and jovial—as evidenced by his name of Big Laugh—it happened that, during the past summer, a roving band of Sioux had camped hard by and begged him out of patience. That morning, too, the threatening weather had spoiled an intended trip to Russel and touched his temper—of which he had a goodly share.

"Can't help it, girl," he snapped. "If we feed every hungry Injun that comes along, we'll soon be out of house and home. Can't do anything for you, boy."

"Him want ba-kin," Batiste said.

"Well, you can just want."

"Iz-le-roy sick, him want ba-kin," the boy pleaded.

His persistence irritated Sterling, and, crowding down the better feeling which spoke for the lad, he sprang up, threw wide the door, and shouted:

"Get, you son of copper sin! Get, now! Quick!"

"Father!" pleaded the girl.

But he took no heed, and held wide the door.

Into Batiste's face flashed surprise, anger and resentment. Surprise, because he had not believed all the things Iz-le-roy had told him of the white men, but had preferred to think them all like Father Francis. But now? His father was right. They were all cold and merciless, their hearts hard as their steel ax-heads, their tongues sharp as the cutting edge. With head held high he marched through the door, away from the hot stove, the steaming coffee, and the delicious smell of frying bacon, out into the cold storm.

"Oh, father!" remonstrated his wife as Sterling closed the door.

"Look here, Mary," he answered testily. "We fed a whole tribe last summer, didn't we?"

"But this lad don't belong to them," she pleaded.

"All the worse," he rejoined. "Do an Injun a good turn an' he never forgets. Give him his breakfast, an' he totes his tribe along to dinner."

"Well," sighed the good woman, "I'm real sorry."

For a few moments both were silent. And presently, as the man's kindly nature began to triumph over his irritation, he hitched uneasily in his chair. Already he felt ashamed. Casting a sheepish glance at his wife, he rose, walked to the door, and looked out. But a wall of whirling white blocked his vision—Batiste was gone beyond recall.

"Where's Avis?" he asked, returning to the stove.

"A-vis!" called her mother.

But there was no answer. For a moment man and wife stared each other in the eye; then, moved by a common impulse, they walked into the kitchen. There, on the table, lay the half of a fresh-cut side of bacon; the bread-box was open and a crusty loaf missing; the girl's shawl was gone from its peg and her overshoes from their corner.

"Good God!" gasped the settler. "The child's gone after him!"

16

They knew the risk. All the morning the storm had been brewing, and now it thundered by, a veritable blizzard. The blizzard! King of storms! It compels the settler to string a wire from house to stables, it sets men to circling in the snow, it catches little children coming home from school and buries them in its monstrous drifts.

Without another word Sterling wound a scarf about his neck, grabbed his badger mitts, and rushed outside.

When Avis softly closed the kitchen door she could just see Batiste rounding a bluff that lay a furlong west of her father's stables. She started after him; but by the time she had covered half the distance a sea of white swept in between and blotted him from view.

She struggled on, and on, and still on, until, in spite of the seventy degrees of frost, the perspiration burst from every pore and the scud melted on her glowing face. This was well enough—so long as she kept moving; but when the time came that she must stop, she would freeze all the quicker for her present warmth.

This, being born and bred of the prairie, Avis knew, and the knowledge kept her toiling, toiling on, until her tired legs and leaden feet compelled a pause in the shelter of a bluff. She was hungry, too. All this time she carried the bread and meat, and now, unconscious of a pair of slant eyes which glared from a willow thicket, she broke the loaf and began to eat. While she ate, the green lights in the eyes flared brighter, a long red tongue licked the drool from grinning jaws, and forth from his covert stole a lank, gray wolf.

'Avis uttered a startled cry. This was no coyote, to be chased with a stick, but a wolf of timber stock, a great beast, heavy, prick-eared, strong as a mastiff. His nose puckered in a wicked snarl as he slunk in half-circles across her front. He was undecided. So, while he circled, trying to make up his mind, drawing a little nearer at every turn, Avis fell back—back towards the bluff, keeping her white face always to the creeping beast.

It was a small bluff, lacking a tree large enough to climb, but sufficient for her purpose. On its edge she paused, threw the bacon to the wolf, and then ran desperately. Once clear of the scrub, she ran on, plunging through drifts, stumbling, falling, to rise again and push her flight. Of direction she took no heed; her only thought was to place distance between herself and the red-mouthed brute. But when, weary and breathless, she paused for rest, out of the drab drift stole the lank, gray shadow.

The brute crouched a few yards away, licking his sinful lips, winking his devil eyes. She still had the loaf. As she threw it, the wolf sprang and snapped it in mid-air. Then she ran, and ran, and ran, as the tired doe runs from the hounds. For what seemed to her an interminable time, though it was less than five minutes, she held on; then stopped, spent, unable to take another step. Looking back, she saw nothing of the wolf; but just when she began to move slowly forward, thinking he had given up the chase, a grap shape loomed right ahead.

Uttering a bitter cry, she turned once more, tottered a few steps, and fainted.

As, wildly calling his daughter's name, Sterling rushed by his stables, the wind smote him with tremendous power. Like a living thing it buffeted him about the ears, tore at his breath, poured over him an avalanche of snow. Still he pressed on and gained the bluff which Avis missed.

As he paused to draw a free breath, his eye picked out a fresh-made track. Full of a sudden hope, he shouted. A voice answered, and as he rushed eagerly forward a dark figure came through the drift to meet him. It was Batiste.

"What do you want?" he asked.

Sterling was cruelly disappointed, but he answered quickly: "You see my girl? Yes, my girl," he repeated, noting the lad's look of wonder. "Young white squaw, you see um?"

"Mooniah papoose?" queried Batiste.

"Yes, yes! She follow you. Want give you bread, want give you bacon. All gone, all lost!" Sterling finished with a despairing gesture.

"Squaw marche to me? Ba-kin for me?" questioned Batiste.

"Yes, yes!" crief Sterling, in a flurry of impatience.

"I find um," he said, softly.

Briefly Batiste laid down his plan, eking out his scanty English with vivid signs. In snow, the white man rolls along like a clumsy buffalo, planting his feet far out to the right and left. And because his right leg steps a little further than the left, he always, when lost, travels in a circle. Wherefore Batiste indicated that they should move along parallel lines, just shouting distance apart, so as to cover the largest possible ground.

"Young squaw marche slow. She there!" He pointed north and east with a gesture. "Yes, there!"

Batiste paused until Sterling got his distance; then, keeping the wind slanting to his left cheek, he moved off north and east. Ever and anon he stopped to give forth a piercing yell. If Sterling answered, he moved on; if not—as happened twice —he traveled in his direction until they were once more in touch. And so, shouting and yelling, they bore off north and east for a long half-hour.

After that, Batiste began to throw his cries both east and west, for he judged that they must be closing on the girl. And suddenly, from the north, came a weird, tremulous answer. He started, and throwing up his head, emitted the wolf's long howl. Leaning forward, he waited—his very soul in his ears—until, shrill yet deep-chested and quivering with ferocity, came back the answering howl.

No coyote gave forth that cry, and Batiste knew it.

"Timber wolf!" he muttered.

Turning due north, he gave the settler a warning yell, then sped like a hunted deer in the direction of the cry. He ran with the long, lithe lope which tires down even the swift elk, and in five minutes covered nearly a mile. Once more he gave forth the wolf howl. An answer came from close by, but as he sprang forward it ended with a frightened yelp. Through a break in the drift he spied a moving figure; then a swirl swept in and blotted it from view.

But he had seen the girl. A dozen leaps and he

was close upon her. Just as he opened his mouth
to speak, she screamed and plunged headlong.

When consciousness returned, Avis was lying in
her own bed. Her mother bent over her; Sterling
stood near by. All around were the familiar things
of life, but her mind still retained a vivid picture
of her flight, and she sprang up screaming:

"The wolf; oh, the wolf!"

"Hush, dearie," her mother soothed. "It wasn't
a wolf, but just the Cree boy."

Batiste had told how she screamed at the sight
of his gray, snow-covered blanket, and the cry had
carried even to her father. But when she recovered sufficiently to tell her story, the father shud-
dered and the mother exclaimed:

"John, we owe that boy more than we can ever
pay!"

"We do!" he fervently agreed.

Just then the latch of the other door clicked, and
a cold blast streamed into the bedroom. Jumping
up, the mother cried:

"Run, John; he's going!"

"Here, young fellow!" shouted the settler.

Batiste paused in the doorway, his hand on the
latch, his slight body silhouetted against the white
of the storm.

"Where you going, boy?"

"To Iz-le-roy," he answered. "Him sick.
Bezhou!"

Sterling strode forward and caught him by the
shoulder. "No, you don't," he said—"not that
way." Then, turning, he called into the bedroom:
"Here, mother! Get out all your wraps while I

hitch the ponies. And fix up our best bed for a sick man.''—From ''The Probationer.''

OCTOBER CLOUDS

By Mary B. Williams

WITH fold on fold in quiet rest
The gray clouds lie along the west—
In sweet repose they lie,
While overhead they sail away
Like phantom ships on a placid bay—
Like ships they sail on high.

And in and out through rifts of blue,
The gray ships tipped in silver hue,
Now idly float along;
And tiny clouds in northern sky
Like flocks of birds prepared to fly
To southland, home of song.

And herd on herd in glowing east,
With here and there a straggling beast,
O'er pastures blue they rove;
Their shining sides are flecked with gold,
They number o'er a thousand fold—
A countless herd they move.

And in the south white domes arise,
Cathedral spires pierce the skies,
And hanging gardens fair,
And palaces in grandeur stand
In ether blue above the land—
My castles in the air.

But what are all these visions grand,
Unless I see the Pilot's hand,
   That sails my cloud-ships by,
Or folds them on the mountain crest,
And keeps them there at perfect rest,
   Along the western sky?

HUMMERS

By FLORENCE A. MERRIAM

CALIFORNIA is the land of flowers and hum-ming-birds. Humming-birds are there the winged companions of the flowers. In the valleys the airy bird hovers about the filmy golden mustard and the sweet-scented primroses; on the blooming hillsides in spring the air is filled with whirring wings and piping voices, as the fairy troops pass and repass at their mad gambols. At one moment the birds are circling methodically around the whorls of the blue sage; at the next hurtling through the air after a distant companion. The great wild gooseberry bushes with red fuchsia-like flowers are like beehives, swarming with noisy hummers. The whizzing and whirring lead one to the bushes from a distance, and on approaching one is met by the brown spindle-like birds, darting out from the blooming shrubs, gleams of gold, green and scarlet glancing from their gorgets.

The large brown hummers probably stop in the valley only on their way north, but the little black-chinned ones make their home there, and the big spreading sycamores and the great live oaks are their nesting grounds. In the big oak beside the ranch house I have seen two or three nests at once; and a ring of live oaks in front of the house held a complement of nests. From the hammock under the oak beside the house one could watch the birds at their work. If the front door was left open, the hummers would sometimes fly inside; and as we stepped out they often darted away from the flowers growing under the windows.

California is the best of all places to study humming-birds. The only drawback is that there are always too many other birds to watch at the same time; but one sees enough to want to see more. I never saw a humming-bird courtship, unless—perhaps one performance I saw was part of the wooing. I was sitting on Mountain Billy under the little lover's sycamore when a buzzing and whirring sounded overhead. On a twig sat a wee green lady and before her was her lover (?), who, with the sound and regularity of a spindle in a machine, swung shuttling from side to side in an arc less than a yard long. He never turned around, or took his eyes off his lady's, but threw himself back at the end of his line by a quick spread of his tail. She sat with her eyes fixed upon him, and as he moved from side to side her long bill followed him in a very droll way. When through with his dance he looked at her intently, as if to see what effect his performance had had upon her. She made some remark, apparently not to his liking, for when he had answered he flew away. She called after him, but as he did not return she stretched herself and flew up on a twig above with an amusing air of relief.

This is all I have ever seen of the courtship; but when it comes to nest-building, I have often been an eyewitness to that. One little acquaintance made a nest of yellow down and put it among the green oak leaves, making me think that the laws of protective coloration had no weight with her, but before the eggs were laid she had neatly covered the yellow with flakes of green lichen. I found her one day sitting in the sun with the top of her head as white as though she had been diving into the flour barrel. Here was one of the wonderful cases of "mutual help" in nature. The flowers supply insects and honey to the humming-birds, and they, in turn, as they fly from blossom to blossom, probing the tubes with the long slender bills that have gradually come to fit the shape of the tubes, brush off the pollen of one blossom to carry it on to the next, so enabling the plants to perfect their flowers as they could not do without help. It is said that, in proportion to their numbers, humming-birds assist as much as insects in the work of cross-fertilization.

Though this little hummer that I was watching let me come within a few feet of her, when a lizard ran under her bush she craned her neck and looked over her shoulder at him with surprising interest. She doubtless recognized him as one of her egg-eating enemies, on which account she put her nest at the tip of a twig too slender to serve as a ladder.

Another humming-bird who built across the way was still more trustful—with people. I used to sit leaning against the trunk of her oak and watch the nest, which was near the tip of one of the long

swinging branches that drooped over the trail.
When the tiny worker was at home, a yard-stick
would almost measure the distance between us. As
she sat on her nest she sometimes turned her head
to look down at the dog lying beside me, and often
hovered over us on going away.

The nest was saddled on a twig and glued to a
glossy, dark green oak leaf. Like the other nest,
it was made of a yellow, spongy substance, probably down from the underside of sycamore leaves;
and like it, also, the outside was coated with lichen
and wound with cobweb. The bird was a rapid
worker, buzzing in with her material and then
buzzing off after more. Once I saw the cobweb
hanging from her needle-like bill, and thought she
probably had been tearing down the beautiful sus-
pension bridges the spiders hang from tree to tree.

It was very interesting to see her work. She
would light on the rim of the nest, or else drop directly into the tiny cup, and place her material
with the end of her long bill. It looked like trying to sew at arm's length. She had to draw back
her head in order not to reach beyond the nest.
How much more convenient it would have been if
her bill had been jointed! It seemed better suited
to probing flower tubes than making nests. But
then, she made nests only in the spring, while she
fed from flowers all the year round, and so could
afford to stretch her neck a trifle one month for the
sake of having a good, long fly-spear during the
other eleven. The peculiar feature of her work was
her quivering motion in moulding. When her material was placed she moulded her nest like a pot-
ter, twirling around against the sides, sometimes

pressing so hard she ruffled up the feathers of her breast. She shaped her cup as if it were a piece of clay. To round the outside she would sit on the rim and lean over, smoothing the sides with her bill, often with the same peculiar tremulous motion. When working on the outside, at times she almost lost her balance, and fluttered to keep from falling. To turn around in the nest, she lifted herself by whirring her wings.

When she found a bit of her green lichen about to fall, she took the loose end in her bill and drew it over the edge of the nest, fastening it securely inside. She looked very wise and motherly as she sat there at work, preparing a home for her brood. After building rapidly she would take a short rest on a twig in the sun, while she plumed her feathers. She made nest-making seem very pleasant work.

One day, wanting to experiment, I put a handful of oak leaves on the nest. They covered the cup and hung down over the sides. When the small builder came, she hovered over it a few seconds before making up her mind how it got there and what she had better do about it. Then she calmly lit on top of it! Part of it went off as she did so, but the rest she appropriated, fastening in the loose ends with the cobweb she had brought.

She often gave a little squeaky call when on the nest as if talking to herself about her work. When going off for material she would dart away and then, as if it suddenly occurred to her that she did not know where she was going, would stop and stand perfectly still in the air, her vibrating wings sustaining her till she made up her mind, when she would shoot off at an angle. It seemed as if she would be worn out before night, but her eyes were bright and she looked vigorous enough to build half a dozen houses.

"There's odds in folks," our great-grandmothers used to say; and there certainly is in bird folks; even in the ways of the same one at different times. Now, this humming-bird was content to build right in front of my eyes, and the hummer down at the little lover's tree, with her first nest, was so indifferent to Billy and me that I took no pains to keep at a distance or disguise the fact that I was watching her. But when her nest was destroyed she suddenly grew old in the ways of the world, and apparently repented having trusted us. In any case, I got a lesson on being too prying. The first nest had not been down long before I found that a second one was being built a few feet away —by the same bird? I imagined so. The nest was only just begun, and being especially interested to see how such buildings were started, I rode close up to watch the work. A roll of sycamore down was wound around a twig, and the bottom of the nest—the floor—attached to the underside of this beam; with such a solid foundation, the walls could easily be supported.

The small builder came when Billy and I were there. She did not welcome us as old friends, but sat down on her floor and looked at us—and I never saw her there again. Worse than that, she took away her nest, presumably to put it down where she thought inquisitive reporters would not intrude. I was disappointed and grieved, having already planned—on the strength of the first experience—to have the mother hummer's picture taken when she was feeding her young on the nest.

At first I thought this suspicion reflected upon the good sense of humming-birds, but after thinking it over concluded that it spoke better for humming-birds than for Billy and me. If this were, as I supposed, the same bird who had to brood her young with Billy gazing at the end of her bill, and if she had been present at the unlucky moment when he got the oak branches tangled in the pommel of the saddle, although her branch was not among them, I can but admire her for moving when she found that the Philistines were again upon her, for her new house was hung at the tip of a branch Billy might easily have swept in passing.

These nests had all been very low, only four or five feet above the ground; but one day I found young in one of the common tree-top nests. I could see it through the branches. Two little heads stuck up above the edge like two small Jacks-in-boxes. Billy made such a noise under the oak when the bird was feeding the youngsters that I took him away where he would not disturb the family, and tied him to an oak covered with poison ivy, for he was especially fond of eating it and the poison did not affect him.

Before the old hummer flew off, she picked up a tiny white feather that she found in the nest, and wound it around a twig. On her return, in the midst of her feeding, she darted down and set the feather flying; but as it got away from her she caught it again. The performance was repeated the next time she came with food; but she did it all so solemnly I could not tell whether she were playing or trying to get rid of something that annoyed her.

She fed at the long intervals that are so trying to an observer, for if you are going to sit for hours with your eyes glued to a nest, it really is pleasant to have something happen once in a while! Though the mother bird did not go to the nest often, she sometimes flew by, and once the sound of her wings roused the young and they called out to her as she passed. When they were awake, it was amusing to see the little midgets stick out their long thread-like tongues, preen their pinfeathers and stretch their wings over the nest.

One fine morning when I went to the oak I heard a faint squeak, and saw something fluttering up in the tree. When the mother came she buzzed about as though not liking the looks of things, for her children were out of the nest, and behold!—a horse and rider were under her tree. She tried to coax the unruly nestlings to follow her up into the upper stories, but they would not go.

Although not ready to be led, one of the infants soon felt that it would be nice to go alone. When a bird first leaves the nest it goes about very gingerly, but this little fellow soon began to feel his strength and the excitement of his freedom. He wiped his tongue on a branch, and then, to my astonishment, his wings began to whirl as though he were getting up steam, and presently they lifted him from his twig, and he went whirring off as softly as a humming-bird moth, among the sprays. His nerves were evidently on edge, for he looked around at the sound of falling leaves, started when Billy sneezed, and turned from side to side very apprehensively, in spite of his out-in-the-world, big-boy airs. He may have felt hampered by his un-used wings, for, as he sat there waiting for his mother to come, he stroked them out with his bill to get them in better working order. That done, he leaned over, rounded his shoulders, and pecked at a leaf as if he were as grown-up as anybody.

Of all the beautiful humming-birds' nests I saw in California, three are particularly noteworthy be-cause of their positions. One cup was set down on what looked like an inverted saucer, in the form of a dark green oak leaf wound with cobweb. That was in the oak beside the ranch house. Another one was on a branch of eucalyptus, set between two leaves like the knot in a bow of stiff ribbon. To my great satisfaction, the photographer was able to induce the bird to have a sitting while she brood-ed her eggs. The third nest belonged, I imagined, to the bird who took up her floor because Billy and I looked at her. If she were, her fate was certainly hard, for her eggs were taken by some one, boy or beast. Her nest was most skillfully supported. It was fastened like the seat of a swing between two twigs no larger than knitting needles, at the end of a long, drooping branch. It was a unique pleasure to see the tiny bird sit in her swing and be blown by the wind. Sometimes she went circling around as though riding in a merry-go-round; and at oth-ers the wind blew so hard her round boat rose and fell like a little ship at sea.—From "A-Birding on a Bronco."

THE FOOTHILLS

BY STEWART EDWARD WHITE

A T once our spirits rose. We straightened in
our saddles, we breathed deep, we joked.
The country was scorched and sterile; the wagon
trail, almost paralleling the mountains themselves
on a long, easy slant toward the high country, was
ankle deep in dust; the ravines were still dry of
water. But it was not the Inferno, and that one
fact sufficed. After a while we crossed high above
a river which dashed white water against black
rocks, and so were happy.

The country went on changing. The change was
always imperceptible, as in growth, or the stealthy
advance of autumn through the woods. From moment to moment one could detect no alteration.
Something intangible was taken away; something
impalpable added. At the end of an hour we
were in the oaks and sycamores; at the end of two
we were in the pines and low mountains of Bret
Harte's Forty-Nine.

The wagon trail felt ever farther and farther into the hills. It had not been used as a stage route
for years, but the freighting kept it deep with dust,
that writhed and twisted and crawled lazily knee-
high to our horses, like a living creature. We felt
the swing and sweep of the route. The boldness of
its stretches, the freedom of its reaches for the opposite slope, the wide curve of its horseshoes, all
filled us with the breath of an expansion which
as yet the broad, low country only suggested.

Everything here was reminiscent of long ago.

17

The very names hinted stories of the Argonauts. Coarse Gold Gulch, Whiskey Creek Grub Gulch, Fine Gold Post Office in turn we passed. Occasionally, with a fine round dash into the open, the trail drew one side to a stage station. The huge stables, the wide corrals, the low living houses, each shut in its dooryard of blazing riotous flowers, were all familiar. Only lacked the old-fashioned Concord coach, from which to descend Jack Hamlin or Judge Starbottle. As for M'liss, she was there, sunbonnet and all.

Down in the gulch bottoms were the old placer diggings. Elaborate little ditches for the deflection of water, long cradles for the separation of gold, decayed rockers, and shining in the sun the tons and tons of pay dirt which had been turned over pound by pound in the concentrating of its treasure. Some of the old cabins still stood. It was all deserted now, save for the few who kept trail for the freighters or who tilled the restricted bottom lands of the flats. Road-runners racked away down the paths; squirrels scurried over worn-out placers; jays screamed and chattered in and out of the abandoned cabins. Strange and shy little creatures and birds, reassured by the silence of many years, had ventured to take to themselves the engines of man's industry. And the warm California sun embalmed it all in a peaceful forgetfulness.

Now the trees grew bigger, and the hills more impressive. We should call them mountains in the East. Pines covered them to the top, straight, slender pines with voices. The little flats were planted with great oaks. When we rode through them, they shut out the hills, so that we might have imagined ourselves in a level, wooded country. There insisted the effect of limitless tree-grown plains, which the warm, drowsy sun, the park-like landscape, corroborated. And yet the contrast of the clear atmosphere and the sharp air equally insisted on the mountains. It was a strange and delicious double effect, a contradiction of natural impressions, a negation of our right to generalize from previous experience.

Always the trail wound up and up. Never was it steep; never did it command an outlook. Yet we felt that at last we were rising, were leaving the level of the Inferno, were nearing the threshold of the high country.

Mountain peoples came to the edges of their clearings and gazed at us, responding solemnly to our salutations. They dwelt in cabins and held to agriculture and herding of the wild mountain cattle. From them we heard of the high country to which we were bound. They spoke of it as you or I would speak of interior Africa, as something inconceivably remote, to be visited only by the adventurous, an uninhabited realm of vast magnitude and unknown dangers. In the same way they spoke of the plains. Only the narrow pine-clad strip between the two and six thousand feet of elevation they felt to be their natural environment. In it they found the proper conditions for their existence. Out of it those conditions lacked. They were as much a localized product as are certain plants which occur only at certain altitudes. Also were they densely ignorant of trails and routes outside of their own little districts.

All this, you will understand, was in what is

known as the low country. The landscape was still brown; the streams but trickles; sage brush clung to the ravines; the valley quail whistled on the side hills.

But one day we came suddenly into the big pines and rocks; and that very night we made our first camp in a meadow typical of the mountains we had dreamed about.—From ''The Mountains.''

''THE JOY OF THE HILLS''

By Edwin Markham

I RIDE on the mountain tops, I ride;
    I have found my life and am satisfied.
Onward I ride in the blowing oats,
Checking the field-lark's rippling notes—
        Lightly I sweep
        From steep to steep:
Over my head through the branches high
Come glimpses of a rushing sky;
The tall oats brush my horse's flanks;
Wild poppies crowd on the sunny banks;
A bee booms out of the scented grass;
A jay laughs with me as I pass.

I ride on the hills, I forgive, I forget
Life's hoard of regret—
All the terror and pain
Of the chafing chain.
Grind on, O cities, grind;
I leave you a blur behind.

I am lifted elate—the skies expand:
Here the world's heaped gold is a pile of sand.
Let them weary and work in their narrow walls:
I ride with the voices of waterfalls!

I swing on as one in a dream—I swing
Down the airy hollows, I shout, I sing!
The world is gone like an empty word:
My body's a bough in the wind, my heart a bird!

—From ''The Man With the Hoe and Other
    Poems.''

DESERT ANIMALS

By John C. Van Dyke

THE Indian and the plant must have *some* water.
    They cannot go without it indefinitely. And
just there the desert animals seem to fit their environment a little snugger than either plant or
human. For, strange as it may appear, many of
them get no water at all. There are sections of the
desert, fifty or more miles square, where there is
not a trace of water in river, creek, arroyo or pocket, where there is never a drop of falling dew; and
where the two or three showers of rain each year
sink into the sand and are lost in half an hour
after they have fallen. Yet that fifty-mile tract
of sand and rock supports its animal, reptile and insect life just the same as a similar tract in Illinois
or Florida. How the animals endure, how—even

on the theory of getting used to it—the jack-rabbit, the ground squirrel, the rat, and the gopher can live for months without even the moisture from green vegetation, is one of the mysteries. A mirror held to the nose of a desert rabbit will show a moist breath-mark on the glass. The moisture came out of the rabbit, is coming out of him every few seconds of the day; and there is not a drop of moisture going into him. Evidently the ancient axiom: "Out of nothing, nothing comes," is all wrong.

It is said in answer that the jack-rabbit gets moisture from roots, cactus lobes and the like. And the reply is that you find him where there are no roots but greasewood, and no cactus at all. Besides there is no evidence from an examination of his stomach that he ever eats anything but dried grass, bark and sage leaves. But if the matter is a trifle doubtful about the rabbit on account of his traveling capacities, there is no doubt whatever about the ground squirrels, the rock squirrels, and the prairie dogs. None of them ever gets more than a hundred yards from his hole in his life, except possibly when migrating. And the circuit about each hole is usually bare of everything except dried grass. There is no moisture to be had. The prairie dog is not found on the desert, but in Wyoming and Montana there are villages of them on the grass prairies, with no water, root, lobe or leaf within miles of them. The old theory of the prairie dog digging his hole down to water has no basis in fact. Patience, a strong arm and a spade will get to the bottom of his burrow in half an hour.

All the desert animals know the meaning of a water famine, and even those that are pronounced water drinkers know how to get on with the minimum supply. The mule-deer, whose cousin in the Adirondacks goes down to water every night, lives in the desert mountains, month in and month out with nothing more watery to quench his thirst than a lobe of the prickly pear or a joint of cholla. But he is naturally fond of green vegetation, and in the early morning he usually leaves the valley and climbs the mountains where with goats and mountain sheep he browses on the twigs of shrub and tree.

The coyote likes water too, but he puts up with sucking a nest of quail eggs, eating some mesquite beans, or at best absorbing the blood from some rabbit. The wild cat will go for weeks without more moisture than the blood of birds or lizards, and then, perhaps, after long thirst, he will come to a water pocket in the rocks to lap only a handful, doing it with an angry, snarling snap as though he disliked it and was doing it under compulsion. The gray wolf is too much a traveler to depend upon any one locality. He will run fifty miles in a night and be back before morning. Whether he gets water or not is impossible to ascertain.

The badger, the coon and the bear are very seldom seen in the more arid regions. They are not, strictly speaking, desert animals because unfitted to endure desert hardships. They are naturally great eaters and sleepers, loving cool weather and their own fatness; and to that the desert is sharply opposed. There is nothing fat in the land of sand and cactus. Animal life is lean and gaunt; if it sleeps at all it is with one eye open; and as for heat it cares very little about it. For the first law of the desert to which animal life of every kind pays allegiance is the law of endurance and abstinence. After that requirement is fulfilled special needs · produce the peculiar qualities and habits of the individual.—From "The Desert."

LEGEND OF THE CHINA LILY

By Idah Meacham Strobridge

L ONG ago—so long that the world, and all in it, was new; even as all now is old, very old— there dwelt in that oldest of all lands, China, a man great, and good, and with money and possessions too plentiful to be counted. And he had wives—two, three, or four, as a rich man may. But only the children of the first two wives have to do with this story. Each wife bore a son. And the first-born—he that was the son of the first wife— was the father's favorite. But the second son it was who loved the father best. This the sire did not know, for the boy hid his great love; yet ever obeying to the most minute particular each request asked of him. For goodness, and honor, and duty, and truth, for loyalty, and for love, this son was one man among ten thousand times ten thousand. But the father went about with an invisible fold of cloth bound across his eyes by an evil spirit, which blinded him to this noble son's worthiness. And the evil spirit removed the bandage whenever the father looked on the elder son, and put, instead, before his eyes a magic glass which made that son's vices seem as virtues, and his treachery as loyalty, and his lies as truth, and his deceitful bearing as love. So the father was ever deceived, and lived out the measure of long life, believing that good was evil and that that which was evil was good.

Then, when the measure of his days was done, he died; and the people mourned. For he had been well beloved for his many virtues and honored for his greatness and his riches.

Now, when his father died the elder son fell to lamenting; and he lamented loudly and long the first day, and lamented less loud the second day, and the third day lamented not at all. For his heart was bad; and in secret he rejoiced that his sire was dead, for now all these great possessions would be his own. Money, and hills where the tea plants grew, and houses in the village, and rice swamps, and riches of many kinds—much of all —were his own. All that his father had left was his. All but one small bit of waste land far up on the side of a great mountain. A barren tract up there in a hollow of the heights was deemed of no worth; for it had never grown tea-tree, nor rice, nor grass, nor flower, nor weed. So this was the father's bequest to the younger son. For the law was that to every son a man had, must be given a portion—little or great—of his lands when he died; and to this son, to whom he wished to leave nothing, he could give no less.

To the elder and favorite went all else; but to the younger, who was worthier than any other child of China, was given but this tract covered with fine bits of broken rock, where no green thing has ever grown and where the ground was dry and forbidding.

Yet against the unjust division this noble son rebelled not; but only mourned the father that was dead. Mourned sincerely—mourned without ceasing and without comfort—that the beloved and honorable being was gone beyond the reach of his gaze.

Of the injustice done him—of the smallness of his portion of the inheritance—he thought little. His father was dead; his father whom he had so loved—whom he still loved beyond all expression—was gone from him. Nothing else mattered.

And days went by. The elder one went abroad among his newly acquired possessions, saying: "This is mine, now; and this, and this also." And, because he was what he was, he forgot the dead man whose gift all these things had been.

But his brother, whose heart was heavy with grief, and who counted not the value of his portion, nor the lack. only longed to see his father's face once more.

Then the new moon came and looked down upon them both—the evil son and the son who was good. And the moon grew to the full—lessened—and waxed old. And in the old of the moon the younger son journeyed to the mountain where his poor inheritance lay; to the miserable and barren land which was awaiting him.

His eyes looked with sadness upon it; not because of its barrenness, but that it was the last gift his father had bestowed upon him.

His heart swelled with sorrow; and tears which scorched and stung flowed down his cheeks as he flung himself on the ground in his grief. He lay there long, so long a time he had lost all count of the hours, mourning as only they can mourn who are true of heart.

It was a great night, full of stars. A night when they burn like fire in the heavens. A band—filmy and far—stretched across the arc like the ragged, white smoke in the wake of a fast-speeding steamer. Meteors shot through the infinite blue-black depth, and the vastness of space could be felt, like the presence of a thing alive, in the vitalized atmosphere.

Though he did not raise his head, he was aware that something most strange had happened. Though hearing no sound, yet he felt near him a presence.

Then a voice spoke to him from out of the heavens; and its vibrations fell upon his ear like the multitudinous cadence of birds in song.

"Why weep you?" the voice asked, and he replied:

"Because I loved my father and he is dead."

"Though he is gone hence, he loves you in measure now as you have ever loved him," he heard the voice say; and it sounded like the ringing of silver bells. And now his heart bounded within him with a great thrill of joy that a father's love was at last his. Yet it was in fear and trembling that he asked, falteringly:

"Even as he loved my brother?"

"Even as he loved your brother once; but he loves not your brother now," the voice of music answered him. "The evil bandage across his eyes has been removed, and the magic glass is broken.

He now sees into his children's hearts with the penetrating eye which belongs to the dead, and he knows the truth at last. Weep no more; your father sees you—touches you—loves you. And because of your faithfulness and loyalty through all trials, your reward shall be great. Here, where only sterility has been, shall henceforth be bountiful yield. Never again will the earth here be dry and barren; for your tears have wetted the ground so that for a thousand times, a thousand years, a generous moisture shall keep the plant-roots healthily growing. The prayers you have breathed here for the dead shall ward off all evil from the living —from you and the family that will be yours. The warmth of your true heart, as it has lain beating and breaking here on the earth, shall call forth blossoms of unearthly beauty.

"Dig into the soil, O most dutiful of dutiful sons, and tell me what it is that you find."

And in the starlight the young man began scraping with his fingers; and digging, he found an unknown bulb.

"What is it?" asked the voice.

"A strange, new kind of root," he answered; "I do not know its name," and he covered it over again with the earth and bits of broken rock. Then once more the voice of sweet music spoke:

"Out of the land from whence your father looks down on you here these roots came, sent by him in his remorseful love; and the flower which grows from the root and stalk is called the Flower of Filial Affection. Go and come again the third day at noon!"

Then the young man went away. And when, at

noontide of the second day, he came again, he was amazed, for green shoots had sprung up from among the stones that were now wetted with water which oozed from the ground.

The voice he had heard before spoke at his elbow. "What see you?"

And he answered: "I see the earth rich with plant-life where it was barren before."

"Even as your father now sees the living evergreen truth of your soul, where once his blinded eyes saw but barrenness! Mourn no more; go, now, and come again to-morrow, which will be the third day, at early morning light when the sun first shines here on the mountain."

At early morning of the third day he came, as he was bidden; and lo! the air was weighted heavy with delicious perfume. It seemed to drop down from the heavens and fall, fold upon fold, on the earth in inexpressible, ineffable sweetness.

All about him green plants were in bloom. From the root came the plant, and the plant bore a beautiful flower. From filial love, rooted deep in the heart of a man, springs all that is noble and good; and the reward of virtues in a good son shall be made manifest. The whole earth seemed to be covered over with blossoms of waxen purity—wax-white blossoms were about him where he stood, like the flowers of heaven that we dream we see under the full moon.

White as snow is white, with a center all yellow as gold; sweet as orange flowers, and altogether lovely. It was as though a feather from some passing angel's wing had fluttered down to fall in the mud and mire of a sty.

A cup of ivory with a heart of gold.

All the world seemed snowed under petals of fragrance; and as he gazed in awe at the wondrous beauty of the scene, he shook with the intensity of his emotions. Moved to helpless weakness by the spirituality of what he saw, he fell upon his knees in worship of the great Power that had caused such exquisite loveliness to grow, and bowed his forehead on the ground.

Then, out of the heavenly surroundings, spoke the voice.

"My son," it said, tenderly, and oh! so sweetly; and now he recognized the loved accents, for it was his father's voice that was speaking—that had been speaking since the hour he had first come to mourn on the mountain—"Oh, my son—son beloved—once a burden you bore, bore it with uncomplaining lips. Life has set no greater task for a child than to be loyal and loving in the face of injustice and misunderstanding. So, for this, your reward shall be great. Because of your heart's loving loyalty these flowers shall henceforth be made sacred to your race, and shall grow only upon this land of yours, and in that way be only for your family. Nowhere else—east or west, north or south—shall they ever be made to grow in the earth to the perfection of blossoming; yet here on this tear-bedewed land shall they forever thrive, on this spot made sacred by your faithfulness. Yours shall they be only; yours, and your sons', and your sons' sons', through all coming generations.

"The bulbs shall grow for you and yours to sell —for others to buy; and riches past all counting shall be yours. Greater riches will be yours than can ever come to him who is your brother. And now I go. Even as I love you I bless you; going hence to await you in that land from whence these white blossoms came. Farewell, beloved child; most honorable son, farewell!''

And the one who was prostrate on the ground raised himself and—though he had seen nothing—knew that the presence had gone, and that he was alone. But in his heart was comfort and everlasting peace.

Only a legend. Only a story made by the fairies for children and these simple-minded folk, who saw its poetic charm as did I. Only a tale brought out of lily-land for those to hear who have the poet-hearts of little children.—From ''Land of Purple Shadows.''

W.S. Rice